Weber Carburettors Owners Workshop Manual

by J H Haynes
Member of the Guild of Motoring Writers

and A K Legg T Eng (CEI), AMIMI

Types covered:

DAF, DCD, DFA, DFV, DFD, DFE, DFM,
DFT, DGV, DIF, IDA, IDF, IDS, IDT,
DCNF, DCOE, DFAV, DFTA, DGAS,
DGAV, IDAP and IDTP carburettors

ISBN 1 85010 061 6
ISBN 1 85010 020 9 (US)

2

Printed in England *(393-7M3)*

Haynes Publishing Group
Sparkford Nr Yeovil
Somerset BA22 7JJ England

Haynes Publications, Inc
861 Lawrence Drive
Newbury Park
California 91320 USA

Acknowledgements

We are indebted to Martin Goodall of Weber Carburettors (UK) Limited, Sunbury-on-Thames, Middlesex, for supplying technical material and for being so helpful with advice and the supply of carburettors used during the compilation of this Manual.

Special thanks must also go to a number of people who were kind enough to lend us carburettors and supply technical information. They include Garry Pollard of Long Beach, California; Josh Sadler of Autofarm, Amersham, Bucks; Terry Batchelor of the Crewkerne Tyre Company, Crewkerne, Somerset; Robin Gould of Pilton Garage, Pilton, Somerset; Pete Wareham of Corville Auto Engineers, Babylon Hill, Sherborne, Dorset; Graham Briginshaw of Western Services, Bristol; Jonathan Evans of the Ilminster Motor Company, Ilminster, Somerset; Tony Bishop of Autoconti Limited, Southwick, Trowbridge, Wiltshire; Martin Hudson and our Chairman John Haynes.

We are also grateful to the Ford Motor Company (GB) Limited, the Champion Sparking Plug Company who supplied the illustrations showing the various spark plug conditions and also to Messrs Derringtons of Kingston, Surrey.

Last, but not least, thanks are due to all of those people at Sparkford who helped in the production of this Manual. Particularly Brian Horsfall and Les Brazier who carried out the mechanical work and photography respectively, Chris Rogers who edited the text and Stanley Randolph who planned the layout of each page.

About this manual

The aim of this Manual is to enable you to obtain the very best from your Weber carburettor, both economically and from the performance angle. Because the carburettor is a fine precision instrument, the Manual assumes that the owner already knows how an engine works and is well acquainted with the basic servicing requirements of the engine.

Part 1 of the Manual contains the theoretical aspects of carburettor care and function, whereas Part 2 describes the practical procedures tabulated under separate chapters covering carburettors of similar type. The operation of the carburettor is fully described so that the owner can diagnose problems quickly, thus saving himself time and money. Although there are a number of special tools available for the servicing of Weber carburettors, alternative methods employing the more common tools are described wherever possible.

Due to the vast number of Weber carburettors that have been manufactured, the scope of this Manual is somewhat limited to the more common types. although information given in Part 1 applies to all Weber carburettors. Information given in Part 2 under the Weber type numbers also applies to Holley and Bressell versions fitted to cars manufactured in the USA and Spain respectively.

The Manual contains two types of illustration: Figures which are numbered according to Chapter and sequence of occurence in that Chapter and photographs which have a reference number on their caption. All photographs apply to the Chapter in which they occur so that the reference figure pinpoints the pertinent Section and paragraph number.

Whilst every care is taken to ensure that the information in this Manual is correct and up to date, it should be realised that modification may be made by the manufacturers at any time. No liability can be accepted by the author or publishers for loss, damage, or injury caused by any errors in, or omission from, the information given.

Contents

Cutaway view of a typical DCOE carburettor

Part 1
Chapter 1 Basic carburation

Contents

1 Function of a carburettor

1 The modern internal combustion engine has been developed considerably from its original concept in a number of ways; including increased power output, greater flexibility and the more efficient combustion of fuel supplied to it. As a direct result of this the role of the carburettor has become an increasingly important factor, requiring frequent modification and the introduction of many previously unheard of devices to improve the function of the carburettor.

Carburettor technology is, of course, a vast subject, and to cover all aspects would require the writing of a volume of books; however, it will be helpful for the reader to be acquainted with the basic factors concerning carburation, as it will then be easier to understand the function of the various components which make up the Weber carburettor.

The prime objective of any carburettor is to meter out a mixture of fuel and air to the engine in a form that can be burnt quickly and completely. In practise this is rarely achieved, although the modern carburettor is much improved on its original counterpart and there is every indication of further advancement. Ideally, for complete combustion, the air/fuel mixture must be supplied to the engine in vapour form. This leads us to the secondary objective of the carburettor, which is to break up or atomise the fuel and disperse it into the air passing into the engine. The efficiency with which the carburettor carries out this process largely determines the efficiency of combustion within the engine.

The third objective of the carburettor in the automotive field is necessary, owing to the constant change of engine speed resulting from the vehicle accelerating and decelerating. The carburettor must be able to vary the amount of fuel supplied to the engine in order to cope with the different speed and power requirements encountered. This also requires that the quantity of air be varied, along with the fuel, to provide a combustible mixture.

2 A/F ratio variation

The theoretical air/fuel ratio for complete combustion is called the stoichiometric A/F ratio and under laboratory conditions is in the region of 15:1 by weight. When the fuel is fully vaporised, the ratio by volume is between 50:1 and 60:1 because fuel vapour is denser than air. However, fuel will tolerate a wide range of mixture ratios varying from about 8:1 to 22:1 by weight.

The stoichiometric A/F ratio does not give maximum power or minimum fuel consumption, these two requirements being obtained with A/F ratios of 12.5:1 and 16:1 respectively, as shown in Fig. 1.1. The curves of the graph are important with regard to the tuning of a carburettor, as they enable the operator to tune the engine for maximum power or maximum economy within defined limits.

It should be observed that an engine will run with A/F ratios outside the 12.5:1 and 16:1 limits, such as when starting (1:1 A/F ratio weakening to 4:1 A/F ratio), but under normal conditions the ratio should be within the limits in order to obtain optimum power or fuel consumption. There are additional adverse effects which occur as a result of A/F ratios outside the limits.

A weak mixture burns considerably slower within the combustion chamber and as a result may still be burning when the piston reaches the end of its power stroke. This leads to overheating and, in extreme cases, burnt valves and piston crowns.

A rich mixture will cause carbon to form rapidly on the combustion chamber and piston crown surfaces; this will necessitate a premature de-coke. Spark plug performance will be impaired and excess fuel will contaminate the engine lubricating oil and cause rapid wear of the cylinder walls.

Excessively rich or lean mixtures also increase the amount of toxic emissions in the exhaust gases. In some countries this has led to the design and introduction of emission control systems. It will therefore be appreciated that mixture control is

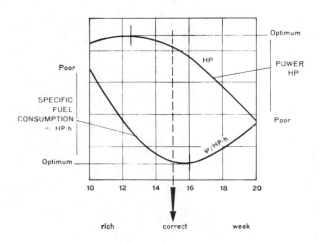

Fig. 1.1 Curves showing the effect of the variation of the air/ fuel ratio on power output and fuel consumption (Sec 2)

extremely critical over the complete range of engine speeds and loads, and the correct functioning of the carburettor is therefore an important if not essential factor.

The mixture content of a particular engine can be tested by using an exhaust gas analyser to determine the amount of carbon monoxide (CO) present. The instrument is particularly helpful when adjusting idle mixture screws in order to supply the correct A/F mixture necessary for good combustion. Exhaust gas analysers are available in many accessory shops and their use may very well become compulsory in the future in view of the trend towards tighter regulations regarding air pollution.

3   The simple carburettor

All modern carburettors are designed around one basic principle. This is illustrated in Fig. 1.2 which is a cross -section of a tube having a curved restriction within it. The restriction in a carburettor is termed a venturi. If air is drawn through this component it will increase in speed in proportion to the cross-sectional diameter of the venturi. Since the air density decreases progressively to a point where its velocity is greatest, the air pressure at the smallest section of the venturi will be considerably less than atmospheric.

In the carburettor, this phenomenon is exploited by inserting a fuel outlet or nozzle into the venturi, this being supplied by a reservoir or float chamber (Fig. 1.3). Note that under static conditions, the fuel level in the float chamber is just below the nozzle outlet in order to prevent it leaking from the nozzle; also the air pressure in the float chamber is identical to that at the nozzle, ie atmospheric. When air is drawn through the venturi arrangement it will be observed that, due to the difference in air pressure at the float chamber and outlet nozzle, the fuel will flow out of the nozzle and mix with the air. On an engine, the resulting mixture is drawn into the cylinders and combustion takes place.

In order to maintain the level of the fuel just below the nozzle outlet, a float controlled inlet valve is incorporated into the float chamber. As the fuel flows out of the nozzle its level drops and the float opens the valve; when the correct level is reached the valve shuts.

To regulate the amount of mixture admitted to the engine, the carburettor is provided with a throttle valve which, when closed, completely seals the engine side of the venturi.

Unfortunately, the simple carburettor has one failing which renders it unsuitable for use in the road vehicle where the engine is operated at variable speeds and loads. In its present form the air/fuel mixture will be consistent provided the air flow remains at a constant speed. If the air flow is increased, its density will decrease in far greater proportion to the liquid fuel, with the result that the mixture becomes progressively richer. If the air flow is decreased the mixture will progressively weaken.

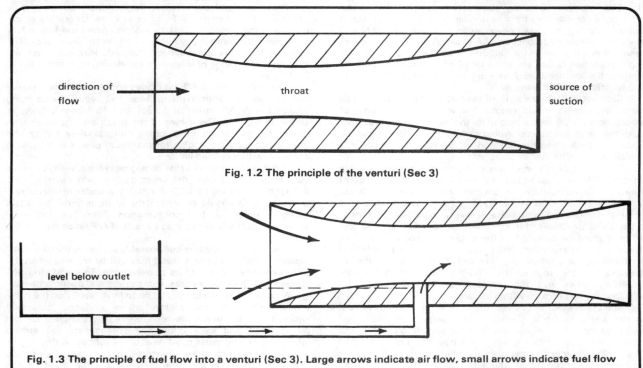

Fig. 1.2 The principle of the venturi (Sec 3)

Fig. 1.3 The principle of fuel flow into a venturi (Sec 3). Large arrows indicate air flow, small arrows indicate fuel flow

Another failing is that the simple carburettor makes no provision for engine idling, acceleration, or cold starting. It is therefore obvious that additional modifications must be made in order to adapt the carburettor for automotive use.

4   The Weber carburettor

Carburettor manufacturers have overcome the deficiencies of the simple carburettor in various ways. With the use of sophisticated test equipment Weber have developed their carburettors to a very high standard and have proved to be leaders in the field of carburettor manufacture.

To overcome the mixture enrichening phenomenon mentioned in Section 4, the Weber carburettor is equipped with an air bleed system. Reference to Fig. 1.4 shows that as the fuel flows from the float chamber to the nozzle in the venturi, it passes a tube (called the emulsion tube), which is vented to atmospheric pressure and additionally has a number of holes drilled throughout its length. The effect of the depression acting on the nozzle will not only draw fuel into the carburettor but also air through the air bleed jet and into the fuel via the holes in the emulsion tube. As the engine speed increases, the fuel level inside the emulsion tube lowers with the result that more air is released into the fuel. The fact that the fuel becomes emulsified also results in better atomization at the nozzle.

In the Weber carburettor the emulsion tube is removable and by varying its diameter, location of holes and diameter of air bleed jet, the mixture strength for a particular engine can be adjusted to fine limits.

At engine idling speed there is insufficient vacuum in the venturi to draw any fuel from the nozzle; so a separate supply of fuel is channelled to the engine side of the throttle valve where there will be greater vacuum, since the throttle is closed. Fig. 1.5 illustrates a typical idling speed circuit and it will be observed that a fuel jet and air corrector jet is incorporated to provide a combustible mixture; the air jet also prevents a syphoning effect through the circuit. A volume of mixture adjustment is also incorporated, so that it is possible to vary the mixture strength as necessary in co-operation with the throttle

valve adjustment screw, which controls the amount of air allowed past the throttle valve at idling.

It should be noted that the idle circuit is supplied from the lower region of the emulsion tube. This arrangement ensures that the idle circuit ceases or is in some instances reversed when the main fuel system is in operation.

The Weber carburettor also includes what is termed as a progression function. When the throttle valve is open slightly after being in the idling position, there is a tendency for the mixture to lean-out and thus cause the engine to misfire. To overcome this problem, one or more transition orifices are drilled into the idling circuit on the inlet side of the throttle valve and in the carburettor barrel. Reference to Fig. 1.6 will show that the vacuum on the engine side of the throttle valve is progressively introduced to the transition orifices and extra fuel is thus provided to cover this stage of increasing engine speed. When the engine reaches sufficient speed to draw fuel from the main nozzle, the progression function will cease.

Where the throttle valve is opened fully and quickly, even the progression orifices are insufficient to enrichen the mixture enough. In this case an accelerator pump must be used. Figs. 1.7 and 1.8 show the two types of accelerator pump used on Weber carburettors.

With the piston type pump, fuel is drawn from the float chamber when the throttle is closed, because this action lifts the pump operating rod by way of a lever. When the throttle is opened, the operating rod is free to move the piston down its bore under the action of the accelerator pump spring. Fuel is channelled past a one-way ball valve, through the pump jet, and thus mixes with the air being drawn into the engine. The fuel is prevented from re-entering the float chamber by a ball and seat in the intake valve, but in order to calibrate the amount of fuel injected, a discharge hole allows a certain amount of fuel to return to the float chamber. The discharge hole also prevents fuel being injected during slow throttle movement.

The diaphragm type pump operates in a similar manner, except that a spring tensioned diaphragm is used instead of a piston.

The final failure of the simple carburettor concerns cold starting. In this respect there are two main methods employed in the Weber carburettor:

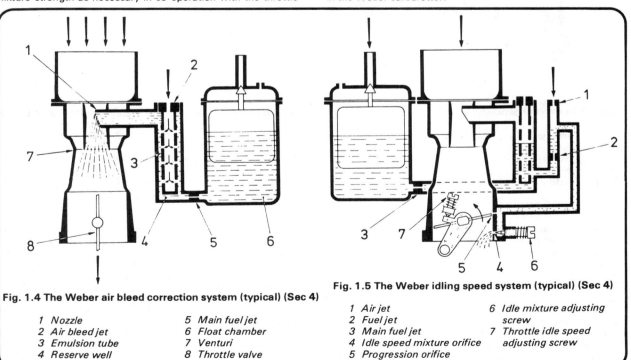

Fig. 1.4 The Weber air bleed correction system (typical) (Sec 4)

1 *Nozzle*	5 *Main fuel jet*
2 *Air bleed jet*	6 *Float chamber*
3 *Emulsion tube*	7 *Venturi*
4 *Reserve well*	8 *Throttle valve*

Fig. 1.5 The Weber idling speed system (typical) (Sec 4)

1 *Air jet*	6 *Idle mixture adjusting*
2 *Fuel jet*	*screw*
3 *Main fuel jet*	7 *Throttle idle speed*
4 *Idle speed mixture orifice*	*adjusting screw*
5 *Progression orifice*	

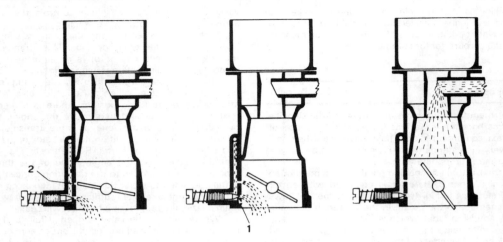

Fig. 1.6 The Weber progression system (Sec 4)

1   Idle speed mixture orifice   *2   Progression orifice*

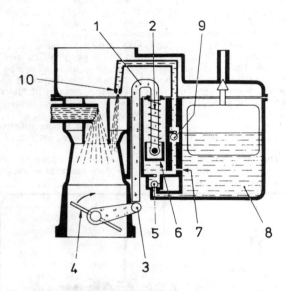

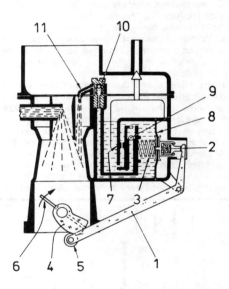

Fig. 1.7 The Weber piston type accelerator pump (Sec 4)   **Fig. 1.8 The Weber diaphragm type accelerator pump (Sec 4)**

1	*Operating rod*	*6*	*Pump piston*
2	*Spring*	*7*	*Discharge jet*
3	*Control lever*	*8*	*Float chamber*
4	*Throttle valve*	*9*	*Delivery valve*
5	*Intake valve*	*10*	*Pump jet*

1	*Operating lever*	*7*	*Discharge jet*
2	*Pump spring*	*8*	*Diaphragm*
3	*Diaphragm return spring*	*9*	*Intake valve*
4	*Cam lever*	*10*	*Delivery valve*
5	*Roller*	*11*	*Pump jet*
6	*Throttle valve*		

The first method employs what is best described as a separate carburettor within the main carburettor. Fig. 1.9 shows the system in basic form. It will be observed that the system can be introduced or regulated by means of a manually controlled valve. The system is designed to give the necessary enrichment of mixture for starting with the throttle valves in the idling position.

The second method is shown in Fig. 1.10 and is termed the strangler or shutter valve type. With this system, an offset valve is positioned in the carburettor inlet and by restricting the amount of air admitted to the carburettor, the quantity of fuel emerging from the nozzle is increased, thus enriching the mixture for starting. Once the engine has started, the mixture

must be weakened and this is automatically taken care of by the offset design of the strangler valve. As soon as the vacuum below it reaches a predetermined level, the larger area of the valve will be drawn downwards against the tension of a calibrated spring and additional air will thus be admitted.

The strangler valve may be operated manually or automatically, but in either case must be returned to its fully open position as soon as the engine reaches its normal operating temperature.

The range of Weber carburettors includes variations of the functions so far described. Where necessary there will be further descriptions in detail in the relevant Chapters of this manual dealing with the individual carburettor types.

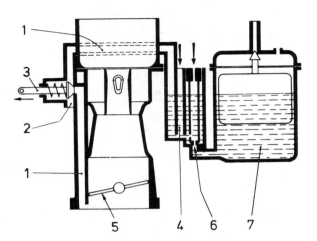

Fig. 1.9 The Weber jet type choke (Sec 4)

1 *Starting mixture channel*
2 *Starting air jet*
3 *Valve*
4 *Reserve well*
5 *Throttle valve*
6 *Starting fuel jet*
7 *Float chamber*

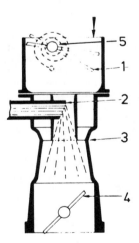

Fig. 1.10 The Weber strangler type choke (Sec 4)

1 *Choke valve*
2 *Nozzle*
3 *Venturi*
4 *Throttle valve*
5 *Calibrated spring*

5 By-pass idle carburettors

A more recent development is the bypass idle carburettor which has been introduced as a result of legislation concerning atmospheric pollution. Weber carburettors equipped with this function have two independent idle systems; the first is the basic idle system which is fitted to all carburettors, and the second is the bypass idle system.

Reference to Fig. 1.11 will show the operation of the bypass idle system. Fuel from the float chamber is drawn through the secondary main jet (A) to the secondary idle jet (B) where it becomes emulsified with air drawn through the calibrated orifice (C). The mixture is then drawn through internal channels and a calibrated drilling and mixes with air supplied through the drilling (D) in the primary choke. The bypass idle adjustment screw (E) controls the amount of mixture admitted to the discharge apertures (F and G) which then is drawn through the inlet manifold and into the engine.

On some by-pass idle carburettors there is a fuel return system to prevent the fuel in the float chamber from being heated excessively, which could otherwise enrich the idle mixture. With this system there is a continuous flow of fuel from the fuel tank to the carburettor inlet and back to the fuel tank.

Another feature included on bypass idle carburettors is the anti-stall or low vacuum enrichment device, which is normally fitted to vehicles with automatic transmission where there is a tendency for the engine to stall when moving the selector. The device comprises a spring tensioned diaphragm and cover, usually located in the vicinity of the float chamber opposite the accelerator pump.Under normal operating conditions, engine vacuum holds the diaphragm against the spring pressure and fuel is drawn into the chamber of the device. If the engine tends to stall, the vacuum will decrease and the spring tension will compress the diaphragm and eject fuel from the chamber. The device is connected by internal channels to the accelerator pump delivery valve and jet, and the fuel is injected into the primary barrel thus providing mixture enrichment in order to overcome the stall.

6 Thermostatically controlled air cleaners

This type of air cleaner ensures a constant temperature of the intake air, so that fuel atomisation in the carburettor takes place using air at the correct temperature. The air cleaner incorporates two inlets; one with fresh air at ambient temperature and the other with air heated by the exhaust manifold. An internal flap determines the quantity of heated or cool air to admit to the carburettor and is controlled by a heat sensor and vacuum assistance.

When the engine is cold, heated air is directed from the exhaust manifold into the air cleaner, but as the engine warms up, cold air is progressively mixed with this heated air. At high ambient temperatures the hot air intake is closed off completely.

7 Tamperproof carburettors

A further recent development as a result of atmospheric pollution control, is the tamperproof carburettor on which various adjustment screws are sealed with plastic plugs. The type of tamperproofing varies according to the carburettor and in some instances special tools are required in order to remove the seals. However before removing them, the owner is advised to be aware of any legislation which may be contravened by removing the seals and making adjustments. In some territories a coloured seal, only available to garages, must replace the removed seal. In this instance, it is recommended that the owner entrusts his car to a suitably equipped agent to carry out any adjustments to the carburettor.

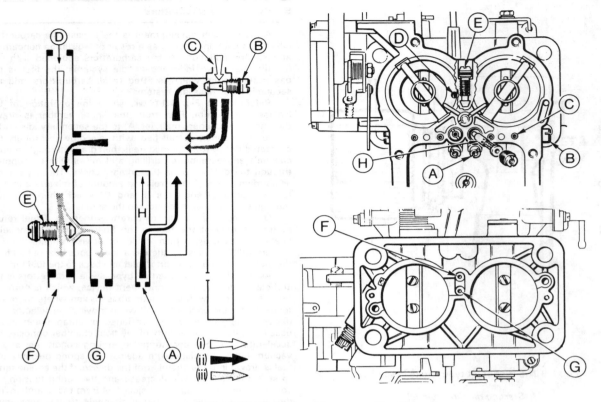

Fig. 1.11 The bypass idle system (Sec 5)

(i)	Air supply	A	Secondary main jet	D	Plain air supply
(ii)	Fuel supply	B	Secondary idle jet	E	Bypass idle adjustment
(iii)	Air/fuel mixture	C	Air bleed		screw

F   Fixed discharge aperture
G   Bypass discharge aperture
H   Secondary emulsion tube

8   USA carburettors

Carburettors used in the USA may have some or all of the following items fitted to them; the exact line-up will depend on local legal requirements:

Deceleration valve

During deceleration this valve supplies an additional flow of air/fuel mixture into the inlet manifold in order to improve combustion within the engine; this in turn lowers the hydrocarbon emission in the exhaust gases. The valve is mounted on the inlet manifold and consists of a spring loaded diaphragm, a control valve, and two ports. Under all driving conditions except deceleration, the spring holds the valve shut, but during deceleration the additional vacuum opens the valve and extra mixture is supplied to the engine. To prevent over-enrichment during the engine warm-up period when the choke is in operation, the control valve, which is temperature sensitive to the cooling system, only operates the deceleration valve when normal operating temperature has been reached.

Evaporative emission control

This system prevents unburnt hydrocarbons in the form of fuel vapour from escaping from the vehicle fuel system into the atmosphere. The fuel system is sealed and the carburettor is vented internally so that the fuel vapour cannot escape when the vehicle is stationary. The build up of vapour in the fuel tank and carburettor is channelled via pipes to a canister containing activated carbon particles which absorb the vapour. When the engine is running, the activated carbon releases the vapour which is then drawn into the air cleaner from where it passes into the engine.

Exhaust gas recirculation (EGR) system

This system reduces the emission of nitrogen oxides from the vehicle exhaust pipe by introducing a small amount of inert exhaust gas into the inlet manifold. The effect of this is to reduce the peak temperatures reached in the combustion chambers, which are responsible for the emission of nitrogen oxides.

The EGR valve is usually operated by vacuum from the carburettor and sometimes uses the same vacuum take-off port as that used for the distributor advance, although normally a separate port is provided.

Ignition advance and retard ports

On some engines the ignition is advanced and retarded by vacuum from the carburettor and inlet manifold. On some carburettors both take-off ports may be incorporated into the carburettor.

Dashpot

This device can be fitted to most carburettors as a bolt-on extra. Its purpose is to retard the action of the throttle lever as it returns to the idling position after releasing the throttle. This prevents an over weak mixture, particularly during deceleration and therefore reduces the emission of certain harmful gases from the exhaust system.

Idle speed step-up valves

On vehicles fitted with air conditioning equipment, a valve is usually incorporated into the carburettor to increase the engine idle speed setting during the period when the air conditioning compressor is in operation. This is necessary because the additional load on the engine would normally cause it to stall. The adjustment of this valve will depend on the type of engine it is fitted to and therefore this information should be obtained from the vehicle manufacturer. However, the overall effect of the step-up valve is to retain the original engine idle speed when the air conditioning compressor is in operation.

A similar type of step-up valve is sometimes fitted to vehicles equipped with automatic transmission, in order to prevent stalling when the selector lever is moved.

Idle cut-off valve

This valve stops the flow of fuel or fuel/air mixture in the idle circuit immediately the ignition is switched off, thus eliminating any tendency for the engine to run-on or 'diesel'. This is particularly important where low octane lead free fuel is used, because the run-on characteristics are more prominent with this type of fuel.

Part 1
Chapter 2 Carburettor fitting

Contents

1   Introduction

Due to the multitude of applications incorporating Weber carburettors, no attempt will be made in this Chapter to detail all the possible arrangements. An outline of the more common arrangements of a particular carburettor is to be found in the relevant Chapter of this manual covering the carburettor in question.

In this Chapter we will consider the general fitting requirements of Weber carburettors, which will already have been catered for if the carburettor is standard equipment on a particular engine. The information will be of special interest to those wishing to fit a Weber carburettor as a non-standard component.

2   Carburettor positioning

The carburettor must be positioned so that all air will have unimpaired access to the inlet and, to prevent turbulence affecting mixture ratios, it is preferable for the air to have as direct a path of entry as is possible.

With sidedraught carburettors, such as the DCOE range, it is permissible for the carburettor to be inclined upwards by 5° from horizontal; the angle being measured from the engine side flange face through the centre-line of the barrels. Where two or more sidedraught carburettors are fitted, rubber fuel proof distance pieces should be fitted between the flange faces of the carburettor and inlet manifold. The outer ends of the carburettors should be supported with a support rod and bracket, also with rubber mountings. The support rod should be attached to the carburettor at one end and the engine block at the other end.

Considering downdraught carburettors, it is important that they are fitted with the barrels vertical, even on engines which are inclined (because of bonnet height for instance). The float chamber should face the front of the vehicle with the float

fulcrum pin axis across the vehicle; this will diminish the effect of acceleration, braking and hill climbing on the fuel level in the float chamber.

Where a carburettor barrel feeds more than one cylinder, the throttle spindle should be parallel to the crankshaft, otherwise there will be unequal distribution of the air/fuel mixture to the cylinders. This applies particularly to in-line engines where the carburettor is mounted on one side of the cylinder head.

3   The inlet manifold

The purpose of the inlet manifold is to convey the previously prepared air/fuel mixture from the carburettor to the engine cylinders, whilst at the same time keeping the composition of the mixture uniform. In general terms the speed of the mixture should be maintained at the identical velocity with which it leaves the carburettor; too large a manifold diameter will cause the mixture to slow down and this may cause condensation of fuel on the manifold walls.

The length of the inlet manifold branches should be as short as possible and as equal in length as possible to ensure that each cylinder receives equal quantities of mixture. The branch bores must have a smooth or even polished surface and all bends must be kept to minimum angles. The use of excessively long horizontal sections of inlet manifold may result in carburation problems when cornering and must therefore be kept to a minimum.

In modern engine applications the inlet manifold is sometimes heated in order to promote vaporisation of the air/fuel mixture. The best method to do this is by passing water from the engine cooling system through a section of the manifold just below the carburettor. This arrangement also has the advantage that it makes possible the use of leaner mixtures throughout the complete engine speed range.

It is important to make sure that each branch of the inlet manifold locates exactly with the inlet bores in the cylinder head

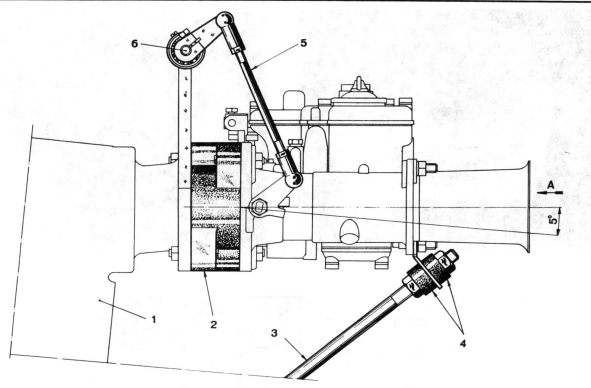

Fig. 2.1 Typical sidedraught carburettor fitting (Sec 2)

1 Cylinder head
2 Anti-vibration flange
3 Support rod
4 Rubber mounting

5 Adjustable throttle control rod
6 Auxiliary shaft and bearings

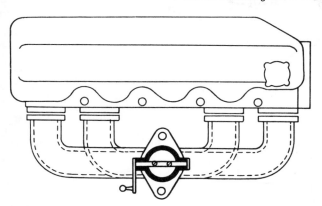

Fig. 2.2 Correct location of a single carburettor feeding four cylinders, showing the position of the throttle spindle (Sec 2)

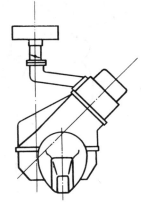

Fig. 2.3 The length of horizontal inlet manifold on this arrangement may cause carburation problems when cornering (Sec 3)

and that manifold gaskets do not obstruct the free passage of air. Failure to take these precautions can lead to quite serious carburation faults.

Although the previous comments are correct for most applications, the design of the inlet manifold is a complicated process involving the use of a dynamometer and the completing of many engine tests. A poor design may result in unsatisfactory vaporisation, unequal mixture distribution, or even insufficient mixture supply and for this reason it is not recommended that a manifold be made up by an inexperienced person. It is a much better idea to purchase a manifold from a conversion specialist who is well versed in the subject.

4 Air cleaners and air horns

The function of the air cleaner is obvious, but it has to perform quite a difficult task and has therefore been the subject of thorough testing and modification. Where an air cleaner is fitted as original equipment, no attempt should be made to alter it in any way as it is usually matched to the particular application on which it is fitted (photos).

Some air cleaners incorporate a vent, whereby fuel vapours which accumulate in the float chamber with the engine stationary are vented to the atmosphere. An alternative method

4.1a Typical air cleaner fitted to a 28/36 DCD type carburettor

4.1b Air filter location after removing the cover

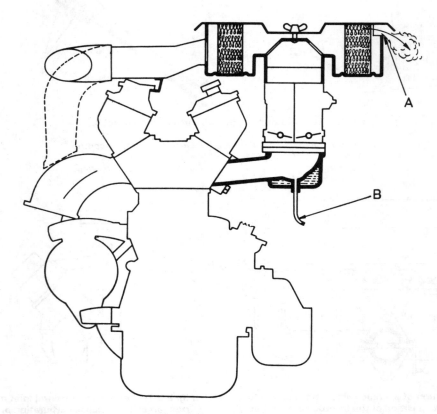

Fig. 2.4 Two methods of dispersing float chamber fuel evaporation (Sec 4)

A *Air cleaner vent*   B *Drain tube*

is to provide a drain tube in the inlet manifold to disperse condensed fuel.

Normally the air cleaner should be mounted on the engine. The use of rubber mountings will prevent vibration being transmitted to the carburettor.

Air horns are fitted to carburettors mainly to prevent turbulence at the air inlet, which would otherwise cause varying mixtures and uneven charging of the combustion chambers. Their purpose is also to reduce the effect of a blow back through the carburettor and in fact, some air horns house a flame trap.

On racing applications the air horns also help to contain fuel mist spraying from the mouth of the carburettor. This phenomenon is sometimes referred to as stand-off and may be attributed to a harmonic effect within the inlet manifold; although where air horns are mounted externally on the vehicle, the effect can be due to air passing across the mouth of the air horn.

A number of different shapes and sizes of air horns are available for the Weber range of carburettors and the choice will in most cases depend on the fitting space available. Angled air

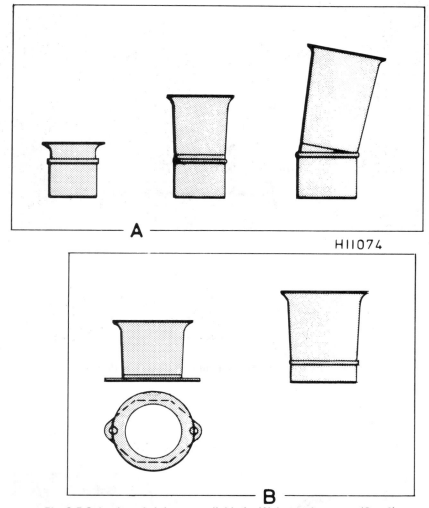

H11074

Fig. 2.5 Selection of air horns available for Weber carburettors (Sec 4)

A Sidedraught carburettors   *B Downdraught carburettors*

horns can be obtained for the more popular side draught DCOE carburettors.

Where an air cleaner is fitted, there is normally no need for an air horn, consequently the usual application is on sports engines where maximum air supply is important.

5 Accelerator and choke controls

All controls must of necessity be strong enough to cope with the loads they will be subjected to. When the accelerator pedal is depressed or the choke operated, the throttle valve or choke device must move smoothly and fully as required. Where multiple carburettors are concerned, the action of the control on each carburettor must be identical. For this purpose it is essential to have some form of adjustment incorporated into the control.

One of the main problems with carburettor controls is that engine vibration is sometimes transmitted to the carburettor, with the result that the fuel in the float chamber becomes emulsioned. This phenomenon can generate a number of adverse characteristics and should be avoided at all costs. To prevent this, it is preferable to use cable rather than rod for the carburettor controls, but only where the prevailing loads will allow this (Fig. 2.6)

A typical rod control is shown in Fig. 2.7, and with this arrangement an auxiliary shaft is mounted along the length of the engine. This shaft must be of 0·4 in to 0·5 in (10 mm to 12 mm) outer diameter and must incorporate two or three self-aligning ball bearings, depending on the linkage length. Each of the operating levers must be identical in length and the balljoints should preferably have spring-loaded end clearance limitation.

It is important to note that the auxiliary shaft is mounted on the engine and not on the body of the vehicle.

6 Fuel lines and hoses

The fuel line should be arranged so that its highest point is always the inlet union on the carburettor. By doing this there is less chance of an air-lock occuring within the fuel line.

The use of flexible hose should be adopted, particularly where the engine fuel line connects with the body fuel line, in order to lessen the effect of engine vibration and prevent fracturing.

Where the vehicle has completed a high mileage, it is possible that the fuel tank and fuel lines may be corroded and sediment may therefore be deposited within the carburettor resulting in its malfunction. In these circumstances it is recom-

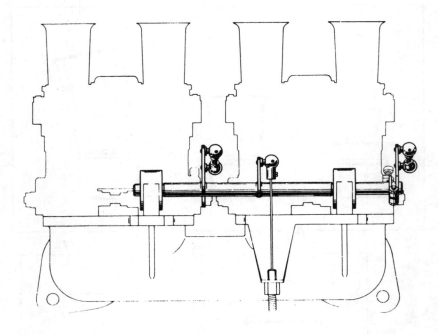

Fig. 2.6 Typical cable and rod throttle control (Sec 5)

Fig. 2.7 Typical rod throttle control also showing the flexible fuel hose location (Sec 5)

mended that a fuel filter be incorporated into the fuel line near the carburettor(s), but it is important that it will be able to pass the quantity of fuel proportionate to the highest fuel consumption likely to be encountered.

7 Vacuum take-off points

On Weber carburettors not fitted with a vacuum take-off

point or spark port for actuation of the ignition advance or retard mechanism on the distributor, no attempt should be made to adapt the carburettor in any way. The vacuum capsule should be removed from the distributor and the apertures blocked, then the centrifugal advance mechanism should be 'recurved' to cover the speed range of the engine. This will entail fitting different centrifugal weights and springs and is therefore best entrusted to a suitable firm specialising in conversions who will have the necessary equipment for testing the distributor.

Part 1
Chapter 3 Maintenance and servicing

Contents

1 Introduction

Maintenance and servicing procedures for all Weber carburettors are identical and are of a straightforward nature.
Engine malfunctions are comparatively rarely a result of carburettor faults and, when they are traced to the carburettor,
there is often an outside factor at work, ie sediment in the fuel.
It is these factors which will be mainly considered in this
Chapter; any specific points in connection with a particular carburettor being detailed in the relevant Chapter of this manual.

The object of the procedures is to maintain the carburation
equipment is first class condition, which will also result in good
engine performance.

2 Intervals

Where the carburettor is standard equipment, servicing and
maintenance should be carried out in accordance with the
manufacturer's recommendations; in the absence of this, the
procedures should be made every 6000 miles (9600 km).

However, if the engine is operated at high speeds for long
periods or in adverse conditions such as dusty terrain, the
procedures must be made more frequently.

3 Cleaning

This is one of the major requirements of the fuel and carburation system. Before attending to any other component it is
essential to clean the exterior of the air cleaner, carburettor,
inlet manifold and, if necessary, the engine. To do this, brush on
a degreasing agent such as Gunk, but where an air cleaner is
not fitted, seal the carburettor apertures with masking tape
before applying the agent. If the engine is being cleaned, place a
polythene bag over the distributor and seal any apertures with
masking tape. The degreasing agent can be washed away with
clean water, together with the dirt and oil deposits.

Remove all masking tape when cleaning is completed; then,
on non air cleaner types, wipe around the air intakes with a
clean lint free cloth.

4 Fuel lines and hoses

1   Check all fuel line unions for security and any signs of
leaking, which, if present, will necessitate the fitting of new
sealing washers.
2   Check all flexible hoses for deterioration and chafing and
renew them if necessary. Check the security of all retaining clips
and if any appear to be seized, renew them.
3   Check that all fuel lines and hoses do not rub against any
sharp objects or contact any hot surfaces, such as the exhaust
system.
4   Where fitted, the fuel pump filter and carburettor fuel inlet
filter should be removed and brushed clean using clean fuel.

5 Air cleaner

1   Where fitted, the air filter should be removed from the air
cleaner and cleaned. The fire resistant foam type are best
cleaned in a household liquid detergent and water solution and
left to dry without the use of any additional heat. The paper type
should be shaken to remove any accumulated dust and dirt.
2   Clean the interior of the air cleaner with a fuel moistened
cloth, then wipe dry with a further lint free cloth.
3   Check the security of the air cleaner and air duct if fitted,
making sure that there is no indication of leaking gaskets.
4   Where a crankcase breather hose communicates with the

air cleaner, it should be cleaned, together with the breather valve.

6 Inlet manifold

1   Check the security of the carburettor mounting nuts and the inlet manifold mounting nuts on the cylinder head.
2   Examine the inlet manifold for fractures and for signs of leaking gaskets, which will often show up as stains on the adjacent metallic surfaces. To detect minor gasket leaks, members of the racing fraternity use a fuel sprayer which consists of a flexible plastic bottle fitted with a 0·012 in to 0·016 in (0·3 mm to 0·4 mm) bore metal tube. With the engine idling, a small quantity of fuel is sprayed around inlet manifold joints and the carburettor throttle spindle exterior locations; if a leak exists, the engine will slow down as a result of the mixture being enrichened. Extreme care must be exercised when using this method in the interests of fire safety and in any case, the procedure must be carried out in an open space.
3   If the inlet manifold is heated by the engine coolant, check the condition and security of the water hoses, tightening the retaining clips as necessary.

7 Throttle and choke controls

1   Check all controls for smooth and complete action and renew any control rods or frayed cables as necessary.
2   Check all balljoints and ball-bearings for signs of deterioration or seizure as well as excessive clearances.
3   Check the tightness of all mounting pedestal nuts and balljoint retaining nuts.
4   Lubricate all bearing surfaces of the complete throttle and choke control linkages, including any carburettor accessory devices with moving parts.

8 Carburettor body

1   Check the security of all fixings and the tightness of all nuts and screws.
2   Where an automatic choke is fitted, check the condition and security of the water hoses and tighten the retaining clips as necessary. Also check that there are no signs of water leakage; if there is, the gasket must be renewed.
3   Check that ignition vacuum connections where fitted, are secure and that the rubber tube is not perished or cracked.
4   Examine the underside of the carburettor for fuel leaks.

9 Tuning

Tuning is probably the most talked about aspect of car maintenance, yet it so often misunderstood and misinterpreted. For instance, carburettors are often spoken of as going 'off-tune', but this is not usually the case, as there are few moving parts which could alter the function of the carburettor to warrant regular 'tuning-up'. Only at high mileages is there significant wear in a carburettor and at this time a complete overhaul must be made. What in fact happens is that the mechanical condition of the engine deteriorates or alters and the carburettor, being a very sensitive instrument, is adversely affected. As shown in Chapter 1, even a change of fuel could influence a carburettor's performance due to an incorrect A/F mixture ratio being delivered.

It is not always appreciated that a change of ambient temperature or air density will influence the operation of the carburettor. For this reason the carburettor may require more frequent tuning than the 6000 mile (9600 km) interval recommended in Section 2.

When tuning a carburettor, the complete procedure should be carried out as given in the relevant Chapter of this manual

A

B

C

D

Fig. 3.1 Plug indication illustration (Sec 10)

A   *Grey/brown deposits indicating correct mixture*   C   *White rusty deposits indicating weak mixture*
B   *Black sooty deposits indicating rich mixture*   D   *Wet oily deposits indicating worn engine*

and, particularly with multiple fittings, it is not advisable to cut short the procedure by trying to guess the correct settings.

10 Engine condition

Carburettor performance depends to a great extent on the condition of the engine. Carburettor adjustments and tuning are only accurate if the general condition of the engine is good. However the average serviceable engine will respond well to carburettor tuning, as this compensates for general wear of the engine components. For example, worn valve guides will admit additional air to the inlet valves and this can be compensated for by adjusting the carburettor slightly richer. Uneven wear in the engine cylinders may result in uneven idling characteristics and this can be corrected by slightly increasing the idling speed adjustment.

The engine components responsible for 'breathing' are of course most important from the point of view of carburation. These include the cylinder head, valves and valve guides, camshaft and cam followers. valve operating gear, piston rings and cylinder bores, and inlet and exhaust systems. Any malfunction of these items must be rectified before accurate carburettor tuning is possible.

With the main engine components in good condition, it is recommended that the ignition timing and valve clearances are checked and adjusted in accordance with the manufacturer's instructions before tuning the carburettor. Spark plugs should be removed, cleaned, and regapped with a feeler gauge. In the absence of manufacturer's data, the average spark plug gap should be set to 0·024 in (0·6 mm), however with electronic ignition fittings, a different gap may be recommended. If possible, always try to obtain the correct spark plug gap for the particular application. It is always helpful to check the appearance of the spark plugs after removing them, as this will give a reliable indication of the general engine operating condition. Fig. 3.1 shows four examples of plug appearance related to carburettor adjustment and engine condition.

Another accurate method of assessing engine condition is to use a compression tester (manometer). This instrument is basically a pressure gauge incorporating a non-return valve and it registers the maximum pressure generated in an engine cylinder (photo). This pressure is termed the compression pressure and is related to the compression ratio. If the engine is of standard specification, the compression pressure and ratio will

10.1 A typical compression tester

normally be stated in the manufacturer's handbook and a comparison can then be made with the actual readings obtained from the engine.

Compression testers are available in various forms, but the more common types are screwed into the spark plug apertures. Before taking readings, the engine should be run until it reaches the normal operating temperature (ie thermostat open). Stop the engine and disconnect the HT lead from the ignition coil, then remove the first spark plug and screw in the compression tester. Fully open the throttle valves, then spin the engine with the starter motor and record the maximum pressure obtained. Repeat the procedure on the remaining cylinders.

If the compression pressure is more than 20% below the specified amount, or if the difference between the cylinder readings is greater than 14·0 lbf in² to 21·0 lbf in² (1·0 kgf cm² to 1·5 kgf cm²), engine repairs are indicated and should be carried out before attempting to tune the carburettor.

If the engine is proved to be in satisfactory condition, the carburettor may be tuned once all the procedures have been carried out as given in the previous Sections of this Chapter.

Part 1
Chapter 4 Overhaul

Contents

1 Introduction

Overhauling of the carburettor becomes necessary when the component parts are worn to such an extent that they are no longer serviceable or efficient in operation. The manufacturers recommend a general overhaul interval of 60 000 miles (97 000 km) but much will depend on the operating conditions and this may well have to be reduced in certain circumstances. However, if the maintenance and servicing procedures as given in Chapter 3 have been regularly carried out from new, this interval is a good guide to work to.

At the time of the overhaul the carburettor must be removed, disassembled, cleaned, inspected, repaired as necessary, reassembled and refitted. This Chapter includes the general overhaul procedures which apply to all carburettors but any special procedures, particularly those including the use of specialized tools, are included in the Chapters dealing with specific carburettor types.

The work involved is within the capabilities of most home mechanics, although in order to effect a first class overhaul it is important not to rush the work. Weber carburettors are manufactured to a high degree of workmanship and therefore must be treated as precision instruments; although they are manufactured to withstand the most adverse road conditions they also incorporate some extremely sensitive mechanisms.

Extensive workshop equipment is not required and the majority of work can be carried out using the normal tools contained in a motorist's tool kit. However there are certain instances where a special tool is required and these are quoted in the relevant Chapters of this Manual.

Before starting work it is recommended that the home mechanic reads all the relevant Chapters of this Manual in order to acquaint himself with all the necessary procedures and spare parts required. By obtaining the spares and tools beforehand, the overhaul will be completed in the shortest time, and there will be little inconvenience due to the car being off the road.

2 Tools

Note: *In addition to the following list, the tools necessary to carry out any special overhaul procedures as given in the relevant Chapter of this Manual, must be obtained.*

Spanners, open-ended metric
Spanners, ring metric
Screwdrivers, large medium and small (flat blade)
Curved metal scraper
Surface plate or thick piece of plate glass
Steel straight-edge
Hard bristle brush, small
Feeler gauges
Vernier calipers or depth gauge
Large clean tray
Open-topped containers suitable for petrol
Pipe cleaners
Foot-operated tyre pump
Light hammer (100 gm)
Centre punch
Small files, flat and round
Hand chuck, small
Flat metal scraper (photo)

2.1 Typical flat metal scraper

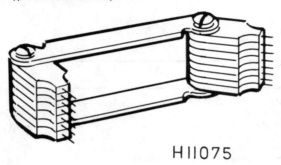
H11075

Fig. 4.1 Set of micron plug jet gauges (Sec 2)

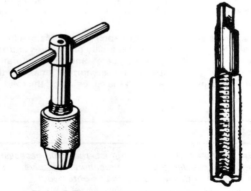
Fig. 4.2 Thread tap and tap holder (Sec 2)

Fig. 4.3 Typical thread die (Sec 2)

Where necessary, the following tools should be obtained from a Weber agent:

Set of jet gauges
Thread tap and tap holder
Thread die and die holder

It is important that all tools are in first class order to prevent damage to the carburettor components. This is particularly relevant to screwdrivers which should be ground flat and square before use. Always enter screwdrivers fully into screw slots and similarly fully engage spanners before attempting to turn them.

3 Materials

Before commencing the overhaul procedure it is advisable to obtain the following materials:

Degreasing fluid (paint stripper or thinners will do)
Petrol
Clean lint-free cloth
Emery cloth (fine)
Engine oil (SAE 30 or SAE 20/50)
Lithium based grease (DCOE and IDA range carburettors with spindle bearings)
Fine grinding paste
Liquid locking agent
Metal polish
Hand cleanser

4 Spare parts

The total amount of spare parts required for the overhaul will not be apparent until the carburettor has been completely dismantled, but at the minimum a gasket set should be obtained prior to commencing work.

The manufacturers currently supply three basic overhaul kits:

A gasket set
A tune-up kit
A master repair kit

The tune-up kit contains the gasket set plus needle valve, float, float fulcrum and accelerator pump diaphragms (if required). The master repair kit contains the tune-up kit plus main jets, air corrector jets, throttle shafts (oversize as necessary), throttle valves and ball bearings (if fitted).

When ordering parts from the manufacturers or agents, it is important to give as much information as you can concerning the carburettor and its application, including jet sizes and carburettor type numbers.

5 Disassembly

The main disassembly procedure is given in the relevant Chapter of this Manual, but it is recommended that the location of the various jets and the position of throttle valves and levers is noted on paper as each component is removed. This will be particularly helpful during the assembly procedure and is essential when working on the progressive or differential type carburettors, where a jet fitted in the incorrect position will completely upset the performance of the carburettor.

If more than one carburettor is being overhauled, it is advisable to work on one unit at a time to prevent accidental interchanging of components.

It is essential to have a large clear area of the workbench available when disassembling the carburettor and each item should be placed in order of removal as far as possible. The workbench must, of course, be scrupulously clean.

Where bypass idle carburettors, tamperproof carburettors and carburettors for use in the USA are fitted, the disassembly procedure may be slightly different to that given in Part 2. USA type carburettors will be fitted with some or all of the items mentioned in Chapter 1 in connection with emission control.

6 Cleaning

This is possibly the most important aspect of overhauling the carburettor as dirt or sediment can lead to many diverse malfunctions. It should be carried out in a well ventilated area and sufficient precautions should be taken to prevent the possibility of fire.

The carburettor body and covers may be cleaned with a degreasant, but only after removing all components such as fibre and rubber washers and seals which may be adversely affected. All traces of gasket should be removed from the flange faces and the internal channels should be blown clear to remove the degreasant. It is advisable to completely immerse the components in fuel as an extra precaution.

The remaining carburettor components should be cleaned in fuel and allowed to dry on a clean tray. In extreme cases, the use of paint thinners will remove the more obstinate accumulation of dirt and sediment.

7 Inspection and repair

With all components cleaned and set out, they must now be inspected for wear and deterioration, in order to decide which are fit for further service, which have to be repaired and which must be renewed.

Special overhaul procedures are given in the relevant Chapter of this Manual but the following Sections give general procedures applicable to all carburettors.

8 Carburettor body and covers

Note: *The body and, on some types, the covers are the only parts of the carburettor which cannot be supplied as spares and therefore, where these items are damaged beyond repair, a new carburettor must be obtained.*

1   Check internally and externally for cracks. These are most likely to be found in the vicinity of the flange mounting holes and are due to overtightening or excessive vibration. On aluminium alloy carburettors it may be possible for a welding specialist to carry out a suitable repair, provided that none of the internal jets and passages are affected. However, great care must be taken to prevent distortion. Carburettors made from zinc alloy (Mazak) cannot be repaired in this way and will either require replacement parts or a new carburettor.

2   Check the flange faces for flatness using a straight-edge (photo). If any undulation or distortion is evident, lap the flange on a sheet of fine emery cloth placed on a surface plate. Where applicable, the carburettor covers may be checked and rectified using the same procedure.

3   Check all tapped (internally threaded) holes for the condition of the thread. It will be observed that the more frequently used threads are fitted with brass inserts and these do not normally deteriorate, but where the thread is tapped directly into the main body the threads may fracture. To repair the latter type of thread, an insert (sometimes called a Helicoil or Cross insert) must be fitted. This is a job best entrusted to a suitably equipped engineering works. An alternative method of repairing the thread is to drill out the threads completely and then tap an oversize thread, but this is only possible in some cases, as the attaching component must be non-standard and it may be necessary to drill adjacent components oversize.

4   Scrape away any corrosion which may have attacked the carburettor metal. This will normally be found in the vicinity of the float chamber on carburettors which have been out of service for a long time (photo). Finish the surface with fine emery cloth but take care not to enlarge any internal bores or channels as this may affect the calibration of the carburettor.

5   Clean any carbon deposits from the carburettor barrels using a curved scraper but ensuring that the barrel walls are not in any way damaged. On differential type carburettors it will be found that the primary barrel is particularly susceptible to carbon build-up which will adversely affect the carburettor performance if not removed. After cleaning, the barrels may be polished lightly with metal polish but make sure that all traces of the polish are removed when the operation is completed.

6   Where a piston type accelerator pump is fitted, check the bore in the carburettor body for scoring and damage. Although the bores are inserted on assembly they cannot be obtained as a spare, and unless an engineering works can effect the repair of a faulty bore, a new carburettor must be obtained.

7   Where applicable, check the condition of all studs fitted to the carburettor body and cover and renew them if necessary.

9 Venturis and chokes

1   Check the auxiliary venturis and chokes for damage; depending on where it is, minor damage may be removed with a fine file and emery cloth, otherwise renew them.

8.2 Checking a carburettor flange with a straight-edge for distortion

8.4 A bad case of corrosion in a 40 IDA 3C carburettor

2   Using a tyre pump, blow through the auxiliary venturi internal channel and nozzle to make sure that it is unobstructed.
3   Where fitted, check that the locating springs are intact and firmly fitted to the auxiliary venturi and choke.

10 Throttle spindles and choke spindles

1   Check the throttle spindles for wear by temporarily refitting them to the body and moving them laterally. If wear is evident, an oversize spindle should be obtained and the body reduced as described in the relevant Chapter of this Manual.
2   Where ball bearings are fitted, spin them by hand and check for any roughness or excessive clearance. The bearing dust seals should be renewed at every overhaul.
3   If the spindle incorporates a cam for operation of the accelerator pump, check this for security and wear.
4   Examine the throttle valve slots in the spindle for signs of distortion; if evident, renew the spindle.
5   Choke spindles (where fitted) should be checked in a similar manner.
6   Check the valve retaining screw threads in the spindle for damage and clear them with a suitable tap if necessary.
7   Where the spindle is discoloured or has score marks, clean it with fine emery tape.

11 Throttle levers and return springs

1   Check all throttle levers and pivots for wear and damage and renew them where necessary.
2   On differential type carburettors, check that the lever slots and associated tags are not excessively worn.
3   Examine the throttle lever retaining nut locktabs for fracturing and, if the tabs appear to be weak, renew them.
4   Check the return springs for damage and renew them if necessary. The springs do not normally lose their tension, but it is worth checking that they return the relevant throttle lever fully when the carburettor is completely assembled.

12 Throttle valves

1   The throttle valves are not normally subject to wear, but the outer periphery of each should be examined for damage which could prevent it fully seating in the barrel.
2   If the throttle lever retaining nut has been tightened with the throttle valve closed, it is possible for the valve to be buckled. To check this, view the valve along its axis and if any distortion is evident, renew it.
3   Polish the throttle valves with metal polish or fine grinding paste to remove any carbon deposits.

13 Choke valves

Check that the choke valves are not distorted and that the periphery is not damaged. Use a fine file if necessary, as irregularities on the periphery may cause the valve to stick shut.

14 Jets and emulsion tubes

1   After cleaning, all jets should be cleared by blowing through them and finally looking through them to check that they are unobstructed. **Note** *Never use wire to clean a jet.*
2   On accelerator pump intake and delivery valves, check that the internal ball is free to move by shaking the valve.
3   Emulsion tubes should be cleaned then blown through with air from a tyre pump.

15 Float assemblies

1   Due to the fact that the float is normally half submerged in petrol, it will not usually require cleaning; however if the carburettor has been out of service for a long time, some corrosion may have accumulated and this should be wiped away.
2   Check visually for any punctures; if fuel has found its way into the float this can be ascertained by shaking it. If any doubt exists, immerse the float in boiling water; a stream of bubbles will issue from the puncture.
3   If a puncture exists, it is usually preferable to renew the float, as the extra weight of any internal fuel and solder used for repair will result in a higher fuel level. However, the weight of the float is usually stamped on the fulcrum tab and if a repair can be effected without exceeding this limit, it is in order to solder the puncture as follows:
4   Thoroughly clean the area around the puncture with fine emery cloth, then immerse the float in boiling water until bubbles cease to issue from the hole. Immediately remove the float, wipe dry, and solder the hole with flux and a lower melting point solder. Remove any excess solder with a small file and emery cloth.
5   Check the float fulcrum pin for wear and renew it if necessary.
6   Where the float assembly consists of two semi-floats, check that they are both level with each other and are at 90° to the fulcrum pin, otherwise in some instances they may foul the sides of the float chamber.

16 Needle valves

1   After cleaning the needle and needle valve seat, dry them and blow through the needle valve seat with air to clear any obstruction.
2   Check the contact surfaces of the needle and seat for wear and if a groove is evident on the needle, renew the complete valve.
3   Check that the ball in the end of the needle is tensioned by the internal spring and that it moves in and out freely.
4   Check the hooked spring on the end of the needle (if fitted); if the original needle valve is being refitted, it is best to fit the hook the same way round as removed but if a new valve is fitted, the hook can be fitted either way round.

17 Fibre washers and diaphragms

1   All fibre washers should be renewed whenever the carburettor is overhauled. Always use genuine Weber washers particularly on the fuel inlet unions, otherwise there is the possibility of a fire risk if a leakage should occur.
2   Examine all diaphragms (accelerator pump, automatic choke, full power valve, etc.) for fractures and renew them if necessary. If the full power valve diaphragm requires renewal, it will be necessary to obtain the complete valve assembly. If the accelerator pump diaphragm requires renewal, the return spring should be renewed at the same time.

18 Accelerator pumps

1   On piston types, check the piston for scoring and damage and check the operating rod for wear and distortion.
2   On diaphragm types, check the mating surfaces of the cover, body and carburettor body. If any corrosion or irregularities are evident remove them with metal polish.
3   Check the operating arm roller (if fitted) for wear and, if worn, obtain a new cover.

19 Screws and washers

1   Check all retaining screws and washers and renew them as necessary. In particular check screw slots for damage. If damage is not excessive, the slot can be reformed using a file and hacksaw blade.
2   If necessary, screw threads can be reformed using a die.
3   Check all idling adjustment screws and springs for damage. The taper on volume control adjustment screws and air compensation screws should also be checked and if it is not smooth and symmetrical, they must be renewed as necessary. If the carburettor is of the bypass idle type, note the comments in Chapter 1 of this Manual.

20 Air horns

The air horns are particularly vulnerable to damage due to their position. However if they are damaged, it is usually a simple matter to beat them back to the original shape using a length of dowel rod and a light hammer.

Part 1
Chapter 5   Carburettor calibration and testing

Contents

1   Introduction

Weber carburettors are manufactured to a high degree of accuracy and initially they are calibrated for the particular engine they are fitted to. This involves extensive testing with a chassis dynamometer in addition to road testing with the aid of many instruments.

The information given in this Chapter is not intended to result in as precise a calibration as the manufacturers can provide. However, since there is quite an interest in fitting carburettors such as the DCOE and 28/36 DCD to engines for which they were not originally intended, it will enable the home mechanic to obtain a satisfactory performance from his carburettor.

It is suggested that the operation of the carburettor being calibrated is fully understood by referring to Part 2 of this Manual and that it is first overhauled and the various jet and choke sizes as given in Sections 2 to 7 inclusive fitted.

In certain territories it will be necessary to check that no emission laws are being violated by altering the original calibration of the carburettor.

With multiple carburettor fittings it may prove beneficial to have the carburettors calibrated by a Weber agent, since the cost of obtaining a selection of jets may be the deciding factor.

2   Choke and auxiliary venturi selection

The diameter of the choke, or main venturi as it is sometimes known, determines the air velocity through the carburettor at all engine speeds and throttle openings. On some carburettors, the choke can be removed but on others it is fixed, however in both instances the choke size (given in mm) refers to the narrowest internal diameter. On fixed choke types the size is

stamped on the outside of the carburettor, whereas on the removable type it is stamped on the inlet side of the choke.

The choke size will be within the limits of 0·7 to 0·9 of the barrel diameter which is measured at the throttle valve end of the carburettor. The correct size of choke for a particular carburettor will depend on the requirements of the engine; a large choke will be required if maximum performance at high engine speed is the objective and a small choke will be required if engine flexibility during lower engine speed is essential. It is always most important to choose a choke size which is the *smallest* consistent with the maximum horse power of the engine.

Figs. 5.1 and 5.2 show graphs which will enable the approximate size to be chosen. On the DCOE carburettor in particular, the choke sizes given in Fig. 5.2 may be rather large for normal road usage where low speed flexibility is desirable. In this instance a reduction in choke area of approximately 10% where one carburettor barrel feeds one cylinder may be required and slightly more where one carburettor barrel feeds more than one cylinder. On the 28/36 DCD carburettor where the chokes are removable, the secondary choke size can be determined from Fig. 5.1 and the primary choke size is normally 1 mm less. If the engine is equipped with a racing cam, the difference between the primary and secondary choke diameters may need to be increased 1 mm or 2 mm in order to give more flexibility at the lower engine speeds.

As to whether the choke selection has been correct will be evident after road testing the car. Any alteration will be decided upon after calibrating the carburettor as described in Sections 8 to 10 inclusive.

The auxiliary venturi is located on the inlet side of the choke and contains the mixture delivery nozzle which operates in conjunction with the main circuit. The size marked in mm indicates the cross-sectional area of the narrowest part of the nozzle channel, which is equal to the area of a circle having the same

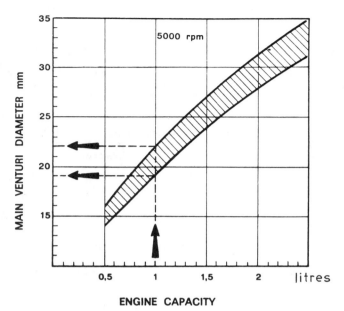

Fig. 5.1 Choke diameter selection chart (Sec 2)

For 4-stroke, 1 to 6-cylinder engines with maximum output at approximately 5000 rpm, fed by one single barrel carburettor (On 2-cylinder engines, multiply the engine capacity by 2)

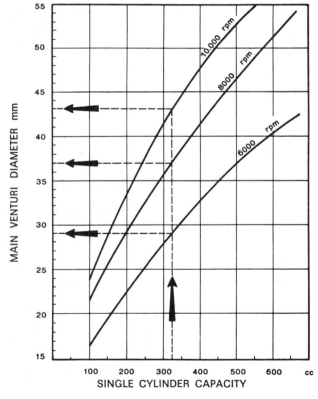

Fig. 5.2 Choke diameter selection chart (Sec 2)

For 4-stroke engines with one carburettor barrel per engine cylinder. The three curves correspond to **maximum** *output engine speeds of 6000, 8000 and 10 000 rpm*

diameter. For instance, the cross-sectional area of a nozzle in a 4·00 mm auxiliary venturi will be $\pi \times 2 \cdot 0$ mm², since πr^2 is the area of a circle.

By fitting a larger size auxiliary venturi, the main mixture supply will be delayed and vice versa. The most common size of auxiliary venturi ranges from 3·00 mm to 4·5 mm, although on some carburettors there is no choice. The eventual size will depend on the results obtained by carrying out the procedure given in the following Sections and therefore as an initial choice, a medium size should be fitted.

3 Air corrector jet selection

The air corrector jet meters air to the emulsion tube and, due to the fact that air is less dense than fuel, the size of jet affects the higher engine speeds rather than the lower speeds. The air corrector jet also works in conjunction with the main fuel jet and both components are therefore calibrated together.

Air corrector jets sizes range from 0·70 mm to 3·40 mm and as a starting point a 2·00 mm size will be in order. On differential type carburettors, the 2·00 mm size air corrector jet should be fitted to the primary main circuit and, as a starting point, a 1·80 mm air corrector jet should be fitted to the secondary main circuit.

4 Main fuel jet selection

The main fuel jet meters fuel to the nozzle in the auxiliary venturi via the emulsion tube. Its size will depend on the requirements of the engine. As it works in direct relationship with the choke, the size of the main jet will vary in relation to the size of the choke. The graph shown in Fig. 5.3 will enable the main jet size to be chosen, although this graph assumes that the air corrector jet size is 2·00 mm.

The final size of main fuel jet and air corrector jet can be chosen after testing the carburettor.

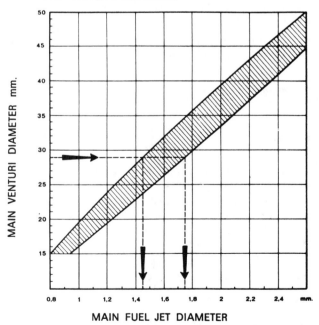

Fig. 5.3 Main fuel jet selection chart (Sec 4)

Showing air corrector jet at a constant 2.00 mm diameter with one choke (main venturi) feeding 4 or 6 cylinders. Where one choke feeds two cylinders, multiply the jet size by 0.90. Where one choke feeds a single cylinder, multiply the jet size by 0.75

5 Emulsion tube selection

The emulsion tube emulsifies air from the air corrector jet with fuel from the main fuel jet and therefore controls the mixture emanating from the nozzle at all engine speeds with the main circuit in operation.

The controlling factors of the emulsion tube are its diameter and the location of the emulsion holes. These factors are included in the code number of the emulsion tube which is always preceded by the letter F. Unfortunately the code numbers do not follow in any particular sequence which would indicate the applicable characteristics, but the following chart shows the emulsion tubes to be wired to correct mixture faults, together with the most common types:

Application	IDF, DCOE, 46/48 IDA	28/36 DCD	Differential and triple choke
Most common type	F16, F11, F7	F30	F6
For low rpm enrichment or slight acceleration enrichment (emulsion holes towards the bottom)	F7	F23, F30	F3, F5, F7, F21
For low rpm weakening or slight acceleration weakening (emulsion holes towards the top)	F2, F3, F11, F14, F15, F16	F8, F26, F33	F20, F33, F34
For high rpm weakening with air corrector jet larger than 2.0 mm (greater number of emulsion holes)	F11, F19	F8, F9, F31	F8, F16, F20
For low rpm acceleration enrichment with larger air corrector jet (smaller diameter tube)	F7, F8	F13	F3, F5, F25
For large main fuel jets or alcohol fuels	F2, F3, F4, F7, F17	F8, F10, F29	F2, F20, F24, F25, F26

Note: *Correction tables for DCNF emulsion tubes are not available, although the most common types are* F36, F25 *and* F27

The operation of the emulsion tube is given in Part 2 of this Manual in the relevant carburettor Chapter. It will be observed that where the emulsion holes are located on the upper section of the tube, the emulsifying action will begin at lower engine speeds. Where the holes are towards the lower section of the tube, the action will begin at higher engine speeds. The diameter of the emulsion tube determines the reserve of fuel in the emulsion tube well; a thin tube will give a large reserve and vice versa. This reserve of fuel has a great effect on the acceleration of the engine and is therefore an important factor.

Due to the number of emulsion tubes available, it is recommended that the advice of a Weber dealer is sought, particularly if there is more than one carburettor, as a wrong choice could prove very expensive. However, in the absence of any information, the most common emulsion tube sizes given in the chart should be used initially.

6 Idling jet selection

The idling jet meters fuel to the idling and progression circuits and, as this circuit is generally used for a large precentage of driving, this size of jet is quite critical both in the interests of economy and engine flexibility.

On DCOE and 46/48 IDA carburettors, the idling jet holders incorporate calibrated air correction holes coded from Rich to Lean in the following sequence:

F6, F12, F9, F8, F11, F13, F2, F4, F5, F7, F1, F3

In carburettor types other than the above, air correction for idling and progression is provided through fixed calibrated holes and these cannot be altered.

Since the choice of idling jet determines the lower to middle engine speed range drivability to a large extent, the final size will be decided during the calibration of the carburettor. However, as a starting point, a 0.50 mm size fuel jet should be fitted.

7 Needle valve selection

The needle valve is operated by the float and admits fuel to the float chamber. The size of the needle valve seat aperture must be sufficient to pass fuel continuously at a rate which the engine requires when it is at maximum power. The size is therefore dependent on the maximum power of the particular engine.

It is recommended that the minimum size needle valve consistent with the maximum engine power is fitted, since the level of fuel in the float chamber is more accurately controlled with smaller sizes.

The following chart indicates the needle valve sizes where one needle valve is fitted; where there is more than one needle valve (ie on triple choke carburettors or multiple carburettor fittings) the maximum hp for the engine should be divided by the number of needle valves to calculate the size for each valve:

hp	mm
Up to 60	*1.50*
61 to 110	*1.75*
111 to 150	*2.00*
151 to 180	*2.25*
181 to 200	*2.50*
Over 200	*3.00*
Alcohol application	*3.00*

8 Calibrating the DCOE carburettor

Having selected and fitted the various jets, chokes, etc as previously described, the time has now come to test the engine for performance and to make any final adjustments as necessary.

1 Start the engine and run it until normal operating temperature has been reached, then adjust the slow running as described in Part 2 of this Manual, Chapter 11. Take care not to set the idle speed screw too far in, otherwise the first progression holes may be uncovered. For this reason the idle screw should be adjusted to give the minimum possible idling speed.

2 As a preliminary check as to whether the idling jet is of the correct size, note the position of the mixture adjustment screw, then screw it in as far as possible then right out. If the idling jet is of the correct size, the idling position of the mixture screw should be approximately midway between fully in and fully out. If the mixture screw needs to be nearly screwed right in, the idling jet is too rich and vice versa. Reset the mixture screw before proceeding.

3 Turn the idling speed adjusting screw to increase the engine speed and at the same time, look through the auxiliary venturis using a torch and mirror if necessary. As soon as mixture starts

to issue from the nozzles, stop turning the idling screw and unscrew it until the mixture stops; at this engine speed (approximately 500 rpm above idling) the progression holes will be brought into action.

4   Note the position of the idling mixture adjustment screw, then turn it in half a turn. This will weaken the mixture slightly and if the engine speed increases as a result, the idling jet is too rich. Alternatively, if the engine speed increases when the mixture screw is turned out the idling jet is too weak.

5   If the idling jet is proved to be incorrect, the mixture may be richened by fitting an idling jet with smaller air holes or a larger fuel jet. It should be noted that, as air is less dense than fuel, the air hole size will affect the higher engine speeds of the progression stage whereas the fuel jet size will affect the complete idling and progression stages. The mixture strength can be checked through the complete progression stage using the procedure given in paragraph 4 with the engine at several different speeds. When completed, the idling speed adjusting screw(s) should be set to its original position.

6   The transfer from the idling to the progression stage should be smooth, but if any flat spot or richness is noticed, the throttle valves may not be seating correctly in the carburettor barrels. Also if the barrels have been polished, the throttle valves may not be positioned against the progression holes correctly. If it is found impossible to cure a flat spot, the progression stage may be brought in earlier by chamfering the throttle valves on the engine side, adjacent to the progression hole (see Fig. 5.4). This action should only be taken after removing the carburettor and thoroughly examining the throttle valve movement. If richness occurs, and this is more common, the opposite (ie choke side of the throttle valves should be chamfered adjacent to the progression hole. This has the effect of delaying the action of the progression holes. An alternative cure for richness which should be employed if other methods fail, is to drill a hole in the throttle valves as shown in Fig. 5.5. This will allow the throttle valves to be closed onto the progression holes without reducing the flow of air. Again, this action should only be taken after thorough investigation and the size of the hole should never exceed 1·5 mm in diameter. Start initially with a 0·7 mm diameter hole.

7   Increase the engine speed from the progression stage until mixture issues from the auxiliary venturi nozzles, indicating that the main circuit is in operation. If the transfer from progression to main circuit produces a flat spot, either the main circuit entry is too late, or the accelerator pump calibration is too weak; the opposite applies if richness occurs. In practice, the auxiliary venturi size selection is comparatively limited and is not as critical as the accelerator pump calibration, therefore the latter should be checked first. It must also be remembered that the accelerator pump injects very little, if any, fuel into the carburettor when the throttle valves are opened slowly. This fact will help decide whether a mixture fault is occurring in the accelerator pump or the auxiliary venturi; if the fault occurs only with fast movement of the throttle, the accelerator pump calibration is likely to be incorrect.

8   Reference to Part 2, Chapter 11 will show that there are a number of variables on the DCOE accelerator pump. The correct selection of components will depend on the particular engine being worked on. Generally it is recommended that the

accelerator pump is calibrated with a weak setting initially and the setting then progressively richened until the correct engine performance is achieved. The following points should be noted:

   (a) *The length of the accelerator pump rod determines the maximum amount of fuel injected through the pump jet. A long rod will allow more fuel to be available*
   (b) *The pump jet meters the fuel into the carburettor throat. A large jet will supply a large amount of fuel but over a short period; all other components remaining the same*
   (c) *The intake and discharge valve determines the amount of fuel returned to the float chamber. A blank discharge valve will enable all the fuel drawn into the accelerator pump chamber to be injected through the pump jet*
   (d) *The accelerator pump spring determines the pressure with which the fuel is forced out of the pump jet and therefore the period over which the injection takes place. A weak spring will increase the injection period, all other components remaining the same*
   (e) *The accelerator pump jet acts as a high speed enrichment jet and its selection should therefore take this aspect into account*

9   Hold the engine speed at several different throttle openings with the main circuit functioning. The engine should run smoothly and evenly if the mixture is correct and the exhaust gases should be clean and not sooty. If there is any indication of a weak or rich mixture, the main jet and/or air corrector jet should be changed. It should be noted that the main jet size affects all engine speeds in the main circuit range, whereas the air corrector jet size affects the higher engine speeds due to the fact that air is less dense than fuel.

10   The relationship between the air corrector jet size and the main jet size is approximately 3 to 1. For instance, an increase in main jet size from 1·60 mm to 1·65 mm is approximately equal to a decrease in air corrector jet size from 2·20 mm to 2·05 mm. This should be taken into account in order to decide where in the engine speed range the mixture needs changing.

11   If it is found impossible to calibrate the main circuit, the choice of emulsion tube may be incorrect and reference should therefore be made to the chart in Section 5 of this Chapter. However, the effect of the emulsion tube is more noticeable at the lower engine speeds of the main circuit. If this range cannot be calibrated correctly by changing the main jet, a change of emulsion tube is indicated.

12   With the carburettor calibrated whilst the car is stationary, the car should now be road tested to find out if any further adjustments are necessary.

13   With the engine at operating temperature, take the carburettor through the progression stage to full throttle stage in each gear, noting the engine performance. If the engine appears to lack performance generally but the mixture calibration seems correct, the choke size may need to be reduced by 1 mm or 2 mm. The complete calibration procedure will need to be repeated if this is proved necessary.

14   The mixture strength at high engine speed is critical if long engine life is to be achieved, as a weak mixture can burn away the piston crowns in extreme cases. As a further check on

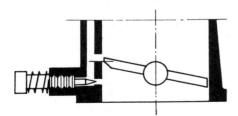

Fig. 5.4 Method of advancing the progression phase of the carburettor (Sec 8)

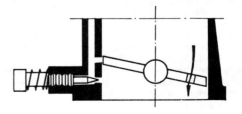

Fig. 5.5 Method of retarding the progression phase of the carburettor (Sec 8)

mixture, it is therefore recommended that the 'plug cut' test is made at several different engine speeds with the car in motion. To do this, keep the engine at the speed being tested over a two or three minute period, then depress the clutch or select neutral (automatic transmission cars) and switch off the ignition. Coast to a halt, then remove the spark plugs and compare them with the chart given in Chapter 3 of this Manual. If there is any tendency for the plugs to be weak or rich, that particular speed range of engine will need recalibration. This test is particularly helpful at maximum engine speed, as the enrichment effect of the accelerator pump jet will be apparent.

15 If an exhaust gas analyser is available, this may be used as a more accurate method of determining the mixture strength at various engine speeds, particularly during the idling and progression phases.

9 Calibrating the 28/36 DCD carburettor

After fitting the various jets and chokes etc as previously described, the engine must now be tested for performance at different stages in order to make any final adjustments and changes as necessary.

1 Start the engine and run it until normal operating temperature has been reached, then adjust the slow running as described in Part 2 of this Manual, Chapter 6.

2 Note the position of the mixture adjustment screw, as this will give a preliminary indication of whether the idling jet size is correct. If the mixture screw is adjusted almost right in, this indicates that the idling jet is too rich, alternatively, if it is on the last few threads, the idling jet is too weak.

3 Turn the idling speed adjusting screw to increase the engine speed and at the same time look through the primary auxiliary venturi. As soon as the mixture starts to issue from the primary nozzle, stop turning the idling screw and unscrew it until the mixture ceases; at this engine speed (approximately 500 rpm above idling) the progression holes will be brought into action.

4 Note the position of the idling mixture adjustment screw, then turn it in half a turn. This action will weaken the mixture and if it is accompanied by an increase in engine speed, the idling jet size is too rich. Alternatively if the engine speed increases as the idling mixture is screwed out, the idling jet is too weak.

5 If the idling jet is proved to be incorrect, the mixture may be richened by fitting a larger size jet. The mixture strength should be checked through the complete idling and progression stages, using the procedure given in paragraph 4, with the engine at different speeds. When completed, reset the idle speed adjusting screw.

6 The transfer from the idling to the progression stage should be smooth and unnoticeable, but if any flat spot or richness occurs, first check that the primary throttle valve is seating correctly in the carburettor barrel. If it is, refer to Section 8 paragraph 6 for details of further checks that can be made.

7 Increase the engine speed from the progression stage until mixture issues from the primary auxiliary venturi nozzle, indicating that the primary main circuit is in operation. If the transfer from progression to main circuit produces a flat spot, either the main circuit entry is too late or the accelerator pump calibration is too weak, and vice versa. Refer to Section 8 paragraph 7 for information on how to diagnose the fault, and if necessary, calibrate the accelerator pump as follows: on the DCD carburettor it is only possible to alter the calibration of the pump jet and the float chamber discharge valve. Start with a small pump jet which will induce the flat spot, then progressively fit larger pump jets until the flat spot ceases. If the flat spot persists with the largest pump jet, progressively decrease the discharge valve size until the correct mixture is obtained.

8 The engine should now be run at several different speeds with the primary main circuit functioning, but without opening the throttle valve more than $\frac{2}{3}$ open (ie without opening the secondary throttle valve which can be wired up to keep it closed if necessary). The engine should run smoothly and evenly if the

mixture is correct and the exhaust gases should be clean and not sooty. If necessary the main jet and/or the air corrector jet for the primary barrel should be changed to obtain the correct mixture. Note that the primary main jet size affects all engine speeds in the primary main circuit range, whereas the primary air corrector jet mainly affects the higher engine speeds.

9 The inter-relationship of the main fuel jet, the air corrector jet and the emulsion tube in the primary barrel is identical to that for the DCOE carburettor; reference should therefore be made to Section 8 paragraphs 9 and 10, in order to decide how to calibrate these components. However, it should be noted that the primary barrel is best calibrated for economy and the main jet size must be kept to a minimum. If the mixture has a tendency to richen with the primary throttle at $\frac{2}{3}$ open, the air corrector jet size should be increased.

10 Increase the engine speed by opening the throttle until the secondary progression circuit is brought into action, but without mixture coming from the secondary nozzle. The exact point where the secondary progression occurs is sometimes difficult to obtain; however if the progression mixture is weak, a flat spot will occur. In order to arrive at the correct secondary progression idling jet size, start with a small jet that will induce the flat spot, then progressively fit larger jets until the flat spot ceases.

11 The main circuit of the secondary barrel must now be calibrated for maximum power, as this barrel only operates when the throttle pedal is more than $\frac{2}{3}$ depressed. The procedure is basically identical to that for the primary barrel as described in paragraphs 8 and 9 but, since the secondary choke is larger than the primary choke, the main jet will be slightly larger. Check the mixture at various engine speeds with the secondary throttle valve at various openings. Although the primary main circuit will obviously be functioning, all adjustments to the mixture during the secondary barrel stage must be made to the secondary main jet, air corrector jet, and emulsion tube. Remember that the secondary main jet will affect the complete secondary engine speed range, whereas the secondary air corrector jet will affect the middle to upper secondary barrel engine speed range. Generally speaking, the secondary air corrector jet is usually approximately 0.20 mm down on the primary air corrector jet size.

12 The carburettor is now calibrated with the car stationary and the calibration must now be checked with the car in motion.

13 With the engine at operating temperature, take the carburettor through the complete primary and secondary stages in each gear, whilst noting the engine performance. The size of the primary choke will have a considerable effect on the flexibility of the engine at low speeds. If there is any indication of a lack of response during this stage, the primary choke size may need to be reduced by 1 mm or 2 mm. It will, of course, be necessary to repeat the calibration procedure if this step is taken.

14 As a final test of mixture strength, carry out the procedures given in Section 8 paragraphs 13 and 14.

Note: *The enrichment effect of the accelerator pump jet does not apply to the 28/36 DCD carburettor.*

10 Calibrating other Weber carburettors

The DCOE and 28/36 DCD type carburettors offer the greatest scope as far as calibration is concerned. The calibration of all other Weber carburettors can be carried out using Section 8 for synchronised throttle opening carburettors and Section 9 for differential throttle opening carburettors. However there are a few points which should be noted where a slightly different approach should be made:

Diaphragm type accelerator pumps

Where these are fitted, the choice of pump jet and intake and discharge valve is identical to that for the plunger type pump. On some types, the pump lever has two pivot positions in order to alter the pump stroke. On the IDAP type, the pump lever stroke can be altered by a threaded adjustment.

Fixed choke carburettors

Unlike the DCOE and 28/36 DCD, some carburettors have fixed chokes and the carburettors described in Chapters 7, 9 and 10 in Part 2 fall into this category. The selection of choke size in relation to the engine size and performance, follows the same procedure as described in Section 2, but it will of necessity need to be as accurate as possible if the carburettor is to function correctly.

High speed enrichment device

Where this is fitted, the mixture is enriched when the engine is at high speed with the throttle valves fully open. Under these conditions additional fuel is drawn from an extra fuel outlet located above the nozzle. It will be necessary to take into consideration the effect of the enrichment device, particularly when calibrating the main jet and air corrector jet.

Full power valve

This valve, when fitted, supplies additional fuel when the throttle valve is opened quickly. It is operated by a channel communicating with the engine side of the throttle valve. It is usually fitted to fixed choke carburettors and its operation is closely related to the choke size. If therefore the choke size is too large for the engine it is fitted to, the power valve may operate too soon in the throttle opening process and thus provide too rich a mixture for the engine speed. Other than changing the carburettor for a smaller choke size, the power valve spring may be changed for a weaker one in order to delay its operation. Unfortunately the spring is not available as a spare and a certain amount of experimenting will be necessary.

Semi-automatic chokes

Where fitted, the semi-automatic choke should be adjusted as described in Part 2 of this Manual under the relevant Chapter. There is very little that can be done in the way of calibration, although if it is found that the mixture during the automatic choke stage is in need of slight adjustment, the thermostat housing may be moved anti-clockwise to prolong the choke action or clockwise to shorten it. The amount of movement should not exceed approximately 0·125 in (3·2 mm) in either direction. On the DFAV type automatic choke, the operating rod stop plate can be adjusted if necessary to limit the initial choke valve opening, but this should only be necessary in an extreme case of incorrect mixture.

Bypass idle carburettors

Selection of the secondary idle jet must take into account the operation of the bypass idle system. When calibrating the jet, the bypass idle adjustment screw should be set at a central position.

Part 2
Chapter 6 Type 28/36 DCD carburettor

Contents

Adjustment data

Float level setting dimensions
	in (mm)
Closed position	0.197 (5.0)
Open position	0.531 (13.5)
Stroke	0.335 (8.5)

1 Introduction

The Weber 28/36 carburettor is of the downdraught type and has two barrels to supply the primary and secondary functions; the primary barrel is of 28.0 mm diameter at the throttle valve location and the secondary barrel is of 3.60 mm diameter. Each throttle valve is mounted on separate shafts and the valves are of the differential or progressive choke type. The linkage between the two throttle valves is arranged so that the secondary throttle valve does not commence to open until the primary throttle valve is $\frac{2}{3}$ open.

The carburettor is normally fitted to the engine as a single unit with both barrels feeding a common inlet manifold, the most common arrangements being as follows:

1 One unit on a four-cylinder in-line engine
2 One unit on a six-cylinder in-line engine

The carburettor identification mark is located on the lower flange outer surface.

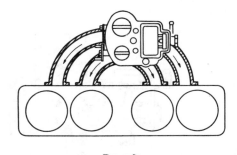

Fig. 6.1 Single carburettor fitted to a four-cylinder in-line engine (Sec 1)

2 Construction

The main body and cover of the Weber 28/36 DCD carburettor are made of die-cast aluminium or zinc alloy (Mazak), the mounting flange being machined flat for fitting on the inlet manifold. The upper face of the cover is also machined flat and incorporates four threaded holes for the fitting of an air cleaner (photo).

The hrottle valves and shafts are of brass and the shafts run directly in the carburettor body. All fuel and air jets and emulsion tubes are of brass construction and are screw fittings into the main body.

Internal channels of the main body and cover are mostly drilled and are sealed with lead plugs where necessary.

The fuel float assembly comprises two semi-floats which are each of two halves soldered together; they are made of thin brass sheet.

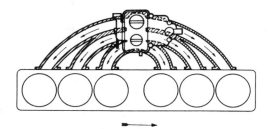

Fig. 6.2 Single carburettor fitted to a six-cylinder in-line engine (Sec 1)

3 Operation

Cold starting

The tarting device fitted to type DCD carburettors operates independently of the main circuit and may be considered as a separate carburettor within the main carburettor.

When the choke cable is pulled, the starting device operating lever turns the control shaft which lifts the starting valve off of its seat. Reference to Fig. 6.3 will show that fuel from the float chamber (7) is driven through the channel (53) to arrive at the starter fuel jet (52). Air entering through the air correction jet (51) and the bypass channel emulsifies the fuel as it i drawn through the starting jet emulsion holes and the bypass channel. The mixture is then drawn through the channel (48) and past the starter valve (50) where additional air from the channel (49) weakens the mixture. The final mixture is drawn through the channel (54) and into both the primary and secondary carburettor barrels at the engine side of the throttle valves.

Once the engine starts, the vacuum in the channels (54) and (57) increases to such an extent that the starter plunger (56) is pulled against spring pressure from the seat (55). Additional air is thus admitted to the mixture to allow the engine to continue running.

The starting device has a progressive action made possible by the tapered shape of the valve head. Lowering the valve will reduce the amount of mixture admitted to the engine. The supply will cease when the valve is completely shut.

Idling and progression

Refer to Fig. 6.4 and note that when the engine is idling the secondary throttle valve (37) is completely shut, but the primary

2.0 Typical air cleaner with the cover removed

throttle (13) is slightly open, according to the throttle idling adjustment screw setting. Fuel is drawn from the float chamber hrough an internal channel to the fuel jet in the idling jet (34). On passing through the fuel jet, air is introduced to the fuel from the calibrated bush (35) and the holes in the idling jet tube. The fuel then becomes emulsified.

The mixture then passes through the channel (32), past the idling mixture adjustment screw (20), through the idling feed hole (31) and into the primary carburettor throat at the engine side of the throttle valve. The idling adjustment screw (20) has a tapered end and can therefore be adjusted to admit more or less fuel/air mixture as necessary.

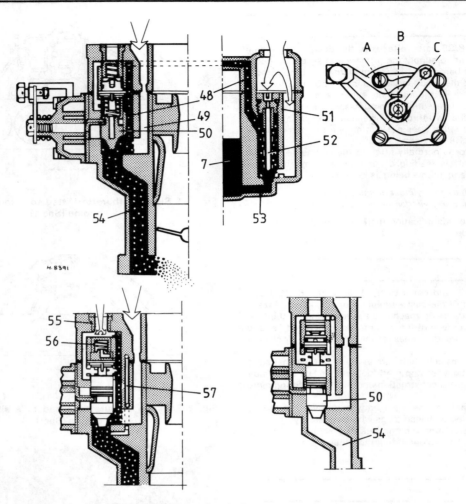

Fig. 6.3 Cold starting device operation (Sec 3)

7	Float chamber	51	Air correction jet	55	Starter air valve seat
48	Channel	52	Starting jet	56	Starter air valve
49	Air channel	53	Fuel channel	57	Transfer channel
50	Starter valve	54	Emulsion channel		

A	Cold starting position
B	Warming up position
C	Closed position

When the primary throttle valve (13) is opened slightly to increase the engine speed, the progression hole (36) is brought into action to provide additional fuel. This is necessary to prevent a flat spot occurring before the main primary fuel supply system comes into operation.

When the primary throttle valve (13) is approximately $\frac{2}{3}$ open, the secondary throttle valve (37) will commence to open. This action causes the secondary progression hole (38) to be brought under engine vacuum. Fuel is then drawn from the float chamber to the secondary idling jet(27), where air is introduced from the calibrated bush (26). The mixture passes through the channel (29) and thus emerges from the progression hole (38).

With either throttle valve fully open, the progression system for the particular carburettor barrel ceases.

Normal running

Under full throttle and high speed cruising conditions, the throttle plates will be sufficiently far from the idling and progression holes to prevent them from admitting fuel and the main fuel supply circuits will be brought into action.

Refer to Fig. 6.5 and note that fuel from the float chamber (7) passes through the main jets (8) and channels (9) to the emulsion tube wells (11). At the same time, air is drawn through the air corrector jets (1), through the centre of the emulsion tubes (12) and via the emulsion tube holes to the fuel. The fuel then becomes emulsified and is drawn through the nozzles (17) and auxiliary venturis (16) and thus mixes with the main air supply as it is drawn through the chokes (15) and into the engine.

Under static conditions the level of fuel in the float chamber and emulsion tube will be identical; however, as the engine speed increases and the fuel flow is faster, the fuel level in the emulsion tube drops. By providing additional holes in the lower part of the emulsion tube, the necessary air correction is made possible at the higher engine speeds.

The main fuel supply circuits of the primary and secondary carburettor barrels operate progressively and there is a certain amount of overlapping as each circuit is brought into action.

Acceleration

To provide the engine with a rich mixture when accelerating, the carburettor is equipped with an acceleration pump which is operated by the primary throttle of the carburettor and injects only into the primary venturi. Reference to Fig. 6.6 will

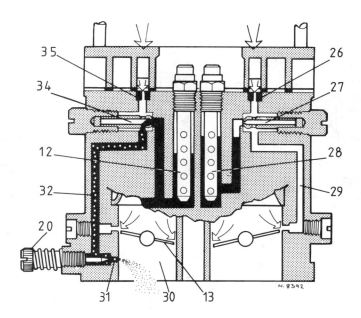

Fig. 6.4 Carburettor idling and progression phase (Sec 3)

12 Primary emulsion tube
13 Primary throttle valve
20 Idling mixture control screw
26 Secondary air jet
27 Secondary idling jet
28 Secondary emulsion tube
29 Secondary progression channel
30 Primary barrel
31 Idle feed orifice
32 Primary idling and progression channel
34 Primary idling jet
35 Primary air jet
36 Primary progression hole
37 Secondary throttle valve
38 Secondary progression hole

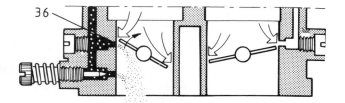

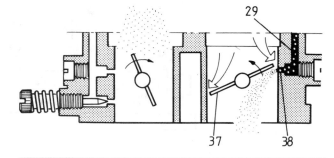

show that when the primary throttle valve is closed, the lever (45) lifts the operating rod (44) under the action of the coil spring. The piston (42) is pulled up the piston bore against the pressure of the spring (41) and fuel is drawn from the float chamber (7) through the intake valve (47).

When the primary throttle valve is opened, the lever (45) moves away from the operating rod (44) and allows the piston (42) to move down the bore under the action of the spring (41). The ball in the intake valve (47) prevents fuel returning to the float chamber (7) and the fuel is forced along the internal channel (43), past the delivery valve (4), through the pump jet (39) and into the primary venturi. The inlet valve (47) may or may not incorporate a discharge orifice according to the application, but where there is one, a certain amount of fuel is discharged back into the float chamber during the ecceleration pump piston stroke. By fine calibration of the discharge orifice, it is possible to determine the exact quantity of fuel injected by the acceleration pump.

4   Removal and refitting

Note: *The following procedure gives a general rather than a specific method of removing and refitting the carburettor, as much will depend on the location within the vehicle.*

1   Unscrew and remove the retaining nuts and withdraw the air cleaner cover and filter gauze. Unscrew the air cleaner retaining screws, being very careful not to drop them into the carburettor barrels.
2   Loosen the fuel supply hose clip and pull the hose from the inlet pipe.
3   Slacken the choke cable retaining screws on the starting device and pull the cable clear.
4   Disconnect the throttle control rod from the throttle lever.
5   Pull the ignition advance tube from the vacuum pipe on the side of the carburettor.

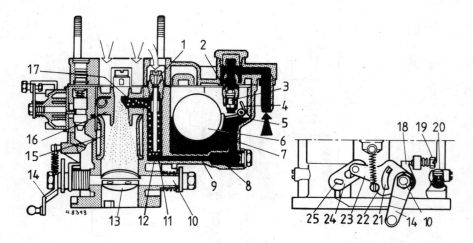

Fig. 6.5 Carburettor normal phase (Sec 3)

1	Air corrector jet	8	Main jet	15	Choke	21	Slot
2	Needle valve seat	9	Channel	16	Auxiliary venturi	22	Sector lug
3	Needle valve	10	Throttle shaft	17	Discharge nozzle	23	Link sector
4	Spring hook	11	Emulsion tube well	18	Throttle sector	24	Secondary lever
5	Fulcrum pin	12	Emulsion tube	19	Idling adjustment screw	25	Secondary throttle shaft
6	Float	13	Throttle valve	20	Idling mixture adjustment		
7	Float chamber	14	Throttle lever		screw		

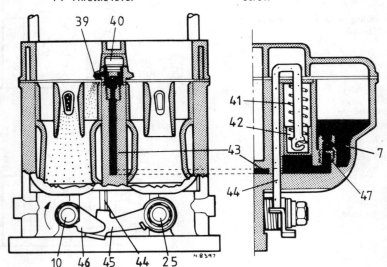

Fig. 6.6 Carburettor acceleration phase (Sec 3)

7	Float chamber	40	Delivery valve	43	Fuel channel	46	Operating cam
10	Primary throttle shaft	41	Accelerator pump spring	44	Operating rod	47	Intake and discharge
25	Secondary throttle shaft	42	Pump piston	45	Lever		valve
39	Pump jet						

6   Where fitted, disconnect the automatic transmission controls from the carburettor.

7   Unscrew and remove the carburettor mounting nuts then withdraw the unit over the mounting studs.

8   Remove the inlet manifold gasket and clean all traces from the contact faces of the inlet manifold and carburettor.

9   Protect the inlet manifold from ingress of foreign matter whilst the carburettor is removed, by sealing it with masking tape.

10 Refitting is a reversal of removal, but the following additional points should be noted:

(a) Always fit a new gasket and tighten the four retaining nuts in diagonal sequence.

(b) When refitting the choke (starting device) cable, first fit the outer cable to the starting device cover, then insert the inner cable into the operating lever nut and push the instrument panel control knob fully in. Tighten the inner cable retaining screw with the operating lever fully released.

(c) The idling adjustment screws should be set as described in Section 7 and finally tuned as described in Section 8.

5 Disassembly

1   Thoroughly clean the carburettor exterior and wipe dry.
2   Referring to Fig. 6.7, unscrew the filter inspection plug (11), remove the gasket (10) and extract the fuel filter (8) (photos).
3   Using a suitable screwdriver, unscrew the carburettor cover retaining screws (3) together with the spring washers, then carefully withdraw the cover (1) from the carburettor body (77). With a new carburettor this is straightforward, but where the seat of the starter plunger spring (7) is a loose fit in the cover (1), it may easily fall out together with the spring (7) and plunger (6) (photo).
4   Remove the gasket (12) from the carburettor cover (1).
5   Invert the carburettor cover (1) so that the float assembly is uppermost, then use a suitable diameter pin punch to release the float fulcrum pin (15) from the two posts.
6   Using a pair of flat pliers, extract the fulcrum pin (15), then carefully withdraw the float (16), at the same time disconnecting the long tab on the float arm from the spring hook on the end of the needle valve needle (photo).
7   Lift the needle from the needle valve (14) seating (photo).
8   Using a 10 mm socket, unscrew the needle valve seating and remove the gasket (13).
9   If the starter plunger spring seat is still retained in the cover (1), use a plastic rod entered through the lockwasher (4) and tap out the seating, spring (7), and plunger (6).
10   The lockwasher (4) is retained in the carburettor cover (1) by local peening and unless the starter plunger seat (5) requires renewal (see overhaul Section 6) neither item should be removed. If removal is necessary, extract the lockwasher (4) and use a small file to remove the peening; the plunger seat (5) can then be driven out from below by using a suitable diameter drift.
11   Unscrew and remove the main jet holders (39) together with the gaskets (37) and place them in separate containers marked 'primary' and 'secondary' as necessary (photo).
12   Unscrew the main jets (38 and 38A) from their respective holders (photo).
13   Unscrew and remove the idling jet holders (36) together with the sealing rings (35) and place them in separate containers marked 'primary' and 'secondary' as necessary (photo).
14   Separate the idling jets (34 and 34A) from their respective holders by pulling apart (photo).
15   Using an 8 mm ring or box spanner, unscrew and remove the emulsion tube assemblies (74 and 74A), keeping them identified for correct refitting (photos).
16   Unscrew the air corrector jets (73 and 73A) from the emulsion tubes (74 and 74A), again keeping them identified for correct refitting (photo).
17   Unscrew and remove the throttle idling adjustment screw (44) and spring (43).
18   Unscrew and remove the idling mixture adjusting screw (41) and spring (42) (photo).
19   Unscrew the accelerator pump delivery valve (70) and withdraw it together with the gaskets (71) and pump jet (72), then separate the jet (72) and gaskets (71) from the valve (70) (photos).
20   Prise the accelerator pump retaining plate (17) from the carburettor body, or alternatively lift the operating rod (18) until the retaining plate (17) comes away (photo). Lift the accelerator pump operating rod (18) from the carburettor body (77) together with the spring (19) and piston (22).
21   Pull the spring (19) away from the piston (22) then unhook the piston by turning it through 90°. Remove the piston (22), spring (19) and retaining plate (17) from the operating rod (18).
22   Unscrew and remove the intake and discharge valve (23) from the bottom of the float chamber (photo).
23   Unscrew and remove the starting air jet (20) and fuel jet (21) assembly, then separate the two components by pulling them apart (photos).

5.2a Removing the filter inspection plug

5.2b Removing the fuel filter

5.3 Example of a loose starter plunger spring seat

5.6 Removing the float fulcrum pin

5.7 Removing the needle from the needle valve

5.11 Removing a main jet holder

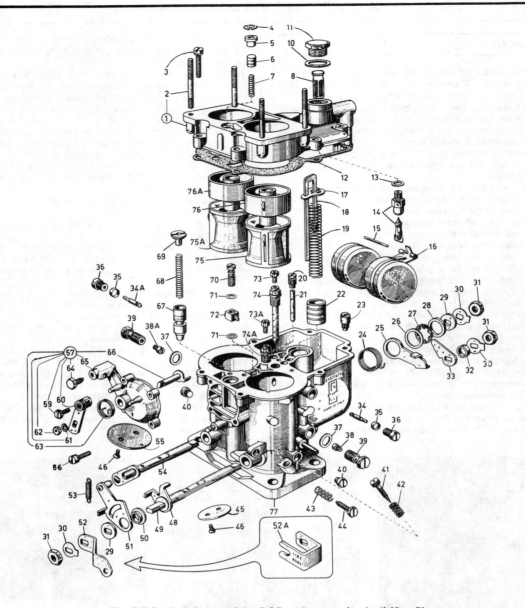

Fig. 6.7 Exploded view of the DCD carburettor (typical) (Sec 5)

1 Carburettor cover	23 Intake and discharge valve	inspection screw plug	61 Spring washer
2 Stud	24 Return spring	41 Idle mixture adjusting screw	62 Nut
3 Cover retaining screw	25 Pump control lever	42 Spring	63 Return spring
4 Lockwasher	26 Washer	43 Spring	64 Screw
5 Starter plunger seat	27 Toothed ring	44 Throttle adjusting screw	65 Starting device cover
6 Starter plunger	28 Washer	45 Primary throttle	66 Shaft
7 Spring	29 Spacer	46 Throttle retaining screw	67 Starting valve
8 Filter	30 Lockwasher	48 Stop sector	68 Spring
10 Gasket	31 Retaining nut	49 Primary shaft	69 Spring guide and retainer
11 Filter plug	32 Spacer bush	50 Bush	70 Pump delivery valve
12 Cover gasket	33 Pump control cam	51 Primary sector	71 Gasket
13 Needle valve gasket	34 Primary idling jet	52 and 52A Alternate throttle control levers	72 Pump jet
14 Needle valve	34A Secondary idling jet	53 Return spring	73 Primary air corrector jet
15 Fulcrum pin	35 Sealing ring	54 Secondary shaft	73A Secondary air corrector jet
16 Float	36 Idle jet holder	55 Secondary throttle	74 Primary emulsion tube
17 Spring retaining plate	37 Gasket	56 Retaining screw	74A Secondary emulsion tube
18 Operating rod	38 Primary main jet	57 Starting device	75 Primary choke
19 Spring	38A Secondary main jet	59 Screw	75A Secondary auxiliary venturi
20 Starting air jet	39 Main jet holder	60 Control lever	77 Carburettor body
21 Starting fuel jet	40 Progression hole		
22 Pump piston			

5.12 Location of a main jet in its holder

5.13 Removing an idling jet holder

5.14 Location of an idling jet in its holder

5.15a Removing an emulsion tube assembly

5.15b An emulsion tube air corrector jet identification number

5.16 Location of an air corrector jet in an emulsion tube

5.18 Removing the idling mixture adjusting screw

5.19a Withdrawing the accelerator pump valve and jet

5.19b The accelerator pump valve and jet

5.20 Removing the accelerator pump assembly

5.22 Location of the accelerator pump intake and discharge valve

5.23a Removing the starting jet assembly

5.23b The starting air and fuel jets

5.24a Removing the starting valve components

5.24b Showing the tapered starting valve head, spring and retainer

5.26 Removing the starting device

5.31 Progression hole inspection screw plug location

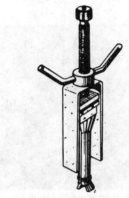

Fig. 6.8 Choke removing tool (Sec 5)

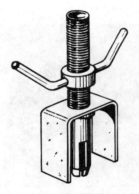

Fig. 6.9 Auxiliary venturi removing tool (Sec 5)

5.33 Typical choke, showing diameter identification mark

5.35 Location of the secondary throttle valve retaining screws

5.36 Removing the secondary throttle valve

5.37 Primary sector return spring location

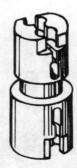

Fig. 6.10 Throttle shaft retaining tool (Sec 5)

24 Using a hooked length of welding rod or similar object, pull the starting valve spring guide and retainer (69) from the carburettor body (77) (photos).

25 Extract the retainer (69) and spring (68) from the starting valve.

26 Unscrew and remove the starting device retaining screws (56) and withdraw the starting control (57) (photo); note the spring washers fitted to the retaining screws (56).

27 Dismantle the starting device by unscrewing the nut (62) and removing the spring washer (61). Lift the control lever (60) over the stop lug, release the spring tension and withdraw it from the shaft (66).

28 Remove the coil spring (63), then withdraw the shaft (66) from the cover (65), noting the relative position of the starting valve operating lug.

29 Unscrew the cable retaining screws (59 and 64).

30 Invert the carburettor body (77) and remove the starting valve (67); if for any reason the valve is difficult to remove, a plastic drift may be inserted from underneath the carburettor and the valve tapped upwards with a light hammer.

31 Unscrew and remove the progression hole inspection screw plugs (40) (photo).

32 Remove the auxiliary venturi (76) and choke (75) from the primary barrel and place them in a suitably marked container. If they will not come out with hand pressure, it will be necessary to obtain Weber tools nos 98009 200 and 98009 100.

33 Remove the auxiliary venturi (76A) and choke (75A) (photo) from the secondary barrel, using the procedure given in paragraph 32. Place them in a suitably marked container.

34 Invert the carburettor and note the location of each throttle plate, marking them with a pencil if necessary.

35 Unscrew and remove the throttle plate retaining screws (46) with the throttle closed, making sure that unnecessary pressure is not exerted on the throttle spindles (49 and 54) as this could distort them (photo).

36 Fully open the throttle and extract the two throttle valves (45 and 55) from their respective spindles using a pair of flat pliers (photo).

37 Unhook the primary sector return spring (53) from the anchoring post and the sector (51) (photo).

38 Bend back the tab washers (30) at both ends of the primary shaft (49) and unscrew the retaining nuts (31). Provided the nuts are not too tight the boss shaft (49) will not be buckled, but if there is any doubt on this matter, it will be necessary to obtain Weber tool no 98011 700 to hold the centre section of the spindle stationary whilst loosening the nuts (photo).

39 Remove the nut (31), tab washer (30), spacer (32) and accelerator pump control cam (33) from the primary shaft (49), then pull the shaft (49) from the carburettor body (77), together with the throttle lever and components and spring (if fitted).

40 Remove the nut (31), tab washer (30), throttle control lever (52 or 52A), spacer (29), primary sector (51), bush (50) and stop sector (48) from the primary shaft (49).

41 Bend back the tab washer (30) at the float chamber end of the secondary shaft (54) and unscrew the retaining nut (31) whilst holding the other end of the shaft stationary (photo). Take care not to buckle the brass shaft (54). If the nut appears to be excessively tight, obtain Weber tool no 98011 700 to hold the centre section of the spindle stationary whilst loosening the nut.

42 Remove the nut (31), tab washer (30) and spacer (29) from the end of the secondary shaft (54). Withdraw the shaft (54) from the carburettor body (77) (photo).

43 If the accelerator pump control lever (25) moves freely on its bearing and the coil spring (24) is not broken, it is recommended that these components are not removed as it is not an easy task to refit them. However, if either component requires renewal, first obtain a new toothed ring (27), otherwise the repair will be in vain, then remove the washer (28) (photo).

44 Using a narrow screwdriver, prise the toothed ring (27) from the bearing lug, edging around the ring a little at a time.

5.38 Removing a primary shaft retaining nut

5.41 Removing the secondary shaft retaining nut

5.42 Withdrawing the secondary shaft from the carburettor body

5.43 Location of the accelerator pump control lever, spring, and toothed ring

45 Prise the spring end from the carburettor body (77) to release all tension, then withdraw the washer (26), control lever (25), and spring (24); it is advisable to place a cloth over the components when prising out the spring, to stop them springing onto the floor.

46 The brass bearing supporting the control lever (25) may be prised from the carburettor body (77), although it cannot be obtained as a spare part.

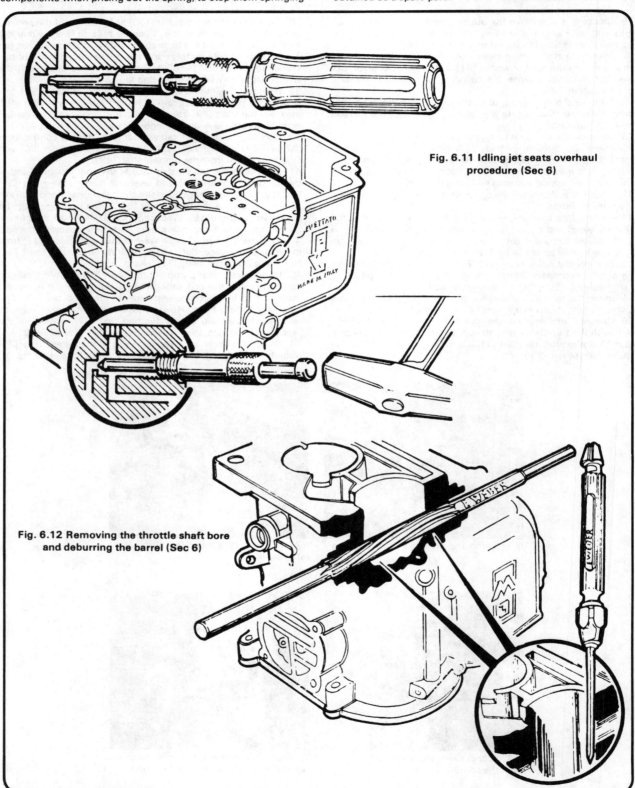

Fig. 6.11 Idling jet seats overhaul procedure (Sec 6)

Fig. 6.12 Removing the throttle shaft bore and deburring the barrel (Sec 6)

6   Special overhaul procedures

After carrying out the general overhaul procedures given in Chapter 4, the following special procedures should be made:

1   Using a hand chuck and Weber tool no 98005 900, reform the idling jet seatings in the carburettor body by carefully rotating the tool in alternate directions. Finish the seatings by inserting Weber tool 98010 500 and gently tapping the centre pin whilst rotating it.

2   Using the same procedure as described in paragraph 1, reform the starter valve seat and bush, using Weber tools nos 98004 100 and 98002 650.

3   Using the same procedure as described in paragraph 1, reform the starting jet seat, using Weber tool nos 98006 300 and 98010 600.

4   If the emulsion tube bores are discoloured and show signs of sediment build up, ream them clear again using Weber tool no 98005 300. Rotate the tool slowly with a hand chuck until it moves quite freely, then remove it whilst still rotating it.

5   If, on disassembly, the throttle shafts (49 and 54) are a tight fit in the carburettor body (77) and they are of original diameter (8.0 mm), use Weber tool no 98003 600 to ream the shaft bores clear with the aid of a hand chuck. Should the shaft bores be excessively worn, oversize shafts of 8.5 mm diameter must be fitted and the bores should be reamed using Weber tool no 98003 500. Note that normally the shaft itself will wear

quicker than its bore, in which case it will only be necessary to renew the shaft.

6   Using a small file, remove any burrs that have formed at the end of the shaft bores as a result of reaming.

7   Check the internal channels of the carburettor body (77) and cover (1), for blockage by injecting fuel with a syringe and observing that it emerges freely from the particular channel being tested. If any are blocked, the lead plugs as shown in Fig. 6.13 must be drilled out and the channels cleared and checked with the special Weber tool.

8   The channels are of three diameters, viz 1.0 mm, 1.5 mm and 2.0 mm. The corresponding tools are Weber tool nos 98014 300, 98014 400, and 98014 500.

9   The carburettor body and cover should be thoroughly cleaned after overhaul to remove swarf and dirt, preferably using clean fuel and air pressure. The lead plugs should be renewed and retained in position by using the Weber tool no 98010 800 as a punch until the plug is expanded into its bore.

10   Check the semi-floats of the float unit for damage and leakage. The seams around each float should be at 90° to the fulcrum pin axis. Check for leakage by shaking the floats and listening for any fuel which may have entered them. If fuel is present, the float assembly must be renewed.

11   Check the contact faces of the starter air valve and seat in the carburettor cover; if either of these components is excessively worn both must be renewed.

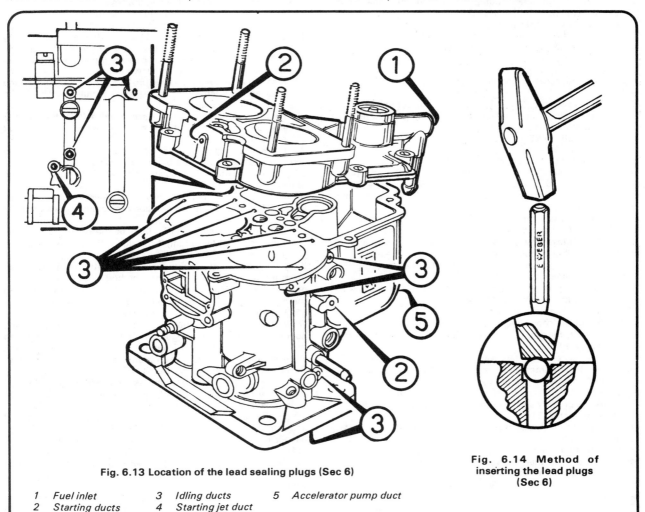

Fig. 6.13 Location of the lead sealing plugs (Sec 6)

Fig. 6.14 Method of inserting the lead plugs (Sec 6)

| 1 | Fuel inlet | 3 | Idling ducts | 5 | Accelerator pump duct |
| 2 | Starting ducts | 4 | Starting jet duct | | |

7 Assembly

Note: *All components should be clean and dry before starting the assembly procedure.*

1 Press the brass bearing which supports the control lever (25) onto the carburettor body (77), largest diameter first.

2 Place the coil return spring (24) over the bearing and insert its straight end into the retaining hole provided in the body (77).

3 The coil spring (24) must now be tensioned so that the control lever (25) can be inserted under the hooked end. One of two methods may be used to do this. Much will depend on the tension of the spring fitted as to how easy its fittings will be. The first method involves one large and one small screwdriver. With the large screwdriver, pass the hooked end of the spring onto the bore of the float chamber, then insert the small screwdriver from the primary shaft end and pass the hook onto the small screwdriver. Lever the small screwdriver around until the hooked end faces the primary shaft; it will be necessary to reposition the spring coils onto the carburettor body using the large screwdriver during the procedure. The second method involves using a length of thin wire firmly secured to the hooked end of the coil spring; the wire is wrapped once around the carburettor body lug and simply pulled to tension the spring.

4 With the coil spring (24) suitably tensioned, fit the control lever (25) onto its bearing, making sure that the square section tab is below the accelerator pump rod (18) aperture, then ease the coil spring hook onto the lever (25).

5 Fit the washer (26), then fit the new toothed ring (27); the teeth of the ring must initially face the carburettor body (77) and the ring should be driven into position using a suitable internal diameter tube (photo).

6 Lightly lubricate the secondary throttle shaft (54) with engine oil then insert it into the bore from the starting device end.

7 Locate the spacer (29), tab washer (30) and nut (31) onto the shaft (54). Tighten the nut (31) whilst holding the other end of the shaft stationary. There is no need to overtighten the nut, but if Weber tool no 98011 700 is available, use this to restrain movement of the shaft (54).

8 Lock the nut (31) by bending the locktab (30).

9 Fit the stop sector (48) to the primary shaft (49) in the position shown in Fig. 6.7, followed by the bush (50), primary sector (51), spacer (29), throttle control lever (52 or 52A), tab washer (30) and retaining nut (31).

10 Where a primary throttle shaft return spring is fitted, locate it on the shaft (49) and hook it over the stop sector (48).

11 Lightly lubricate the primary throttle shaft (49) with engine oil, then insert it into the bore from the starting device end.

12 Pull the spring, if fitted, and tension it before pushing the shaft (49) fully home.

13 Engage the primary sector (51) with the slot in the end of the secondary throttle shaft (54) (photo).

14 Fit the accelerator pump control cam (33) to the primary shaft (49), lift the control lever (25) and push the cam (33) fully onto the shaft, making sure that its angled section abuts the control lever (25).

15 Fit the spacer (32), tab washer (30) and nut (31) to the shaft (49), then tighten both nuts (31). If necessary use the special tool as described in paragraph 7.

16 Lock the nuts (31) by bending the locktabs (30).

17 Hook the primary sector return spring (53) to the anchoring post and the sector (51).

18 With both throttle shafts in the open position, fit the throttle valves (45 and 55) into their respective locations, then close the throttle shafts to allow the valves to centralise within the barrels. Make sure that the valves (45 and 55) are fitted the correct way round so that the angled perimeters seat correctly; the hole in the secondary valve (55) should face the primary barrel, ie opposite the progression orifices (photo).

19 Insert the throttle plate retaining screws (46) and tighten them finger tight, then move each throttle shaft in turn until both shafts and valves are centralised. Tighten the screws (46)

evenly without exerting excessive pressure on the shafts. It is recommended that new screws are always fitted as it is quite easy to cross-thread previously peened screws. Lock the screws (46) by peening with Weber tool no 98010 900 whilst supporting the shafts with a length of wood. Alternatively, coat the screw threads with a liquid locking agent (fuel resistant) prior to inserting them.

20 Check that both throttle valves operate smoothly and fully without any trace of binding or sticking.

21 Fit the choke (75A) and auxiliary venturi (76A) into the secondary barrel, locating the springs into the location groove; make sure that the choke identification number faces away from the throttle valve and the long centre section of the auxiliary venturi faces the throttle valve (photos).

22 Fit the choke (75) and auxiliary venturi (76) into the primary barrel using the same method as described in paragraph 21.

23 Fit and tighten the progression hole inspection screw plugs (40).

24 With the carburettor upright, insert the starting valve (67) into its bore.

25 Assemble the shaft (66) to the starting device cover (65) with the operating lug facing away from the cover extension (photo).

26 Fit the coil spring (63) to the cover (65) and insert the straight end in the location hole.

27 Tension the coil spring (63), then fit the control lever (60) with the cable securing nut facing the cover.

28 Fit the spring washer (61) and tighten the nut (62).

29 Fit the cable retaining screws (59 and 64).

30 Offer the starting device (57) up to the carburettor body (77) and locate the operating lug in the starting valve groove; check for correct engagement by operating the lever and checking that the valve moves up and down (photo).

31 Insert the retaining screws (56) together with the spring washers and tighten them in diagonal sequence; check the operation of the device again.

32 Fit the spring (68) to the starting valve (67), then fit the retainer (69) and press it into the carburettor body using the flat blade of a screwdriver.

33 Press the starting fuel jet (21) into the air jet (20), then screw it into the carburettor body (77) and tighten.

34 Screw the intake and discharge valve (23) into the bottom of the float chamber.

35 Fit the retaining plate (17) to the accelerator pump operating rod (18) with the spring location facing downwards, then fit the spring (19).

36 Compress the spring (19), then fit the piston (22) to the operating rod (18) by turning it through 90°; release the spring (19) into the piston (22).

37 Fit the accelerator pump to the carburettor body (77), then press the retaining plate (17) into the body, using the flat blade of a screwdriver. Check the operation of the pump by operating the throttle lever; there must be no signs of sticking.

38 Fit a gasket (71) to the accelerator pump delivery valve (70), followed by the pump jet (72) with the hole facing downwards and a further gasket (71). Locate the assembly into the carburettor body (77) with the locating lug in the corresponding cut-out, then tighten the valve (70). Note that the ball in the valve must move freely.

39 There is no accelerator pump stroke checking procedure for the 28/36 DCD carburettor as it is identical on all versions and cannot be adjusted.

40 Fit the spring (42) to the idling mixture adjusting screw (41) and screw it into the carburettor body (77).

41 Fit the spring (43) to the throttle idling adjustment screw (44) and screw it into the carburettor body (77).

42 Tighten the air corrector jets (73 and 73A) into the tops of the emulsion tubes (74 and 74A) keeping them identified as when removed.

43 Using an 8 mm ring or box spanner, tighten the emulsion tube assemblies (74 and 74A) into their respective locations in the carburettor body (77).

44 Press the idling jets (34 and 34A) into their respective

7.5 Correct assembled position of the accelerator pump control lever

7.13 Correct assembled position of the primary sector

Fig. 6.15 Angled perimeter of the throttle valves (Sec 7)

7.18 Showing the bypass hole in the secondary throttle valve

7.21a The choke and auxiliary venturi locating groove

7.21b Fitting a choke

7.21c Fitting an auxiliary venturi

7.25 The correct location of the starter device operating lug

7.30 Starter valve control grooves (upper) and operating lug groove (lower dark area)

holders (36), then tighten each holder into the carburettor body (77) making sure that the nylon seals (35) are positioned correctly and that the correct jet is fitted to both the primary and secondary locations.

45 Tighten the main jets (38 and 38A) into the main jet holders (39), keeping them identified as when removed.

46 Locate a new gasket (37) to each main jet holder (39), then tighten them into their respective locations in the carburettor body (77).

47 If the starter plunger seat (5) has been removed, fit the new seat and insert the lockwasher (4). Retain the lockwasher (4) by local peening in two or three places.

48 Invert the carburettor cover (1) and insert the starter plunger (6) followed by the spring (7). The spring seat is a press fitting and should be fitted by pressing with a flat blade screwdriver. If the seat is a loose fit as a result of continual removal, extra care must be exercised to locate it when fitting the cover (1) to the body (77).

49 Fit a new gasket (13) to the needle valve (14) seating, then tighten it into the carburettor cover (1) using a 10 mm socket or ring spanner.

50 Insert the needle into the needle valve (14) seating with the spring hook aligned across the cover (1).

51 Carefully locate the float (16) into position, at the same time inserting the long tab under the needle spring hook.

52 Fit the fulcrum pin (15) through the float arm and two posts and very carefully pinch the split post to secure the pin using a pair of pliers.

53 The float level adjustment must now be checked in the following manner. Hold the carburettor cover (1) vertically so that the floats are hanging from the fulcrum and the float level arm is in light contact with the needle ball (ie without the ball being depressed). Obtain a drill or dowel rod of 5.0 mm diameter and check that the distance from the cover surface to the nearest part of the floats is correct (Fig. 6.16). The annular seams of the semi-floats should not be taken into consideration,

and for this reason two small grooves must be filed on the checking rod (photo).

54 If the dimension is not correct, bend the long tab on the float arm accordingly.

55 Tilt the cover (1) so that the floats move away from the cover and the short tab makes contact with the needle valve seating. Now, using the same method as described in paragraph 53, check the needle valve fully open dimension which should be 13.5 mm and if necessary, bend the short tab to correct (photo).

56 The difference between the dimensions checked in paragraphs 53 and 55 is the needle valve stroke which must be 8.5 mm.

57 Fit a new gasket (12) to the carburettor cover (1), then lower the cover (1) onto the carburettor body (77). Make sure that the gasket is located correctly and aligns with the various drillings in the cover. Where the starter plunger spring seating is loose, it is better to fit the gasket to the top of the carburettor body, then to place the seating on the gasket before lowering the cover (1) (photo).

58 Insert the cover retaining screws (3) together with spring washers and tighten them evenly in diagonal sequence.

59 Fit the fuel filter (8) into the cover (1), fit a new gasket (10) to the filter inspection plug (11) and tighten the plug into the cover (1).

60 With the carburettor completely assembled, the idling adjustment screws should be turned to their preliminary settings. To do this, first screw in the throttle idling adjustment screw (44) until it just touches the throttle lever lug, then continue turning for a further $\frac{1}{2}$ turn. Working on the idling mixture volume screw (41), fully screw it in until it is in light contact with its seat, then back it off 2 full turns. Final adjustments will be necessary when the carburettor is fitted on the engine (refer to Section 8).

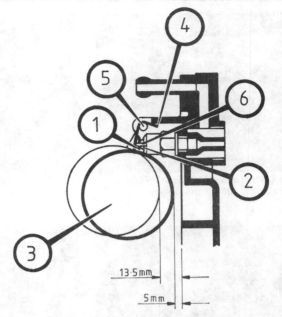

Fig. 6.16 Float level adjustment (Sec 7)

1	Long adjusting tab	4	Short adjusting tab
2	Spring tensioned ball	5	Fulcrum pin
3	Float	6	Spring hook

7.53 Checking the closed position of the floats using a length of dowel rod

7.55 Checking the open position of the floats using a length of dowel rod

7.57 Lowering the carburettor cover assembly onto the carburettor body

8 Tuning

Note: *Refer to Chapter 3 for general notes on tuning.*

1 The idling adjustment screws should be set to their preliminary positions as described in Section 7 paragraph 60.

2 Connect a tachometer to the engine in accordance with the manufacturer's instructions.

3 Start the engine and run until normal operating temperature has been reached (ie the thermostat has opened).

4 Turn the throttle valve adjusting screw so that the engine runs at the recommended idling speed for the particular engine being worked on; this will be between 600 and 800 rpm for touring models and approximately 1000 rpm for sports car models.

5 Turn the idle mixture adjustment screw in or out until the engine runs at the highest rpm.

6 Re-adjust the throttle valve adjusting screw if necessary, to bring the engine speed within limits.

7 Repeat the procedure given in paragraphs 5 and 6, then switch off the engine and remove the tachometer.

9 Fault diagnosis

Symptom	Reason/s
Engine will not start	Faulty starter device Blocked fuel filter or jets Starter air valve sticking
Uneven idling	Leaking manifold or carburettor flange gasket Loose idling jets Excessive sediment or water in carburettor Starter valve not seating Starter device not returning Throttle spindle or carburettor body excessively worn Secondary throttle valve partially sticking open Leaking ignition advance vacuum tube
Carburettor floods	Worn needle valve Leaking or damaged semi-floats Incorrect float level adjustments Excessive sediment in fuel
Engine lacks performance	Incorrect tuning adjustments Incorrect float level adjustments Excessive sediment in fuel Throttle valves do not fully open Accelerator pump jamming
Excessive fuel consumption	Faulty starter device Needle valve not seating Leaking or damaged semi-floats Incorrect float level adjustments Choked air filter

Part 2
Chapter 7 Type 32 DFD, 32 DFE, 32 DFM, 32 DIF, 32 DAF, 32 DGV, 32/36 DFV, 32/36 DGV, 32/36 DFAV, 32/36 DGAV carburettors

Contents

Chapter 7 Type 32 DFD, 32 DFE, 32 DFM, 32 DIF,
32 DAF, 32 DGV, 32/36 DFV, 32/36 DGV, 32/36 DFAV, 32/36 DGAV carburettors

49

Adjustment data

Manual choke types

Fast idle primary throttle valve opening:	in (mm)
32 DFD	0.04 (1.0)
32 DFE	0.035 (0.9)
32 DFM	0.04 (1.0)
32 DIF	0.047 (1.2)
32 DGV	0.03 (0.8)
32/36 DFV	0.047 (1.2)
32/36 DGV	0.033 (0.85)

Automatic choke types

Fast idle primary throttle valve opening

32/36 DGAV type:	in (mm)
Series 1A, 01A, 1B, 01B	0.03 to 0.035 (0.8 to 0.9)
Series 2A, 02A, 2B, 02B, 11A, 011A, 12A, 012A 13A, 013A	0.039 to 0.043 (0.95 to 1.05)
Series 3A, 03A, 3B, 03B, 4A, 04A, 4B, 04B	0.04 to 0.045 (1.0 to 1.10)
Series 6A, 06A	0.03 to 0.033 (0.8 to 0.85)
Series 8A, 08A, 10A, 010A	0.035 to 0.04 (0.9 to 1.0)
Series 9A, 09A	0.045 to 0.049 (1.15 to 1.25)
DFAV and DAF types	0.049 (1.25)

Spindle to shaft clearance

	in (mm)
32/36 DGAV (except series 3A)	0.008 to 0.016 (0.2 to 0.4)
32/36 DGAV (series 3A)	0.008 to 0.1 (0.2 to 2.5)
32/36 DFAV and DAF	0.008 (0.2) min

Choke valve clearance

At minimum shaft travel

DGAV types:	in (mm)
Series 1A, 01A, 1B, 01B	0.18 ± 0.006 (4.5 ± 0.15)
Series 2A, 02A, 2B, 02B, 9A, 09A	0.12 ± 0.006 (3.0 ± 0.15)
Series 3A, 03A, 3B, 03B, 4A, 04A, 4B, 04B, 8A, 08A, 10A, 010A, 11A, 011A, 12A, 012A, 13A, 013A	0.16 ± 0.006 (4.0 ± 0.15)
Series 6A, 06A	0.14 ± 0.006 (3·5 ± 0.15)

At maximum shaft travel

	in (mm)
Series 1A, 01A, 1B, 01B, 2A, 02A, 2B, 02B, 12A, 012A, 13A, 013A	0.26 ± 0.02 (6.5 ± 0.5)
Series 3A, 03A, 3B, 03B, 4A, 04A, 4B, 04B, 8A, 08A, 9A, 09A, 10A, 010A, 11A, 011A	0.24 ± 0.02 (6.0 ± 0.5)
Series 6A, 06A	0.22 ± 0.02 (5.5 ± 0.5)

Choke valve pull down

	in (mm)
32/36 DFAV and DAF	0.187 to 0.207 (4.75 to 5.25)

Choke valve opening

Low fast idle cam position

32/36 DGAV types:	in (mm)
Series 1A to 06A inclusive	0.08 to 0.1 (2.0 to 2.5)
Series 8A to 011A inclusive	0.06 to 0.08 (1.5 to 2.0)
Series 12A to 13A inclusive	0.1 to 0.12 (2.5 to 3.0)

Float level setting dimensions

	Closed position (A) in (mm)	Stroke (B) in (mm)
32 DFD	0.256 (6.5)	0.315 (8.0)
32 DFE	0.285 (7.25)	0.315 (8.0)
32 DFM	0.256 (6.5)	0.315 (8.0)
32 DAF, 32 DIF	0.276 (7.0)	0.315 (8.0)
32 DGV	1.535 (39.0)	0.433 (11.0)
32/36 DFV, 32/36 DFAV	1.437 (36.5)	0.394 (10.0)
32/36 DGV, 32/36 DGAV	1.535 (39.0)	0.433 (11.0)

1 Introduction

The carburettor types covered in this Chapter are all of downdraught design and are of dual barrel construction to supply the primary and secondary functions.

Each throttle valve is mounted on a separate shaft and they are of differential or progressive choke type. The linkage between the two throttle valves is arranged so that the secondary valve does not commence to open until the primary throttle valve is $\frac{2}{3}$ open.

DAF, DFAV and DGAV types are equipped with a semi-automatic choke control.

The carburettor is normally fitted to the engine as a single

**Chapter 7 Type 32 DFD, 32 DFE, 32 DFM, 32 DIF,
32 DAF, 32 DGV, 32/36 DFV, 32/36 DGV, 32/36 DFAV, 32/36 DGAV carburettors**

50

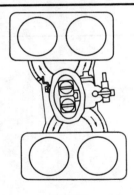

**Fig. 7.1 Single carburettor fitted to a four-cylinder V-engine
(Sec 1)**

unit with both barrels feeding a common inlet manifold, the
most common arrangements being as follows:

1 *One unit on a four-cylinder in-line engine*
2 *One unit on a four-cylinder V engine*

The carburettor identification mark is located on the lower
flange outer surface.

2 Construction

The main body and cover of the carburettor types covered
in this Chapter are of die-cast aluminium or zinc alloy (Mazak)
construction. The mounting flange is machined flat for fitting
purposes. The cover incorporates a mounting flange for the air

cleaner assembly and is equipped with four mounting studs.

The throttle valves are of brass and the throttle shafts,
which run directly in the carburettor body, are of steel.

All fuel and air jets are of brass construction and are
screwed into the main body; the emulsion tubes are also of
brass.

Internal channels of the main body and cover are mostly
drilled and are sealed with lead plugs where necessary.

Single fuel float assemblies are fitted to 32 DFD, 32 DFE,
32 DFM, 32 DIF and 32 DAF types and are of brass construction; two semi-floats are fitted to remaining types and they are
of plastic or brass construction.

3 Operation

Cold starting – manually operated choke

Refer to Fig. 7.2 and note that when the lever (53) is moved
to position A, the choke valves (50) close the air intake. At the
same time the fast idle lever (55) partially opens the primary
throttle valve (35).

When the engine is cranked, a rich mixture is drawn from
the nozzle (9) to facilitate starting. As soon as the engine fires,
the additional vacuum causes the choke valves (50) to partially
open, due to the offset pivot shaft, against the tension of the
spring (51).

As the engine warms up the control cable is progressively
shut, until at position B the choke valves are fully open and the
primary throttle (35) is returned to its idling position. The choke
valves (50) are held open by the lever extension (52).

Cold starting – automatically operated choke

Refer to Fig. 7.3 and note that when the engine is cold and
the throttle pedal has been depressed once, the bi-metallic

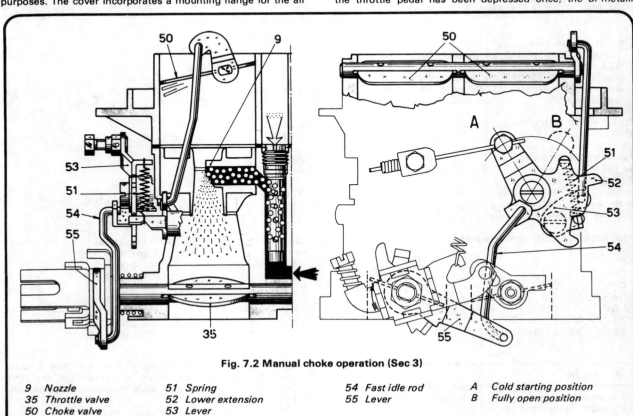

Fig. 7.2 Manual choke operation (Sec 3)

9 Nozzle	51 Spring	54 Fast idle rod	A Cold starting position
35 Throttle valve	52 Lower extension	55 Lever	B Fully open position
50 Choke valve	53 Lever		

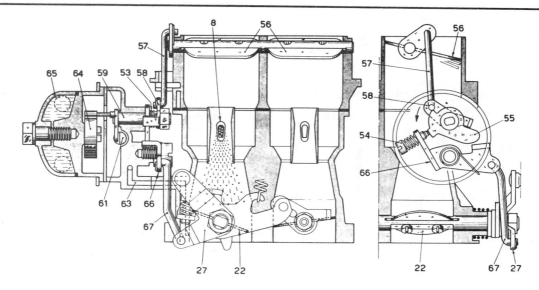

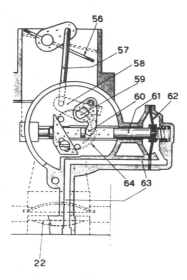

Fig. 7.3 Automatic choke operation (Sec 3)

8	Nozzle	59	Spindle
22	Throttle valve	60	Lever
27	Lever	61	Shaft
53	Spring	62	Diaphragm
54	Fast idle adjustment	63	Channel
55	Fast idle cam	64	Bi-metallic spring
56	Choke valve	65	Cover
57	Operating rod	66	Lever
58	Lever	67	Rod

spring (64) rotates the spindle (59) and closes the choke valves (56). At the same time, the fast idle cam (55) prevents the throttle valve (22) from completely closing.

When the engine is cranked, a rich mixture is drawn from the nozzle (8) to facilitate starting. As soon as the engine fires, vacuum from below the throttle valve is relayed through channel (63) to diaphragm (62) and the shaft (61) moves and partially opens the choke valves (56) against the action of the bi-metallic spring (64). If the throttle is opened at this stage, the vacuum will cease and the choke valves (56) will close; however, the passage of air will open the choke valves against the action of the bi-metallic spring (64) and the auxiliary spring (53).

As the engine warms up, the bi-metallic spring (64) progressively opens the choke valves (56), until at normal operating temperature they are held fully open. The fast idling screw (54) does not now rest on the fast idling cam (55) since the latter has been rotated by the bi-metallic spring and therefore the throttle valve (22) is free to return it to its normal idling position.

Idling and progression

Refer to Fig. 7.4 and note that when the engine is idling both throttle valves (12 and 22) are shut. Fuel is drawn from the float chamber, through an internal channel to the primary well (14) and then passes along the channel (36) to the idling jet (37) where air is introduced from the calibrated bush (38). The fuel and air is now an emulsion and continues through channel (35), past the idling mixture control screw (34) through the idling feed hole (33) and into the primary carburettor throat at the engine side of the throttle valve (22).

Refer to Fig. 7.5 and note that 32 DFD, 32 DFE and 32 DFM type carburettors have idling channels to both primary and secondary carburettor barrels and the mixture adjusting screw is located in the secondary barrel.

When the primary throttle valve is opened slightly to increase the engine speed, the progression holes (Fig. 7.4) (39) are brought into action to provide extra fuel.

When the primary throttle valve (22) is $\frac{2}{3}$ open, the secondary throttle valve (12) will commence to open and the secondary progression holes provide mixture to the secondary barrel.

When either throttle valve is sufficiently open, the idling and progression system ceases and the main fuel supply system operates.

Normal running

Under full throttle and high speed cruising conditions, the

**Chapter 7 Type 32 DFD, 32 DFE, 32 DFM, 32 DIF,
32 DAF, 32 DGV, 32/36 DFV, 32/36 DGV, 32/36 DFAV, 32/36 DGAV carburettors**

52

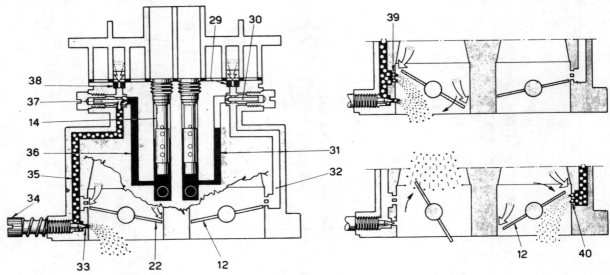

Fig. 7.4 Carburettor idling and progression phase (Sec 3)

12 Secondary throttle valve	31 Secondary channel	screw	37 Primary idling jet
14 Primary well	32 Secondary progression	35 Primary progression	38 Calibrated bush
22 Primary throttle valve	channel	channel	39 Progression holes
29 Calibrated bush	33 Idling feed hole	36 Primary channel	40 Progression holes
30 Secondary idling jet	34 Idling mixture control		

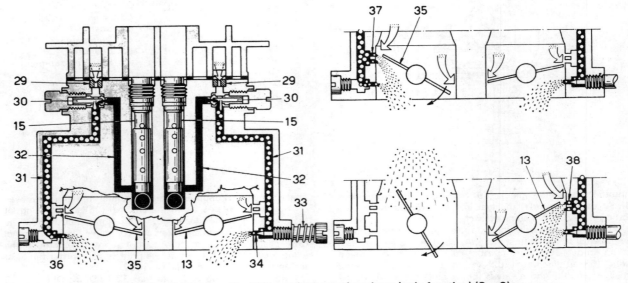

Fig. 7.5 Carburettor idling and progression phase (twin function) (Sec 3)

13 Secondary throttle valve	31 Channel	34 Feed hole	37 Primary progression holes
15 Secondary well	32 Channel	35 Primary throttle valve	38 Secondary progression
29 Calibrated bush	33 Idling mixture control	36 Feed hole	holes
30 Idling jets	screw		

main fuel supply circuit is brought into action. Refer to Fig. 7.6 and note that fuel from the float chamber (18) passes through the main jets (15) to the emulsion tube wells (14). At the same time air is drawn through the air corrector jets (8), through the holes in the emulsion tubes (13) and emulsifies the fuel which is then drawn through the nozzles (9) and auxiliary venturis (10). The mixture then mixes with the main air supply as it is drawn

through the chokes (11) and into the engine.

When the throttle valves are both open fully, the overfeed enrichment circuit is brought into action to provide full power. Under these conditions the air velocity through the carburettor is high and extra fuel is drawn out of the calibrated orifice located at the top of the secondary barrel. The arrangement varies in the different carburettors; on DGV and DGAV types the

Chapter 7 Type 32 DFD, 32 DFE, 32 DFM, 32 DIF,
32 DAF, 32 DGV, 32/36 DFV, 32/36 DGV, 32/36 DFAV, 32/36 DGAV carburettors

53

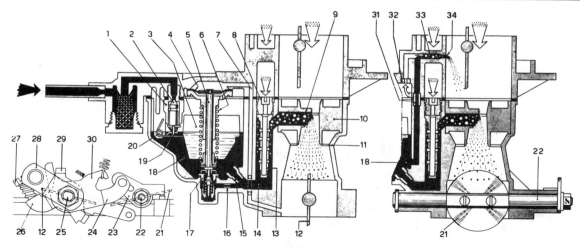

Fig. 7.6 Carburettor normal phase (Sec 3)

1 Needle seat	10 Auxiliary venturi	19 Spring hook	27 Adjusting screw
2 Needle	11 Choke	20 Pivot	28 Lever
3 Float	12 Throttle valve	21 Secondary throttle	29 Lever
4 Diaphragm	13 Emulsion tube	22 Shaft	30 Lever
5 Rod	14 Well	23 Lever	31 Calibrated bush
6 Spring	15 Main jet	24 Lever	32 Calibrated bush
7 Channel	16 Calibrated bush	25 Shaft	33 Channel
8 Air jet	17 Full power valve	26 Lever	34 Calibrated orifice
9 Nozzle	18 Float chamber		

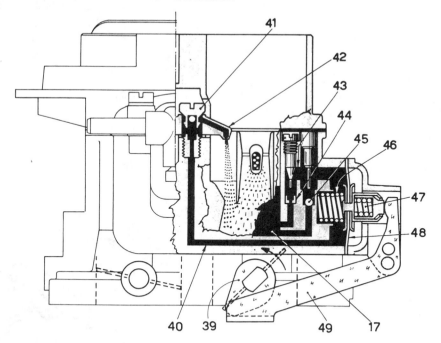

**Fig. 7.7 Carburettor acceler-
ation phase (Sec 3)**

17 Float chamber
39 Throttle shaft cam
40 Channel
41 Delivery valve
42 Jet
43 Channel
44 Calibrated bush
45 Ball
46 Return spring
47 Buffer spring
48 Diaphragm
49 Lever

circuit does not include air correction and on 32 DFE and 32 DFM types the circuit emerges directly above the secondary nozzle.

DFV, DFAV, DGV and DGAV carburettors are also equipped with a full power valve which operates immediately the primary throttle valve is opened quickly. Under these conditions the vacuum through channel (7) is insufficient to draw the diaphragm (4) against the spring (6) and the operating rod (5) therefore opens the full power valve (17). The fuel level in the primary emulsion tube well (14) immediately rises and the mixture drawn from the nozzle (9) is enriched. When the primary throttle valve is partially open, the vacuum through channel (7) overcomes the tension of the spring (6) and the full power valve shuts.

Acceleration

To provide the engine with a rich mixture when accelerating, the carburettor is provided with a diaphragm type accelerator pump which is operated by the primary throttle shaft and injects only into the primary venturi. Reference to Fig. 7.7 will show that when the primary throttle valve is closed, the accelerator pump diaphragm (48) draws fuel from the float

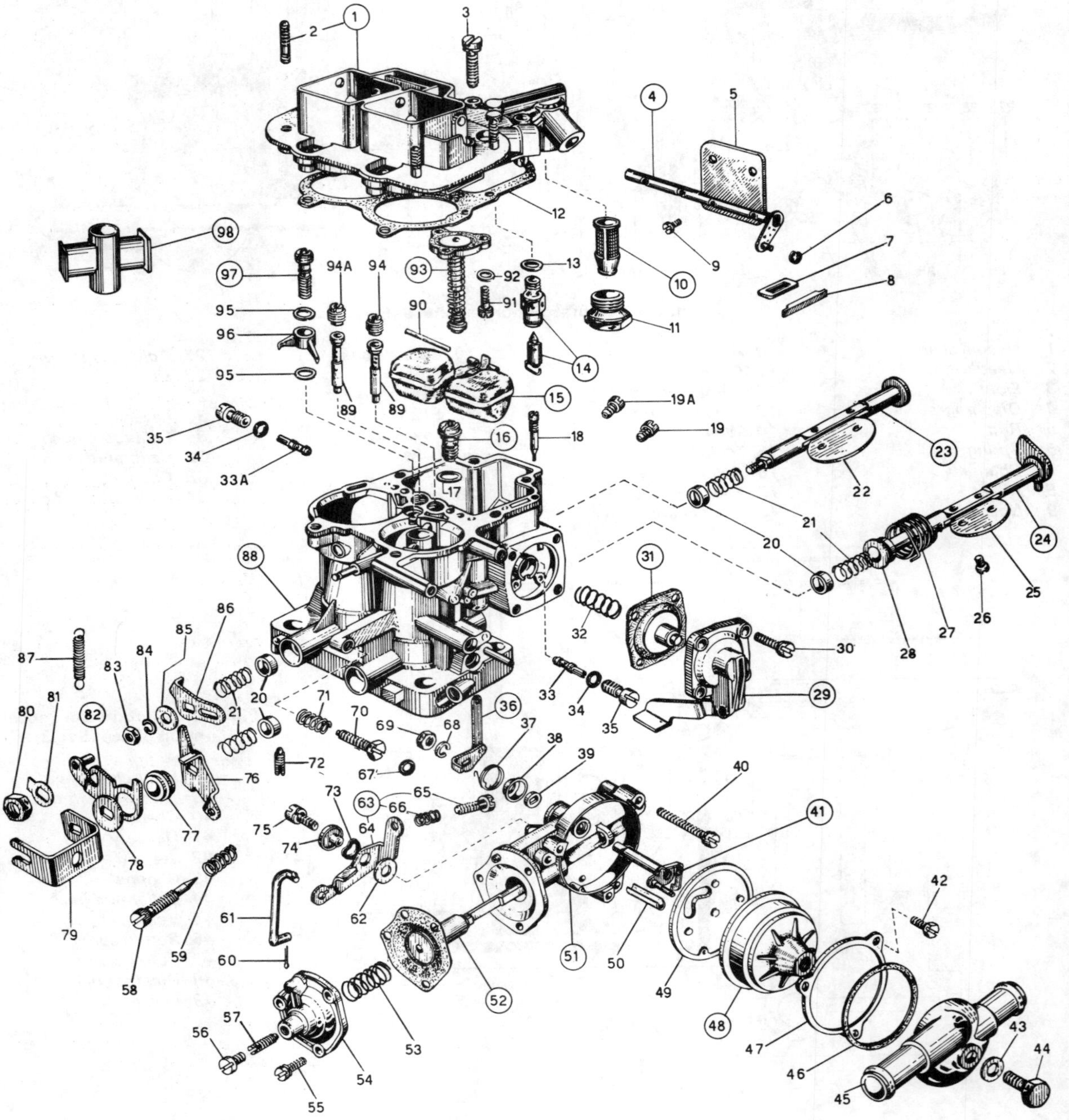
1
2
3
4
5
6
7
8
9
10
11
12
13
14
15
16
17
18
19A
19
20
21
22
23
24
25
26
27
28
29
30
31
32
33A
33
34
35
36
37
38
39
40
41
42
43
44
45
46
47
48
49
50
51
52
53
54
55
56
57
58
59
60
61
62
63
64
65
66
67
68
69
70
71
72
73
74
75
76
77
78
79
80
81
82
83
84
85
86
87
88
89
90
91
92
93
94A
94
95
96
97
98

chamber (17), through the ball valve (45) into the pump chamber. When the primary throttle valve is opened, the cam (39) moves the lever (49) and fuel is forced along the channel (40), through the delivery valve (41) and out of the pump jet (42). The spring (47) absorbs the initial movement of the lever (49) and extends the fuel delivery period. Excess fuel and any accumulated air is discharged into the float chamber (17) through the channel (43) and calibrated bush (44). The lever (49) incorporates two pivot holes by which the pump stroke may be varied.

4 Removal and refitting

Note: *The following procedure gives a general rather than a specific method of removing and refitting the carburettor, as much will depend on the location within the vehicle.*

1 Unscrew and remove the retaining nuts and withdraw the air cleaner cover (screws are fitted to some models).
2 Lift out the air filter element.
3 Bend back the locktabs and unscrew the air cleaner body retaining nuts.
4 Unscrew and remove the mounting bracket bolts and remove the air cleaner together with the reinforcement plate.
5 On automatic choke models, partially drain the cooling system and disconnect the two water hoses.
6 On manual choke models, disconnect the choke cable.
7 Disconnect the fuel supply pipe and return pipe where fitted.
8 Release the distributor automatic advance pipe from the side of the carburettor.
9 Disconnect the throttle control shaft from the throttle lever.

10 Unscrew and remove the carburettor mounting nuts then withdraw the unit over the mounting studs.
11 Remove the inlet manifold gasket and clean all traces of gasket from the contact faces of the inlet manifold and carburettor.
12 Protect the inlet manifold from ingress of foreign matter by sealing it with masking tape.
13 Refitting is a reversal of removal, but the following additional points should be noted:

> *(a) Always fit a new gasket and tighten the four retaining nuts in diagonal sequence*
> *(b) When refitting the choke cable, first secure the outer cable then insert the inner cable fully and tighten the retaining screw*
> *(c) On automatic choke models, refill the cooling system in accordance with the manufacturer's instructions*
> *(d) The idling adjustment screws should be set as described in Section 8 and finally tuned as described in Section 9*

5 Disassembly

Note: *Throughout the disassembly and assembly Sections, reference will be made to the illustrations of 32/36 DGAV, 32/36 DGV and 32 DFE/DFM carburettors. The remaining carburettor types covered in this Chapter are very similar in construction although the individual components may be located in different areas, or in some instances omitted.*

1 Thoroughly clean the carburettor exterior and wipe dry.
2 Referring to Fig. 7.8, unscrew and remove the fuel filter inspection plug (11) and extract the filter (10) (photo).

Fig. 7.8 Exploded view of the 32/36 DGAV carburettor (typical) (Sec 5)

1 Carburettor cover assy	33 Primary idle jet	66 Spring
2 Stud bolt	33A Secondary idle jet	67 Auto-choke O-ring seal
3 Cover fixing screw	34 Gasket for idling jet holder	68 Spring washer
4 Choke shaft and lever assy	35 Idling jet holder	69 Throttle shaft fixing nut
5 Starting throttle valve	36 Choke control lever assy	70 Primary throttle adjusting screw
6 Spring ring	37 Spring for fast idle cam	71 Spring for throttle adjusting screw
7 Dust seal plate	38 Spring retaining cover	72 Secondary throttle adjusting screw
8 Dust seal plug	39 Washer for shaft	73 Wave washer for loose lever
9 Choke plates fixing screw	40 Choke fixing screw	74 Bushing for loose lever
10 Strainer assy	41 Auto-choke shaft and lever assy	75 Loose lever fixing screw
11 Strainer inspection plug	42 Plate screw	76 Primary throttle control lever
12 Cover gasket	43 Washer for water cover fixing screw	77 Bushing for loose lever
13 Needle valve gasket	44 Water cover fixing screw	78 Washer for loose lever
14 Needle valve assy	45 Auto-choke water chamber	79 Throttle valve control lever
15 Float assy	46 Water chamber seal gasket	80 Throttle shaft fixing nut
16 Full power needle valve assy	47 Thermostat assy locking ring	81 Lockwasher
17 Power valve gasket	48 Auto-choke thermostat assy	82 Loose lever assy
18 Pump discharge blanking needle	49 Gasket to auto-choke body	83 Secondary shaft fixing nut
19 Primary main jet	50 Plate for choke shaft	84 Spring washer
19A Secondary main jet	51 Auto-choke body assy	85 Washer for loose lever
20 Shafts retaining bush	52 Choke diaphragm assy	86 Secondary throttle control lever
21 Bush retaining spring	53 Diaphragm loading spring	87 Spring for loose lever
22 Secondary throttle valve	54 Auto-choke cover	88 Carburettor body
23 Secondary shaft	55 Auto-choke cover fixing screw	89 Emulsioning tube
23 Secondary shaft assy oversize	56 Screw plug	90 Float fixing pin
24 Primary shaft	57 Diaphragm adjusting screw	91 Control valve retaining screw
24 Primary shaft assy oversize	58 Idle adjusting screw	92 Washer for control valve screw
25 Primary throttle valve	59 Spring for idle adjusting screw	93 Power valve assy
26 Throttle plates fixing screw	60 Split pin	94 Primary air corrector jet
27 Shaft return spring	61 Fast idling control rod	94A Secondary air corrector jet
28 Spacer	62 Washer for loose lever	95 Pump jet gasket
29 Accelerator pump cover assy	63 Fast idling loose lever assy	96 Accelerator pump jet
30 Pump cover fixing screw	64 Lever	97 Pump delivery valve assy
31 Accelerator pump diaphragm assy	65 Screw	98 Auxiliary venturi
32 Pump loading spring		

5.2 Removing the fuel filter inspection plug and filter

5.3 Disconnecting the choke operating rod

5.4 Removing the carburettor cover (DFAV type shown)

5.5a Withdrawing the float fulcrum pin ...

5.5b ... needle valve and return hook

5.8 Removing the full power valve assembly

5.9 Removing the needle valve seating

5.10a Withdrawing the accelerator pump cover ...

5.10b ... and spring

5.11 Removing the accelerator pump delivery valve and jet

5.13 The accelerator pump discharge blanking needle

5.14 Removing the primary main jet

3 Disconnect the choke plate operating rod (36) at its upper end by removing the split pin or prising off the circlip (6). On automatic types, slightly open the throttle if necessary to allow the choke plates to fully close (photo).

4 Unscrew and remove the carburettor cover retaining screws (3) together with the spring washers, then carefully lift the cover (1) from the main body (88) at the same time disengaging the choke operating rod (36) by tilting the cover (photo).

5 Invert the carburettor cover (1) so that the float assembly is uppermost, then extract the float fulcrum pin (90) and withdraw the float assembly (15) together with the needle of the needle valve (14). If necessary, use a suitable diameter pin punch to tap the pin from the two posts. **Note**: *On no account prise the slotted post apart (photos).*

6 Unhook the needle from the float assembly (15).

7 Lift the gasket (12) from the cover (1).

8 Where fitted, unscrew the three screws (91) and remove them together with the spring washers (92), then lift the power valve assembly (93) from the cover (1) being careful not to damage the thin diaphragm (photo).

9 Using a 10 mm box spanner or socket, unscrew the needle valve (14) seating and remove the gasket (13) (photo).

10 Unscrew the four screws (3) and withdraw the accelerator pump cover (29) from the carburettor body (88) together with the diaphragm (31) and spring (32). If necessary, carefully peel the diaphragm assembly (31) from the cover (29) (photos).

11 Unscrew the accelerator pump delivery valve (97) and remove it together with the pump jet (96) and gaskets (95). Note that on some types with an upper tapered seating, only one lower gasket is fitted (photo).

12 Separate the delivery valve (97), gaskets (95) and pump jet (96).

13 Unscrew and remove the accelerator pump discharge blanking needle (18) (photo).

14 Unscrew the primary (19) and secondary (19A) main jets

from the bottom of the float chamber, noting their correct locations (photo).

15 Unscrew the primary (94) and secondary (94A) air corrector jets from the carburettor body (88), noting their correct locations (photos).

16 Invert the carburettor body and extract the primary and secondary emulsion tubes (89); if these are tight due to overtightening of the air corrector jets, use a selftapping screw to remove them, but take care not to damage the tubes (photo).

17 Unscrew the idling jet holders (35) from each side of the carburettor and place them in separate marked containers (photo).

18 Remove the gaskets (34) if fitted, then separate the idling jets (33 and 33A) from their holders (photo).

19 Unscrew and remove the idling mixture adjusting screw (58) and spring (59). Where fitted, remove the plug from the opposite end of the carburettor flange (photo).

20 Unscrew and remove the throttle idling adjustment screw (70) and spring (71); on some types these are located on the throttle linkage.

21 Note the location of each choke valve (5) and mark them if necessary with a pencil.

22 Unscrew the retaining screws (9) and remove the choke valves (5) from the shaft (4), then remove the shaft (4) from the cover (1) (photo). Note that some types are fitted with brushes and circlips.

23 Where fitted, prise the dust cover (8) from the cover (1) then extract the dust seal (7).

24 *On manually operated choke types follow paragraphs 25 or 26 as applicable:*

25 Refer to Fig. 7.9 and, on DGV type carburettors, unscrew the retaining screw (46) and withdraw the bush (45), control lever (41) and return spring (44), together with the choke operating rod (7). Detach the rod (7) from the lever and remove the screw (43). Extract the split pin (50) and detach the fast idle

5.15a Location of the primary and secondary air corrector jets

5.15b Removing the primary air corrector jet

5.16 Removing the primary emulsion tube

5.17 An idling jet holder location

5.18 An idling jet separated from its holder

5.19 Removing the idling mixture adjusting screw

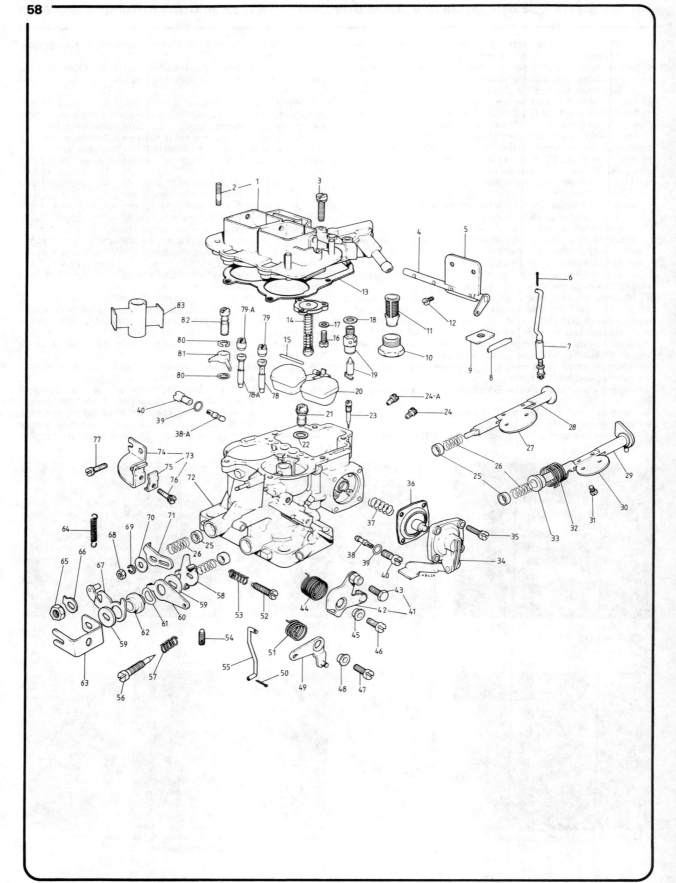

**Fig. 7.9 Exploded view of the 32/36 DGV carburettor
(typical) (Sec 5)**

1   Carburettor cover assy
2   Stud bolt
3   Cover fixing screw
4   Choke shaft and lever
    assy
5   Choke throttle valve
6   Split pin
7   Choke rod
8   Dust seal plug
9   Dust seal plate
10 Strainer inspection plug
11 Strainer assy
12 Choke plates fixing screw
13 Cover gasket
14 Power valve assy
15 Float fixing pin
16 Control valve retaining
    screw
17 Washer for control valve
    screw
18 Needle valve gasket
19 Needle valve assy
20 Float assy
21 Full power needle valve
    assy
22 Power valve gasket
23 Pump discharge blanking
    needle
24 Primary main jet
24A Secondary main jet
25 Shaft retaining bush
26 Bush retaining spring
27 Secondary throttle valve
28 Secondary shaft
28 Secondary shaft assy
    oversize
29 Primary shaft
29 Primary shaft assy
    oversize
30 Primary throttle valve
31 Throttle plates fixing
    screw
32 Shaft return spring
33 Spacer
34 Accelerator pump cover
    assy
35 Pump cover fixing screw
36 Accelerator pump
    diaphragm assy
37 Pump loading spring
38 Primary idle jet
38A Secondary idle jet
39 Gasket for idling jet
    holder
40 Idling jet holder
41 Choke control lever assy

42 Lever
43 Screw securing wire
44 Spring for choke lever
45 Bushing for choke lever
46 Choke lever fixing screw
47 Square lever fixing screw
48 Bushing for square lever
49 Fast idle control square
    lever assy
50 Split pin
51 Spring for square lever
52 Primary throttle adjusting
    screw
53 Spring for throttle
    adjusting screw
54 Secondary throttle
    adjusting screw
55 Fast idling control rod
56 Idle adjusting screw
57 Spring for idle adjusting
    screw
58 Primary throttle control
    lever
59 Washer for loose lever
60 Fast idling loose lever
61 Wave washer
62 Bushing for loose lever
63 Throttle valve control
    lever
64 Spring for loose lever
65 Throttle shaft fixing nut
66 Lockwasher
67 Loose lever assy
68 Secondary shaft fixing nut
69 Spring washer
70 Washer for loose lever
71 Secondary throttle control
    lever
72 Carburettor body
73 Sheat support assy
74 Sheat support
75 Sheat securing plate
76 Sheat support fixing
    screw
77 Sheat support fixing
    screw
78 Primary emulsioning tube
78A Secondary emulsioning
    tube
79 Primary air corrector jet
79A Secondary air corrector
    jet
80 Pump jet gasket
81 Accelerator pump jet
82 Pump delivery valve assy
83 Auxiliary venturi

5.22 Removing a choke valve

rod from the lever (60), then remove the retaining screw (47) and withdraw the brush (48), lever (49) and spring (51). Disengage the fast idle rod (55) from the lever (49).
26 Refer to Fig. 7.10 and, on all but DGV type carburettors, extract the split pin (6) and detach the fast idle rod (40) from the lever (50). Unscrew the retaining screw (34) and unhook the spring (27). Remove the washer (33), lever assembly (30) and spring (29) from carburettor body, then disengage the rod (40) from the lever (31) and remove the screw (32). Extract the split pin (6), remove the washer (67) and detach the operating rod (9) from the lever (26). Extract the split pin (6A), remove the washer (28) and withdraw the lever (26) from the carburettor body.
27 *On automatically operated choke types, follow paragraphs 28 to 40 inclusive.*
28 Unscrew and remove the three screws (42) and lift the automatic choke thermostat assembly (48) away from the body (51) (photo).
29 Remove the gasket (49), then unscrew and remove the three retaining screws (40) and spring washers. Withdraw the automatic choke body (51), at the same time disengage the fast idling control rod (61) from the throttle lever (76). Note that some models have a retaining split pin (60) instead of an offset lug (photos).
30 Unscrew the water housing retaining bolt (44) together with the gasket (43), then separate the housing (45) from thermostat assembly (48); cut the gasket (46) from the assembly if it is stuck.
31 Remove the retaining ring (47).
32 Note the location of the individual components of the automatic choke body (51) before dismantling them.
33 Prise the O-ring seal (67) from the rear of the unit.
34 Unscrew and remove the retaining nut (69) and spring washer (68), then withdraw the lever (36), spring (37), cover (38), if fitted, and spacer (39). The shaft (41) can now be removed (photos) extract the split pin and separate the rod from the lever (36) where these are separate items.
36 Unscrew the screw (75) and remove it together with the spring washer and fast idling lever (63), then remove the brush (74), wave washer (73) where fitted, washer (62), adjusting screw (65) and spring (66) (photo).
37 On 32/36 DFAV and 32 DAF types, mark the location of the adjusting stop plate in the automatic choke body, then remove the screw and lift the plate out (photo).
38 On all types, unscrew the diaphragm cover retaining screws (55) and lift off the cover (54) and spring (53). Where fitted, remove the screw plug (56) and adjusting screw (57), noting how many turns are necessary to remove the plug (photo).

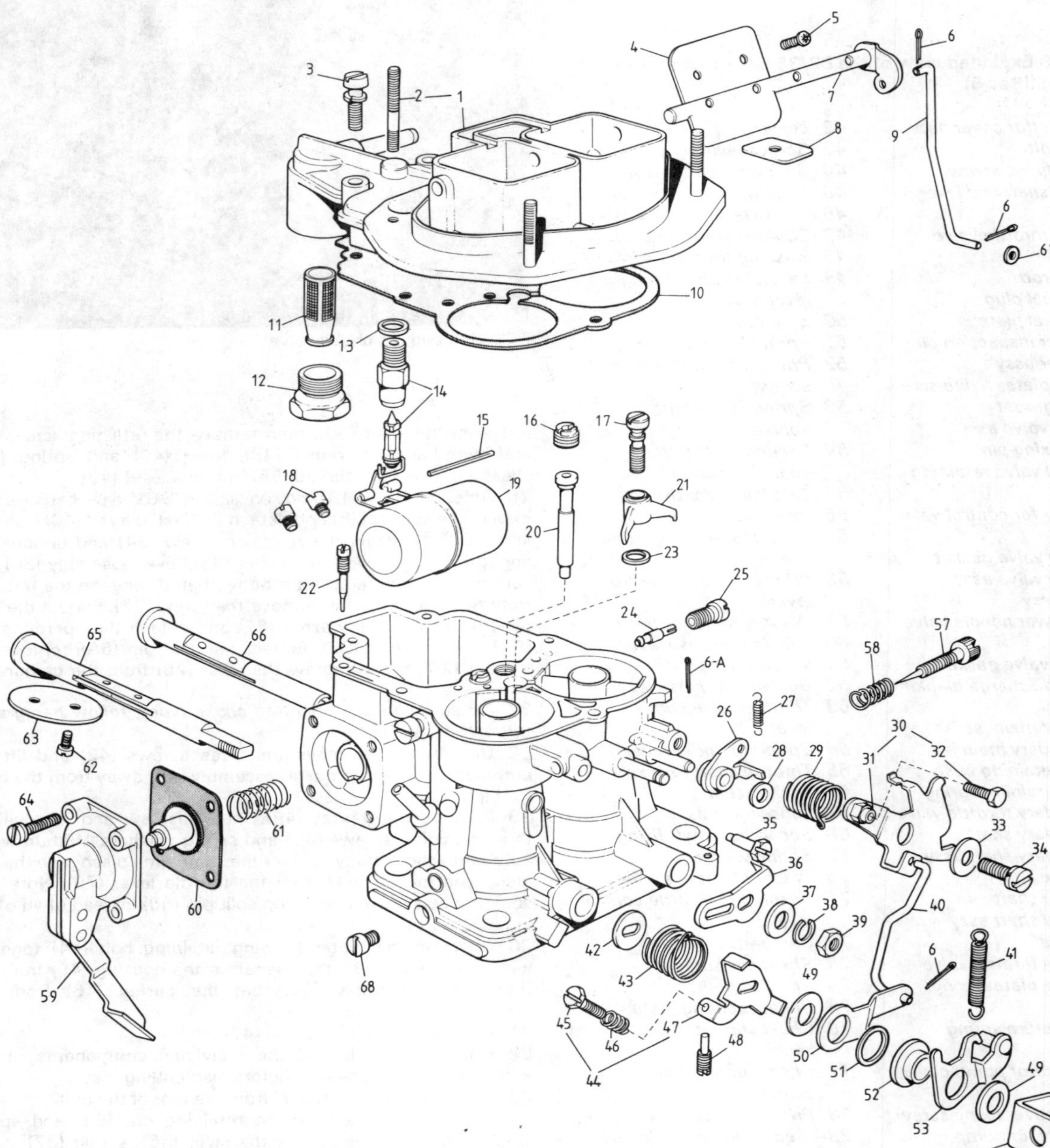
1
2
3
4
5
6
7
8
9
10
11
12
13
14
15
16
17
18
19
20
21
22
23
24
25
6-A
26
27
28
29
30
31
32
33
34
35
36
37
38
39
40
41
42
43
44
45
46
47
48
49
50
51
52
53
54
55
56
57
58
59
60
61
62
63
64
65
66
67
68

5.28 Withdrawing the automatic choke thermostat assembly (DFAV type shown)

5.29a Location of the automatic choke disc gasket (DFAV type shown)

5.29b Disengaging the fast idle control rod (DFAV type shown)

5.34a Removing the automatic choke lever ...

5.34b ... spacer ...

5.34c ... spring ...

Fig. 7.10 Exploded view of the 32 DFE and 32 DFM carburettor (typical) (Sec 5)

1 Air horn and plugs assy
2 Air cleaner retaining stud
3 Horn and plug assy fixing screw and washer
4 Choke plate
5 Choke plate screw
6 Control rod split pin
6 Choke/throttle interconnecting rod split pin
6A Choke lever pivot split pin
7 Choke shaft and lever assy
8 Air cleaner dust seal
9 Choke control rod
10 Air horn to throttle body gasket
11 Fuel inlet strainer assy
12 Fuel inlet strainer plug
13 Fuel intake valve washer
14 Fuel inlet valve and seat assy
15 Float lever shaft
16 Starting air adjusting jet (Primary)
16A Starting air adjusting jet (Secondary)
17 Accelerator pump discharge valve assy
18 Main primary jet
19 Float assy
20 Emulsion tube
21 Pump discharge nozzle

22 Accelerator pump discharge blanking needle
23 Nozzle bar gasket
24 Idling jet (Primary)
24A Idling jet (Secondary)
25 Idling jet holder
26 Choke lever assy
27 Choke lever spring
28 Choke lever pivot washer
29 Choke lever return spring
30 Choke control lever assy
31 Lever
32 Screw securing wire
33 Washer
34 Screw and washer
35 Screw securing sheath
36 Full throttle stop lever
37 Geared sector adjusting screw washer
38 Auto-choke lever fixing nut spring washer
39 Auto-choke lever fixing nut
40 Faet idle rod
41 Throttle control return spring (RH Secondary)
42 Throttle lever and shaft assy washer (Primary)
43 Throttle control return spring (LH

Primary)
44 Fast idle adjustment lever assy
45 Screw
46 Spring
47 Lever
48 Screw
49 Primary throttle shaft assy washer
50 Choke/throttle interconnecting lever
51 Throttle shaft (Primary) wave washer
52 Throttle shaft bushing
53 Throttlecontrol leler
54 Throttle lever
55 Throttle shaft (Primary) tab washer
56 Throttle shaft (Primary) nut
57 Idle adjustment needle
58 Idle adjusting needle spring
59 Accelerator pump cover assy
60 Accelerator pump diaphragm assy
61 Accelerator pump rod spring
62 Throttle plate screw
63 Throttle plate
64 Accelerator pump cover fixing screw and washer
65 Throttle shaft assy (LH Primary)
66 Throttle shaft assy (RH Secondary)
67 Rod/choke control washer
68 Idle primary duct plug

**Chapter 7   Type 32 DFD, 32 DFE, 32 DFM, 32 DIF,
32 DAF, 32 DGV, 32/36 DFV, 32/36 DGV, 32/36 DFAV, 32/36 DGAV carburettors**

62

5.34d ... and shaft (DFAV type shown)

5.36 Automatic choke control levers (DFAV type shown)

5.37 Location of the automatic choke adjusting stop plate (DFAV type shown)

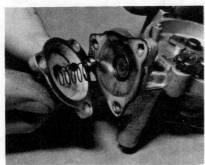

5.38 Removing the automatic choke diaphragm cover and spring (DFAV type shown)

5.39 Withdrawing the automatic choke operating rod (DFAV type shown)

5.41 Removing the full power valve from the float chamber

39 Carefully release the thin diaphragm, then withdraw the operating rod (52) from the body (51) (photo).

40 The automatic choke body (51) is supplied complete with the fast idle cam and shaft bush and it is therefore of no consequence to remove the bush and cam.

41 Where fitted, unscrew the full power valve (16) from the base of the float chamber and remove the gasket (17) (photo).

42 Mark the position and location of the auxiliary venturis (98), then remove them from the primary and secondary barrels. If they are tight, open each throttle valve in turn and use a plastic or wooden rod to tap them out. Failure of this method to remove the auxiliary venturis will necessitate obtaining Weber tool no 9610 150 0035 (photo).

43 Unhook the spring (87) from the lever (82) and the carburettor body, then bend back the tab washer (81) and unscrew the nut (80) from the end of the primary throttle shaft. If the nut is tight, Weber tool no 9610 315 1514 should be used to hold the shaft stationary, otherwise the shaft could be buckled (photo).

44 Remove the nut (80), tab washer (81), lever (79), washer (78), lever (82), bush (77), lever (76) and return spring (27). On DGV and DGAV types, the return spring (27) is located on the opposite end of the primary shaft and cannot be removed until the shaft has been removed (photos).

45 Remove the spring (21) and bush (20) on DGV and DGAV types. Remove the spacer on all other types (photo).

46 With the primary throttle valve closed, unscrew and remove the retaining screws (26), then mark the valve (25) with a pencil so that it can be refitted in its original position.

47 Fully open the primary throttle and remove the valve (25) from the shaft (24), then withdraw the primary shaft (25) from the carburettor body (88) (photos).

48 On DGV and DGAV types, remove the bush (20), spring (21), spacer (28) and spring (27).

49 Unscrew the nut (83) from the end of the secondary throttle

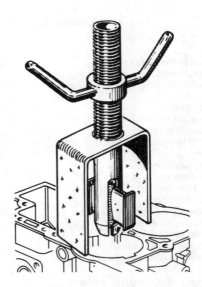

Fig. 7.11 Removing the primary auxiliary venturi with the special tool (Sec 5)

shaft (23); if it is tight, use Weber tool no 9610 315 1514 to hold the shaft stationary (photo).

50 Remove the nut (83), spring washer (84), plain washer (85), and lever (86); additionally on DGV and DGAV types, remove the bush (20) and spring (21).

51 With the secondary throttle valve closed, unscrew and remove the retaining screws (26) then mark the valve (22) with a pencil to identify its location and position (photo).

5.42 Withdrawing the primary auxiliary venturi

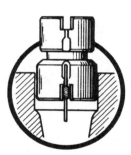

Fig. 7.12 Using the special tool to hold the throttle shaft stationary (Sec 5)

5.43 Primary throttle lever components

5.44a Removing the primary throttle shaft lever ...

5.44b ... bush ...

5.44c ... idling lever ...

5.44d ... and return spring

5.45 Removing the primary throttle shaft spacer

5.47a Removing the primary throttle valve ...

5.47b ... and throttle shaft

5.49 Secondary throttle lever components

5.51 Secondary throttle valve retaining screws

52 Fully open the secondary throttle and remove the valve (22) from the shaft (23), then withdraw the secondary shaft (23) from the carburettor body (88).
53 On DGV and DGAV types, remove the bush (20) and spring (21) from the shaft (23).

6 Special overhaul procedures

After carrying out the general overhaul procedures given in Chapter 4, the following special procedures should be made.
1 Using a hand chuck and Weber tool no 9600 325 1047, reform the idling jet seats by carefully rotating the tool in alternate directions. Finish the seatings by inserting Weber tool no 9610 315 1202 and gently tapping the top of the tool whilst rotating it.

being tested. If any are blocked, the lead plugs must be drilled out and the channels cleared and checked with the special Weber tool.
7 The channels are of three diameters (1.0 mm, 1.5 mm, and 2.0 mm) and the corresponding tools are Weber tool nos 98014 300, 98014 400 and 98014 500. Fig. 7.17 shows the location of the various channels.
8 The carburettor body and cover should be thoroughly cleaned after overhaul to remove swarf and dirt, preferably using clean fuel and air pressure. The lead plugs should be renewed and retained in position by using Weber tool nos 9610 315 0822 and 9610 315 0823 to expand them into their bores.
9 Check the float unit for damage and leakage; shake the float to determine whether fuel has entered. If the float is damaged or fuel is present, it must be renewed.

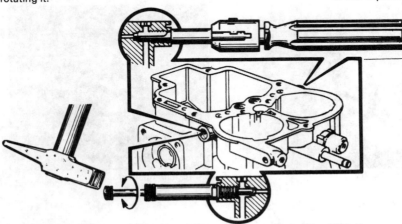

Fig. 7.13 Overhauling the idling jet seats (Sec 6)

2 If the emulsion tube bores are discoloured and show signs of sediment build up, ream them clear again using Weber tool no 9600 325 0765. Rotate the tool slowly with a hand chuck until it moves quite freely, then remove it while still rotating it.
3 If on disassembly, the choke shaft (4) (Fig. 7.8) is a tight fit in the carburettor cover (1) and it is of original diameter (6.0 mm), use Weber tool no 9600 035 0540 to ream the shaft bore clear with the aid of a hand chuck. Should the shaft bores be excessively worn, a new carburettor cover (1) must be obtained, but note that normally, the shaft itself will wear quicker than its bore, in which case a new shaft will cure the problem.
4 If on disassembly, the throttle shafts (23 and 24) are a tight fit in the carburettor body (88) and they are of original diameter (8.0 mm), use Weber tool no 9600 035 0407 to ream the shaft bores clear with the aid of a hand chuck. Should the shaft bores be excessively worn, oversize shafts of 8.5 mm diameter must be fitted and the bores should be reamed using Weber tool no 9600 035 0406.
5 Using a small file remove any burrs, which have been formed as a result of reaming as described in paragraphs 3 and 4.
6 Check the internal channels of the carburettor body (88) and cover (1) for blockage, by injecting fuel with a syringe and observing that it emerges freely from the particular channel

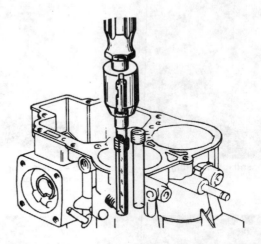

Fig. 7.14 Reaming the emulsion tube bores (Sec 6)

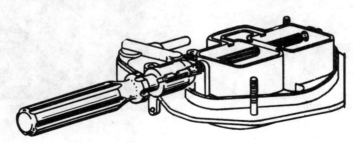

Fig. 7.15 Reaming the choke shaft bore (Sec 6)

Fig. 7.16 Reaming the throttle shaft
bore (Sec 6)

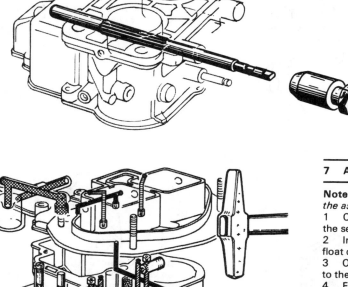

Fig. 7.17 Location of the carburettor internal channels and
method of fitting the lead plugs (Sec 6)

10 Where a power valve is fitted, check the condition of the diaphragm seat in the carburettor cover. If necessary clean the seat with a little metal polish.
11 During the manufacture of the carburettor a ball is inserted into the accelerator pump channel and retained by a brass plug (see Fig. 7.18). To check that this ball is free and unobstructed, shake the carburettor body (88) and listen to the ball movement.
12 On carburettors fitted with an automatic choke, check that the internal channel of the automatic choke body (51) is free and unobstructed. Also check that the diaphragm (52) and corresponding surfaces are serviceable; if necessary clean the surfaces with metal polish.
13 Check the accelerator pump diaphragm and corresponding surfaces in the same manner to that described in paragraph 12.
14 Renew the diaphragm assemblies checked in paragraphs 12 and 13 if necessary.
15 Check the accelerator pump lever for wear, especially on the type fitted with a roller bearing and renew it as necessary.
16 Check the walls of the choke intake, where the choke valves rest when they are fully shut; if there is a deep wear ridge, this could cause the valves to temporarily stick shut especially after an engine 'blowback' (photo). The ridge should be removed using fine emery tape.

7 Assembly

Note: *All components should be clean and dry before starting the assembly procedure.*
1 On DGV and DGAV types, fit the spring (21) (Fig. 7.8) to the secondary shaft (23) followed by the bush (20).
2 Insert the shaft (23) into the carburettor body (88) from the float chamber end.
3 On DGV and DGAV types, fit the spring (21) and bush (20) to the remaining end of the secondary shaft (23).
4 Fit the lever (86), plain washer (85), spring washer (84) and nut (83) to the secondary shaft (23) and tighten the nut (83). If available, use the Weber tool no 9610 315 1514 to hold the shaft stationary while the nut is tightened.
5 Insert the secondary valve (22) into the shaft slot, then turn the lever (86) onto the adjusting screw (72) or stop. Check that the angled perimeter of the valve (22) seats correctly in the secondary barrel. If necessary loosen the screw (72) during this procedure.
6 With the throttle valve (22) held closed, insert the valve retaining screws (26) and tighten them evenly but without exerting excessive pressure on the shaft. It is recommended that new screws are always fitted as it is quite easy to cross-thread previously peened screws. Lock the screws (26) by peening with Weber tool no 98010 900 while supporting the shaft (23) with a block of wood. Alternatively, coat the screw threads with a liquid locking agent (fuel resistant) prior to inserting them (Figs. 7.19 and 7.20).
7 On DGV and DGAV types, fit the spring (27), spacer (28), spring (21) and bush (20) to the primary throttle shaft (24).
8 Insert the shaft (24) into the carburettor body (88) from the float chamber end and tension the spring (27) where fitted.
9 On DGV and DGAV types, fit the bush (20) and spring (21) to the remaining end of the primary shaft (24); on all other types, fit the spacer and return spring.
10 Fit the lever (76) and bush (77), then fit the lever (82) and enter its lug into the secondary lever (86).
11 Fit the washer (78), lever (79), tab washer (81) and nut (80). Note that the accelerator pump cam on the end of the primary shaft (24) should be facing the well at the bottom of the float chamber while fitting the components.
12 Tighten the nut (80) and lock it by bending the tab washer (81); if available, use the Weber tool no 9610 315 1514 to hold the shaft stationary.
13 Insert the primary valve (25) into the shaft slot and check that when it is closed the angled perimeter seats correctly in the primary barrel (photo).
14 With the throttle valve (25) held closed, insert the valve retaining screws (26) and tighten them evenly but without exerting excessive pressure on the shaft. Refer to paragraph 6 for details of locking the screws.
15 Hook the spring (87) to the lever (82) and the carburettor body extension.
16 Check that both the primary and secondary throttle valves

Chapter 7 Type 32 DFD, 32 DFE, 32 DFM, 32 DIF,
32 DAF, 32 DGV, 32/36 DFV, 32/36 DGV, 32/36 DFAV, 32/36 DGAV carburettors

66

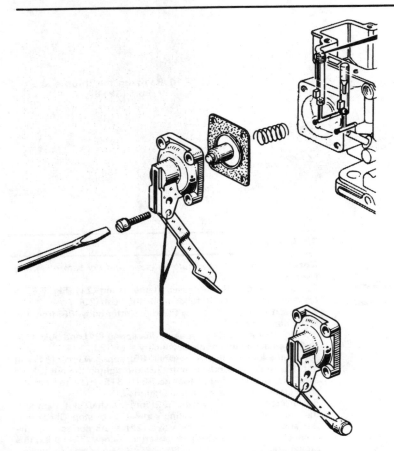

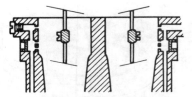

Fig. 7.18 Location of the accelerator
pump inlet ball valve (Sec 6)

Fig. 7.19 Correct attitude of the
throttle valve angled perimeters when
fitted to the carburettor (Sec 7)

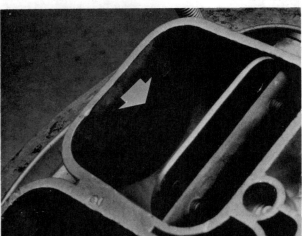

6.16 Showing the wear ridge on the choke intake walls

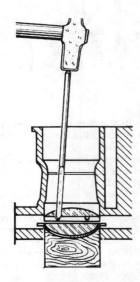

Fig. 7.20 Peening the throttle valve retaining screws (Sec 7)

operate smoothly and fully without any signs of sticking.
17 Fit the auxiliary venturis (98) into their respective positions
as noted previously, making sure that the supply channels are
adjacent and that the extended venturis face the throttle valves.
18 Fit the gasket (17) to the full power valve (16) then tighten
the valve into the base of the float chamber (where this component is fitted).
19 *On automatically operated choke types follow paragraphs
20 to 37 inclusive:*
20 Lubricate the operating rod (52) with a little engine oil, then
insert it into the automatic choke body (51) and locate the

diaphragm over the brass tube.
21 Locate the spring (53) into the cover (54) then fit it over the
diaphragm making sure that the spring seats correctly in the
diaphragm plate.
22 Press the operating rod (52) towards the cover (54) and
insert the retaining screws (55) and spring washers; tighten the
screws evenly.
23 Fit the adjusting screw (57) and plug (56), where fitted, to
the previously noted adjustment.
24 Check that the diaphragm is sealing properly by placing a
finger over the brass entry pipe after lifting the operating rod

7.13 The primary throttle valve (the angle relates to the total movement of the valve)

7.34 Refitting the fast idling control rod and the automatic choke assembly

7.36 Location of the automatic choke bi-metal spring

(52) against the spring (53); it should hold its position, but if it slowly moves to the rest position, a leak is indicated.

25 On 32/36 DFAV types, fit the adjustment stop plate to its previously noted position and tighten the retaining screw.

26 Fit the adjustment screw (65) and spring (66) to the fast idling lever (63), then fit the screw (75) to the lever together with the bush (74), wave washer (73) where fitted, and washer (62).

27 Tighten the screw (75) into the body (51) and check that the adjustment screw (65) locates on the fast idle cam correctly.

28 Where applicable, fit the rod to the lever (36) and insert the split pin, bending the legs back to secure.

29 Lubricate the shaft (41) with engine oil then insert it into the body (51) and locate the lever against the operating rod (52).

30 Fit the spacer (39), cover (38) if fitted, spring (37), lever (36), spring washer (68) and nut (69). Hook the spring (37) onto the lever (36) and tighten the nut (69). Position the cam towards the adjusting screw (65) during this operation and make sure that the lug of the lever (36) locates on top of the smooth part of the fast idle cam.

31 Press the rubber O-ring seal (67) to the rear of the unit.

32 Fit the retaining ring (47) to the thermostat assembly (48), then fit the gasket (46).

33 Locate the housing (45) to the assembly (48), then insert and tighten the retaining bolt (44) and gasket (43) making sure that the inlet and outlet pipes are facing the correct way.

34 Engage the fast idling control rod (61) to the lever (64) making sure that the single retaining lug end is fitted, then engage the remaining end with the throttle lever (76) and fit the split pin where necessary (photo).

35 Fit the auto-choke body (51) to the carburettor body (88) and tighten the retaining screws (40) and spring washers, noting that they are different lengths.

36 Locate the gasket (49) over the operating shaft arm and the location peg. Fit the thermostat assembly (48), at the same time locating the bi-metal spring end over the shaft arm (photo).

37 Align the marks on the thermostat assembly (48) and body (51), then insert the screws (42) and tighten them evenly. It may be necessary to reposition the housing (45) during this operation. If a new body (51) has been fitted, it will be necessary to make the fast idle adjustments given in Section 8, then to make an alignment mark using Weber tool no 98028 600, at the same time keeping the choke valves completely shut.

38 *On manually operated choke types paragraphs 39 or 40 as applicable:*

39 Refer to Fig. 7.10 and, on all but DGV type carburettors, fit the lever (26) to the carburettor body followed by the washer (28) and split pin (6). Fit the operating rod (9) to the lever (26), then locate the washer (67) and split pin (6). Insert the screw (32) into the lever (31), then engage the rod (40) to the lever (31) and fit the spring (29), lever assembly (30) and washer (33)

to the carburettor body. Insert and tighten the screw (34) and spring washer, then hook the spring (27) to the lever assembly (30) and lever (26). Locate the rod (40) to the lever (50) and fit the split pin (6).

40 Refer to Fig. 7.9 and, on DGV type carburettors, engage the fast idle rod (55) to the lever (49) then fit the bush (48) and lever (49) to the retaining screw (47). Mount the spring (51) to the carburettor, then fit and tighten the screw (47); hook the spring (51) over the lever (49). Locate the lower end of the rod (55) to the lever (60) and fit the split pin (50). Insert the screw (43) through the lever (42), then fit the rod (7) to the lever (42). Mount the return spring (44) to the carburettor body and fit the lever (41), bush (45) and retaining screw (46). Tighten the screw (46), hook the spring (44) to the lever (41) and make sure that the cam abuts the peg on the lever (49).

41 Referring to Fig. 7.8, fit the dust seal (7) and dust cover (8) to the carburettor cover (1).

42 Lubricate the choke shaft (4) with a little engine oil and insert it into the cover (1), together with bushes and circlips where fitted.

43 With the choke shaft (4) in the open position, fit the choke valves (5) into their location slots, then close the shaft to allow the valves to centralise (photo).

44 Holding the shaft closed, insert the valve retaining screws (9) and tighten them evenly without exerting excessive pressure on the brass shaft (4). It is recommended that new screws are always fitted as it is quite easy to cross-thread previously peened screws. Lock the screws (9) by peening with Weber tool no 9610 315 0833, or alternatively by coating the threads with a liquid locking agent (fuel resistant) prior to inserting them. If the tool method is used, support the shaft (4) with a piece of wood.

45 Fit the spring (71) to the throttle idling adjustment screw (70) and locate the screw in the carburettor body or linkage as applicable.

46 Fit the spring (59) to the idling mixture adjusting screw (58) and locate the screw in the carburettor body.

47 Where fitted, tighten the plug into the carburettor flange.

48 Prise the idling jets (33 and 33A) into their respective holders (35) and fit the gaskets (34) if fitted.

49 Tighten each idling jet into their primary and secondary locations in the carburettor body (88).

50 Insert the primary and secondary emulsion tubes (89) into the carburettor body (88), then fit and tighten the primary (94) and secondary (94A) air corrector jets.

51 Fit and tighten the primary (19) and secondary (19A) main jets to the bottom of the float chamber.

52 Fit and tighten the accelerator pump discharge blanking needle (18).

53 Fit a gasket (95) to the accelerator pump delivery valve (97) followed by the pump jet (96) and a further gasket (95). Note that on some types the upper gasket is omitted.

54 Fit and tighten the delivery valve (97) to the carburettor body (88).

68

**Chapter 7 Type 32 DFD, 32 DFE, 32 DFM, 32 DIF,
32 DAF, 32 DGV, 32/36 DFV, 32/36 DGV, 32/36 DFAV, 32/36 DGAV carburettors**

7.43 Choke lever position with the valves shut

55 Locate the diaphragm (31) to the accelerator pump cover (29) and insert the screws (30) through the cover and diaphragm.

56 Place the carburettor body on end and locate the spring (32) into the housing, then lower the diaphragm and cover into the spring and tighten the retaining screws in diagonal sequence. Make sure that the roller or arm, as applicable, locates on the primary shaft (24) cam.

57 Fit the gasket (13) to the needle valve (14) seating then tighten it into the carburettor cover (1) using a 10 mm box spanner or socket.

58 Locate the power valve (93) (where fitted) on the inverted cover (1) then depress the valve with one hand and lift the valve cover slightly to settle the diaphragm. While keeping the valve depressed, insert and tighten the retaining screws (91) together with spring washers (92). Check the operation of the valve by depressing it and placing a finger over the brass connecting channel; the valve should remain in the closed position but, if it

moves, a leak is indicated in the diaphragm.

59 On all but DFV, DFAV, DGV and DGAV type carburettors, locate the gasket (12) to the carburettor cover (1). On the types given, the gasket is fitted after checking the float level.

60 Hook the needle onto the wide tab of the float (15), then lower both items into position and insert the fulcrum pin (90) into the two posts. Lightly pinch the slotted post with a pair of flat pliers to retain the pin.

61 The float level adjustment must now be checked in the following manner, remembering that DFV, DFAV, DGV and DGAV types must *not* have the gasket (12) in position. Hold the carburettor cover vertically so that the float(s) is hanging from the fulcrum pin and the float arm is in light contact with the needle ball (ie the ball is not depressed).

62 On DFV, DFAV, DGV and DGAV types, use vernier calipers to determine the distance from the cover to the further edge of the floats as indicated in Fig. 7.21. On all other types obtain a drill or dowel rod of diameter equal to the closed checking dimension and check that the distance from the cover gasket to the nearest part of the float is correct. The annular seam must not be taken into consideration for the check and for this reason a groove must be filed in the checking rod.

63 If the dimension obtained in paragraph 62 is not correct, carefully bend the wide tab on the float as necessary.

64 Tilt the carburettor cover so that the float(s) moves away from the cover and the narrow tab makes contact with the needle valve seating. Now, using the same methods as described in paragraph 62, check the needle valve fully-open dimension. The difference between the dimension and the closed dimension is the needle valve stroke. If this is not correct, bend the narrow tab as necessary.

65 On DFV, DFAV, DGV and DGAV types, place the gasket (12) onto the cover (1) making sure that it is the correct way round.

66 Tilt the cover (1) and insert the choke operating rod (36) through the dust seal (7), then lower the cover (1) onto the carburettor body (88) (photo).

67 Fit the retaining screws (3) together with the spring washers and tighten then evenly in diagonal sequence.

68 Engage the choke plate operating rod (36) to the choke shaft (4) and retain with the circlip (6) or split pin as applicable.

69 Fit the fuel filter (10) and tighten the inspection plug (11) into the cover (1).

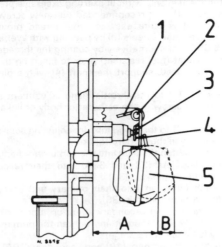

Fig. 7.21 Checking the float level adjustment (DFV, DFAV, DGV, DGAV types) (Sec 7)

1	Stop tab	5	Float
2	Fulcrum pin	A	Closed dimension
3	Contact tab	B	Stroke
4	Needle valve		

Fig. 7.22 Checking the float level adjustment (DFD, DFE, DFM, DIF, DAF types) (Sec 7)

1	Stop tab	5	Float
2	Fulcrum pin	6	Seam
3	Contact tab	A	Closed dimension
4	Needle valve	B	Stroke

7.66 The main carburettor body ready for assembly of the cover (DFAV type shown)

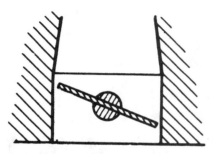

Fig. 7.23 Fast idle throttle opening checking location (Sec 8)

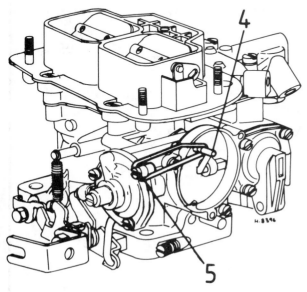

Fig. 7.24 Checking the automatic choke shaft setting on DGAV type carburettors (Sec 8)

  4   Spindle arm   5   Elastic band

8   Carburettor adjustments

With the carburettor completely assembled, the following adjustments must be made prior to fitting it to the engine:

1   Turn the throttle idling adjustment screw until it just touches the throttle lever (DGV and DGAV types) or carburettor lug (all other types), then continue to screw it in 2 further turns. On automatic choke types, it will be necessary to first open the throttle fully, hold the choke valves open, then release the throttle; it is preferable to hold the choke valves open while making the adjustment.

2   Turn the idling mixture screw in until it is in light contact with its seat, then back it off 1 complete turn.

3   Turn the secondary throttle adjustment stop until a gap of 0.05 mm (0.002 in) exists between the outer edge of the secondary throttle valve and the secondary barrel. Check the gap with feeler gauges.

Fast idle adjustment – manual choke

4   Fully operate the choke lever and, while keeping the lever stationary, check that the gap between the primary throttle valve and the outer primary barrel bore is as given in the adjustment data. If not, bend the fast idle operating rod accordingly. Check the gap with a drill of the correct diameter inserted into the barrel.

Fast idle adjustment – DGAV automatic choke

5   Fully open and close the throttle and check that the fast idling adjustment screw (Fig. 7.8) (65) is resting on the high part of the fast idle cam.

6   Refer to the adjustment data and determine the fast idle throttle opening for the the carburettor being worked on, then obtain a drill or length of dowel rod of the same diameter and insert it between the primary throttle valve and the outer barrel wall. Turn the adjusting screw as necessary to obtain the correct clearance.

7   Fully open the throttle, then hold the choke valves open and release the throttle. Slowly release the choke valves until the fast idle adjusting screw rests on the lower part of the fast idle cam (against the step).

8   Refer to the adjustment data and determine the correct choke valve opening, then check the clearance between the longest choke valve section and the intake wall using a drill or length of dowel rod. If necessary, bend the lever which contacts the fast idle cam to obtain the correct clearance.

Choke valve pull down – DGAV automatic choke

9   Remove the thermostat housing (Fig. 7.8) (48) and the gasket disc.

10   Open and close the throttle so that the choke valves fully close under finger pressure, then holding the choke valves shut, check that there is a clearance between the diaphragm spindle (Fig. 7.8) (52) and the shaft arm (Fig. 7.8) (41) equal to the dimension given in the adjustment data. If not, the diaphragm may be stretched or the shaft arm bent. Check and rectify both of these items before proceeding.

11   Connect an elastic band between the shaft arm and the diaphragm cover so that the choke valves are held shut.

12   Open and close the throttle so that the choke valves shut, then using a small electrician's screwdriver or length of welding rod, push the outer diameter of the diaphragm spindle hard against the adjustment screw by inserting it into the spindle bore. The tension of the elastic band must be sufficient to overcome the tension of the spring inside the diaphragm spindle. This can be checked by temporarily opening the choke valves and observing whether the visible section of the spindle moves.

13   Check that the clearance between the longest section of the choke valve and the intake wall is not less than the dimension given in the adjustment data. If it is, use a narrow screwdriver to adjust the setting screw (Fig. 7.8) (57).

14   Using the blade of a screwdriver, press both sections of the spindle hard against the adjustment screw; the clearance

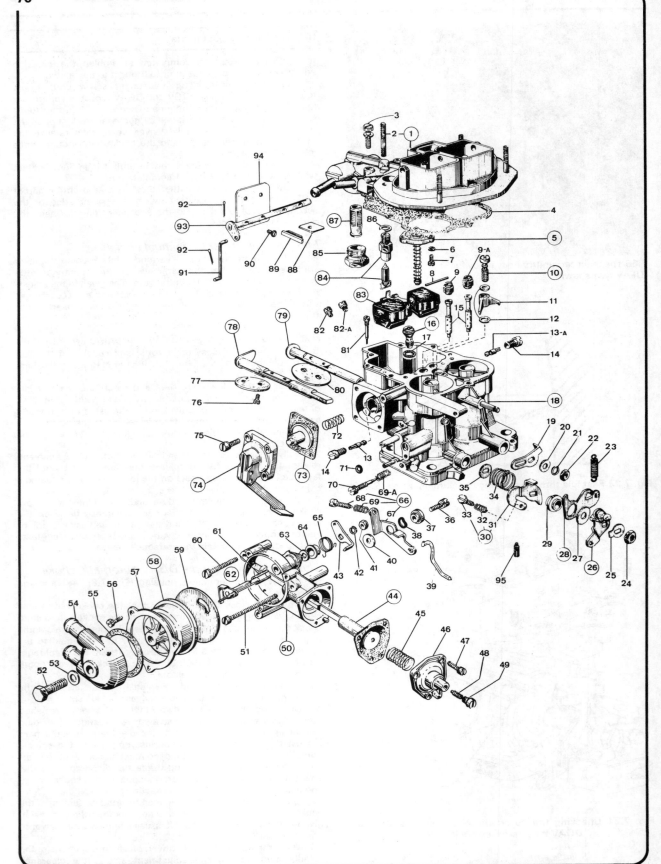

between the lower edge of the choke valves and the intake wall should now be as given in the adjustment data. If not, the internal spring of the spindle is faulty and the spindle should be renewed.

15 Remove the elastic band and refit the gasket and thermostat housing.

Fast idle adjustment – DAF and DFAV automatic choke

16 Fully open and close the throttle and check that the fast idling adjustment screw (Fig. 7.25) (68) is resting on the high part of the fast idle cam.

17 Refer to the adjustment data and determine the fast idle throttle opening for the carburettor being worked on, then obtain a drill or length of dowel rod of the same diameter and insert it between the primary throttle valve and the outer barrel well. Turn the adjusting screw as necessary to obtain the correct clearance.

Choke valve pull down – DAF and DFAV automatic choke

18 Remove the thermostat housing (Fig. 7.25) (58) and the gasket disc.

19 Open and close the throttle so that the choke valves fully close under finger pressure, then holding the choke valves shut, check that there is a clearance between the diaphragm spindle (Fig. 7.25) (62) and the shaft arm (Fig. 7.25) (44) of at least 0.008 in (0.2 mm). Make the check with feeler gauges and, if incorrect, check the shaft arm or linkage for damage. If any damage is found, they should be bent back to the original shape; alternatively the diaphragm may be found to be damaged.

20 Using an elastic band, hold the primary throttle valve fully open, then move the diaphragm spindle so that it abuts the stop plate. Move the shaft arm against the spindle central stop and check that the clearance between the choke valve longest section and the intake well is between 0.187 in (4.75 mm) and 0.207 in (5.25 mm). Use a drill to make the check and if incorrect, adjust the position of the stop plate as necessary.

21 Remove the elastic band and refit the gasket and thermostat housing.

9 Tuning

Note: *Refer to Chapter 3 for general notes on tuning.*

1 The idling adjustment screws should be set to their preliminary positions as described in Section 8 paragraphs 1 and 2.

2 Connect a tachometer to the engine in accordance with the manufacturer's instructions.

3 Start the engine and run until normal operating temperature has been reached (ie the thermostat has opened).

4 Turn the throttle valve adjusting screw so that the engine runs at the recommended idling speed for the particular engine being worked on; this will be between 600 and 800 rpm for touring models and approximately 1000 rpm for sports car models.

5 Turn the idle mixture adjustment screw in or out until the engine runs at the highest rpm commensurate with even running.

6 Re-adjust the throttle valve adjusting screw if necessary, to bring the engine speed within limits.

7 Repeat the procedure given in paragraphs 5 and 6, then switch off the engine and remove the tachometer.

8 On bypass idle type carburettors, the procedure is similar but the bypass idle adjustment screw should first be fully

---

Fig. 7.25 Exploded view of the 32/36 DFAV carburettor (typical) (Sec 8)

1 Carburettor cover assy	33 Screw	67 Lever
2 Stud bolt	34 Primary shaft return spring	68 Screw
3 Cover fixing screw	35 Washer	69 Spring
4 Cover gasket	36 Loose lever fixing screw	69A Spring for idle adjusting screw
5 Power valve	37 Bushing for loose lever	70 Idle adjusting screw
6 Washer for power valve screws	38 Wave washer	71 Auto-choke O-ring seal
7 Control valve retaining screw	39 Fast idling control rod	72 Pump loading spring
8 Float fixing pin	40 Washer for loose lever	73 Accelerator pump diaphragm assy
9 Primary air corrector jet	41 Shaft fixing nut	74 Accelerator pump cover assy
9A Secondary air corrector jet	42 Spring washer	75 Pump cover fixing screw
10 Pump delivery valve assy	43 Lever for rod	76 Throttle plates fixing screw
11 Pump jet	44 Choke diaphragm assy	77 Primary throttle valve
12 Pump jet gasket	45 Spring for diaphragm	78 Primary shaft assy
13 Primary idling jet	46 Cover for diaphragm	78 Primary shaft assy oversize
13A Secondary idling jet	47 Diaphragm cover fixing screw	79 Secondary shaft assy
14 Idling jet holder	48 Diaphragm adjusting screw	79 Secondary shaft assy oversize
15 Emulsioning tube	49 Screw plug	80 Secondary throttle valve
16 Full power needle valve assy	50 Auto-choke body assy	81 Pump discharge blanking needle
17 Power valve gasket	51 Auto-choke fixing screw	82 Primary main jet
18 Carburettor body assy	52 Water cover fixing screw	82A Secondary main jet
19 Secondary throttle control lever	53 Gasket for water cover	83 Float assy
20 Washer for lever	54 Auto-choke water chamber	84 Needle valve assy
21 Spring washer	55 Water chamber seal gasket	85 Strainer inspection plug
22 Secondary shaft fixing nut	56 Plate fixing screw	86 Gasket for needle valve
23 Spring for loose lever	57 Thermostat assy locking ring	87 Strainer assy
24 Primary shaft fixing nut	58 Auto-choke thermostat assy	88 Dust seal plate
25 Lockwasher	59 Gasket for auto-choke body	89 Dust seal plug
26 Throttle valve control lever assy	60 Auto-choke cover fixing screw	90 Choke plates fixing screw
27 Washer for loose lever	61 Plate for choke shaft	91 Choke control rod
28 Primary loose lever assy	62 Auto-choke shaft and lever assy	92 Split pin
29 Bushing for loose lever	63 Washer for shaft	93 Choke shaft and lever assy
30 Idle adjusting screw lever assy	64 Spring retaining cover	94 Choke throttle valve
31 Lever	65 Spring for fast idle cam	95 Secondary throttle adjusting screw
32 Spring	66 Fast idle loose lever assy	

screwed in, then screwed out 1 full turn. The basic idle adjustment is then made in the normal way and the bypass idle adjustment used for any final adjustment of speed. If an exhaust analyser is available, the percentage of CO should be made on the basic idle adjustment, prior to making the final speed adjustment on the bypass idle screw.

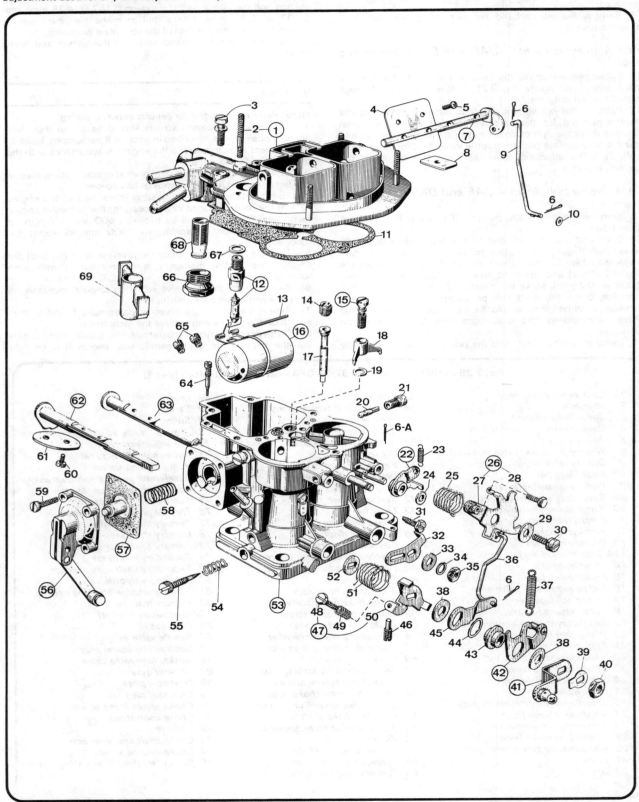

10 Fault diagnosis

Symptom	Reason/s
Engine will not start	Faulty choke linkage Faulty automatic choke Blocked fuel filter or jets
Uneven idling	Leaking carburettor flange or manifold gasket Loose idling jets or auxiliary venturis Excessive sediment or water in carburettor Throttle spindle or carburettor body excessively worn Secondary throttle valve partially sticking open Leaking ignition advance tube
Carburettor floods	Worn needle valve Leaking or damaged float assembly Incorrect float level adjustments Excessive sediment in fuel
Engine lacks performance	Incorrect tuning adjustments Incorrect float level adjustments Excessive sediment in fuel Acceleration pump seized Throttle valves do not fully open
Excessive fuel consumption	Needle valve not seating Choked air filter Leaking or damaged float assembly Faulty automatic choke (when fitted) Incorrect float level adjustments

Fig. 7.26 Exploded view of the 32 DIF carburettor (typical) (Sec 9)

1   Air horn and plugs assy
2   Air cleaner retaining stud
3   Horn and plug assy fixing screw and washer
4   Choke plate
5   Choke plate screw
6   Choke control rod split pin
6A Choke lever pivot split pin
7   Choke shaft and lever assy
8   Air cleaner dust seal
9   Choke control rod
10 Choke rod washer
11 Air horn to throttle body gasket
12 Fuel inlet valve and seat assy
13 Float lever shaft
14 Starting air adjusting jet
15 Accelerator pump discharge valve assy
16 Float assy
17 Fuel jet
18 Pump discharge nozzle
19 Nozzle bar gasket
20 Idling secondary jet
21 Idling jet holder
22 Choke lever assy
23 Choke lever spring
24 Choke lever pivot washer
25 Choke lever return spring

26 Choke control lever assy
27 Lever
28 Screw securing wire
29 Choke control lever assy retaining washer
30 Choke control lever assy retaining screw and washer
31 Screw securing sheath
32 Full throttle stop lever
33 Full throttle stop washer
34 Full throttle stop lockwasher
35 Full throttle stop nut
36 Fast idle rod
37 Throttle control return spring (RH Secondary)
38 Primary throttle shaft assy washer
39 Throttle shaft (Primary) tab washer
40 Throttle shaft (Primary) nut
41 Throttle lever
42 Throttle control lever
43 Throttle shaft bushing
44 Throttle shaft (Primary) wave washer
45 Choke/throttle interconnecting lever
46 Fast idling adjustment screw
47 Fast idle adjustment lever assy
48 Screw

49 Spring
50 Lever
51 Throttle control return spring (LH Primary)
52 Throttle lever and shaft assy (Primary) washer
53 Carburettor body
54 Fast idle adjusting screw spring
55 Idle adjustment needle
56 Accelerator pump cover assy
57 Accelerator pump diaphragm assy
58 Accelerator pump rod spring
59 Accelerator pump cover fixing screw and washer
60 Throttle plate screw
61 Throttle plate
62 Throttle shaft assy oversize (LH Primary)
63 Throttle shaft assy (RH Secondary)
64 Accelerator pump discharge blanking needle
65 Main primary jet
65A Main secondary jet
66 Fuel inlet strainer plug
67 Fuel intake valve washer
68 Fuel inlet strainer assy
69 Fuel discharge units

Part 2
Chapter 8 Type 46 IDA, 48 IDA,
40 IDA 3C, 40 IDS 3C, 40 IDT 3C,
46 IDA 3C, 40 IDAP 3C, 40 IDTP 3C,
40 IDTP 13C carburettors

Contents

Chapter 8 Type 46 IDA, 48 IDA, 40 IDA 3C, 40 IDS 3C
40 IDT 3C, 46 IDA 3C, 40 IDAP 3C, 40 IDTP 3C, 40 IDTP 13C carburettors

75

1 Introduction

The carburettors covered by this Chapter are of the vertical downdraught type and each barrel of the carburettor is of an identical diameter.

The throttle valves are of the synchronized, simultaneous operation type.

The carburettor may be fitted on the engine in several different arrangements, the most common being listed as follows:

1 Two twin choke units on a four-cylinder horizontally opposed engine, ie one barrel to each cylinder
2 Two triple choke units on a six-cylinder horizontally opposed engine, ie one barrel to each cylinder
3 Four twin choke units on an eight-cylinder V-configuration engine, ie one barrel to each cylinder

The carburettor identification mark is located on the side of the main body.

2 Construction

The main body and cover of the carburettors covered in this Chapter are of die-cast aluminium construction. The mounting flanges are machined flat for fitting on the inlet manifold assemblies.

The throttle spindles are made of steel and the throttle valves of brass. The retaining screws on 46 IDA and 48 IDA types are made of brass; on triple choke types however, they are made of steel.

The air intake horns are of steel construction and are attached to the carburettor cover by studs and nuts.

All fuel and air jets and emulsion tubes are of brass construction and, with the exception of the emulsion tubes on triple choke types, are screw fittings into the main body.

The internal channels of the main body are mainly drilled and where necessary, sealed with lead plugs.

On twin choke types, the throttle spindles are supported by two ball-bearings mounted in the main body. Spring tensioned seals are incorporated at each end of the spindle to prevent air being drawn through the bearings.

On triple choke types, the throttle spindles run directly in the carburettor body.

The fuel float assemblies are constructed of thin brass sheet and comprise two halves soldered together.

On twin choke types, the accelerator pump is of the piston type and the piston is of brass construction.

On triple choke types, the accelerator pump is of the diaphragm type and the housing and cover are of die-cast aluminium.

3 Operation

Idling and progression
46 IDA and 48 IDA types

Refer to Fig. 8.3 and note that when the engine is idling with the throttle valves (19) closed, fuel is drawn from the float chamber (13) to the idling jets (15) where it becomes emulsified with air entering through the calibrated orifices in the idling jet holders (14). The mixture then travels through the channel (16), past the adjustable mixture screws (17), through the idling feed holes (18) and into the carburettor throats at the engine side of the throttle valves. The idling mixture screws (17) have tapered ends and can therefore be adjusted to admit more or less mixture as necessary.

When the throttle valves are opened slightly to increase the engine speed, the progression holes (20) are brought into action to provide additional fuel and to enable the engine to reach the speed when the main system starts to function.

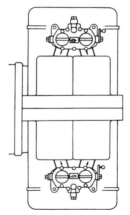

Fig. 8.1 Two carburettors fitted to a 4-cylinder opposed engine (Sec 1)

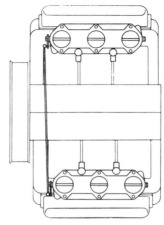

Fig. 8.2 Two carburettors fitted to a 6-cylinder opposed engine (Sec 1)

Triple choke types

Refer to Fig. 8.4 and note that when the engine is idling with the throttle valves (18) closed, fuel is drawn from the emulsion tube wells (12), along the channel (22) to the idling jets (23) where it becomes emulsified with air entering through the calibrated orifices (24). The mixture then passes through the channel (21), past the mixture screws (20), through the idling feed holes (19) and into the carburettor throats at the engine side of the throttle valves. The idling mixture screws (20) have tapered ends and can be adjusted to admit more or less mixture as necessary.

When the throttle valves are opened slightly to increase the engine speed, the progression holes (15) are brought into action to provide additional fuel until the main system starts to function.

In order to ensure that each carburettor barrel passes identical amounts of air, three air compensation adjustment screws (16) are incorporated whereby air can bypass the throttle valves. This system ensures identical vacuum below each throttle valve and the idling and progression mixtures in each barrel are therefore identical.

Normal running
46 IDA and 48 IDA types

Refer to Fig. 8.5 and note that under full throttle and cruise conditions, fuel is drawn from the float chamber (13), through the channel (12) and main jets (11) and then through the orifices in the emulsion tubes (8).

The fuel then becomes emulsified with air drawn in through

76

Chapter 8 Type 46 IDA, 48 IDA, 40 IDA 3C, 40 IDS 3C
40 IDT 3C, 46 IDA 3C, 40 IDAP 3C, 40 IDTP 3C, 40 IDTP 13C carburettors

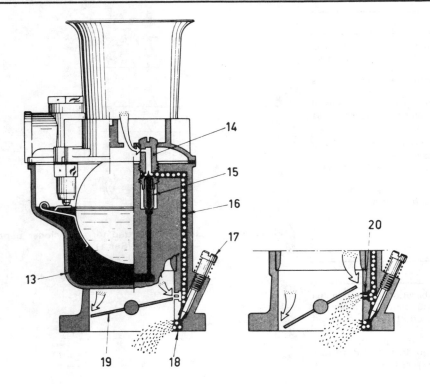

Fig. 8.3 Idling and progression phase (46 IDA and 48 IDA) (Sec 3)

13 Float chamber
14 Idling jet holders
15 Idling jets
16 Channel
17 Mixture volume screw
18 Idling feed holes
19 Throttle valves
20 Progression holes

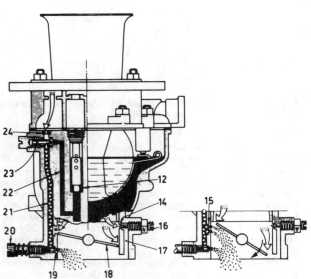

Fig. 8.4 Idling and progression phase (triple choke types) (Sec 3)

12 Wells
14 Air compensation jet
15 Progression holes
16 Adjustment screw
17 Channel
18 Throttle valve
19 Idling feed holes
20 Idling mixture screw
21 Channel
22 Channel
23 Idling jets
24 Calibrated bush

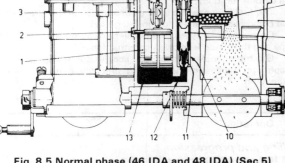

Fig. 8.5 Normal phase (46 IDA and 48 IDA) (Sec 5)

1 Float
2 Fulcrum pin
3 Needle valve
4 Needle valve seat
5 Air corrector jet
6 Nozzle
7 Auxiliary venturi
8 Emulsion tube
9 Choke
10 Well
11 Main jet
12 Channel
13 Float chamber

the air corrector jets (5) and is then drawn through the nozzles (6) and chokes (9) and into the engine.

Triple choke types

Refer to Fig. 8.6 and note that under full throttle and cruise

conditions, fuel is drawn from the float chambers (6) through the main jets (10) and channels (11) to the emulsion tube wells (12). The fuel becomes emulsified with air drawn in through the air corrector jets (3) and, after leaving the emulsion tubes (4), is drawn through the nozzles (2) and chokes (13) into the engine.

Chapter 8 Type 46 IDA, 48 IDA, 40 IDA 3C, 40 IDS 3C
40 IDT 3C, 46 IDA 3C, 40 IDAP 3C, 40 IDTP 3C, 40 IDTP 13C carburettors

77

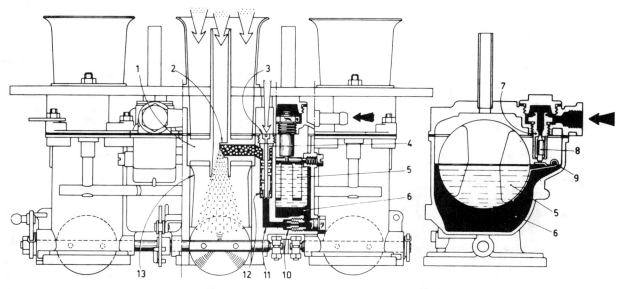

Fig. 8.6 Normal phase (triple choke types) (Sec 3)

1	Auxiliary venturi	5	Float	8	Needle valve	11	Channel
2	Nozzle	6	Float chamber	9	Fulcrum pin	12	Well
3	Air corrector jet	7	Needle valve seat	10	Main jet	13	Choke
4	Emulsion tube						

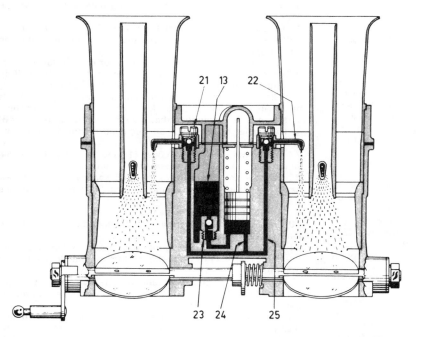

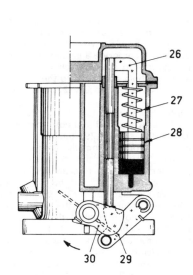

Fig. 8.7 Acceleration phase (46 IDA and 48 IDA) (Sec 3)

13	Float chamber	23	Inlet and discharge valve	26	Operating rod	29	Lever
21	Delivery valve	24	Channel	27	Spring	30	Cam
22	Pump jet	25	Channel	28	Piston		

Acceleration
46 IDA and 48 IDA types

Refer to Fig. 8.7 and note that when the throttle valves are closed, the lever (29) under the action of its spring, lifts the accelerator pump operating rod (26). Fuel is then drawn from

the float chamber (13) through the inlet valve (23) into the pump chamber. When the throttle valves are opened, the cam (30) moves the lever (29) away from the bottom of the operating rod (26) and the piston (28) moves down the pump bore under the action of the spring (27). The inlet valve ball then

Chapter 8 Type 46 IDA, 48 IDA, 40 IDA 3C, 40 IDS 3C
40 IDT 3C, 46 IDA 3C, 40 IDAP 3C, 40 IDTP 3C, 40 IDTP 13C carburettors

78

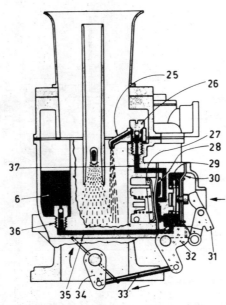

Fig. 8.8 Acceleration (triple choke types) (Sec 3)

6 *Float chamber*	31 *Operating lever*
25 *Pump jet*	32 *Cam*
26 *Delivery valve*	33 *Linkage*
27 *Release plate*	34 *Lever*
28 *Diaphragm*	35 *Channel*
29 *Spring*	36 *Inlet and discharge valve*
30 *Diaphragm*	37 *Channel*

closes and fuel is forced through the channels (24 and 25), through the delivery valves (21) and pump jets (22) into the barrels in the vicinity of the auxiliary venturis. The inlet valve (23) may incorporate a calibrated discharge hole whereby some fuel returns to the float chamber; by varying the size of the discharge hole according to the application, the amount of fuel injected by the pump jets (22) can be varied.

Triple choke types

Refer to Fig. 8.8 and note that when the throttle valves are closed, the spring (29) pushes the diaphragm (30) outwards and fuel is drawn from the float washers (6), through the inlet valves (36), along the channels (35) and into the pump chamber. When the throttle valves are opened, the lever (34) pulls the linkage (33) and the cam (32) causes the lever (31) to depress the diaphragm (30) against the tension of the spring (29). Fuel is forced past the release diaphragm (28) when the plate (27) moves against the reaction spring and then travels through the channels (37) to the delivery valves (26). It is then injected through the pump jets (25) into the carburettor barrels in the vicinity of the auxiliary venturis. The inlet valve(s) (23) may incorporate a calibrated discharge hole whereby some fuel returns to the float chambers; the size of the hole depending on the particular application.

IDS type carburettors are equipped with booster jets located at the mouth of each auxiliary venturi. Their purpose is to provide mixture enrichment during high speed conditions.

4   Removal and refitting

Note: *The following procedure gives a general rather than a specific method of removing and refitting the carburettor, as much will depend on the location of the carburettor within the*

vehicle. On some applications for instance, the retaining nuts may not be accessible without removing surrounding components.

1   Disconnect all hoses from the air cleaner, if fitted. Remove the air cleaner cover and extract the air cleaner element.
2   Detach the air cleaner base from the carburettor, if fitted.
3   Disconnect the throttle linkage from the throttle lever.
4   Disconnect the fuel inlet hose or pipe (withdraw the filter on triple choke types).
5   Unscrew and remove the carburettor retaining nuts and spring washers and withdraw the carburettor complete over the mounting studs.
6   Remove the gaskets from the inlet manifold and clean all traces of gasket from the contact faces of the manifold and carburettor.
7   Protect the inlet manifold from ingress of foreign matter whilst the carburettor is removed by sealing it with masking tape.
8   Refitting is a reversal of removal but the following additional points should be noted:

    (a) *Always fit new gaskets and tighten the retaining nuts evenly in diagonal sequence*
    (b) *The idling adjustment screws should be set as described in Sections 8 and 9, and finally tuned as described in Section 10*

5   Disassembly (46 IDA and 48 IDA types)

1   Thoroughly clean the carburettor exterior and wipe dry.
2   Referring to Fig. 8.9, unscrew and remove the retaining nuts (61) and withdraw the filter gauze (64) (photo).
3   Unscrew and remove the retaining nuts (60), remove the plates (59) and withdraw the air intake horns (58).
4   Unscrew and remove the filter inspection plug (57), remove the washer (56) and extract the fuel filter (55) and retaining bush (63) (photo).
5   Unscrew and remove the carburettor cover retaining nuts (62) and carefully lift the cover from the carburettor body (65), making sure that the gasket (14) is not broken (photo).
6   Lift the gasket (14) from the carburettor body (65). If it is necessary to retain the gasket for any reason and it has become shrunk, it is recommended that the emulsion tube holders (48) and idling jet holders (50) are removed before removing the gasket.
7   Invert the carburettor cover (1) and unscrew the needle valve (12), then remove the washer (13) (photo).
8   Remove the locking wire from the float fulcrum pin screw head (17), then unscrew and remove it together with the washer (16) (photos).
9   Lift the float (15) from the float chamber.
10   Unscrew and remove the float chamber drain plug (23) and washer (22) (photo).
11   Unscrew and remove the accelerator pump inlet and discharge valve (11) from the bottom of the float chamber (photo).
12   Unscrew the emulsion tube holders (48) from the carburettor body (65) and lift out the emulsion tube assemblies (photo).
13   Separate the emulsion tubes (46) from the holders (48) and then pull the main jets (45) and air corrector jets (47) from the emulsion tubes (46). Take care not to damage the jets when removing them and if pliers are used, interpose a piece of paper or card to prevent the brass being scratched (photo).
14   Unscrew the idling jet holders and air corrector jets (50) from the carburettor body (65) and then separate the idling jets (49) (photos).
15   Unscrew and remove the accelerator pump delivery valves (8) together with the pump jets (10) and washers (9), then separate the washers and jets from the valves (photos).
16   Lift the accelerator pump operating rod (4) against the tension of the spring (6) until the retainer (5) is released from the carburettor body (65), then withdraw the complete

5.2 Removing the filter gauze (twin choke type)

5.4 Removing the fuel filter (twin choke type)

5.5 Removing the carburettor cover (twin choke type)

5.7 Removing the needle valve (twin choke type)

5.8a Fulcrum pin locking wire location (twin choke type)

5.8b Removing the float fulcrum pin (twin choke type)

5.10 Removing the float chamber drain plug (twin choke type)

5.11 Location of the pump inlet and discharge valve (twin choke type)

5.12 Removing an emulsion tube (twin choke type)

5.13 Emulsion tube components (twin choke type)

5.14a Removing the idling jets (twin choke type)

5.14b The idling jet and holder (twin choke type)

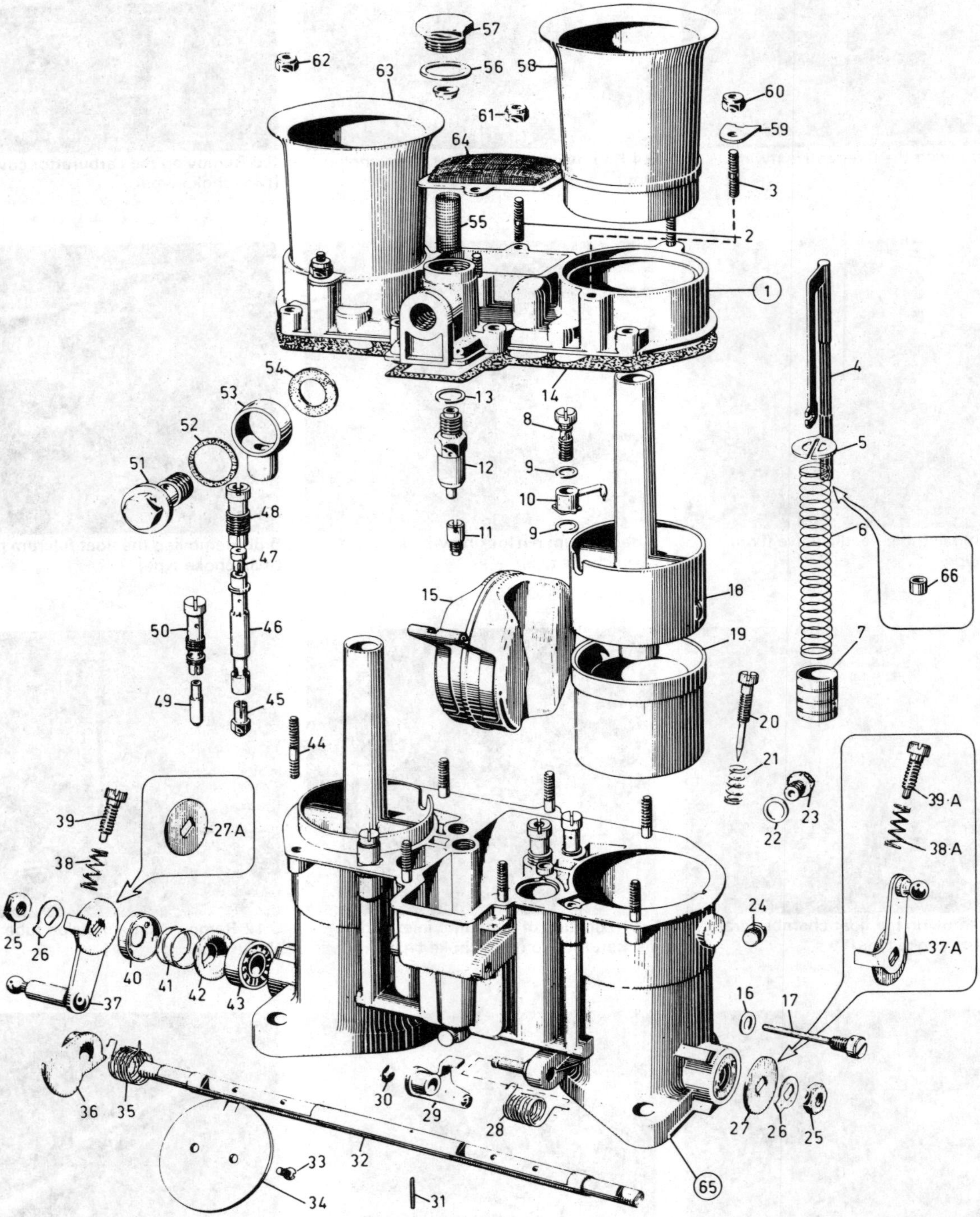
57
62
56
58
63
60
61
59
64
3
55
2
1
4
54
13
14
53
8
5
52
12
9
51
48
10
6
9
11
66
47
15
18
50
46
19
7
49
45
20
44
21
39
27·A
23
22
39·A
38
38·A
24
25
26
40
41
42
43
37
37·A
16
17
36
35
30
29
28
27
26
25
33
32
65
34
31

**Chapter 8 Type 46 IDA, 48 IDA, 40 IDA 3C, 40 IDS 3C,
40 IDT 3C, 46 IDA 3C, 40 IDAP 3C, 40 IDTP 3C, 40 IDTP 13C carburettors**

81

5.15a Location of the accelerator pump delivery valve(twin choke type)

5.15b Pump delivery valve and jet components (twin choke type)

5.17 Accelerator pump components (twin choke type)

5.19 Removing the auxiliary venturis (twin choke type)

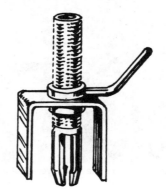

Fig. 8.10 Auxiliary venturi removal tool (Sec 5)

5.20a Removing the chokes (twin choke type)

accelerator pump assembly.

17 Lift the accelerator pump piston (7) against the spring (6) and disconnect it from the operating rod by turning it through 90°. Remove the piston (7), spring (6) and retainer (5) from the operating rod (4) (photo).

18 On 46 IDA types, remove the accelerator pump operating rod bush (66).

19 Note the location of the auxiliary venturis (18) and mark them, if necessary, with a pencil to ensure correct refitting, then withdraw them from the carburettor body (65) (photo). If necessary, use a wooden or plastic dowel rod inserted from the throttle valve end of the barrel, to tap the auxiliary venturis free. If they are excessively tight, it will be necessary to obtain Weber tool no 9610 150 0035.

20 Remove the chokes (19), noting that the end with the

smaller internal diameter is uppermost (photos). If these are excessively tight it will be necessary to obtain Weber tool no 9610 150 0034.

21 Unscrew and remove the idling mixture adjusting screws (20) and springs (21) from the carburettor body (65) (photo).

22 Unscrew and remove the idling adjusting screw (39 or 39A) and spring (38 or 38A) from the carburettor body (65).

23 Bend back the locktabs (26) on each end of the throttle spindle (32) and unscrew the nuts (25) (photo). If the nuts are tight, use Weber tool no 98023 700 to hold the spindle while the nut is loosened; if this precaution is not taken, the spindle (32) may become buckled. **Note:** *Under no circumstances should the nuts be loosened or tightened with the throttle valves being forced against the barrel walls.*

24 Remove the nuts (25), tab washers (26), spacer (27 or 27A)

Fig. 8.9 Exploded view of the 46 IDA and 48 IDA carburettor (Sec 5)

1	Cover	18	Auxiliary venturi	34	Throttle valve	50	Holder
2	Stud	19	Choke	35	Spring	51	Bolt
3	Stud	20	Mixture adjustment screw	36	Cam	52	Washer
4	Pump rod	21	Spring	37 and 37A	Lever	53	Union
5	Retainer	22	Washer	38 and 38A	Spring	54	Washer
6	Spring	23	Plug	39 and 39A	Idling adjustment	55	Fuel filter
7	Piston	24	Progression hole		screw	56	Washer
8	Delivery valve		inspection plug	40	Retainer	57	Plug
9	Washers	25	Nut	41	Spring	58	Air intake horn
10	Pump jet	26	Tab washer	42	Dust seal	59	Plate
11	Inlet and discharge valve	27 and 27A	Spacer	43	Bearing	60	Nut
12	Needle valve	28	Spring	44	Stud	61	Nut
13	Washer	29	Lever	45	Main jet	62	Nut
14	Gasket	30	Clip	46	Emulsion tube	63	Bush
15	Float	31	Roll pin	47	Air corrector jet	64	Filter gauze
16	Washer	32	Throttle spindle	48	Holder	65	Carburettor body
17	Fulcrum pin	33	Screw	49	Idling jet	66	Bush

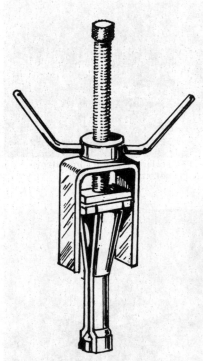

Fig. 8.11 Choke removal tool (Sec 5)

5.20b Choke diameter size location (twin choke type)

5.21 Idling mixture screw location (twin choke type)

5.23 Throttle spindle stop lever location (twin choke type)

5.25 Throttle valve retaining screw location (twin choke type)

5.27 Removing a throttle valve (twin choke type)

5.28 Accelerator pump lever location (twin choke type)

5.30 Removing the spring retainers (twin choke type)

5.31 Removing the throttle shaft springs (twin choke type)

Chapter 8 Type 46 IDA, 48 IDA, 40 IDA 3C, 40 IDS 3C
40 IDT 3C, 46 IDA 3C, 40 IDAP 3C, 40 IDTP 3C, 40 IDTP 13C carburettors

83

and lever (37 or 37A) from the throttle spindle (32).

25 Unscrew and remove the throttle valve retaining screws (33), being careful not to exert excessive pressure on the spindle (32) (photo).

26 Note the position of the throttle valves in relation to the barrels, and if necessary mark them with a pencil.

27 Turn the spindle to the fully open position and withdraw the two throttle valves (34) from their location slots (photo).

28 Using a small screwdriver, prise the C-clip (30) from the accelerator pump lever pivot then withdraw the lever (29) and spring (28) (photo).

29 Using a suitable pin punch, drive the roll pin (31) through the cam (36) and spindle (32). To ensure correct refitting, mark the cam and spindle in relation to each other.

30 Remove the spring retainers (40) from each end of the throttle spindle by inserting two self-tapping screws into the holes and pulling them with pliers (photo).

31 Remove the springs (41) and dust seals (42) (photo).

32 Using a plastic or wooden mallet, tap one end of the spindle (32) until the bearing (43) emerges from the opposite end of the carburettor body (65).

33 Continue to drive the spindle out with a length of dowel rod, at the same time recover the cam (36) and spring (35).

34 Mount the spindle loosely in a soft jaw vice, then tap the spindle (32) through the bearing (43).

35 Temporarily reinsert the spindle (32) into the carburettor body and remove the remaining bearing (43) using the method described in paragraphs 32, 33, and 34.

36 If the bearings are excessively worn, it is possible for the inner race to separate from the outer race leaving the latter in the carburettor body. If this happens, gently heat the body with a gas blow lamp until the race can be removed. On no account use excessive heat, otherwise the main body may be permanently distorted. It is not possible to obtain this component as a spare.

6 Disassembly (triple choke types)

1 Thoroughly clean the carburettor exterior and wipe dry.

2 Referring to Fig. 8.12, unhook the throttle lever return spring (where fitted), then unscrew and remove the carburettor cover retaining nuts (4A) and spring plate (where fitted) (photo).

3 Lift the cover (1) from the carburettor body, being careful not to break the gasket (11) (photo).

4 On 46 IDA 3C types, remove the screws (77) and lift off the gauze filters (76).

5 Unscrew and remove the retaining nuts (4) and withdraw the three air intake horns (3) and gasket (where fitted) (photo).

6 Carefully lift the gasket (11) from the carburettor body.

7 Unscrew both fuel inlet union bolts (14) and withdraw the unions (9 and 10) from the cover (1). Separate the sealing washers (8 and 13) from the unions and bolts and withdraw the fuel filter gauzes (12).

8 Pull the intermediate hose from the inlet unions (9 and 10).

9 Unscrew and remove the needle valve housing plugs (7) and washers (6) (photo).

10 Unscrew and remove the needle valves (5), noting the quantity of washers (75) fitted to them (photo).

11 Remove the locking wire from the float fulcrum pin screw heads (18), then remove the fulcrum pins together with the washers (17) (photo).

12 Lift the two floats (15) from the float chambers.

13 Unscrew and remove the drain plugs (64) and washers (63) (photo).

14 Unscrew and remove the main jet holders (61) and washers (59), then unscrew the main jets (60) from the holders (61) (photos).

15 Unscrew and remove the idling jet holders (66), then pull out the idling jets (65) (photos).

16 Unscrew and remove the air corrector jets (74), then invert

6.2 Throttle lever return spring location (triple choke type)

6.3 Removing the carburettor cover (triple choke type)

6.5 Removing the air intake horns (triple choke type)

6.9 Removing the needle valve housing plug (triple choke type)

6.10 Removing the needle valves (triple choke type)

6.11 Removing the float fulcrum pin (triple choke type)

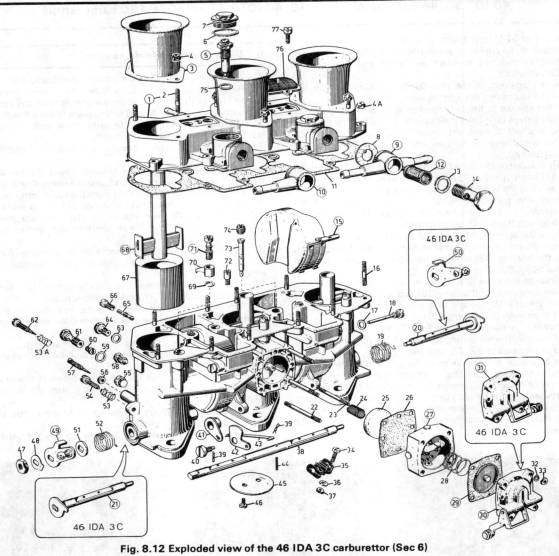

Fig. 8.12 Exploded view of the 46 IDA 3C carburettor (Sec 6)

1 Cover	28 Spring	53 and 53A Spring
2 Stud	29 Diaphragm	54 Idling adjustment screw
3 Air horn	30 Cover	55 Progression hole inspection plug
4 and 4A Nut	31 Cover	56 Locknut
5 Needle valve	32 Spring washer	57 Air compensating adjustment screw
6 Washer	33 Nut	58 Choke retaining screw
7 Plug	34 Screw	59 Washer
8 Washer	35 Linkage	60 Main jet
9 Union	36 Washer	61 Holder
10 Union	37 Nut	62 Mixture adjustment screw
11 Gasket	38 Throttle spindle	63 Washer
12 Fuel filter	39 Clip	64 Drain plug
13 Washer	40 Pivot	65 Ilding jet
14 Bolt	41 Arm	66 Holder
15 Float	42 Cam	67 Choke
16 Stud	43 Linkage	68 Auxiliary venturi
17 Washer	44 Roll pin	69 Washer
18 Fulcrum pin	45 Throttle valve	70 Pump jet
19 Spring	46 Screw	71 Delivery valve
20 Throttle spindle	47 Nut	72 Inlet and discharge valve
21 Throttle spindle	48 Tab washer	73 Emulsion tube
22 and 23 Stud	49 Lever	74 Air corrector jet
24 Spring	50 Lever	75 Washer
25 Plate	51 Spacer	76 Filter gauze
26 Diaphragm	52 Spring	77 Screw
27 Accelerator pump housing		

Chapter 8 Type 46 IDA, 48 IDA, 40 IDA 3C, 40 IDS 3C
40 IDT 3C, 46 IDA 3C, 40 IDAP 3C, 40 IDTP 3C, 40 IDTP 13C carburettors

85

6.13 Removing the drain plugs (triple choke type)

6.14a Removing a main jet (triple choke type)

6.14b A main jet and holder (triple choke type)

6.15a Removing an idling jet (triple choke type)

6.15b An idling jet and holder (triple choke type)

6.16a Removing the air corrector jets (triple choke type)

6.16b Removing an emulsion tube (triple choke type)

6.17 Location of an accelerator pump inlet and discharge valve (triple choke type)

6.18 Location of an accelerator pump delivery valve (triple choke type)

the carburettor body and extract the emulsion tubes (73). If they are a tight fit due to overtightening of the air jets, careful use of a selftapping screw may be necessary to extract the emulsion tubes (photos).

17 Unscrew and remove the accelerator pump inlet valves (72) from the bottom of the float chambers (photo).

18 Unscrew the accelerator pump delivery valves (71) and remove them together with the washers (69) (photo).

19 Withdraw the washers (69) and pump jets (70), then, on IDS types, remove the retaining screws and withdraw the booster jet assemblies.

20 Unscrew the accelerator pump retaining nuts (33) and remove them together with the spring washers (32) (photo).

21 Withdraw the accelerator pump cover (30) and body (27) over the location studs; at the same time recover the reaction spring (24) and plate (25) (photo).

22 Carefully remove the release diaphragm (26) from the body (27).

23 Separate the cover (30) from the body (27) and remove the return spring (28).

24 Carefully peel the pump diaphragm (29) from the cover (30).

25 Remove the locking wire from the choke retaining screws (58) then unscrew and remove them.

26 Note the location of the auxiliary venturis (68) and mark them with a pencil if necessary to ensure correct refitting; then withdraw them from the carburettor body (photos). If necessary, use a wooden or plastic dowel rod inserted from the throttle valve end of the barrel to tap the auxiliary venturis free but, if they are excessively tight, it will be necessary to obtain Weber tool no 9610 150 0035.

27 Remove the chokes (67), noting that the end with the

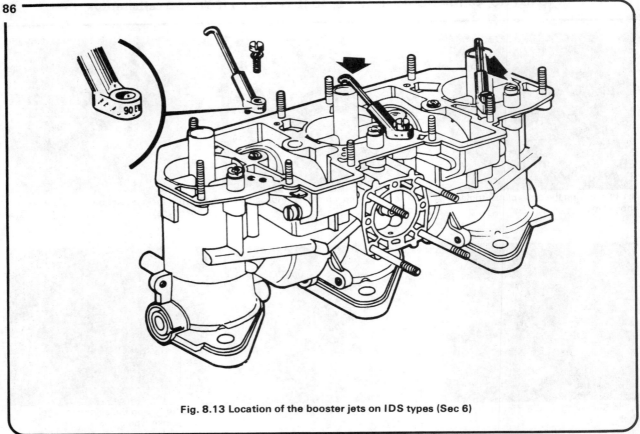

Fig. 8.13 Location of the booster jets on IDS types (Sec 6)

6.20 Accelerator pump cover location (triple choke type)

6.21 Removing the pump reaction plate and spring (triple choke type)

6.26a Removing an auxiliary venturi (triple choke type)

6.26b Auxiliary venturi and size identification (triple choke type)

6.27a Removing a choke (triple choke type)

6.27b Choke and size identification (triple choke type)

smaller internal diameter is uppermost (photos). If these are excessively tight it will be necessary to obtain Weber tool no 9610 150 0034.

28 Unscrew and remove the throttle valve retaining screws (46), being careful not to exert excessive pressure on the spindles (20 and 38) (photo).

29 Turn the spindles to the fully open position and withdraw the three throttle valves (45) from their location slots (photos).

30 Slacken the intermediate linkage screws (34) and withdraw the short spindle (20) from the carburettor body (photo). Note that on some types the linkage incorporates grub screws instead of nuts.

31 Remove the return spring (19) from the spindle (20).

32 Remove the linkage (35) from the long spindle (38).

33 Extract the spring clip (39) from the linkage (43) then detach the linkage from the lever (41) (where applicable).

34 Extract the spring clip (39) and unscrew the pivot (40) then withdraw the accelerator pump cam (42) (photo).

35 Using a suitable pin punch, drive the roll pin (44) through the spindle (38), at the same time mark the lever (41) and spindle (38) in relation to each other to facilitate refitting.

36 With a suitable length of dowel rod, carefully tap the spindle (38) out of the carburettor body and through the lever (41).

37 Bend back the locktab (48) and unscrew the nut (47). If necessary, mount the spindle in a soft jaw vice during this operation.

38 Remove the nut (47), tab washer (48), lever (49), spacer (51) and spring (52) from the spindle (38), noting the relative position of the lever.

39 On some types the location of the short and long throttle spindles is reversed and it is therefore important to note the

6.28 Throttle valve retaining screw location (triple choke type)

6.29a Removing a throttle valve (triple choke type)

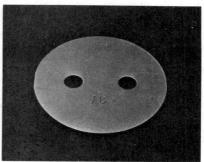

6.29b A throttle valve (triple choke type)

6.30 Intermediate linkage (triple choke type)

6.34 Accelerator pump cam location (triple choke type)

6.40 Removing the air compensation adjustment screws (triple choke type)

6.41 Removing the idling mixture screws (triple choke type)

6.42 Removing the progression hole inspection plugs (triple choke type)

correct fitted position of these items.

40 Looser the locknuts (56) then unscrew and remove the air compensation adjustment screws (57) (photo).

41 Unscrew and remove the idling mixture adjustment screws (62) and springs (53A); on some models a plain washer and seal are fitted to the screws (photo).

42 Unscrew and remove the progression hole inspection plugs (55) (photo).

43 Unscrew and remove the idling adjustment screw (54) and spring (53).

7 Special overhaul procedures

After carrying out the general overhaul procedures given in Chapter 4, the following special procedures should be followed:

46 IDA and 48 IDA types

1 Using a hand chuck and the special Weber tool, reform the main jet seatings at the bottom of the emulsion tube housing wells by carefully rotating the tool in alternate directions. Finish the seatings by inserting the further Weber tool and gently tapping the top of the tool whilst rotating it.

2 Using the same procedure as described in paragraph 1 reform the idling jet seats.

Triple choke types

3 Using a hand chuck and Weber tool no 9600 325 0767, reform the idling jet seats by carefully rotating the tool in alternate directions. Finish the seatings by inserting Weber tool no 9610 315 0816 and gently tapping the top of the tool whilst rotating it.

4 If the emulsion tube wells are discoloured and considerable sediment has accumulated, the bores must be reamed using Weber tool no 9600 325 0762 and a hand chuck. Turn the tool carefully until it moves freely then continue turning it whilst removing it.

5 If on disassembly, the throttle spindles are a tight fit in the carburettor body and they are of original diameter (8.0 mm), use Weber tool no 9600 035 0542 to ream the spindle bores clear with the aid of a hand chuck. Should the spindle bores be excessively worn, oversize spindles of 8.5 mm diameter must be fitted. The bores should be reamed using Weber tool no 9600 035 0556.

6 Using a small file, remove any burrs which have been formed as a result of reaming as described in paragraphs 4 and 5.

All types

7 Check the internal channels for blockage by injecting fuel from a syringe and observing whether it emerges freely from the particular channel being tested. If any are blocked, it will be necessary to drill out the lead plugs as shown in Fig. 8.15, 8.16 and 8.17.

8 The channels are of the diameters viz 1.0 mm, 1.5 mm and 2.0 mm. The Weber tool nos 9620 175 1846, 9620 175 1847 and 9620 175 1848 should be used to check that the channels are clear from their full lengths.

9 The carburettor body should be thoroughly cleaned after overhaul to remove any swarf and dirt, preferably using clean fuel and air pressure. The lead plugs should be renewed and retained in position by using the Weber tool no 9610 315 0823 as a punch until the plugs are expanded into their bores.

10 Check the throttle spindles for high spots which could cause them to seize and if necessary, clean the spindles with fine emery tape.

8 Assembly (46 IDA and 48 IDA types)

Note: *All components should be clean and dry before starting the assembly procedure.*

1 Using a suitable diameter length of tubing, drive one

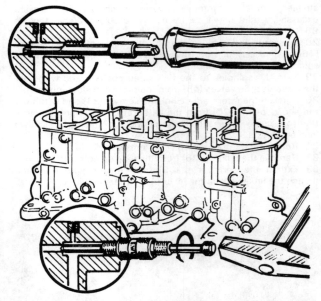

Fig. 8.14 Overhauling the idling jet seats (triple choke types) (Sec 7)

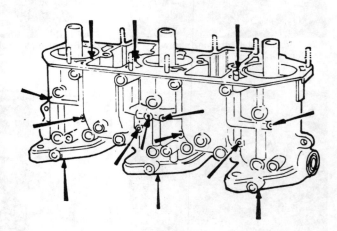

Fig. 8.15 Lead plug location points (Sec 7)

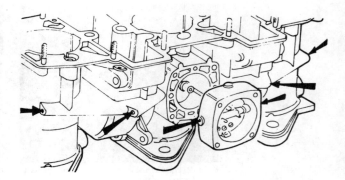

Fig. 8.16 Accelerator pump channel lead plug location points (Sec 7)

Chapter 8   Type 46 IDA, 48 IDA, 40 IDA 3C, 40 IDS 3C
40 IDT 3C, 46 IDA 3C, 40 IDAP 3C, 40 IDTP 3C, 40 IDTP 13C carburettors

89

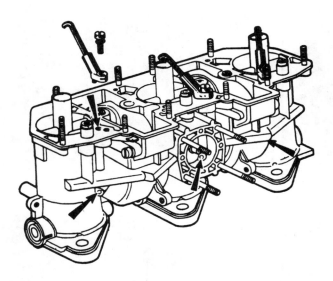

Fig. 8.17 Booster jet channel lead plug location points (IDS types) (Sec 7)

Fig. 8.18 Method of retaining the lead plugs (Sec 7)

4   Lightly lubricate the spindle (32) and bearings (43) with engine oil, then insert the spindle into the carburettor body (65) and through the spring (35) and cam (36). Make sure that the spring and cam are located correctly so that they will operate the lever (29) (photo).

5   Drive the bearing (43) into the carburettor body using tubing located on the outer diameter; if necessary support the opposite bearing during this operation to ensure that both bearings are fully entered (photo).

6   Fit the dust seals (42) and springs (41) over each end of the spindle (32), then tap the spring retainers into the carburettor body (65).

7   If the original spindle (32) and cam (36) are being refitted, align the previously made marks and drive the roll pin (31) into the spindle until it is in a central position, then locate the spring (35) (photo).

8   Turn the spindle (32), against the tension of the spring (35) if already fitted, until the throttle valve slots can be seen from the flange end of the carburettor; then insert the throttle valves (34), entering the indented ends first, and close the spindle. Make sure that the throttle valves are fitted the correct way round so that the angled perimeters seat in the bores and the indentations are adjacent to the barrel progression holes.

9   Snap the valves shut several times in order to centralise them, then insert and tighten the valve retaining screws (33) without exerting excessive pressure on the spindle. It is recommended that new screws are always fitted, as it is quite easy to cross-thread previously peened screws. Lock the screws (33) by peening with Weber tool no 98010 900 whilst supporting the spindle with a length of wood. Alternatively, coat the threads with a liquid locking agent (fuel resistant) prior to inserting them.

10   If a new spindle (32) or cam (36) is being fitted, both must be drilled with a 0.078 in (2.0 mm) drill to accommodate the roll pin (31). To do this it is essential to obtain the special Weber fixture. Drive in the roll pin when completed until it is in a central position, then locate the spring (35).

11   Fit the spring (28) to the accelerator pump lever pivot, followed by the lever (29) with the lug uppermost. Press the C-clip onto the pivot and then check that the lever moves freely when the throttle spindle is turned.

12   Fit the throttle lever (37 or 37A), spacer (27 or 27A), tab washers (26) and nuts (25) to their respective ends of the spindle (32). Tighten the nuts and lock them by bending the locktabs (26) (photo). Do not overtighten the nuts and under no circumstances force the throttle valves against the barrel walls.

13   Fit the spring (38 or 38A) to the idling adjustment screw (39 or 39A) and fit it to the carburettor body.

14   Fit the springs (21) to the idling mixture adjustment screws (20) and fit them to the carburettor body.

15   Insert the chokes (19) into the barrels with the smaller diameters and choke reference numbers uppermost.

16   Fit the auxiliary venturis (18), making sure that the location springs engage with the grooves in the barrels and that the

bearing (43) fully into the carburettor body (65) (Fig. 8.9).

2   Mount the spindle (32) in a soft jaw vice and drive the remaining bearing (43) onto the spindle (32) with tubing located on the inner diameter. Make sure that it is fitted to the correct end so that the roll pin hole is towards the lever (29) end of the carburettor.

3   If a new cam (36) or spindle (32) is being fitted, ream the cam as necessary so that it is a firm sliding fit on the spindle.

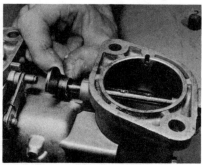

8.4 Fitting the throttle shaft (twin choke type)

8.5 Fitting the throttle shaft bearing (twin choke type)

8.7 Correct location of the accelerator pump cam (twin choke type)

8.12 Fitting a throttle lever (twin choke type)

Fig. 8.19 Fitting the accelerator pump (twin choke type)

8.20 Fitting the accelerator pump delivery valves (twin choke type)

8.26 Fitting the float (twin choke type)

8.27a Using a rubber wedge to set the float (twin choke type)

8.27b Checking the float level (twin choke type)

supply channels are in alignment with those in the carburettor body (65). The extended venturis must also be uppermost.

17 On 46 IDA types, fit the accelerator pump operating rod bush (66).

18 Fit the spring (6) to the operating rod (4) followed by the piston (7); engage the piston with the rod by turning it through 90°.

19 Fit the retainer (5) over the spring (6) with the tab facing the operating rod, then lower the assembly into the carburettor body (65) and press the retainer into its location with the flat side of a screwdriver (photo). If the retainer refuses to hold, it should be gently prised apart to give it the necessary tension.

20 Fit a washer (9) to the accelerator pump delivery valves (8) followed by the pump jets (10) and a further washer (9), then fit and tighten the assemblies into the carburettor body (65) (photo).

21 Press the idling jets (49) into the holders (50) and tighten the holders into the carburettor body (65).

22 Press the main jets (45) and air corrector jets (47) into each end of the emulsion tubes (46), then press the emulsion tubes (46) into the holders (48).

23 Insert the emulsion tube assemblies into the carburettor body (65) and tighten them.

24 Fit and tighten the accelerator pump inlet and discharge valve (11) to the bottom of the float chamber.

25 Fit the washer (22) to the drain plug (23) and tighten the plug into the carburettor body (65).

26 Lower the float (15) into the float chamber with the operating tube facing upwards, then fit and tighten the fulcrum pin (17) together with the washer (16) (photo). Lock the pin with locking wire threaded through the adjacent holes in the body.

27 The float level adjustment must now be checked in the following manner: Obtain a rubber or plastic wedge approximately 0.25 in (6.4 mm) thick (tubing is ideal for the procedure). Insert the wedge between the float and the outer carburettor body, then lift the float until the distance from the carburettor upper face to the float tab is 0.953 in (24.2 mm) (photo). If a depth gauge is not available, use vernier calipers and a feeler gauge as shown in photo 9.33b but make allowance for the thickness of the feeler. With the float held in this position by the wedge, check that the distance from the carburettor upper face to the top of the float is between 0.216 in and 0.236 in (5.5 mm and 6.0 mm). Make the check at the highest point of the float perimeter but not on the annular seam (photo). If the dimension obtained is incorrect, carefully bend the float tab as necessary and remove the wedge when the checking is complete.

28 Screw the needle valve (12) into the carburettor cover (1) without any washers. Check the distance from the cover face to the needle ball apex with the needle valve in the closed position and without the needle ball being depressed. Make the check with vernier calipers and deduct the result from 0.984 in (25.0 mm) to give the thickness of washers required.

29 Fit the washer(s) (13) to the needle valve (12) and tighten it into the carburettor cover (1). Check that the dimension described in paragraph 28 is still 0.984 in (25.0 mm).

30 Place the gasket (14) onto the top face of the carburettor body (65).

31 Lower the carburettor cover (1) onto the main body and over the studs, then fit the retaining nuts (62) and tighten them a little at a time in diagonal sequence.

32 Insert the fuel filter (55) into the carburettor cover (1), followed by the retaining bush (63), washer (56) and filter inspection plug (57); tighten the plug into the cover.

33 Fit the air intake horns (58) to the cover (1). Fit the plates (59) and tighten the retaining nuts (60).

34 Locate the filter gauze (64) over the cover studs (2) and fit and tighten the retaining nuts (61).

Chapter 8   Type 46 IDA, 48 IDA, 40 IDA 3C, 40 IDS 3C
40 IDT 3C, 46 IDA 3C, 40 IDAP 3C, 40 IDTP 3C, 40 IDTP 13C carburettors

91

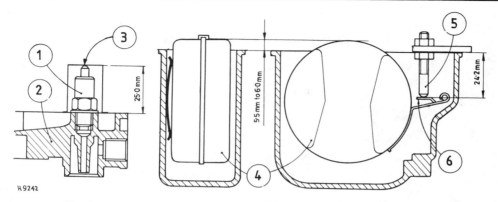

Fig. 8.19 Float level adjustment dimensions on 46 IDA and 48 IDA types (Sec 8)

| 1 | Needle valve | 3 | Needle ball | 5 | Gauge |
| 2 | Cover | 4 | Float | 6 | Tab |

35 With the carburettor completely assembled, the idling adjustment screws should be turned to their preliminary settings. To do this, first screw in the throttle idling adjustment screw until it just touches the throttle lever, then continue turning for a further 2 turns. Working on the idling mixture volume screws in turn, fully screw them in until they are in firm contact with their seats, then back them off 2 complete turns. Final adjustments will be necessary when the carburettor is fitted on the engine (refer to Section 10).

9   Assembly (triple choke types)

Note: *All components should be clean and dry before starting the assembly procedure.*

1   Fit the spring (53) (Fig. 8.12) to the idling adjustment screw (54) and fit the screw to the carburettor body, turning it on two or three threads only.
2   Fit and tighten the progression hole inspection plugs (55).
3   Fit the springs (53A) to the idling mixture adjustment screws (62) together with the plain washers and seals where fitted, then fit the screws into the carburettor body.
4   Fit the air compensating adjustments screws (57) fully, then fit and tighten the locknuts (56).
5   Fit the spring (52) to the spindle (38) followed by the spacer (51), lever (49), tab washer (48) and nut (47). Make sure that the lever is in its correct position as previously noted and tighten the nut with the spindle mounted in a soft jaw vice. Lock the nut by bending the tab washer.
6   If a new lever (41) or spindle (38) is being fitted, ream the lever as necessary so that it is a firm sliding fit on the spindle.

7   Lightly lubricate the throttle spindle (38) with engine oil, then insert it into the carburettor body, at the same time locating the lever (41) between the two barrels. If the original lever (41) is being refitted, make sure that it is the correct way round as previously noted, then insert the roll pin (44) and drive it through the lever and spindle until it is in a central position (photos).
8   Fit the accelerator pump cam (42) to the pivot (40). Fit the pivot and insert the spring clip (39). On IDAP and IDTP types, it will first be necessary to engage the linkage to the lever (41) but, if a new lever (41) or spindle (38) is being fitted, delay fitting the cam (42) until the roll pin hole has been drilled.
9   Fit the linkage (35) to the long spindle (38) but do not tighten the screws at this stage.
10   Fit the return spring (19) to the short spindle (20) and lubricate the spindle with a little engine oil.
11   Insert the short spindle (20) into the carburettor body and locate it into the linkage (35).
12   Make sure that the return springs (19 and 52) are correctly located (photo), then turn each spindle in turn to their fully open positions and insert the throttle valves (45) into their location slots. Close the throttle valves and allow them to centralise within the barrels; make sure that they are fitted the correct way round so that the angled perimeters seat in the bores.
13   Insert and tighten the valve retaining screws (39) without exerting excessive pressure on the spindles. It is recommended that new screws are always fitted as it is quite easy to cross-thread previously peened screws. Lock the screws (39) by peening with Weber tool no 98010 900 whilst supporting the spindle with a length of wood. Alternatively, coat the threads with a liquid locking agent (fuel resistant) prior to inserting them.

9.7a Fitting the long throttle spindle (triple choke type)

9.7b Correct location of the throttle lever (triple choke type)

9.7c Inserting the roll pin into the spindle (triple choke type)

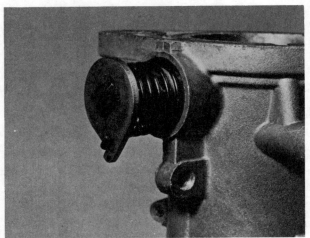

9.12 Correct location of the short throttle spindle return spring (triple choke type)

9.14 Fitting the intermediate linkage (triple choke type)

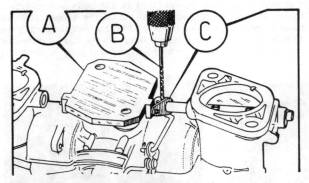

Fig. 8.20 Drilling the throttle spindle (triple choke types) (Sec 9)

A Gauge   B Drill   C Arm

14 With the throttle valves (45) fully closed, tighten the intermediate linkage screws (34) (photo).

15 If a new lever (41) or spindle (38) is being fitted, the spindle must be drilled with a 0.079 in (2.0 mm) drill to accommodate the roll pin (44). To do this it is essential to obtain the Weber

gauge no 9620 175 2949. Fit the gauge to the central barrel flange with the lever (41) attached to the location peg, then drill through the lever and spindle whilst holding the throttle valves fully shut.

16 Insert the roll pin (44) and drive it through the lever and spindle until it is in a central position.

17 On IDAP and IDTP types, engage the cam and linkage to the lever (41), fit the cam to the pivot (40), tighten the pivot and fit the retaining spring clip (39). On all other types, engage the linkage (43) to the lever (41) then connect the remaining end to the cam (42) and fit the retaining spring clip (39).

18 Insert the chokes (67) into the barrels with the smaller inside diameters and choke reference numbers uppermost. Make sure that the location drillings coincide with the retaining screw (58) holes (photo).

19 Insert and tighten the choke retaining screws (58), then lock them with locking wire threaded through the holes in the carburettor body (photo).

20 Fit the auxiliary venturis (68), making sure that the supply channels are in alignment with those in the carburettor body and also that the cut away sections of the nozzles face the throttle valves.

21 With the carburettor body on its side, locate the reaction spring (24) into the accelerator pump chamber and locate the plate (25) onto the spring, concave side towards the body (photo).

22 Place the release diaphragm (26) onto the plate and the accelerator pump body (27) onto the diaphragm with the spring locating pegs facing outwards as shown in Fig. 8.12 (photos).

23 Fit the return spring (28) over the pegs, followed by the diaphragm (29) and cover (30) (photos).

24 Make sure that the accelerator pump lever roller is seated on the cam (42), then depress the cover and fit the retaining nuts (33) and spring washers (32) (photo). Tighten the nuts (33) in diagonal sequence then check the operation of the pump by operating the throttle lever.

25 On IDS types, fit the booster jet assemblies and tighten the retaining screws.

26 Fit the pump jets (70) to the accelerator pump delivery valves (71) followed by the washers (69), then fit and tighten the assemblies into the carburettor body.

27 Fit and tighten the accelerator pump inlet valve(s) (72) to the bottom of the float chamber(s).

28 Insert the emulsion tubes (73) into the carburettor body then fit and tighten the air corrector jets (74).

29 Press the idling jets (65) into their holders (66) and tighten the holders into the carburettor body.

30 Tighten the main jets (60) into the holders (61) and tighten the holders into the carburettor body.

31 Fit the washers (63) to the drain plugs (64), then tighten the plugs into the carburettor body.

32 Lower the floats (15) into the float chambers with the operating tabs facing upwards, then fit and tighten the fulcrum pins (18) together with washers (17). Lock the pins with locking wire threaded through the adjacent holes in the body (photo).

33 The float level adjustment must now be checked in the following manner: obtain a length of rubber or a plastic wedge approximately 0.25 in (6.35 mm) thick (tubing is ideal for the procedure). Insert the rubber or plastic between the float and the outer carburettor body, then lift the float until the distance from the carburettor upper face to the float tab is 0.709 in (18.0 mm) (photos). If a depth gauge is not available, use vernier calipers and a feeler gauge as shown in photo 9.33b but make allowance for the thickness of the feeler. With the float held in this position by the wedge, check that the distance from the carburettor upper face to the top of the float is between 0.492 in and 0.512 in (12.5 mm and 13.0 mm) (photo). Do not take into consideration the float seam and make the check at the highest point of the float perimeter. If the dimension obtained is incorrect, carefully bend the float tab accordingly (Fig. 8.21).

34 Check and adjust the float level adjustments of both floats using the procedure described in paragraph 33.

35 Screw the needle valves (5) into the carburettor cover (1)

9.18 The choke and locating hole (triple choke type)

9.19 Locking wire attached to the choke retaining screw (triple choke type)

9.21 Correct location of the accelerator pump reaction spring (triple choke type)

9.22a Fitting the accelerator pump release diaphragm ...

9.22b ... and body (triple choke type)

9.23a Fitting the accelerator pump return spring (triple choke type)

9.23b Fitting the accelerator pump diaphragm (triple choke type)

9.24 Correct location of the accelerator pump lever and cam (triple choke type)

9.32 Float fulcrum pin locking wire location (triple choke type)

9.33a Using a rubber wedge to set the float height (triple choke type)

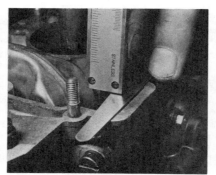
9.33b Checking the float tab height with a vernier and feeler gauge (triple choke type)

9.33c Checking the float height (triple choke type)

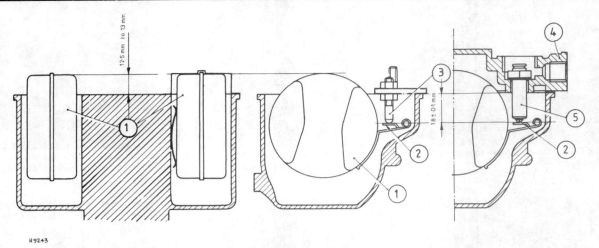

Fig. 8.21 Float level adjustment dimensions on triple choke types (Sec 9)

1 Floats	2 Tab	3 Gauge	4 Cover	5 Needle valve

9.35 Checking the needle valve height (triple choke type)

without any washers and check the distance from the cover face to the needle ball apex with the needle valves in the closed position and without the needle balls being depressed. Make the check with vernier calipers and deduct the result from 0.709 in (18.0 mm) to give the thickness of washers required (photo).

36 Fit the washers (75) to the needle valves (5) and tighten them into the carburettor cover (1). Check that the dimensions described in paragraph 35 are now 0.709 ± 0.004 in (18.0 ± 0.1 mm).

37 Fit the washers (6) to the needle valve housing plugs (7) and tighten them into the carburettor cover (1).

38 Connect the intermediate hose to the fuel inlet unions (9 and 10).

39 Fit the washers (13) to the inlet union bolts (14) followed by the filter gauzes (12), then fit the bolt assemblies to the unions (9 and 10) and fit the sealing washers (8).

40 Locate the fuel unions to the carburettor cover (1) and tighten the union bolts (14).

41 Carefully locate the gasket (11) to the carburettor body over the studs (16).

42 Lower the carburettor cover (1) over the locating studs and onto the gasket, then fit the retaining nuts (4A) and spring plate

(where fitted). Tighten the nuts a little at a time in diagonal sequence.

43 Where fitted, locate the gasket over the cover (1).

44 Fit the air intake horns (3) and tighten the retaining nuts (4).

45 On 46 IDA 3C types, fit the gauze filters (76) and tighten the retaining screws (77).

46 Hook the throttle lever return spring to the throttle lever and spring plate (where fitted).

47 With the carburettor completely assembled, the idling adjustment screws should be turned to their preliminary settings. To do this, first screw in the throttle idling adjustment screw until it just touches the throttle lever, then continue turning for a further 2 turns. Working on the idling mixture volume screws in turn, fully screw them in until they are in light contact with their seats then back them off 2 turns. Final adjustments will be necessary when the carburettor is fitted on the engine (refer to Section 10).

10 Tuning

Note: *Refer to Chapter 3 for general notes on tuning.*

1 The idling adjustment screws should be set to their preliminary positions as described in Sections 8 and 9.

2 Connect a tachometer to the engine in accordance with the manufacturer's instructions.

3 The carburettors must be synchronized in order to deliver equal amounts of air/fuel mixture to each individual cylinder. To check the adjustment it will be necessary to obtain a length of tubing of approximately 1 metre in length and of about 5 mm to 10 mm (0.25 in to 0.05 in) internal diameter. Alternatively and preferably, a synchronizer may be used (photo).

4 Remove the air cleaner(s) if fitted, then start the engine and run until normal operating temperature has been reached (ie the thermostat has opened). To ensure that the engine is really hot enough, drive it hard over at least a 5 mile distance.

5 Switch off the engine and disconnect the accelerator rod connections from each carburettor.

6 Start the engine and if necessary, adjust each idling speed adjusting screw by equal amounts until the engine is idling at the approximate recommended idling speed (usually between 600 and 800 rpm for touring models and approximately 1000 rpm for sports car models).

7 On triple choke types only, loosen the three compensation adjustment screw locknuts and screw the adjustment screws in until they are in light contact with their seats. If the engine falters as a result, turn the idle speed adjustment screw on each carburettor by equal amounts until the engine runs evenly

10.3 Weber carburettor synchronizer

again. Place one end of the synchronizing tube in the middle of one air intake and listen at the other end to the amount of hiss present. Alternatively, use the synchronizer to record the air flow of the air intake. Check each air intake of the carburettor to determine which one is passing the greatest volume of air, then adjust the remaining carburettor barrels to give identical volumes and finally tighten the adjustment locknuts. Carry out this procedure independently on each carburettor fitted to the engine.

8   On all carburettor types, each carburettor must now be synchronized with the remaining carburettors. To do this, allow the engine to idle and check the volume of air flowing through one air intake of each carburettor using the length of tube or the synchronizer. Determine the carburettor which is passing the

medium volume of air and adjust the idle speed adjustment screws of the remaining carburettors until they also pass identical volumes of air. Where the throttle linkage is arranged from a common shaft, the individual throttle levers will have to be adjusted by loosening the locknuts.

9   If necessary, turn each idling speed adjustment screw by equal amounts to bring the engine speed within the recommended idling limits.

10   The mixture screw adjustments on each carburettor must now be set and synchronized. Since each screw was turned to its preliminary setting, we must assume that they are reasonably synchronized to start with. With the engine idling, turn each screw by equal amounts ($\frac{1}{2}$ a turn initially) and observe whether the engine speed falls or increases. Make several adjustments in a similar manner until the engine runs at the highest speed commensurate with even firing.

11   If necessary, again turn each idling speed adjustment screw by equal amounts to bring the engine speed within the recommended idling limits.

12   The final mixture screw synchronization can be determined by allowing the engine to idle, then to remove each spark plug lead in turn and observe the reduction in engine rpm on the tachometer. The reduction should be identical for each cylinder, then proving that the mixture strength is also identical for each cylinder. A further check can be made by removing the spark plugs after the engine has been idling for approximately 15 minutes, then checking that they are all in identical condition. Any with black sooty deposits indicate that the particular cylinder is running rich.

13   If necessary, adjust the idling speed screws on each carburettor by equal amounts to bring the engine speed within the recommended limits.

14   Note that on some applications it may be advisable to fit 'hotter' spark plugs while adjusting the carburettors to prevent misfiring, but the original plugs must always be refitted after completing the adjustment.

15   Switch off the engine and reconnect the throttle linkages, making adjustments as necessary to prevent the carburettor settings from being affected.

16   Remove the tachometer from the engine and refit the air cleaner(s) if fitted.

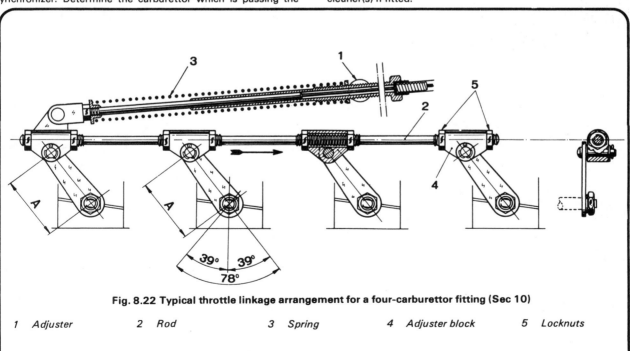

Fig. 8.22 Typical throttle linkage arrangement for a four-carburettor fitting (Sec 10)

| 1 Adjuster | 2 Rod | 3 Spring | 4 Adjuster block | 5 Locknuts |

Note: *Dimensions A and lever angles must all be identical*

Chapter 8 Type 46 IDA, 48 IDA, 40 IDA 3C, 40 IDS 3C
40 IDT 3C, 46 IDA 3C, 40 IDAP 3C, 40 IDTP 3C, 40 IDTP 13C carburettors

96

11 Fault diagnosis

Symptom	Reason/s
Engine will not start	Blocked fuel filter or jets Flooded engine as a result of depressing accelerator pedal
Uneven idling	Leaking manifold or carburettor flange gaskets Loose idling jets or auxiliary venturis Excessive sediment or water in carburettor Throttle spindle dust covers broken (46 IDA and 48 IDA) Throttle spindles worn Incorrect tuning adjustments
Carburettor floods	Worn needle valve(s) Leaking or damaged float(s) Incorrect float level adjustments Excessive sediment in fuel
Engine lacks performance	Incorrect tuning adjustments Incorrect float level adjustments Excessive sediment in fuel Throttle valves not fully opening Accelerator pump faulty Accelerator pump leaking (triple choke types)
Excessive fuel consumption	Needle valve not seating Leaking or damaged float(s) Incorrect float level adjustments Choked air filter (if fitted)

Part 2
Chapter 9 Type 40 DFA,
40 DFAV, 34 DGAS, 38 DGAS carburettors

Contents

Adjustment data

Fast idle throttle valve opening

	in (mm)
High cam position:	
40 DFA and 40 DFAV types	0.029 to 0.031 (0.75 to 0.80)
34 DGAS and 38 DGAS types:	
38 DGAS 1A	0.026 to 0.028 (0.65 to 0.70)
38 DGAS 7A	0.025 to 0.027 (0.65 to 0.70)
38 DGAS 3A and 34 DGAS	0.027 to 0.029 (0.70 to 0.75)
38 DGAS 4A	0.029 to 0.031 (0.75 to 0.80)
Low cam position:	
38 DGAS 4A	0.080 to 0.100 (2.05 to 2.55)
38 DGAS 7A	0.080 to 0.100 (2.05 to 2.55)
38 DGAS 1A	0.100 to 0.120 (2.55 to 3.05)
38 DGAS 3A	0.100 to 0.120 (2.55 to 3.05)

Choke valve pull down clearance

	in (mm)
38 DGAS types:	
Minimum:	
All types	0.112 to 0.124 (2.85 to 3.15)
Maximum:	
38 DGAS 4A and 7A	0.177 to 0.216 (4.5 to 5.5)
38 DGAS 1A and 3A	0.196 to 0.236 (5.0 to 6.0)

Float level setting dimension

	Closed position	Open position	Stroke
40 DFA and 40 DFAV types	0.236 in (6.0 mm)	0.551 in (14.0 mm)	0.315 in (8.0 mm)
34 DGAS and 38 DGAS types (brass float)	1.57 in (40.0 mm)	1.968 in (50.0 mm)	0.393 in (10.0 mm)
34 DGAS and 38 DGAS types (plastic float)	1.35 in (34.3 mm)	1.744 in (44.3 mm)	0.393 in (10.0 mm)

1 Introduction

The carburettor types covered in this Chapter are of dual downdraught design. Each throttle valve is mounted on a separate shaft, but the shafts are linked by toothed sectors and their action is synchronised.

Semi-automatic choke controls are fitted to all carburettor types included in this Chapter.

The carburettor is normally fitted to the engine as a single unit, the most common arrangements being as follows:

1   One unit on a six-cylinder in-line engine, ie each barrel feeds three cylinders separately
2   One unit on a six-cylinder V-engine, ie each barrel feeds one bank of three cylinders

The carburettor identification mark is located on the lower flange outer surface.

2 Construction

The main body and cover of the carburettor types covered in this Chapter are of die cast aluminium construction and the mounting flange is machined flat for fitting purposes. The cover incorporates a mounting flange for the air cleaner assembly and is equipped with four mounting studs.

The throttle valves are of brass and the throttle shafts are of steel. The throttle shafts run on Teflon (PTFE) bearings mounted in the main body. The choke valves are cadmium plated steel and the choke shaft is of steel on DGAS types and brass on DFA and DFAV types.

All fuel and air jets are of brass construction and are screwed into the main body. The emulsion tubes are also constructed of brass.

Internal channels of the main body and cover are mostly drilled and are sealed with lead plugs where necessary.

The fuel float assemblies are of brass construction; DFA and DFAV types have a single float and DGAS types have two semi-floats.

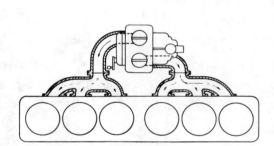

Fig. 9.1 Single carburettor fitted to a six-cylinder in-line engine (Sec 1)

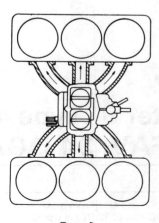

Fig. 9.2 Single carburettor fitted to a six-cylinder V-engine (Sec 1)

3   Operation

Cold starting

Refer to Fig. 9.3 and note that when the engine is cold and the throttle pedal has been depressed once, the bi-metallic spring (51) rotates the spindle (52) and closes the choke valves (55). At the same time the fast idle cam (59) prevents the throttle valves (12) from completely closing.

When the engine is cranked, a rich mixture is drawn from the nozzle (9) to facilitate starting. As soon as the engine fires, vacuum from below the throttle valve is relayed through the channel (53) to the diaphragm (47). The shaft (50) then moves and partially opens the choke valves (55) against the action of the bi-metallic spring (51). If the throttle is opened at this stage,

the vacuum will cease and the choke valves (55) will close, however the passage of air will open the choke valves against the action of the bi-metallic spring (51) due to the offset construction of the choke valves (55). On DGAS types, the action of the shaft (50) is modulated by an internal spring (49).

As the engine warms up, the bi-metallic spring (51) progressively opens and the choke valves (55), until at normal operating temperature they are held fully open. The fast idling screw (62) does not now rest on the fast idling cam (59) since the latter has been rotated by the bi-metallic spring and therefore the throttle valves (12) are free to return to the normal idling position.

Idling and progression

Refer to Fig. 9.4 and note that when the engine is idling, the

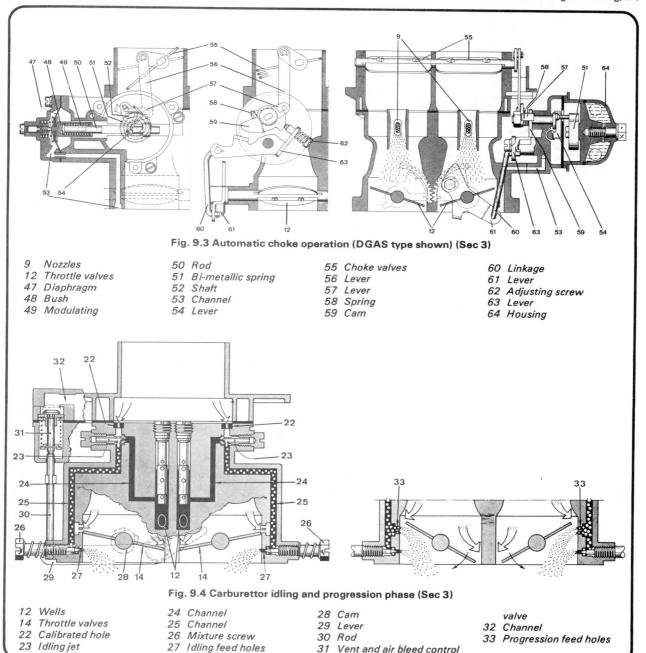

Fig. 9.3 Automatic choke operation (DGAS type shown) (Sec 3)

9 Nozzles	50 Rod	55 Choke valves	60 Linkage
12 Throttle valves	51 Bi-metallic spring	56 Lever	61 Lever
47 Diaphragm	52 Shaft	57 Lever	62 Adjusting screw
48 Bush	53 Channel	58 Spring	63 Lever
49 Modulating	54 Lever	59 Cam	64 Housing

Fig. 9.4 Carburettor idling and progression phase (Sec 3)

12 Wells	24 Channel	28 Cam	valve
14 Throttle valves	25 Channel	29 Lever	32 Channel
22 Calibrated hole	26 Mixture screw	30 Rod	33 Progression feed holes
23 Idling jet	27 Idling feed holes	31 Vent and air bleed control	

throttle valves (14) are shut. Fuel is drawn from the float chamber through internal channels to the emulsion tube wells (12) and then passes along the channels (24) to the idling jets (23) where air is introduced through the calibrated bushes (22). The fuel and air is now an emulsion and continues through the channels (25), past the idling mixture control screws (26), through their idling feed holes (27) and into the carburettor throats at the engine side of the throttle valves (14) (photo). When the throttle valves (14) are opened slightly to increase the engine speed, the progression holes (33) are brought into action to provide extra fuel. Note that on DGAS types, three progression holes are provided in each barrel.

When the throttles valves (14) are sufficiently open, the

idling and progression system ceases and the main fuel supply system operates.

DFAV types are provided with a float chamber vapour discharge valve (31) which prevents the build up of vapour within the float chamber. The valve is open when the throttle valves are fully shut or fully open and additionally controls the overfeed enrichment air bleed.

Normal running

Under full throttle and high speed cruise conditions, the main fuel supply circuit is brought into action. Refer to Fig. 9.5 and note that fuel from the float chamber (9) passes through the main jets (10) to the emulsion tube wells (12). Air is drawn through the air corrector jets (2), through the holes in the emulsion tubes (13) and emulsifies the fuel which is then drawn through the nozzles (18) and auxiliary venturis (17). The mixture then combines with the main air supply as it is drawn through the chokes (16) and into the engine.

At high engine speeds with the throttle valves (14) open, the overfeed enrichment circuit is brought into action (not 40 DFA types) and additional fuel is supplied through the calibrated tubes (1) via the calibrated bushes (4).

DGAS type carburettors are also equipped with a full power valve which operates immediately the throttle valves are opened quickly. Refer to Fig. 9.6 and note that under these conditions the vacuum through the channel (7) is insufficient to draw the diaphragm (4) against the spring (6). The operating rod (5) therefore opens the full power valve (17). The fuel level in the emulsion tube wells (14) immediately rises and the mixture drawn from the nozzle (9) is enriched. When the throttle valves (12) are partially open, the vacuum through the channel (7) overcomes the tension of the spring (6) and the full power valve shuts.

Acceleration

To provide the engine with a rich mixture when accelerating, the carburettor is provided with a diaphragm type acceleration pump which is operated by the primary throttle shaft but

3.2 Location of the idling and progression holes (40 DFAV type)

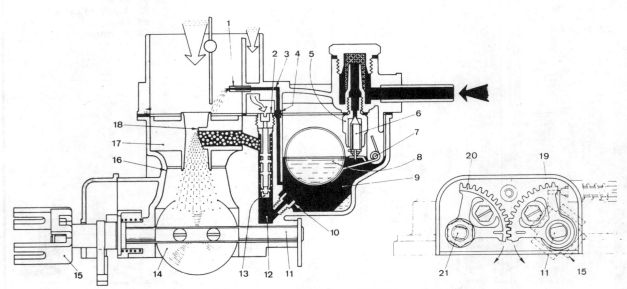

Fig. 9.5 Carburettor normal phase (DFAV types) (Sec 3)

1 Enrichment tube	7 Fulcrum pin	12 Well	17 Auxiliary venturi
2 Air corrector jet	8 Float	13 Emulsion tube	18 Nozzle
3 Channel	9 Float chamber	14 Throttle valve	19 Primary sector
4 Calibrated bush	10 Main jet	15 Lever	20 Secondary sector
5 Needle valve seating	11 Throttle shaft	16 Choke	21 Throttle shaft
6 Needle			

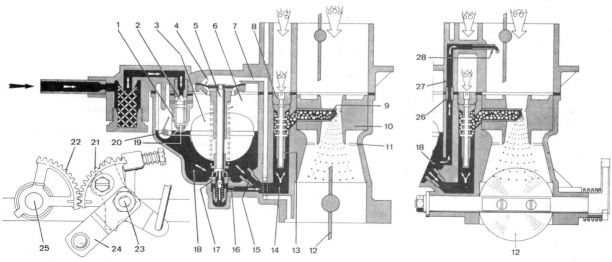

Fig. 9.6 Carburettor normal phase (DGAS types) (Sec 3)

1 Needle valve seating	8 Air corrector jet	15 Main jet	22 Secondary sector
2 Needle	9 Nozzle	16 Calibrated bush	23 Throttle shaft
3 Float	10 Auxiliary venturi	17 Full power valve	24 Lever
4 Diaphragm	11 Choke	18 Float chamber	25 Throttle shaft
5 Rod	12 Throttle valve	19 Hook	26 Calibrated bush
6 Spring	13 Emulsion tube	20 Fulcrum pin	27 Channel
7 Channel	14 Well	21 Primary sector	28 Enrichment tube

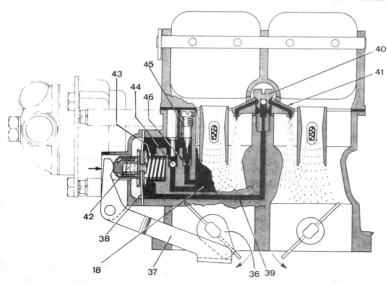

Fig. 9.7 Carburettor acceleration phase (Sec 3)

18 Float chamber
36 Cam
37 Lever
38 Diaphragm
39 Channel
40 Delivery valve
41 Pump jet
42 Spring
43 Return spring
44 Ball
45 Blanking needle
46 Discharge jet

injects into both venturis. Reference to Fig. 9.7 will show that when the throttle valves are closed, the accelerator pump diaphragm (38) draws fuel from the float chamber (18), through the ball valve (44) into the pump chamber. When the throttle valves are opened, the cam (36) moves the lever (37) and fuel is forced along the channel (39), through the delivery valve (40) and out of the pump jet (41). The spring (42) absorbs the initial movement of the lever (37) and prolongs the fuel delivery period. Excess fuel and any accumulated air is discharged into the float chamber (18) through the channel (45) and calibrated bush (46).

DGAS types are fitted with a discharge blanking needle which determines the amount of fuel returned to the float chamber (18).

DFAV types are equipped with an accelerator pump lever incorporating two pivot holes whereby the pump stroke can be varied.

4 Removal and refitting

Note: The following procedure gives a general rather than a specific method of removing and refitting the carburettor, as much will depend on the location within the vehicle.

1   Unscrew and remove the retaining nuts and withdraw the air cleaner cover (screws are fitted to some models).

2   Lift out the air filter element.

3   Bend back the locktabs and unscrew the air cleaner body retaining nuts.

4   Unscrew and remove the mounting bracket bolts and

remove the air cleaner together with the reinforcement plate and gasket.

5   Partially drain the cooling system and disconnect the two water hoses.

6   Disconnect the fuel supply pipe and return pipe (where fitted) and release the vent tube from the top of the float chamber.

7   Release the distributor automatic advance pipe from the side of the carburettor.

8   Disconnect the throttle control shaft from the throttle lever.

9   Disconnect the crankcase ventilation pipe from the heat insulator spacer, if fitted.

10   Unscrew and remove the carburettor mounting nuts then withdraw the unit over the mounting studs.

11   Remove the inlet manifold gasket and spacer (if fitted) and clean all traces of gasket from the inlet manifold and carburettor flange.

12   Protect the inlet manifold from ingress of foreign matter by sealing it with masking tape.

13   Refitting is a reversal of removal, but the following additional points should be noted:

    (a)   Always fit new gaskets and tighten the mounting nuts in diagonal sequence
    (b)   Note that on some fittings the lower gasket has two metal V-notches which must locate within the inlet manifold
    (c)   Refill the cooling system in accordance with the manufacturer's instructions
    (d)   The idling adjustment screws should be set as described in Sections 8 and 9 and finally tuned as described in Section 10

5   Disassembly (40 DFA and 40 DFAV types)

1   Thoroughly clean the carburettor exterior and wipe dry.

2   Referring to Fig. 9.8, unscrew and remove the fuel filter inspection plug (4) and extract the filter (5) (photo).

3   Disconnect the choke plate operating rod (16) from the lever (39) by removing the split pin (15).

4   Unscrew and remove the carburettor cover retaining screws (3) together with the spring washers, then carefully lift the cover (1) from the main body (photo).

5   Invert the carburettor cover (1) so that the float assembly is uppermost, then extract the float fulcrum pin (14) and withdraw the float assembly (13) together with the needle of the needle valve (12). If necessary, use a suitable diameter pin punch to tap the pin from the two posts, but on no account prise the slotted post apart (photo).

6   Unhook the needle from the float assembly (13).

7   Lift the gasket (9) from the cover (1).

8   On 40 DFAV types only, unscrew and remove the vent and power valve (92) from the cover (1) (photo).

9   Unscrew and remove the needle valve (12) seating and

remove the gasket (11) (photo).

10   Unscrew the two main jets (17) and remove them from the bottom of the float chamber in the main body (photos).

11   Unscrew the idling jet holders (83) from each side of the carburettor body, then separate the idling jets (84) from their holders (photos).

12   Unscrew and remove the air corrector jets (88) from the carburettor body (photos).

13   Invert the body and extract the emulsion tubes (89). If these are tight due to overtightening of the air corrector jets, use a selftapping screw to remove them but take care not to damage the tubes (photos).

14   Unscrew and remove the idling adjusting screws (81) and springs (82) from the body.

15   Unscrew and remove the throttle idling adjustment screw (28) and spring (27).

16   Unscrew the accelerator pump delivery valve (87) and remove it together with the pump jet (86) and gasket (85), then separate the gasket and jet from the valve (photos).

17   Unscrew and remove the accelerator pump discharge blanking plug (18) (photo).

18   Unscrew the four screws (26) and withdraw the accelerator cover (25) together with the diaphragm (24) and spring (23). If necessary, peel the diaphragm assembly (24) from the cover (25) (photos).

19   Working on the carburettor cover (1), extract the split pin (15) and detach the operating rod (16) from the choke spindle arm.

20   Pull the rod (16) through the seal (10), then prise the plug (101) and seal (10) from the cover (1) (photo).

21   Note the location of each choke valve (7) and if necessary, mark them with a pencil.

22   Unscrew the retaining screws (6) and remove the choke valves (7) from the shaft (8), then remove the shaft (8) from the cover (1).

23   Working on the carburettor body, unscrew the automatic choke water housing retaining bolt (58) and remove it together with the gasket (57).

24   Remove the cover (56) and gasket (54); cut the gasket from the thermostat assembly (53) if it is stuck.

25   Unscrew and remove the retaining screws (59) and lift the automatic choke thermostat assembly (53) from the body (47), then remove the retaining ring (55) (photo).

26   Remove the disc gasket (52), then unscrew and remove the three retaining screws (51) and spring washers. Withdraw the automatic choke body (47) at the same time disengage the fast idling control rod (61) from the throttle lever (71) by extracting the split pin (60) (photos).

27   Disconnect the rod (61) from the fast idle lever (29) by extracting the split pin (60), if fitted.

28   Note the location of the individual components on the automatic choke body (47) before dismantling them.

29   Prise the O-ring seal (35) from the side of the carburettor (photo).

5.2 Removing the fuel filter (DFAV type)

5.4 Removing the carburettor cover (DFAV type)

5.5 Withdrawing the float fulcrum pin (DFAV type)

5.8 Location of the vent and air bleed valve (DFAV type)

5.9 Removing the needle valve seat (DFAV type)

5.10a Location of the main jets (DFAV type)

5.10b Location of the main jet size (DFAV type)

5.11a Removing the idling jets (DFAV type)

5.11b Idling jet and holder (DFAV type)

5.11c Idling jet size location (DFAV type)

5.12a Removing the air connector jets (DFAV type)

5.12b Air corrector jet size location (DFAV type)

5.13a Removing the emulsion tubes (DFAV type)

5.13b Emulsion tube size location (DFAV type)

5.16a Removing the accelerator pump delivery valve (DFAV type)

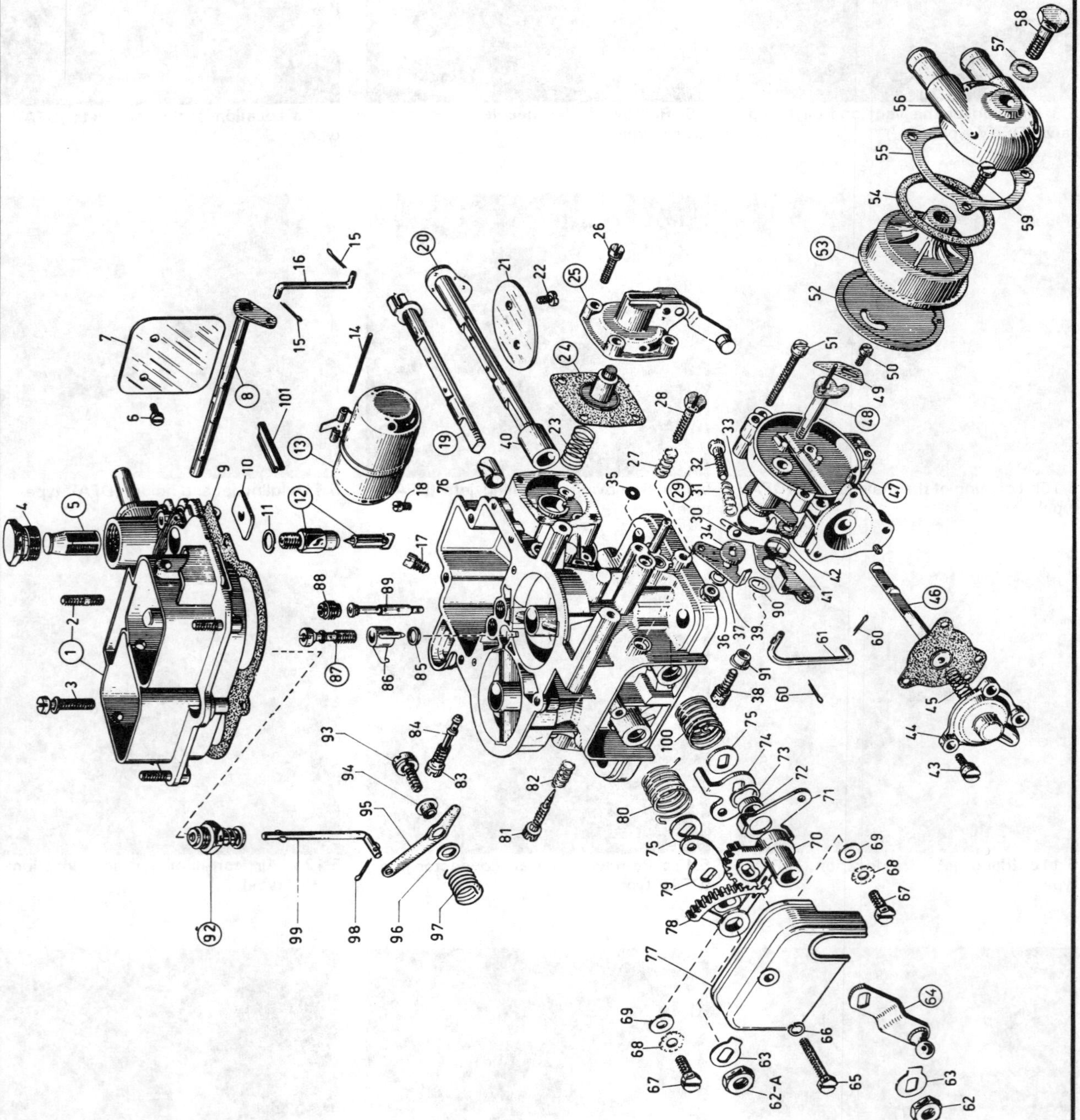
1
2
3
4
5
6
7
8
9
10
11
12
13
14
15
16
17
18
19
20
21
22
23
24
25
26
27
28
29
30
31
32
33
34
35
36
37
38
39
40
41
42
43
44
45
46
47
48
49
50
51
52
53
54
55
56
57
58
59
60
61
62
62-A
63
64
65
66
67
68
69
70
71
72
73
74
75
76
77
78
79
80
81
82
83
84
85
86
87
88
89
90
91
92
93
94
95
96
97
98
99
100
101

Fig. 9.8 Exploded view of the 40 DFAV carburettor (typical) (Sec 5)

1 Carburettor cover assembly
2 Carburettor to air cleaner stud
3 Cover screw and washer
4 Strainer inspection plug
5 Fuel inlet strainer assy
6 Choke plate screw
7 Choke plate
8 Choke shaft and lever assy
9 Cover to throttle body gasket
10 Air cleaner dust seal
11 Fuel intake valve gasket
12 Fuel inlet needle valve assy
13 Float assy
14 Float lever shaft
15 Auto-choke control rod split pin
16 Auto-choke operating rod
17 Main jet
18 Accelerator plug discharge plug
19 Throttle left-hand shaft
20 Throttle right-hand shaft assy
21 Throttle plate
22 Throttle plate screw
23 Accelerator pump self-loading spring
24 Accelerator pump diaphragm assy
25 Accelerator pump cover assy
26 Accelerator pump cover screw and washer
27 Idling adjusting screw spring
28 Idling adjustment screw
29 Fast idling adjusting lever assy
30 Lever
31 Spring
32 Screw
33 Auto-choke shaft spring
34 Auto-choke shaft spacer
35 Auto-choke body O-ring seal
36 Auto-choke lever fixing nut
37 Spring washer
38 Fast idle lever pivot screw and washer
39 Auto-choke lever
40 Right-hand shaft spacer
41 Fast idle lever spring
42 Fast idle lever washer
43 Auto-choke cover screw and washer
44 Auto-choke cover
45 Auto-choke vacuum diaphragm spring
46 Auto-choke vacuum diaphragm and shaft assy
47 Auto-choke body assy
48 Auto-choke shaft and lever assy
49 Auto-choke shaft adjusting plate
50 Screw
51 Auto-choke body to throttle body screw and washer
52 Auto-choke body gasket
53 Auto-choke thermostat assy
54 Water chamber to thermostat assy
55 Locking ring
56 Water chamber
57 Washer
58 Bolt
59 Screw
60 Fast idle rod split pin
61 Fast idle rod
62 Throttle shaft nut
63 Lockwasher
64 Throttle lever
65 Geared sector cover screw
66 Spring washer
67 Geared sector adjusting screw
68 External tooth washer
69 Washer
70 Geared sector (right-hand)
71 Fast idling lever
72 Throttle shaft bushing
73 Wave washer
74 Full throttle stop lever
75 Washer
76 Throttle shaft bearing
77 Geared sectors cover
78 Geared sector (left-hand)
79 Geared sector adjusting lever
80 Throttle control return spring (left-hand)
81 Idle adjustment needle screw
82 Spring
83 Idling jet holder
84 Idle jet
85 Nozzle bar gasket
86 Accelerator pump jet
87 Accelerator pump valve assy
88 Air corrector jet
89 Emulsion tube
90 Auto-choke wave washer
91 Fast idling adjusting lever bush
92 Power valve
93 Lever fixing screw
94 Bushing
95 Valve control lever
96 Washer
97 Spring
98 Split pin
99 Valve control rod
100 Return spring (right shaft)
101 Dust seal plug

5.16b Accelerator pump jet size location (DFAV type)

5.17 Removing the accelerator pump discharge plug (DFAV type)

5.18a Accelerator pump location (DFAV type)

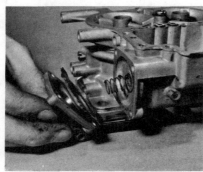

5.18b Removing the accelerator pump cover (DFAV type)

5.20 Removing the cover dust seal (DFAV type)

5.25 Withdrawing the thermostat housing (DFAV type)

5.26a Insulation gasket location (DFAV type)

5.26b Location of the fast idling control rod (DFAV type)

5.29 Automatic choke O-ring seal location (DFAV type)

5.33 Removing the automatic choke shaft (DFAV type)

5.34 Removing the stop plate (DFAV type)

5.35 Removing the diaphragm cover (DFAV type)

5.36 Withdrawing the diaphragm rod (DFAV type)

5.39a Removing the auxiliary venturi (DFAV type)

5.39b Auxiliary venturi size location (DFAV type)

Fig. 9.9 Tool for holding throttle shaft (DFA and DFAV types) (Sec 5)

5.46 Vent valve operating arm location (DFAV type)

5.48 Throttle valve retaining screw location (DFAV type)

5.49a Removing a throttle valve (DFAV type)

5.49b Throttle valve showing the idle bleed hole (DFAV type) (arrowed)

5.50a Removing a throttle shaft (DFAV type)

5.50b Removing a Teflon bush (DFAV type)

5.51 Removing the primary throttle shaft (DFAV type)

30 Unscrew and remove the retaining screw (38) and bush (91) then withdraw the wave washer (90).

31 Remove the fast idle lever (29) and spring (41) noting the position of the latter, then remove the washer (42).

32 Unscrew and remove the adjusting screw (32) and spring (31) from the lever (30).

33 Unscrew and remove the retaining nut (36) and spring washer (37), then withdraw the lever (39), spring (33) and spacer (34). The shaft (48) can now be removed (photo).

34 Mark the location of the adjusting stop plate (49) on the body (47), then remove the screw (50) and lift the plate out (photo).

35 Unscrew and remove the retaining screws (43) lift off the cover (44) and spring (45) (photo).

36 Carefully release the thin diaphragm, then withdraw the operating rod (46) from the body (47) (photo).

37 Unscrew and remove the starting duct inspection plug from the bottom of the body (47).

38 The automatic choke body is supplied complete with the fast idle cam and it is therefore not necessary to dismantle this item. However if a second-hand part is being fitted, the cam and bush may be driven out of the body using a suitable diameter metal drift.

39 Mark the position and location of the auxiliary venturis, then remove them from the carburettor barrels. If they are tight, open the throttle valves and use a plastic or wooden rod to tap them out. Failure of this method to remove the auxiliary venturis will necessitate obtaining Weber tool no 9610 150 0035 (photos).

40 Unscrew and remove the retaining screw (65) and spring washer (66) then withdraw the cover (77).

41 Invert the carburettor body, then bend back the tab washers (63).

42 Unscrew and remove the nuts (62 and 62A) from the ends of each throttle shaft. If they are tight, Weber tool no 9610 315 1201 should be used to hold the shaft stationary, otherwise the shaft could be buckled.

43 From the throttle shaft (20) located at the automatic choke side of the carburettor, remove the tab washer (63), throttle lever (64), toothed sector (70), lever (71), bush (72), wave washer (73), stop lever (74), spacer (75) and spring (100), if fitted.

44 From the throttle shaft (19) located furthest from the automatic choke mounting, remove the tab washer (63), toothed sector (78), lever (79), spacer (75) and spring (80).

45 Unscrew and remove the adjustment screws (67) from the toothed sectors, together with the lock washers (68) and plain washers (69), in order to separate the levers from the toothed sectors.

46 On DFAV types only, unscrew and remove the retaining screw (93) and withdraw the vent valve operating arm (95) and rod (99). Remove the bush (94), washer (96) and spring (97), then separate the rod from the arm by extracting the split pin (98) (photo).

47 Close each throttle valve in turn and mark the valves (21) with a pencil so that they can be refitted in their original positions.

48 Unscrew and remove the retaining screws (22) (photo).

49 Fully open the throttles and remove the valves (21) from the shafts (19 and 20) (photos).

50 Remove the shaft (19) from the carburettor body, then extract the Teflon bushes and mark them relative to their locations (photos).

51 Remove the shaft (20) from the carburettor body, withdraw the spacer (40), then extract the Teflon bushes and again mark them relative to their locations (photo).

6 Disassembly (34 DGAS and 38 DGAS types)

1 Thoroughly clean the carburettor exterior and wipe dry.

2 Referring to Fig. 9.10, unscrew and remove the fuel filter inspection plug (11) and extract the filter (10).

3 Disconnect the choke plate operating lever (37) from the choke shaft (4) after prising out the C-clip with a small screwdriver.

4 Unscrew and remove the carburettor cover retaining screws (3) together with the spring washers, then carefully lift the cover (1) from the main body (86) (photo).

5 Invert the carburettor cover (1) so that the float assembly (15) is uppermost, then extract the float fulcrum pin (90) and withdraw the float assembly (15) together with the needle of the needle valve (14). If necessary, use a suitable diameter pin punch to tap the pin from the two posts, but on no account prise the slotted post apart (photo).

6 Unhook the needle from the float assembly (15).

7 Lift the gasket (12) from the cover (1).

8 Unscrew and remove the retaining screws (91) and spring washers (92) and lift the power valve assembly (93) from the cover (1), taking care not to damage the diaphragm (photo).

9 Using a 10 mm socket or ring spanner, unscrew and remove the needle valve (14) seating and remove the gasket (13) (photo).

10 Unscrew the two main jets (19) and remove them from the bottom of the float chamber in the main body (photo).

11 Unscrew the idling jet holders (36) from each side of the carburettor body, then separate the idling jets (34) from their holders and remove the gaskets (35) (photos).

12 Unscrew and remove the air corrector jets (94) from the carburettor body (photo).

13 Invert the body and extract the emulsion tubes (89). If these are tight due to overtightening of the air corrector jets, use a selftapping screw to remove them but take care not to damage the tubes (photos).

14 Unscrew and remove the idling mixture adjusting screws (87) and springs (88) from the body (photo).

15 Unscrew and remove the throttle idling adjustment screw (73) and spring (74).

16 Unscrew and remove the full power valve (18) and gasket (17) from the bottom of the float chamber (photo).

17 Unscrew the accelerator pump delivery valve (97) and remove it together with the pump jet (96) and gaskets (95), then separate the gaskets and jet from the valve (photo).

18 Unscrew and remove the accelerator pump discharge blanking needle (16) (photo).

19 Unscrew the four screws (31) and withdraw the accelerator pump cover (41) together with the diaphragm (32) and spring (33). If necessary, peel the diaphragm assembly (32) from the cover (41) (photos).

20 Working on the carburettor cover (1), prise out the plug (8) and seal (7) using a screwdriver.

21 Note the location of each choke valve (5) and if necessary, mark them with a pencil.

22 Unscrew and remove the retaining screws (9), then withdraw the choke valves (5) from the shaft (4); the shaft (4) can now be removed from the cover (1).

23 Working on the carburettor body, unscrew the automatic choke water housing retaining bolt (46) and remove it together with the gasket (45) (photo).

24 Remove the cover (47) and gasket (48). Cut the gasket from the thermostat assembly (50) if it is stuck.

25 Unscrew and remove the retaining screws (44) and lift the automatic choke thermostat assembly (50) from the body (53), then remove the retaining ring (49) (photo).

26 Remove the disc gasket (51), then unscrew and remove the three retaining screws (42) and spring washers. Withdraw the automatic choke body (53), at the same time disengage the fast idling control rod (61) from the lever (64) (photo).

27 Disconnect the rod (61) from the fast idle lever (75) by extracting the split pin (60) (photo).

28 Note the location of the individual components of the automatic choke before dismantling them.

29 Prise the O-ring seal (69) from the side of the carburettor (photo).

30 Unscrew and remove the retaining screw (72) together with the lever (63) and washers (photo).

31 Separate the washer (62), lever (63), wave washer (70) and

6.4 Removing the carburettor cover (DGAS type)

6.5 Withdrawing the float fulcrum pin (DGAS type)

6.8 Removing the full power valve assembly (DGAS type)

6.9 Needle valve seating (DGAS type)

6.10 Main jet location (DGAS type)

6.11a Removing an idling jet (DGAS type)

6.11b Idling jet and holder (DGAS type)

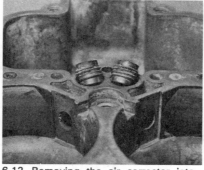
6.12 Removing the air corrector jets (DGAS type)

6.13a Removing the emulsion tubes (DGAS type)

6.13b The emulsion tube (DGAS type)

6.14 Location of an idling mixture adjusting screw (DGAS type)

6.16 Removing the full power valve (DGAS type)

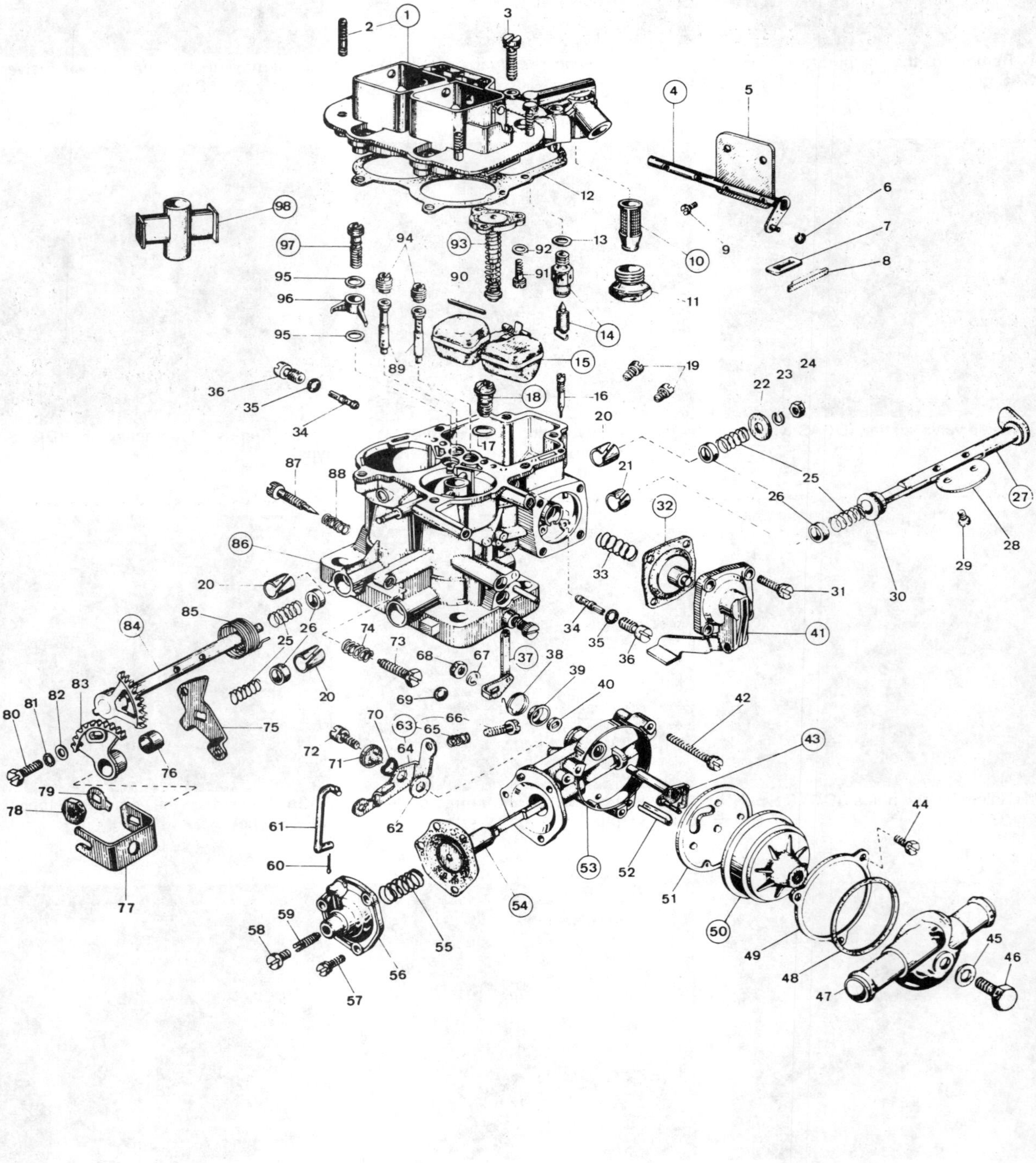
2
1
3
4
5
98
12
6
9
7
97
94
93
92
13
10
95
91
8
90
11
96
95
14
89
15
19
24
36
35
18
16
23
22
34
17
20
87
88
21
32
25
26
27
28
86
33
29
30
31
20
85
84
26
25
74
73
34
35
36
41
68
67
37
38
39
40
20
83
69
42
80
81
82
75
76
70
63
66
65
43
72
64
71
79
78
61
62
53
52
44
60
77
51
54
59
55
50
58
56
49
45
46
57
48
47

6.17 Removing the accelerator pump delivery valve (DGAS type)

6.18 Removing the discharge blanking needle (DGAS type)

6.19a Acceleration pump cover location (DGAS type)

6.19b Removing the accelerator pump cover (DGAS type)

6.23 Automatic choke cover location (DGAS type)

6.25 Removing the thermostat assembly (DGAS type)

Fig. 9.10 Exploded view of the 38 DGAS carburettor (typical) (Sec 6)

1 Carburettor cover assy	34 Idling jet	67 Spring washer
2 Stud	35 Gasket for idling jet holder	68 Throttle shaft fixing nut
3 Carburettor cover fixing screw	36 Idling jet holder	69 Auto-choke O-ring seal
4 Choke shaft and lever assy	37 Choke control lever assy	70 Washer for idle loose lever
5 Choke throttle valve	38 Spring for fast idle cam	71 Bushing for idle loose lever
6 Lock ring	39 Spring retaining cover	72 Screw securing fast idle loose lever
7 Dust seal plate	40 Washer for shaft	73 Throttles adjusting screw
8 Dust seal plug	41 Accelerator pump cover assy	74 Spring for throttle adjusting screw
9 Choke plates fixing screw	42 Choke fixing screw	75 Toothed sector control lever
10 Strainer assy	43 Auto-choke shaft and lever assy	76 Bushing for toothed sector
11 Strainer inspection plug	44 Screw for plate	77 Throttle control lever
12 Carburettor cover gasket	45 Seal for water cover fixing screw	78 Primary shaft fixing nut
13 Gasket for needle valve	46 Water cover fixing screw	79 Lockwasher
14 Needle valve assy	47 Auto-choke water chamber	80 Toothed sector fixing screw
15 Float assy	48 Water cover gasket	81 Wave washer
16 Pump discharge blanking needle	49 Thermostat assy locking ring	82 Flat washer
17 Gasket for power valve	50 Auto-choke thermostat assy	83 Primary toothed sector
19 Main jet	51 Gasket for auto-choke body	84 Secondary main shaft assy
20 Plate for shafts	52 Plate for auto-choke shaft	85 Shaft return spring
21 Plate for shafts	53 Auto-choke body assy	86 Carburettor body
22 Washer for secondary shaft	54 Choke diaphragm assy	87 Idle adjusting screw
23 Spring washer	55 Spring for diaphragm	88 Spring for idle adjusting screw
24 Secondary shaft fixing nut	56 Auto-choke cover	89 Emulsioning tube
25 Bush retaining spring	57 Screw securing auto-choke cover	90 Float fixing pin
26 Bushing for shafts	58 Plug	91 Screw securing power valve
27 Primary main shaft assy	59 Diaphragm adjusting screw	92 Flat washer
28 Throttle valve	60 Pin for fast idle rod	93 Power valve assy
29 Throttle valve fixing screw	61 Fast idling control rod	94 Air corrector jet
30 Spacer	62 Washer for fast idle loose lever	95 Pump jet gasket
31 Screw securing pump cover	63 Fast idle loose lever assy	96 Pump jet
32 Accelerator pump diaphragm assy	64 Lever	97 Pump delivery valve assy
33 Pump loading spring	65 Spring	98 Auxiliary venturi
	66 Screw	

6.26 Insulation disc gasket location (DGAS type)

6.27 Location of the fast idle rod (DGAS type)

6.29 Automatic choke O-ring location (DGAS type)

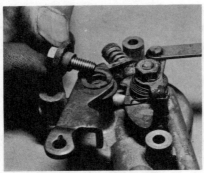

6.30 Removing the fast idle lever (DGAS type)

6.33a Removing the choke lever and spring (DGAS type)

6.33b Removing the shaft cover (DGAS type)

6.34 Removing the diaphragm cover and spring (DGAS type)

6.35 Removing the operating rod (DGAS type)

6.38 Removing the auxiliary venturi (DGAS type)

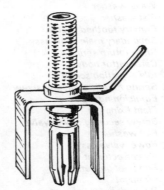

Fig. 9.11 Tool for removing the auxiliary venturis (Sec 6)

6.44 Withdrawing the primary throttle shaft (DGAS type)

6.45 Location of the Teflon bushes (DGAS type)

6.47 Removing a throttle valve (DGAS type)

6.50 Removing the secondary throttle shaft (DGAS type)

bush (71) from the screw (72).

32 Unscrew and remove the adjusting screw (66) and spring (65) from the lever (64).

33 Unscrew and remove the retaining nut (68) and spring washer (67), then withdraw the lever (37), spring (38), cover (39) and spacer (40). The shaft (43) can now be removed and the bearing (52) extracted from the body (53) (photos).

34 Unscrew and remove the retaining screws (57) and lift off the cover (56) and spring (55) (photo).

35 Carefully release the thin diaphragm, then withdraw the operating rod (54) from the body (53) (photo).

36 Unscrew and remove the plug (58) and adjusting screw (59) from the cover (56), noting the position of the screw.

37 The automatic choke body is supplied complete with the fast idle cam and it is therefore not necessary to dismantle this item. However if a second-hand part is being fitted, the cam, bush and spacer may be prised from the body using a wide blade screwdriver.

38 Mark the position and location of the auxiliary venturis (98) then remove them from the carburettor barrels (photo). If they are tight, open the throttle valves and use a plastic or wooden rod to tap them out. Failure of this method to remove the auxiliary venturis will necessitate obtaining Weber tool no 9610 150 0035.

39 Invert the carburettor body then bend back the tab washer (79).

40 Unscrew the nut (78). Provided that the lug on the fast idle lever (75) is intact, no harm can be done to the throttle valves or shaft; however if the lug is broken, the special Weber tool must be used to hold the shaft stationary while the nut is loosened.

41 Remove the nut (78), tab washer (79), lever (77) (noting its location), toothed sector assembly (83), spring (25) and bush (26). Gently tap the body to remove the bush (26) if necessary.

42 Unscrew and remove the sector screw (80), lock washer (81) and plain washer (82). Separate the lever (75) and bush (76) from the toothed sector (83).

43 Unscrew and remove the throttle valve retaining screws (29) from the throttle shaft with the accelerator pump cam fitted. Withdraw the throttle valve, noting which way round it is located. Mark it with a pencil if necessary.

44 Remove the throttle shaft (27) from the body, then remove the bush (26), spring (25) and spacer (30) (photo).

45 Extract the Teflon bushes (20 and 21) from the body and mark them relative to their locations (photo).

46 Hold the remaining throttle valve (28) closed and unscrew the nut (24). If this nut is excessively tight, it will be necessary to obtain the special Weber tool to hold the shaft stationary while the nut is loosened.

47 Unscrew and remove the throttle valve retaining screws (29), then open the valve against the spring tension and remove the throttle valve (28) (photo).

48 Release the spring tension and note the location of the return spring (85).

49 Remove the nut (24), spring washer (23), washer (22) and spring (25) and gently tap the body to remove the bush (26).

50 Remove the throttle shaft (84) from the body, then remove the bush (26), spring (25) and return spring (85) (photo).

51 Extract the Teflon bushes (20) from the body and mark them relative to their locations.

7 Special overhaul procedures

After carrying out the general overhaul procedures given in Chapter 4, the following special procedures should be made:

1 Using a hand chuck and Weber tool no 9600 325 1047, reform the idling jet seats by carefully rotating the tool. Finish the seatings by inserting Weber tool no 9610 315 1202 and gently tapping the top of the tool whilst rotating it (Fig. 9.12).

2 If the emulsion tube bores are discoloured and have signs of sediment build up, ream them clear again using Weber tool no 9600 325 0765. Rotate the tool slowly with a hand chuck until it moves quite freely, then remove it whilst still rotating it.

3 If on disassembly the choke shaft (8) is a tight fit in the carburettor cover (1) and it is of original diameter (6.0 mm), use Weber tool no 9600 035 0540 to ream the shaft bore clear with the aid of a hand chuck (Fig. 9. 14). Should the shaft bores be excessively worn, a new carburettor cover (1) must be obtained, but note that normally the shaft itself will wear quicker than its bore, it which case a new shaft will cure the problem.

4 If the Teflon bushes which support the throttle shafts are worn, they should be renewed.

5 Check the internal channels of the carburettor body and cover for blockage by injecting fuel with a syringe and observing that it emerges freely from the particular channel being tested. If any are blocked, the lead plugs must be drilled out and the channels cleared and checked with the special Weber tool.

6 The channels are of three diameters, viz 1.0 mm, 1.5 mm and 2.0 mm. The corresponding tools are Weber tool nos 9620 175 1846, 9620 175 1847 and 9620 175 1848. Fig. 9.15 shows the location of the various channels.

7 The carburettor body and cover should be thoroughly cleaned after overhaul to remove swarf and dirt, preferably using clean fuel and air pressure. The lead plugs should be renewed and retained in position by using Weber tool nos 9610

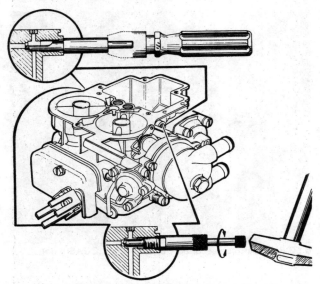

Fig. 9.12 Reforming the idling jet seats (Sec 7)

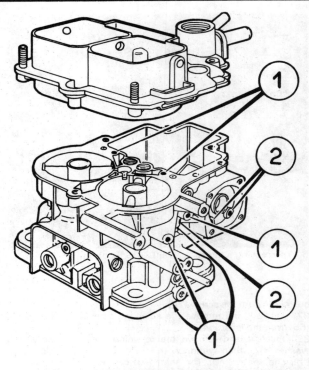

Fig. 9.15 Location of the internal channels of the carburettor body (Sec 7)

1   Idling channels   2   Accelerator pump channels

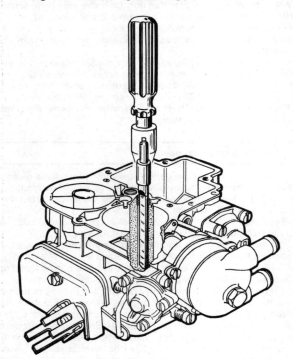

Fig. 9.13 Reaming the emulsion tube bores (Sec 7)

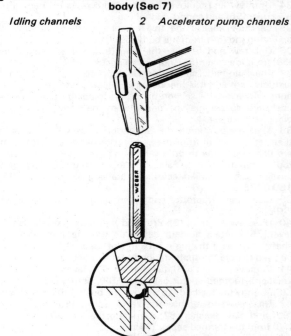

Fig. 9.16 Method of fitting the lead plugs (Sec 7)

315 0822 and 9610 315 0823 to expand them into their bores.

8   On 38 DGAS types, check the condition of the power valve diaphragm and diaphragm seat; if necessary, clean the seat with a little metal polish.

9   During the manufacture of the carburettor, a ball is inserted into the accelerator pump channel and retained by a brass plug (see Fig. 9.17). To check that this ball is free and unobstructed, shake the carburettor body and listen to the ball movement.

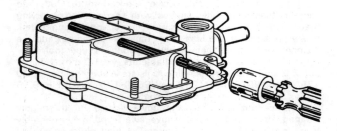

Fig. 9.14 Reaming the choke shaft bore (Sec 7)

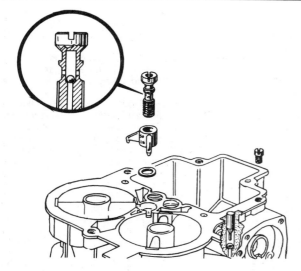

Fig. 9.17 Location of the acclerator pump ball valve (Sec 7)

8.9 Correct toothed sector alignment (DFAV type)

8.11 Fitting the sector adjustment screws (DFAV type)

10 Check that the internal channel of the automatic choke body is free and unobstructed. Also check that the diaphragm and corresponding surfaces are serviceable; if necessary clean the surfaces with metal polish.

11 Check the accelerator pump diaphragm and corresponding surfaces in the same manner to that described in paragraph 10.

12 Renew the diaphragm assemblies checked in paragraph 10 and 11 if necessary.

13 Check the accelerator pump lever for wear, especially on the type fitted with a roller bearing. Renew the lever if necessary.

14 Check the walls of the choke intake, where the choke valves rest when they are fully shut. If there is a deep wear ridge, this could cause the valves to temporarily stick shut, especially after an engine 'blow back'. The ridge should be removed using fine emery tape.

15 On 38 DGAS types, check the automatic choke shaft Teflon bush for wear and renew it if necessary.

8 Assembly (40 DFA and 40 DFAV types)

Note: *All components should be clean and dry before starting the assembly procedure.*

1 Fit the spacer (40) to the throttle shaft (20).

2 Insert the four Teflon bushes (76) into the carburettor body and lightly lubricate them with engine oil.

3 Insert the throttle shafts (19 and 20) into their correct locations in the carburettor body, making sure that the Teflon bushes are not displaced.

4 With the carburettor body inverted and the largest section of the accelerator pump cam on the shaft (20) uppermost, insert the throttle valve (21) and turn the shaft until the valve is shut. Make sure that the angled perimeter of the valve seats correctly in the barrel. The by-pass hole in the valve should be adjacent to the idling and progression holes in the barrel.

5 Insert the valve retaining screws (22) and tighten them evenly but without exerting excessive pressure on the shaft. It is recommended that new screws are always fitted as it is quite easy to cross thread previously peened screws. Lock the screws (22) by peening with Weber tool no 98010 900 whilst supporting the shaft (20) with a block of wood. Alternatively, coat the screw threads with a liquid locking agent (fuel resistant) prior to inserting them.

6 Insert the throttle shaft (19) and fit the throttle valve (21) in the same manner as described in paragraphs 4 and 5. On 40 DFAV types, the valve must be fitted with the vent operating lugs uppermost (with the carburettor inverted).

7 On DFAV types only, locate the vent operating rod (99) in the body, then fit it to the arm (95) and retain with the split pin (98). Locate the spring (97) to the body, then fit the bush (94), operating arm (95) and washer (96) to the retaining screw (93) and tighten the screw into the body. Tension the spring (97) and hook it over the arm (95) which should now rest on the lugs at the end of the throttle shaft.

8 Fit to the throttle shaft (19), the spring (80), spacer (75), lever (79), toothed sector (78) and tab washer (63); then fit and tighten the nut (62A) finger tight.

9 Fit to the throttle shaft (20) the spring (100) (if fitted), spacer (75), stop lever (74), bush (72), wave washer (73) and lever (71); then with both throttle valves shut, fit the toothed sector (70) so that the alignment marks on both sectors face each other (photo).

10 Fit the throttle lever (64), tab washer (63) and nut (62), tightening the latter finger tight only.

11 With both throttle valves held fully closed and the alignment marks on the two sectors facing each other, insert and tighten the two screws (67) together with the lockwashers (68) and plain washers (69) (photo).

12 Tighten the retaining nuts (62 and 62A) and lock them by bending the tab washers (63); if available, use the Weber tool no 9610 315 1201 to hold the shafts stationary. Alternatively, insert and tighten the idling adjustment screw (28) whilst

tightening the nuts.

13 Check that the two throttle shafts operate smoothly and that both throttle valves are synchronised exactly. If not, it will be necessary to loosen the nuts (62) and reset the adjustment screws (67).

14 Tension the return springs (80 and 100) (if fitted), using a length of welding rod hooked at one end and locate them onto the levers (74 and 79). Make sure that the springs are tensioned sufficiently and that no coils are trapped between the spacers and the main body.

15 Lubricate the toothed sectors with a little grease, then locate the cover (77) onto the body and tighten the retaining screw (65) together with the spring washer (66).

16 Fit the auxiliary venturis into their respective positions as noted previously, making sure that the supply channels are adjacent and that the nozzle cut away sections face the throttle valves.

17 Fit the fast idle cam and bush into the automatic choke body (47) if removed, making sure that the cam is positioned as shown in Fig. 9.8 (photo). Use a suitable diameter metal drift and support the body on a block of wood.

18 Insert and tighten the starting duct inspection plug into the bottom of the body (47).

19 Insert the operating rod (46) into the body (47) and locate the diaphragm over the brass dowel peg.

20 Locate the spring (45) and press the cover (44) onto the body (47), then insert and tighten the retaining screws (43) evenly.

21 Check that the operating rod (46) moves freely with the blade of a screwdriver.

22 Fit the adjusting stop plate (49) to the body (47) in its pre-viously marked location, then tighten the retaining screw (50).

23 Lightly lubricate the shaft (48) with engine oil then insert it into the body (47).

24 Rotate the shaft (48) until it contacts the operating rod (46), then fit the spacer (34), spring (33), lever (39), spring washer (37) and retaining nut (36). Make sure that the lever is positioned as shown in Fig. 9.8 then tighten the nut (36) (photo).

25 Hook the spring (33) over the fast idle cam and the lever (39) lug so that both are kept in contact by the spring tension.

26 Fit the adjusting screw (36) and spring (31) to the fast idle lever (30).

27 Locate the bush (91) on the retaining screw (38), followed by the wave washer (90), lever (29), spring (41) and washer (42), then tighten the screw (38) into the body (47). Make sure that the spring (41) is located correctly so that the tension moves the adjusting screw (32) off of the fast idle cam (photo).

28 Press the O-ring seal (35) onto the brass dowel at the side of the carburettor.

29 Engage the rod (61) to the front idle lever (29) and then insert the split pin (60) (if fitted) and bend the legs to retain it.

30 Locate the automatic choke to the carburettor body, insert the three retaining screws (51) and spring washers, and tighten the screws evenly (photos).

31 Engage the fast idling control rod (61) with the throttle lever (71), insert the split pin (60), and bend the legs to retain it.

32 Working on the carburettor cover (1), lightly lubricate the choke shaft (8) with engine oil then insert it into the cover.

33 With the choke shaft (8) in the open position, fit the choke valves (7) into their location slots, then close the shaft to allow the valves to centralise.

34 Holding the shaft closed, insert the valve retaining screws (6) and tighten them evenly without exerting excessive pressure on the brass shaft (8). It is recommended that new screws are always fitted as it is quite easy to cross-thread previously peened screws. Lock the screws (6) by peening with Weber tool no 98010 900, or alternatively by coating the threads with a liquid locking agent (fuel resistant) prior to inserting them. If the tool method is used, support the shaft (8) with a piece of wood.

8.17 Correct positioning of fast idle cam (DFAV type)

8.24 Fitting the choke rod and lever (DFAV type)

8.27 Correct positioning of fast idle lever (DFAV type)

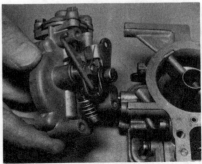

8.30a Fitting the automatic choke body (DFAV type)

8.30b Location of the fast idle levers (DFAV type)

8.49 Inserting the needle into the valve seat (DFAV type)

35 Fit the seal (10) and plug (101) into the cover (1).

36 Insert the choke operating rod (16) through the seal (10) and engage it with the choke spindle arm, then retain it by inserting the split pin (15) and bending the pin legs.

37 Locate the diaphragm assembly (24) to the accelerator pump cover (25) then, with the carburettor body on end, fit the spring (23) into the pump chamber and lower the diaphragm and cover onto it.

38 Insert the accelerator pump cover retaining screws (26), depress the cover and tighten the screws in diagonal sequence. Make sure that the roller locates on the throttle shaft cam.

39 Fit and tighten the accelerator pump discharge blanking plug (18).

40 Fit the pump jet (86) to the accelerator pump delivery valve (87) followed by the gasket (85), then locate the pump jet into the carburettor body and tighten the delivery valve (87).

41 Fit the spring (27) to the throttle idling adjustment screw (28) and locate the screw in the carburettor body.

42 Fit the springs (82) to the idling mixture adjusting screws (81) and locate them in the carburettor body.

43 Insert the emulsion tubes (89) into the body then fit and tighten the air corrector jets (88).

44 Press the idling jets (84) into their respective holders (83) then tighten the holders into the carburettor body.

45 Fit and tighten the main jets (17) to the bottom of the float chamber.

46 Fit the gasket (11) to the needle valve (12) seating and tighten the seating into the carburettor cover (1).

47 On 40 DFAV types only, fit and tighten the vent and power valve (92) to the cover (1).

48 With the cover (1) inverted, fit the gasket (9).

49 Lower the needle into the needle valve (12) seating then insert the float tab beneath the needle hook and insert the fulcrum pin (14) through the two posts and float (photo).

50 The float level adjustment must now be checked in the following manner: Obtain a drill or dowel rod of 0.236 in (6.0 mm) diameter. Hold the carburettor cover vertically so that the float hangs from the fulcrum pin and the float arm is in light contact with the needle ball (ie the ball is not depressed). Using the drill, check that the distance from the cover gasket to the nearest part of the float is 0.236 in (6.00 mm). The annular seam must not be included in the distance and for this reason a groove must be filed or ground in the drill (photo).

51 If the dimension obtained in paragraph 50 is not correct, carefully bend the wide tab on the float as necessary.

52 Tilt the carburettor cover so that the float moves away from the cover and the narrow tab makes contact with the needle valve seating. Now, using a drill or dowel rod of 0.551 in (14.0 mm) diameter, check the needle valve fully open dimension using the method described in paragraph 50 (photo).

53 If the dimension obtained in paragraph 52 is not correct, carefully bend the narrow tab on the float as necessary (photo).

54 The difference between the dimension obtained in paragraphs 50 and 52 represents the needle valve stroke which

should be 0.315 in (8.0 mm).

55 Lower the carburettor cover (1) onto the main body, making sure that the vent valve operating rod (99) locates on the vent valve (92).

56 Fit the cover retaining screws (3) together with the spring washers and tighten them evenly in diagonal sequence.

57 Engage the choke plate operating rod (16) with the lever (39) and retain with the split pin (15) by bending the pin legs.

58 Fit the fuel filter (5) and tighten the inspection plug (4) into the cover (1).

59 With the carburettor completely assembled, the automatic choke and idling adjustments must be made. To do this, first turn the throttle idling adjustment screw (28) until it just touches the throttle lever (74), then continue to screw it in 2 complete turns. Note that if this adjustment is being made with the automatic choke completely assembled, it will be necessary to first open the throttle fully, hold the choke valves open and release the throttle. It is preferable to hold the choke valves open while making the adjustment.

60 Turn both idling mixture screws (81) until they are in light contact with their seats, then back them off one complete turn each.

61 To adjust the automatic choke, first operate the throttle and hold the choke valves in their closed position. Using a 0.008 in

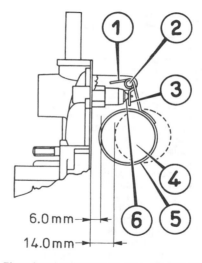

Fig. 9.18 Float level adjustment diagram (40 DFA and 40 DFAV types) (Sec 8)

1	Stroke adjustment	4	Float
2	Fulcrum pin	5	Seam
3	Closed adjustment	6	Needle

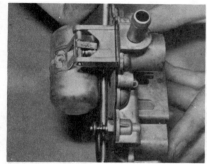

8.50 Checking the closed float level clearances (DFAV type)

8.52 Checking the open float level clearance (DFAV type)

8.53 Float arm narrow tab location and float weight (DFAV type)

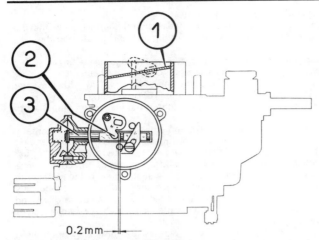

0·2 mm

Fig. 9.19 Automatic choke minimum clearance check location (40 DFA and 40DFAV types) (Sec 8)

1   *Choke valves*   3   *Rod*
2   *Shaft arm*

(0.2 mm) feeler gauge, check that there is at least 0.008 in (0.2 mm) clearance between the automatic choke shaft arm (48) and the contact face of the operating rod (46). If not, the operating rod diaphragm may be twisted and the shaft arm bent. This should be rectified before proceeding.

62 Loosen the fast idle adjustment screw (32), then while still holding the choke valves shut under finger pressure, use the blade of a screwdriver to move the operating rod (46) against the stop plate (49). With the shaft arm in contact with the operating rod abutment, the distance from the lower edge of the choke valves and the intake wall must be between 0.137 in and 0.157 in (3.5 mm and 4.0 mm). Use a suitable drill shank to make the check and if necessary, adjust the position of the stop plate (49) to obtain the correct clearance (photos).

63 If a new automatic choke body (47) has been fitted, the alignment mark must now be stamped on the top of the body. To do this it is essential to obtain Weber tool no 9620 175 2951. The mark is made while keeping the choke valves completely shut by applying light pressure on the tool.

64 Fit the disc gasket (52) to the automatic choke body (47).

65 Fit the thermostat assembly (53) to the body (47) at the same time locating the bi-metallic spring onto the shaft (48), then fit the retaining ring (55) and insert the three screws (59).

66 Whilst holding the thermostat assembly (53) so that the alignment mark is opposite the mark on the body (47), tighten the three screws (59) evenly (photo).

67 Fit the gasket (54) and the cover (56) then insert and tighten the retaining bolt (58) with the gasket (57).

68 The automatic choke fast idling adjustment must now be made. Open and close the throttles and make sure that the fast idling adjustment screw (32) is against the fast idle cam highest point with the choke valves completely shut. Using a small drill or a feeler gauge, check that the distance from the throttle valves to the outer wall of the barrels by the progression holes is between 0.029 in and 0.031 in (0.75 mm and 0.80 mm). If not, adjust the fast idling screw (32) to give the correct clearance.

9   Assembly (34 DGAS and 38 DGAS types)

Note: *All components should be clean and dry before starting the assembly procedure.*

1   Insert the Teflon bushes (20) into the secondary throttle shaft bore of the carburettor body (86) and lightly lubricate them with a little engine oil.

2   Locate the return spring (85), spring (25) and bush (26) to the secondary throttle shaft (84), then insert it into the carburettor body from the side opposite the float chamber. Make sure that the Teflon bushes are not displaced and locate the

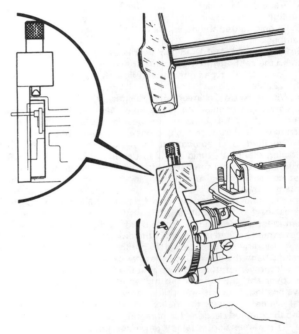

Fig. 9.20 Alignment marking tool for new automatic choke bodies (40 DFA and 40 DFAV types) (Sec 8)

8.62a Checking the choke valve clearance with a drill (DFAV type)

8.62b Adjusting the automatic choke stop plate (DFAV type)

8.66 Automatic choke alignment marks (DFAV type)

return spring (85) in the special hole.

3   Fit the bush (26), spring (25), washer (22), spring washer (23) and nut (24) to the end of the throttle shaft (84), then tighten the nut (84) whilst holding the shaft stationary with a screwdriver inserted through the toothed sector.

4   Tension the spring (85) by turning the toothed sector, then insert the throttle valve into the throttle shaft (84) and close the valve. Make sure that the angled perimeter of the valve seats correctly in the barrel and allow it to snap shut several times to centralise it.

5   Insert the throttle valve retaining screws (29) and tighten them evenly but without exerting excessive pressure on the shaft. It is recommended that new screws are always fitted to avoid cross-threading previously peened screws. Lock the screws (29) by peening with Weber tool no 98010 900 whilst supporting the shaft with a block of wood. Alternatively, coat the screw threads with a liquid locking agent (fuel resistant) prior to inserting them.

6   Insert the Teflon bushes (20 and 21) into the primary throttle shaft bore of the carburettor body (86) and lightly lubricate them with a little engine oil. Note that the smaller bush (21) is located at the float chamber end.

7   Locate the spacer (30), spring (25) and bush (26) to the primary throttle shaft (27) with the smaller diameter of the spacer against the accelerator pump operating cam.

8   Insert the throttle shaft (27) into the carburettor body from the float chamber side, making sure that the Teflon bushes are not displaced (photo).

9   With the accelerator pump cam facing the centre of the float chamber, fit the bush (26), spring (25) and lever (75), making sure that the threaded hole in the lever (75) is towards the secondary toothed sector (photos).

10   Fit the bush (76) to the throttle shaft (27) then press on the toothed sector (83) and mesh it with the secondary sector so that the alignment marks are in line (photo).

11   Fit the lever (77), tab washer (79) and nut (78).

12   Locate the spring (74) on the throttle idling adjustment screw (73), then insert the screw into the carburettor body and screw it in as far as it will go. The nut (78) may now be fully tightened and the locktab (79) bent. Fully unscrew the adjustment screw (73) but leave it in the carburettor body.

13   Open the primary throttle shaft (27) and insert the throttle valve (28), observing the procedure given in paragraphs 4 and 5 to centralise it. Fit the retaining screws (29).

14   Insert the sector screw (80) with lockwasher (81) and plain washer (82) and tighten it whilst holding both throttle valves completely shut; this will synchronise the throttle valves (photo).

15   Lubricate the toothed sectors with a little grease and check that the throttle valves operate smoothly and fully.

16   Fit the auxiliary venturis (98) into their respective positions as noted previously, making sure that the supply channels are adjacent and that the nozzle cut away sections face the throttle valves.

17   If removed, locate the fast idle cam on the bush followed by the spacer, then press the bush onto the rear of the automatic choke body (53) using a suitable diameter length of tubing. Note that when fitted the round contour of the cam must face the diaphragm end of the body with the flat edge uppermost (photo).

18   Fit the screw (59) and plug (58) to the cover (56), positioning the screw as previously noted.

19   Fit the operating rod (54) to the body (53), at the same time locate the diaphragm over the brass dowel.

20   Locate the spring (55) into the cover (56) then fit the cover to the body making sure that the spring locates in the diaphragm plate.

21   Insert and tighten the retaining screws (57) evenly.

22   Insert the Teflon bearing (52) into the body (53).

23   Lightly lubricate the shaft (43) with engine oil and fit it in

9.8 Inserting the primary throttle shaft (DGAS type)

9.9a Fitting the spring to the primary throttle shaft (DGAS type)

9.9b Fitting the lever to the primary throttle shaft (DGAS type)

9.10 Aligning the toothed sectors (DGAS type)

9.14 Fitting the sector adjustment screw (DGAS type)

9.17 Correct location of the fast idle cam (DGAS type)

the body (53) (photo).

24 Fit the spacer (40), cover (39), spring (38), lever (37), spring washer (67) and nut (68). Tighten the nut, being careful not to bend the arm on the end of the shaft (43). Make sure that the lever and spring are assembled as shown in Fig. 9.10 with the lever resting on the flat edge of the fast idle cam.

25 Fit the spring (65) to the adjusting screw (66) and fit the screw to the lever (64).

26 Locate the spring washer, bush (71), wave washer (70), lever (63) and washer (62) to the retaining screw (72), then tighten the screw into the body (53). Make sure that the fast idle screw (66) can locate on the stepped edge of the fast idle cam (photo).

27 Press the O-ring seal (69) to the side of the carburettor.

28 Engage the rod (61) to the fast idle lever (75) and retain it with the split pin (60).

29 Engage the rod (61) with the fast idle lever (64), then fit the automatic choke body (53) to the carburettor body (86). Insert the retaining screws (42) and spring washers and tighten them evenly.

30 Working on the carburettor cover (1), lightly lubricate the choke shaft (4) with engine oil and insert it into the cover.

31 With the choke shaft (4) in the open position, fit the choke valves (5) into their location slots, then close the shaft to allow the valves to centralise.

32 Holding the shaft closed, insert the valve retaining screws (9) and tighten them evenly without exerting excessive pressure on the shaft (4). It is recommended that new screws are always fitted to avoid cross-threading previously peened screws. Lock the screws (9) by peening with Weber tool no 98010 900 or alternatively, by coating the threads with a liquid locking agent (fuel resistant) prior to inserting them. If the tool method is used, support the shaft (4) with a piece of wood.

33 Fit the seal (7) and plug (8) into the carburettor cover (1).

34 Locate the accelerator pump diaphragm assembly (32) to the cover (41) then, with the carburettor body on end, fit the spring (33) into the pump chamber and lower the diaphragm and cover onto it.

35 Insert the accelerator pump cover retaining screws (31), depress the cover and tighten the screws in diagonal sequence, making sure that the pump lever locates on the throttle shaft cam.

36 Fit and tighten the accelerator pump discharge blanking needle (16).

37 Fit a gasket (95) to the accelerator pump delivery valve (97) followed by the pump jet (96) and a further gasket (95), then locate the pump jet into the carburettor body and tighten the delivery valve (97).

38 Fit and tighten the full power valve (18) and gasket (17) to the bottom of the float chamber.

39 Fit the springs (88) to the idling adjusting screws (87) and locate them in the carburettor body.

40 Lower the emulsion tubes (89) into the body (86) then fit and tighten the air corrector jets (94).

41 Press the idling jets (34) into their holders (36) and fit the gaskets (35), then tighten the holders (36) into the body (86).

42 Fit and tighten the main jets (19) to the bottom of the float chamber.

43 Fit the gasket (13) to the needle valve (14) seating and tighten the seating into the carburettor cover (1) using a 10 mm socket or ring spanner.

44 With the cover (1) inverted, locate the power valve assembly (93), then depress the valve with one hand and lift the valve cover slightly to settle the diaphragm. While keeping the valve depressed, insert and tighten the retaining screws (91) complete with spring washers (92).

45 Lower the needle into the needle valve (14) seating, then locate the float assembly (15) and insert the float tab beneath the needle hook (photo).

46 Insert the fulcrum pin (90) through the two posts and float.

47 The float level adjustment must now be checked in the following manner. Hold the carburettor cover vertically so that the float assembly hangs from the fulcrum pin and the float arm is in light contact with the needle ball (ie the ball is not depressed). Using vernier calipers, check that the distance from the cover to the furthest part of the two semi-floats is as given in the adjustment data. If not, carefully bend the wide tab on the float arm as necessary (photo).

48 Tilt the carburettor cover so that the float assembly moves away from the cover and the narrow tab makes contact with the needle valve seating. The distance from the cover to the furthest part of the two semi-floats should now be as given in the adjustment data. If not, carefully bend the narrow tab on the float arm as necessary (photo).

49 The difference between the dimensions obtained in paragraphs 47 and 48 represents the needle valve stroke which should be 0.393 in (10.0 mm).

50 Locate the gasket (12) onto the carburettor body (86) then lower the carburettor cover (1) onto the main body (86), at the same time inserting the choke control lever (37) through the dust seal (7).

51 Fit the cover retaining screws (3) together with the spring washers and tighten them evenly in diagonal sequence.

52 Engage the choke plate operating lever (37) with the choke shaft (4) and retain by pressing the C-clip into the groove (photo).

53 Fit the fuel filter (10) and tighten the inspection plug (11) into the cover (1).

54 With the carburettor completely assembled, the idling and automatic choke adjustments must be made. To do this, first turn the throttle idling adjustment screw (73) until it just touches the fast idle lever (75), then continue to screw in 2 complete turns. Note that if this adjustment is being made with the automatic choke completely assembled, it will be necessary to first open the throttle fully, hold the choke valves open and release the throttle. It is preferable to hold the choke valves open whilst making the adjustment.

55 Turn both idling mixture screws (87) until they are in light

9.23 Fitting the automatic choke shaft (DGAS type)

9.26 Fitting the fast idle lever (DGAS type)

9.45 Fitting the float (DGAS type)

9.47 Checking the closed float level adjustment (DGAS type)

9.48 Checking the open float lever adjustment (DGAS type)

9.52 Fitting the choke operating lever (DGAS type)

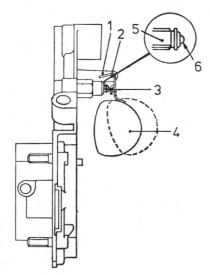

Fig. 9.21 Float level adjustment diagram (34 DGAS and DGAS types) (Sec 9)

1   Stroke adjustment   4   Float
2   Fulcrum pin   5   Needle
3   Closed adjustment   6   Spring tensioned ball

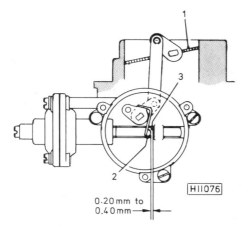

0.20 mm to
0.40 mm

H11076

Fig. 9.22 Checking the shaft arm to rod clearance (DGAS types) (Sec 9)

1   Choke valves   3   Rod abutment
2   Shaft arm

contact with their seats, then back them off one complete turn each.

56 To adjust the automatic choke, first fully unscrew the fast idle adjustment screw (66). The choke valve pull down dimension must now be checked.

57 Connect an elastic band between the automatic choke shaft (43) and the diaphragm cover (56) so that the choke valves are held shut. With the operating rod (54) in the rest position, the clearance between the shaft (43) arm and the rod (54) abutment must be between 0.007 in and 0.015 in (0.2 mm and 0.4 mm). Make the check with a feeler gauge. If it is not correct the diaphragm may be stretched or the shaft arm bent. Check and rectify both of these items before proceeding (photo).

58 Using a small electrician's screwdriver or length of welding rod, push the outer diameter of the operating rod (54) hard against the adjustment screw (59) by inserting it into the rod bore. The tension of the elastic band must be sufficient to overcome the tension of the spring inside the operating rod (54). This can be checked by temporarily opening the choke valves and observing whether the visible section of the rod (54) moves. Check that the distance from the lower edge of the choke valves to the intake wall is between 0.112 in and 0.124 in (2.85 mm and 3.15 mm). Make the check using a drill shank and if not correct, adjust the screw (59) as necessary, after first removing the plug (58) (photo).

59 Using the blade of a screwdriver, press both sections of the rod (54) hard against the screw (59). The distance from the lower edge of the choke valves to the intake well should now be the maximum choke valve gap given in the adjustment data. Make the check using a drill shank and if not correct, renew the operating rod (54) (photo).

60 If a new automatic choke body (53) has been fitted, the alignment mark must now be stamped on the top of the body. To do this it is essential to obtain Weber tool no 98028 600. The mark is made while keeping the choke valves completely shut by applying light pressure on the tool.

61 Fit and tighten the plug (58) into the diaphragm cover (56).

62 Fit the disc gasket (51) to the automatic choke body (53).

63 Fit the thermostat assembly (50) to the body (53), at the same time locating the bi-metallic spring onto the shaft (43), then fit the retaining ring (49) and insert the three screws (44) (photo).

64 Whilst holding the thermostat assembly (50) so that the alignment mark is opposite the mark on the body (53), tighten the three screws (44) evenly (photo).

65 Fit the gasket (48) and the cover (47), then insert and tighten the retaining bolt (46) with the gasket (45).

66 The automatic choke fast idling adjustment must now be made. Open and close the throttles and make sure that the fast idling adjustment screw (66) is against the fast idle cam highest point with the choke valves completely shut. Using a small drill or a feeler gauge, check that the distance from the throttle valves to the outer wall of the barrels by the progression holes is as given in the adjustment data. If not, adjust the fast idling

9.57 Checking the shaft arm to rod clearance (DGAS type)

9.58 Adjusting the rod stop screw (DGAS type)

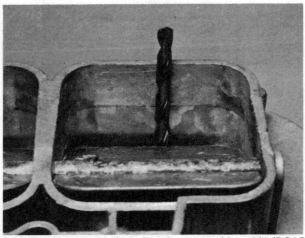

9.59 Checking the choke valve clearance with a drill (DGAS type)

9.63 Automatic choke thermostat bi-metallic spring (DGAS type)

9.64 Automatic choke alignment marks (DGAS type)

screw (66) to give the correct clearance.

67 Slightly open the throttles and, by moving the choke valves, position the adjustment screw (66) into the step on the fast idling cam. The distance from the lower edge of the choke valves to the intake walls must now be as given in the adjustment data.

68 Fully open the throttles and slowly close the choke valves. The fast idle cam should rotate until the adjustment screw (66) rests against the step. If not, re-check the idling screw (73) adjustment and the fast idling screw (66) adjustment and correct so that the above check is achieved.

10 Tuning

Note: *Refer to Chapter 3 for general notes on tuning.*

1 The idling adjustment screws should be set to their preliminary positions as described in Sections 8 and 9.

2 Connect a tachometer to the engine in accordance with the manufacturer's instructions.

3 Start the engine and run until normal operating temperature has been reached (ie the thermostat has opened).

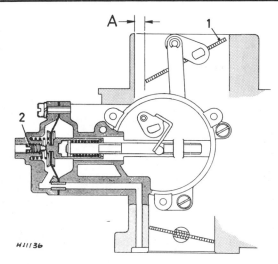

Fig. 9.23 Automatic choke minimum gap setting (DGAS types) (Sec 9)

1 *Choke valves*   *A Choke valve clearance*
2 *Adjustment screw*

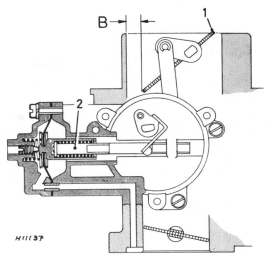

Fig. 9.24 Automatic choke maximum gap setting (DGAS types) (Sec 9)

1 *Choke valves*   *B Choke valve clearance*
2 *Operating rod*

4   Turn the throttle valve idling adjusting screw so that the engine runs at the recommended idling speed for the particular engine being worked on; this will be between 600 rpm and 800 rpm for touring models and approximately 1000 rpm for sports car models.
5   Turn the idle mixture adjustment screws in or out by equal amounts until the engine runs at the highest rpm commensurate with even running.
6   Re-adjust the throttle valve adjusting screw, if necessary, to bring the engine speed within limits.
7   Ideally a vacuum gauge should be used to make the adjustment described in paragraph 5, in which case the mixture adjustment screws are adjusted to give the maximum vacuum reading.
8   When the adjustment is completed, switch off the engine and remove the tachometer and vacuum gauge if fitted.
9   On bypass idle type carburettors, the procedure is similar but the bypass idle adjustment screw should be first fully screwed in, then screwed out 1 full turn. The basic idle adjustment is then made in the normal way and the bypass idle adjustment used for any final adjustment of speed. If an exhaust analyser is available, the percentage of CO should be made on the basic idle adjustment, prior to making the final speed adjustment on the bypass idle screw.

11 Fault diagnosis

Symptom	Reason/s
Engine will not start	Faulty automatic choke Blocked fuel filter or jets
Uneven idling	Leaking carburettor flange or manifold gasket Loose idling jets or auxiliary venturis Excessive sediment or water in carburettor Throttle shafts and bearings or carburettor body excessively worn Faulty automatic choke Leaking ignition advance tube
Carburettor floods	Worn needle valve Leaking or damaged float assembly Incorrect float level adjustments Excessive sediment in fuel
Engine lacks performance	Incorrect tuning adjustments Incorrect float level adjustments Excessive sediment in fuel Faulty acceleration pump Throttle valves do not fully open
Excessive fuel consumption	Needle valve not seating Leaking or damaged float assembly Incorrect float level adjustments Faulty automatic choke Choked air filter

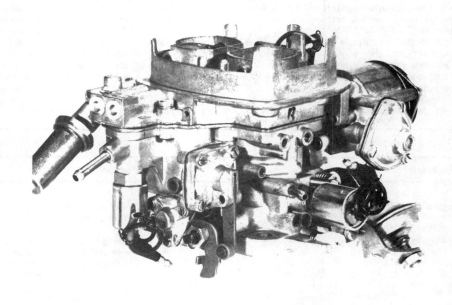

Part 2
Chapter 10 Type 32 DFT,
32 DFTA, 32 DFTA1 carburettors

Contents

Adjustment data

	Closed position	Open position	Stroke
Float level setting dimensions			
32 DFT type (UK)	0·315 in (8·0 mm)	0·630 in (16·0 mm)	0·315 in (8·0 mm)
32 DFTA and 740 types (USA)	0·276 in (7·0 mm)	0·630 in (16·0 mm)	0·354 in (9·0 mm)

	Maximum	Minimum
Automatic electric choke vacuum pull down		
32 DFT type	0·197 in to 0·236 in (5·0 mm to 6·0 mm)	0·128 in to 0·148 in (3·25 mm to 3·75 mm)
32 DFTA type		0·108 in to 0·128 in (2·75 mm to 3·25 mm)
740 type	0·196 in to 0·198 in (4·98 mm to 5·02 mm)	

Automatic electric choke phasing
32 DFT and 32 DFTA types . . . .   0·157 in to 0·177 in (4·0 mm to 4·5 mm)

Automatic electric choke de-choke   in (mm)
32 DFT type . . . .   0·157 to 0·236 (4·0 to 6·0)
32 DFTA type . . . .   0·118 to 0·197 (3·0 to 5·0)
740 type . . . .   0·157 (4·0) minimum

Automatic electric choke fast idle primary throttle valve opening
                                                                 in (mm)
32 DFT type . . . .   0·020 to 0·022 (0·50 to 0·55)
32 DFTA type . . . .   0·024 to 0·026 (0·60 to 0·65)
740 type . . . .   0·078 to 0·080 (1·98 to 2·02)

Dashpot positive opening
32 DFTA and 740 types . . . .   0·020 in to 0·022 in (0·50 mm to 0·55 mm)

Approximate CO percentage at idle speed
(Refer to engine manufacturer's specification for
correct amount) . . . .   1·5%

1 Introduction

The carburettor types covered in this Chapter are all of downdraught design and are of dual barrel construction to supply the primary and secondary functions.

Each throttle valve is mounted on a separate shaft and is of differential or progressive choke type. The linkage between the two throttle valve shafts is arranged so that the secondary valve does not commence to open until the primary throttle valve is $\frac{2}{3}$ open.

A semi-automatic fully electric choke control is incorporated and the idle circuit includes a solenoid operated cut-off valve.

The USA version incorporates a solenoid operated vent valve, an additional vacuum take off point and a dashpot.

The carburettor is fitted to the engine as a single unit with both barrels feeding a common inlet manifold. The most common fitting is on a transverse, four-cylinder in-line engine.

The carburettor identification mark is located on the lower flange outer surface (photo).

1.6 Carburettor identification location

2 Construction

The main body and cover are of die-cast zinc alloy (Mazak) construction. The mounting flange is machined flat for fitting purposes. The cover incorporates a mounting flange for the air cleaner assembly.

The throttle valves are of brass and the throttle shafts, which run in Teflon (PTFE) bushes, are of steel. The choke valves are of cadmium plated steel. The choke shafts, which also run in Teflon bushes, are also of steel.

With the exception of the accelerator pump delivery valve and jet which is die cast, all fuel and air jets are of brass construction and are screwed into the main body.

Internal channels of the main body and cover are mostly drilled and are sealed with lead plugs where necessary.

The float assembly comprises two plastic semi-floats.

3 Operation

Cold starting

Refer to Fig. 10.5. When the engine is cold and the throttle pedal has been depressed once, the bi-metallic spring in the electric choke housing (19) rotates the shaft (15) and closes the choke valves. At the same time, the fast idle cam within the automatic choke housing (27) prevents the primary throttle valve (59) from completely closing.

When the engine is cranked, a rich mixture is drawn from the nozzle in the auxiliary venturi (88) to facilitate starting. As soon as the engine fires, vacuum from below the throttle valve is relayed through a channel to the diaphragm (26). The shaft (15) then moves and partially opens the choke valves against the action of the bi-metallic spring. If the throttle is opened at this stage, the vacuum will cease and the choke valves will close; however, the passage of air will open the choke valves against the action of the bi-metallic spring and the internal auxiliary spring, due to the valve fulcrums being offset.

As soon as the engine is running, current from the alternator is relayed to the electric choke and a heating element commences to heat the bi-metallic spring which progressively opens the choke valves over a predetermined engine warm-up period. At the end of this period the choke valves are held fully open and the fast idle cam is rotated so that the throttle valve (59) and lever (46) is free to return to its normal idling position.

Idling and progression

When the engine is idling, fuel is drawn from the float chamber, through internal channels to the primary well. It is then drawn through the primary idle fuel jet and is emulsified with air entering through a calibrated bush. The fuel and air is then drawn past the idling mixture adjustment screw (66), through the idling feed hole and into the primary carburettor throat at the engine side of the primary throttle valve (59).

When the primary throttle valve is opened slightly to increase the engine speed, the progression holes are brought into action to provide extra fuel.

When the primary throttle valve is $\frac{2}{3}$ open, the secondary throttle valve will commence to open. The secondary progression holes will then provide mixture to the secondary barrel through the secondary idle jet and calibrated bush.

When either throttle valve is sufficiently open, the idling and progression system ceases and the main fuel supply system operates.

Normal running

Under normal cruising conditions the main fuel supply circuit is brought into action. Fuel flows from the float chamber to the primary emulsion tube well, through the main jet (38) and is emulsified with air entering through the air corrector jet (34) and through the holes in the emulsion tube (35). The fuel/air mixture is then drawn through the nozzle in the auxiliary venturi (88) and mixes with the main air supply as it is drawn through the primary choke into the engine.

The secondary main fuel supply operates in an identical manner as the primary, but commences at a higher engine speed.

With both throttle valves fully open, the overfeed enrichment circuit is brought into action to provide full power. Under these conditions the air velocity through the carburettor is high

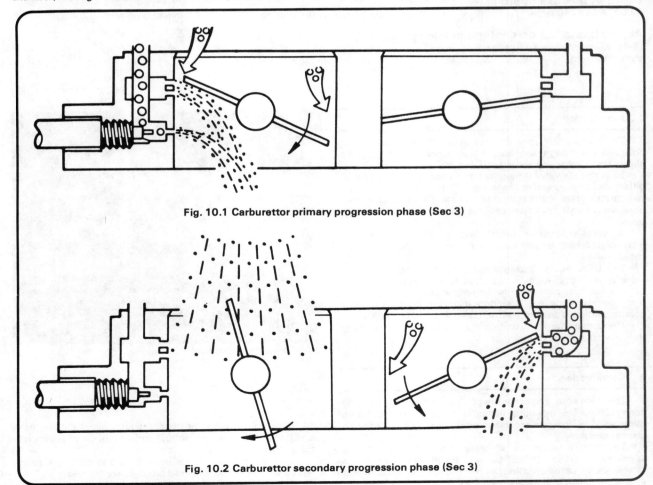

Fig. 10.1 Carburettor primary progression phase (Sec 3)

Fig. 10.2 Carburettor secondary progression phase (Sec 3)

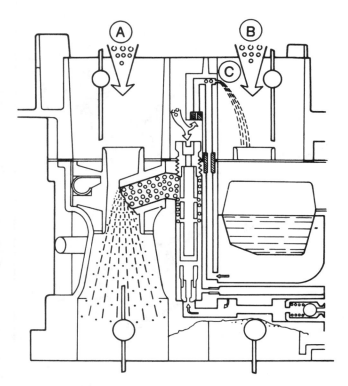

Fig. 10.3 Carburettor full power overfeed phase (Sec 3)

A   Primary barrel
B   Secondary barrel
C   Enrichment aperture

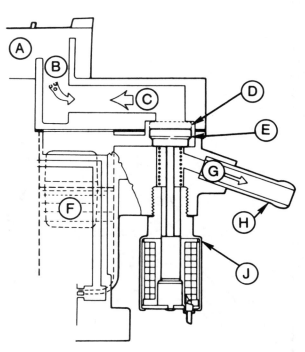

Fig. 10.4 Float chamber vent valve operation (Sec 3)

A   Carburettor intake   F   Float
B and C Vapour movement   G   Vapour movement with
         with ignition on   ignition off
D   Valve seat position with   H   Canister tube connection
     ignition off   J   Solenoid
E   Valve seat

and extra fuel is drawn out of the orifice located at the top of the secondary intake horn. At the same time air is drawn through a calibrated bush to emulsify the fuel.

To provide full power immediately the primary throttle valve is opened quickly, the carburettor incorporates a full power valve. Under these conditions the vacuum through an internal channel is insufficient to draw the diaphragm (78) against the spring (77) and the full power valve is therefore opened. The fuel level in the primary emulsion tube well immediately rises and the mixture drawn from the primary nozzle is enrichened. When the primary throttle valve is partially open, the vacuum at the engine side of the secondary throttle valve is relayed through the internal channel and is now sufficient to overcome the tension of the spring (77). The full power valve then shuts and the spring-loaded ball contacts the valve seat.

Acceleration

To provide the engine with a rich mixture when accelerating, the carburettor is provided with a diaphragm type acceleration pump which is operated by the primary throttle shaft and injects only into the primary venturi.

When the primary throttle valve is closed, the accelerator pump diaphragm draws fuel from the float chamber through an internal ball-valve and into the pump chamber. When the primary throttle valve is opened, the cam (74) moves the lever on the cover (70) and fuel is forced along a channel and through the delivery valve and pump jet (87). A spring in the diaphragm assembly (71) absorbs the initial movement of the lever and extends the fuel delivery period. Excess fuel and any accumulated air is discharged into the float chamber through a channel and calibrated bush.

Idle cut-off valve operation

As soon as the ignition is switched off, this valve stops the flow of fuel mixture from the idle circuit. With the ignition switched on, the idle circuit operates normally.

The valve eliminates any tendency for the engine to run on when the ignition is switched off.

Float chamber vent valve operation (USA types only)

The valve controls two separate vent circuits. When the ignition is on and the engine running, the float chamber is vented to the air cleaner through an internal channel. In this condition the valve solenoid is energised and the rubber seating is pulled against the tension of the return spring. When the ignition is switched off, the solenoid is de-energised and the spring then pushes the seating to shut the air cleaner vent passage and open the passage to the evaporative emission carbon canister.

Dashpot operation (USA types only)

When the throttle valve is released, the dashpot retards the action of the throttle as it approaches the idling position; this prevents an over weak mixture and therefore reduces the emission of certain harmful gases from the exhaust system.

---

4   Removal and refitting

Note: *The following procedure gives a general rather than a specific method of removing and refitting the carburettor, as the fitting may vary with different vehicle models.*

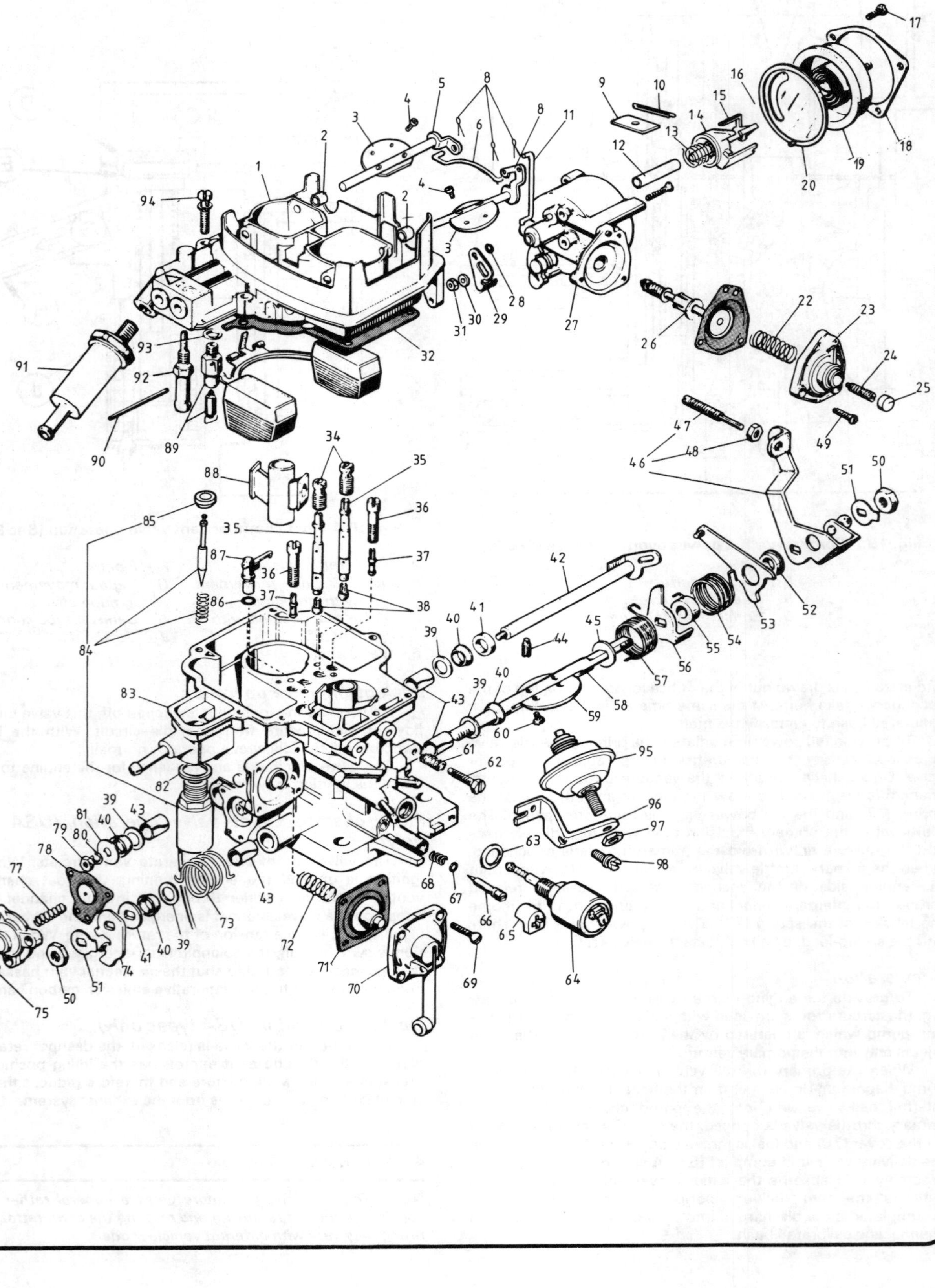
17
8
5
9
10
16
15
4
8
11
14
3
6
13
18
2
12
19
1
20
4
94
2
3
28
31
30
29
27
22
23
26
93
32
24
91
92
25
89
47
49
90
48
46
34
50
88
35
51
85
36
35
87
36
37
42
37
38
52
41
53
40
45
39
54
84
86
44
55
56
57
58
83
43
39
40
59
60
61
95
62
82
39
43
81
40
79
80
96
78
77
97
63
98
68
76
67
73
66
65
72
40
39
43
41
74
71
69
51
64
50
70
75

1 Disconnect the battery earth lead.
2 Remove the air cleaner cover, air filter element and air cleaner body.
3 Disconnect the accelerator cable from the carburettor throttle lever.
4 Pull off the distributor and EGR valve vacuum pipes as applicable.
5 Pull off the external vent pipe, if fitted.
6 Disconnect the fuel inlet hose and return hose.
7 Disconnect the electric choke and idle cut off solenoid supply wires.
8 Disconnect the vent valve solenoid supply wire, where fitted.
9 Unscrew and remove the carburettor mounting nuts and spring washers then withdraw the unit over the mounting studs.
10 Remove the inlet manifold gasket and clean all traces from the contact faces of the inlet manifold and carburettor.
11 Protect the inlet manifold from the ingress of foreign matter by sealing it with masking tape.
12 Refitting is a reversal of removal, but the following additional points should be noted:
    (a) Always fit a new gasket and tighten the four retaining nuts in diagonal sequence
    (b) The idling adjustment screws should be set as described in Section 8 and finally tuned as described in Section 9

5 Disassembly

Note: Throughout the disassembly and assembly Sections, reference will be made to the illustration of the 32 DTFA carburettor which is fitted on vehicles operating in the USA. The 32 DFT carburettor (UK type) is basically the same, although some of the external control components are not fitted.
1 Thoroughly clean the carburettor exterior and wipe dry.
2 Referring to Fig. 10.5, unscrew and remove the fuel filter (91) (photo).

3 Unscrew the carburettor cover retaining screws (94) together with the spring washers. Open the throttle so that the fast idle adjusting screw (47) clears the automatic choke aperture and carefully lift the cover (1) from the main body (83) (photo).
4 Invert the carburettor cover (1) so that the float assembly is uppermost, then extract the float fulcrum pin (90) and withdraw the float assembly (33) together with the needle of the needle valve (89). If necessary, use a suitable diameter pin punch to tap the pin from the two posts, but on no account prise the slotted post apart (photos).
5 Unhook the needle from the float assembly (33).
6 Lift the gasket (32) from the cover (1).
7 Using a box spanner or socket, unscrew the needle valve (89) seating and remove the gasket (93).
8 Unscrew and remove the fuel return pipe check valve (92).
9 Unscrew the electric cable retaining screws (17) and withdraw the retaining ring (18) and housing (19) (photos).
10 Remove the insulation disc (20) (photo), then unscrew and remove the automatic choke housing retaining screws (21). It will be necessary to rotate the choke valve mechanism in order to reach all of the screws.
11 Disengage the choke lever (29) from the primary choke link (11) and withdraw the automatic choke assembly (photo).
12 Prise the rubber O-ring seal (28) from the rear of the housing (27) (photo).
13 Unscrew and remove the choke pull down cover retaining screws (49) and withdraw the cover (23) and spring (22) (photo).
14 Carefully release the thin diaphragm then withdraw the operating rod and diaphragm assembly (26) (photos).
15 Note the location of the internal components of the automatic choke, then unscrew and remove the shaft nut (31) and lockwasher (30).
16 Remove the choke lever (29) then withdraw the shaft (15) and remove the Teflon (PTFE) sleeve (12).
17 Withdraw the lever (14) together with the fast idle cam

Fig. 10.5 Exploded view of the 32 DFTA carburettor (Sec 5)

1	Cover	34	Air corrector jets	67	O-ring seal
2	Bush	35	Emulsion tubes	68	Spring
3	Choke valves	36	Idle jet holders	69	Screw
4	Retaining screws	37	Idle jets	70	Accelerator pump cover
5	Secondary choke shaft	38	Main jets	71	Diaphragm
6	Link	39	Washer	72	Spring
7	Spring clips	40	Teflon seal	73	Return spring
8	Primary choke shaft	41	Secondary shaft spacer	74	Pump cam
9	Seal	42	Secondary throttle shaft	75	Screw
10	Plug	43	Teflon bushes	76	Power valve cover
11	Link	44	Secondary throttle stop screw	77	Spring
12	Teflon sleeve	45	Spacers	78	Diaphragm
13	Spring	46	Throttle lever	79	Nut
14	Choke lever	47	Fast idle adjustment screw	80	Lockwasher
15	Choke shaft	48	Locknut	81	Washer
16	Auxiliary spring	49	Screw	82	Washer
17	Screw	50	Nut	83	Main body
18	Retaining ring	51	Locktab	84	Vent valve assembly
19	Electric choke unit	52	Bush	85	Valve seat
20	Insulator	53	Intermediate lever	86	O-ring seal
21	Screw	54	Return spring	87	Pump delivery valve and jet
22	Spring	55	Spacer	88	Auxiliary venturi
23	Pull down cover	56	Stop	89	Needle valve
24	Adjusting screw	57	Return spring	90	Fulcrum pin
25	Seal	58	Primary throttle shaft	91	Fuel filter
26	Diaphragm and spindle assembly	59	Throttle valve	92	Fuel return check valve
27	Choke housing	60	Retaining screw	93	Gasket
28	O-ring seal	61	Spring	94	Screw
29	Lever	62	Idle speed screw	95	Dashpot
30	Lockwasher	63	Washer	96	Bracket
31	Nut	64	Idle cut-off solenoid	97	Locknut
32	Gasket	65	Limiter cap	98	Screw
33	Float	66	Idle mixture screw		

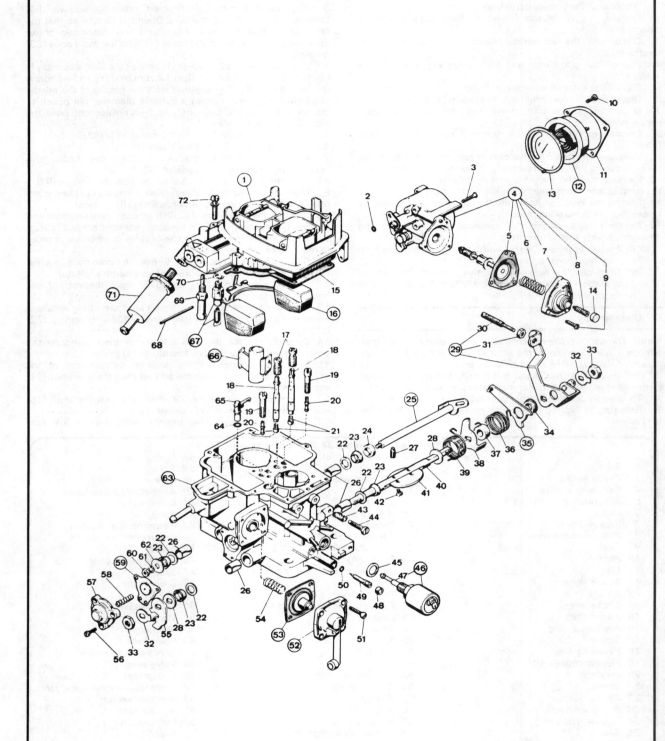

5.2 Removing the fuel filter

5.3 Lifting the carburettor cover

5.4a Extracting the float fulcrum pin

5.4b Removing the float and needle valve

5.9a Removing the electric choke housing

5.9b Showing the location of the electric choke bi-metallic spring

Fig. 10.6 Exploded view of the 32 DFT carburettor (Sec 5)

1 Cover	25 Secondary throttle shaft	49 Idle mixture adjusting screw
2 O-ring seal	26 Teflon bushes	50 O-ring seal
3 Screw	27 Secondary throttle stop screw	51 Screw
4 Automatic choke	28 Spacer	52 Accelerator pump cover
5 Diaphragm and spindle assembly	29 Throttle lever	53 Diaphragm assembly
6 Spring	30 Adjustment screw	54 Spring
7 Cover	31 Locknut	55 Pump cam
8 Adjusting screw	32 Tab washer	56 Screw
9 Screw	33 Nut	57 Power valve cover
10 Screw	34 Bush	58 Spring
11 Retaining ring	35 Intermediate lever	59 Diaphragm
12 Electric choke unit	36 Return spring	60 Nut
13 Insulator	37 Spacer	61 Lockwasher
14 Seal	38 Stop lever	62 Washer
15 Gasket	39 Return spring	63 Main body
16 Float assembly	40 Primary throttle shaft	64 O-ring seal
17 Air corrector jets	41 Throttle valve	65 Pump delivery valve and jet
18 Emulsion tubes	42 Retaining screw	66 Auxiliary venturi
19 Idle jet holders	43 Spring	67 Needle valve
20 Idle jets	44 Idle speed screw	68 Fulcrum pin
21 Main jets	45 Washer	69 Fuel return check valve
22 Washer	46 Idle cut-off valve	70 Gasket
23 Teflon seal	47 Needle	71 Fuel filter
24 Secondary throttle shaft spacer	48 Tamperproof seal	72 Screw

5.10 Electric choke heat insulation disc location

5.11 Disengaging the electric choke lever

5.12 O-ring seal location on the rear of the electric choke

5.13 Removing the choke pull down cover and spring

5.14a Withdrawing the electric choke operating rod

5.14b Locking bush location on the electric choke operating rod

5.18 Location of the electric choke fast idle cam and weight

5.19 Choke link locations on the carburettor cover

5.24a Removing the accelerator pump cover ...

5.24b ... diaphragm and spring

5.25 Extracting the accelerator pump delivery valve and jet

5.26 Removing the idle cut-off valve

spring (13), then remove the spring (13) from the slot in the lever.

18 Using a suitable diameter metal rod, drive the bush through the automatic choke housing and remove the fast idle cam and weight (photo).

19 Extract the spring clips (7) from the choke links (6 and 11) and remove the links (photo). The lower link (6) must be turned behind the automatic choke mounting before it can be removed.

20 Note the location of each choke valve (3) and mark them, if necessary, with a pencil.

21 Close each choke valve (3) in turn and unscrew the retaining screws (4).

22 Withdraw the choke valves (3) and remove the choke shafts (5 and 8) together with the Teflon bushes (2). Keep the shafts and bushes separate to ensure correct refitting.

23 Using a screwdriver, prise the plug (10) and seal (9) from the cover (1).

24 Unscrew and remove the accelerator pump cover retaining screws (69), then withdraw the cover (70), gasket and diaphragm (71) and spring (72) (photos). *Do not attempt to separate the gasket from the diaphragm as these items are adhered together on manufacture.*

25 Using a screwdriver, prise the accelerator pump delivery valve and jet (87) from the main body (photo), then prise the O-ring seal (86) from the valve.

26 Unscrew and remove the idle cut-off valve (64) and note the number of gaskets (63). Remove the needle from the valve (photo).

27 On USA types only, unscrew and remove the float chamber vent solenoid (84) and washer (82) and withdraw the rod and spring. Pull the rubber seal (85) from the rod (photos).

28 Unscrew and remove the power valve retaining screws (75) and withdraw the cover (76), spring (77) and diaphragm (78) (photos). Take care not to damage the diaphragm (78) and if necessary, ease it away with a thin screwdriver. Do not attempt to remove the brass insert from the main body.

29 Where fitted on USA types, unscrew the dashpot mounting screw (98) and spring washer and remove the assembly (photo). If necessary, unscrew the nut (97) and remove the dashpot (95) from the bracket (96).

30 Pull the idle limiter cap (65) from the idle mixture adjusting screw (66), then unscrew and remove the screw (66) and spring (68) (photo).

31 Prise the O-ring seal (67) from the adjusting screw (66).

32 Mark the position and location of the auxiliary venturis (88), then remove them from the primary and secondary barrels (photos). If they are tight, open each throttle valve in turn and use a plastic or wooden rod to tap them out. Failure of this method to remove the auxiliary venturis will necessitate obtaining a special Weber removal tool.

33 Unscrew the primary and secondary idle jet holders (36) from the carburettor body and place them in separate marked containers.

34 Separate the idle jets (37) from the holders (36) by pulling them apart (photos).

35 Unscrew the primary and secondary air corrector jets (34), remove them and place them in separate marked containers.

36 Separate the air corrector jets (34), emulsion tubes (35) and main jets (38) by pulling them apart (photo). If they are tight, pliers may be used, but interpose a piece of wood to avoid damaging the surface of the jets.

37 Unscrew and remove the idle speed adjustment screw (62) and spring (61).

38 Bend back the tab washer (51) and unscrew the nut (50) from the end of the primary throttle shaft (58) (photo). If the nut is excessively tight, temporarily fit the idle speed adjustment screw (62) less the spring (61), and turn it almost fully in; this will prevent any damage to the primary throttle valve (59) and shaft (58).

39 Remove the nut (50), tab washer (51), throttle lever (46),

5.27a Removing the float chamber vent solenoid (USA type)

5.27b Removing the vent solenoid valve (USA types)

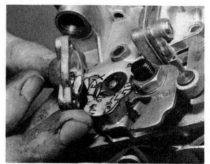

5.28a Lifting off the power valve cover, spring ...

5.28b ... and diaphragm

5.29 Dashpot location (USA types)

5.30 Idle mixture adjusting screw

5.32a Removing an auxiliary venturi

5.32b An auxiliary venturi showing size identification

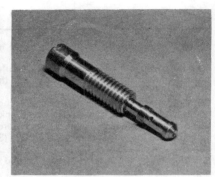

5.34a Idle jet components

5.34b Idle jet and emulsion tube locations in the main body

5.36 An air corrector jet and emulsion tube

5.38 Primary throttle shaft tab washer and lever location

5.39 Primary throttle shaft with lever removed

5.40 Primary throttle shaft stop lever location

5.42 Primary throttle valve and retaining screws

5.51 Removing the secondary throttle shaft nut

5.52 Removing the secondary throttle valve retaining screws

5.55 Showing the correct location of the secondary throttle shaft spacer, seal and washer

lever (53) and bush (52). It will be necessary to disengage the lever (53) from the return spring (54) (photo).

40 Remove the spring (54) and spacer (55), then remove the stop lever (56) whilst tensioning it against the spring (57) (photo).

41 Disengage the stop lever (56) then withdraw the spring (57) and spacer (45).

42 Mark the primary throttle valve (59) with a pencil so that it can be refitted in its original position, then unscrew and remove the retaining screws (60) (photo).

43 Fully open the primary throttle and remove the valve (59) from the shaft (58) whilst holding the shaft against the tension of the spring (73).

44 Check that the throttle shaft (58) is not damaged where the retaining screws have been peened; if it is, carefully file the shaft with a fine file. If this precaution is not taken, the Teflon bushes (43) may be damaged when the shaft is removed. If the retaining screws (60) are tight due to previous peening, use a file to remove the ends of the screws completely; this will also prevent damage to the shaft (58).

45 Carefully withdraw the primary throttle shaft (58) from the main body, at the same time release the tension on the spring (73).

46 Remove the return spring (73), then prise the outer Teflon seals (40) and washers (39) from the main body.

47 Using a screwdriver, extract the Teflon bushes (43) from the main body; identify them for refitting.

48 Mount the primary throttle shaft (58) in a shaft jaw vice and note the position of the accelerator pump cam.

49 Bend back the tab washer (51) and unscrew the nut (50).

50 Remove the nut (50), tab washer (51), pump cam (74) and spacer washer (45).

51 Unscrew and remove the secondary throttle shaft nut (79) and remove the spring washer (80) and spacer (81) (photo).

52 Close the secondary throttle and mark it with a pencil so that it can be refitted in its original position, then unscrew and remove the retaining screws (60) (photo). If they are tight, remove the peened ends of the screws with a file.

53 Fully open the secondary throttle and remove the valve (59) from the shaft (42).

54 Check the secondary throttle shaft (42) for damage in the vicinity of the retaining screw holes. Use a fine file to remove any irregularities.

55 Withdraw the secondary throttle shaft (42) from the main body, then prise out the outer Teflon seals (40) and washers (39). Remove the spacer (41) (photo).

56 Using a screwdriver, extract the Teflon bushes (43) from the secondary shaft bore in the main body. Identify them so that they can be refitted in their original locations (photo).

5.56 Removing a Teflon bush from the secondary throttle shaft bore

6 Special overhaul procedures

After carrying out the general overhaul procedures given in Chapter 4, the following special procedures should be made:

1 Reform the idling jet seats using the special Weber tool, carefully rotating it in alternate directions. Finish the seatings with the further Weber tool by gently tapping the tool whilst rotating it.

2 Reform the main jet seats at the bottom of the emulsion tube bores using the same procedure described in paragraph 1.

3 Check the Teflon bushes and seals of the choke and throttle valve shaft bores for deterioration and wear and renew them if necessary.

4 Check the choke and throttle shafts for distortion (as a result of peening) in the area around the valve retaining screws. Use a small file to remove any irregularities.

5 Check the internal channels of the main body and cover for blockage by injecting fuel with a syringe and observing that it emerges freely from the particular channel being tested. If any are blocked in the main body, the lead plugs must be drilled out and the channels cleared and checked with Weber tool nos 98014 300, 98014 400 and 98014 500. The channels are of three diameters, ie 1.0 mm, 1.5 mm and 2.0 mm.

6 The main body and cover should be thoroughly cleaned after overhaul, preferably using clean fuel and air pressure. The lead plugs should be renewed and retained in position by using a flat punch to expand them into their bores.

7 Check the condition of the power valve and accelerator pump diaphragms and internal surfaces and renew the diaphragms as necessary. Remove any corrosion or deposits from internal surfaces with a little metal polish.

8 During the manufacture of the carburettor, a ball is inserted into the accelerator pump channel and retained by a brass plug. Check that this ball is free and unobstructed by shaking the carburettor and listening to the ball movement.

9 Check the internal channel of the automatic choke for freedom of blockage. Make sure that the diaphragm and corresponding surfaces are serviceable; if necessary, clean the surfaces with metal polish.

10 Check the roller fitted to the accelerator pump lever for wear and renew it if necessary.

11 It is recommended that the in-line fuel filter is renewed every time the carburettor is dismantled for major overhaul.

12 Check the idle cut-off valve needle and vent valve seating (USA types only) for wear and deterioration. The valve solenoids can be checked for correct operation by connecting a 12 volt positive supply to the lead wires and negative supply to the solenoid bodies. If either valve is proved faulty, renew it.

13 Check the operation of the dashpot (USA types only) and renew it if necessary.

14 Check that the power valve ball and spring are free to operate when depressed with a screwdriver. If the valve is defective, it cannot be renewed and the only course of action is to obtain a new carburettor.

7 Assembly

Note: *All components should be clean and dry before starting the assembly procedure.*

1 Insert the Teflon bushes (43) into the secondary shaft bore in the main body. To do this, curl them into a small diameter and expand them into the bores making sure that they are fully entered.

2 Fit the washers (39) and outer Teflon seals (40) making sure that the closed ends of the latter are entered first (photo).

3 Fit the spacer (41) to the secondary throttle shaft (42), then fit the shaft to the main body so that the lever lug locates against the secondary throttle stop screw (44).

4 Fit the spacer (81), spring washer (80), and secondary throttle shaft nut (79). Tighten the nut (79) with the lever against the bottom of the float chamber.

5   Close the secondary throttle shaft against the stop screw then open it approximately 90°.

6   Insert the secondary throttle valve (59) into the shaft slot, then close the valve and check that the angled perimeter seats correctly in the secondary barrel.

7   With the throttle valve (59) held firmly closed, insert the retaining screws (60) and tighten them evenly. It is recommended that new screws are always fitted as it is quite easy to cross-thread previously peened screws. Lock the screws (60) by peening with the Weber tool no 98010 900 whilst supporting the shaft (42) with a block of wood. Alternatively, coat the screw threads with a liquid locking agent (fuel resistant) prior to inserting them.

8   Mount the primary throttle shaft (58) in a soft jaw vice with the short cutaway uppermost, then fit the spacer washer (45), pump cam (74), tab washer (51) and nut (50); tightening the latter finger tight.

9   Insert the Teflon bushes (43) into the primary bore of the main body using the procedure given in paragraph 1.

10   Fit the washers (39) and outer Teflon seals (40) making sure that the closed ends of the latter are entered first.

11   Check that the pump cam (74) on the primary shaft (58) is facing the same way as the countersunk valve retaining screw holes.

12   Fit the return spring (73) (the thick, heavy spring) to the main body making sure that the angled end is fully entered in the locating hole.

13   Insert the primary throttle shaft (58) from the accelerator pump end of the carburettor. At the same time engage the pump cam with the hooked end of the spring (photo).

14   Tension the spring (73) through approximately 180°, fully enter the shaft and release it so that it rests against the power valve casting.

15   Fit the spacer (45) and spring (57), making sure that the angled end of the latter is fully entered in the locating hole.

16   Locate the stop lever (56) over the primary throttle shaft (58), push it fully on and turn it to position the flat edge against the idle speed adjusting screw (62) aperture.

17   Using a small screwdriver, tension the return spring (57) and hook it over the stop lever (56).

18   Fit the spacer (55) and spring (54), making sure that the angled end of the latter is fully entered in the locating hole.

19   Locate the intermediate lever (53) over the primary throttle shaft (58) and engage it with the hooked end of the spring (54).

20   Turn the lever (53) to tension the spring (54), then insert the dowel on the end of the lever (53) into the elongated hole on the end of the secondary throttle shaft (42).

21   Fit the bush (52) into the lever (53) and press both items fully onto the shaft (58), making sure that no coils of the spring (54) are trapped behind the lever.

22   Fit the throttle lever (46), tab washer (51) and nut (50); tightening the latter finger tight.

23   Fully open the primary throttle shaft (58) and insert the primary throttle valve (59) into the shaft slot. Close the valve

and check that the angled perimeter seats correctly in the primary barrel.

24   With the throttle valve (59) held firmly closed, insert the retaining screws (60) and tighten them evenly. Refer to paragraph 7 for details of recommendations for the fitting of the retaining screws.

25   Hold the throttle lever (46) stationary in the closed position and tighten the shaft nuts (50). Do not overtighten the nuts.

26   Bend the tab washers (51) to lock the nuts. Check that the primary and secondary throttle valves operate smoothly and fully.

27   Locate the spring (61) to the idle speed adjustment screw (62) and fit the screw into the main body.

28   Press the main jets (38) fully into the bottom of the emulsion tubes (35), then press the top of the emulsion tubes (35) fully into the air corrector jets (34) making sure that the primary and secondary components are kept separate and identified.

29   Insert the emulsion tubes into their correct locations in the main body and tighten the air corrector jets (34).

30   Press the idle jets (37) fully into their holders (36) keeping the primary and secondary components separate.

31   Insert the idle jets into their correct locations in the main body and tighten the holders (36).

32   Fit the auxiliary venturis (88) into their respective positions as noted previously, making sure that the supply channels are adjacent and that the nozzle cutaway apertures face the throttle valves. Press the auxiliary venturis fully home (photo).

33   Locate the O-ring seal (67) in the groove on the idle mixture adjusting screw (66).

34   Locate the spring (68) on the idle mixture adjusting screw (66), then fit the screw (66) to the main body.

35   Where applicable on USA types, fit the dashpot (95) to the bracket (96), then fit and tighten the nut (97). Locate the bracket (96) to the main body and tighten the retaining screw (98) and spring washer. The dashpot must be adjusted as described later in Section 8.

36   Locate the power valve diaphragm (78) onto the main body with the small dowel entered against the valve ball.

37   With the carburettor on its side, place the spring (77) in the centre of the diaphragm plate and lower the cover (76).

38   Press the cover (76) against the diaphragm, then insert and tighten the retaining screws (75).

39   On USA types only, locate the washer (82) onto the float chamber vent solenoid (84), then tighten the solenoid into the main body. Press the rubber seal (85) over the rod and locate the spring onto the rod, then lower the rod into the valve solenoid from the top of the carburettor.

40   Insert the needle into the idle cut-off valve (64) and fit the gaskets (63) in the same quantity as previously noted, then tighten the valve (64) into the main body.

41   Locate the O-ring seal (86) onto the accelerator pump delivery valve and jet (87), then press the jet (87) firmly into the main body, using the flat blade of a screwdriver if necessary.

42   With the carburettor on end, insert the spring (72) into the

7.2 Assembled seals and washer in the secondary throttle shaft bore

7.13 Engaging the primary throttle shaft return spring with the accelerator pump cam

7.32 Inserting an auxiliary venturi

7.43 Correct fitted position of the accelerator pump cover

7.47 Correct fitted position of the choke links

7.67 Float assembly location on the carburettor cover

accelerator pump chamber, then position the gasket and diaphragm (71) onto the spring with the extended section uppermost.

43 Lower the cover (70) onto the gasket and press it firmly against the main body, then insert and tighten the retaining screws (69) evenly and in diagonal sequence (photo).

44 Insert the seal (9) into the cover (1) and retain by pressing the plug (10) into the slot.

45 Insert the Teflon bushes (2) in the choke shaft bores, locating the shorter ones at the inlet end of the cover.

46 Insert the choke shafts (5 and 8) into their correct locations as previously noted; refer to Fig. 10.5 if necessary.

47 Fit the choke links (6 and 11) and retain with the spring clips (7). Make sure the links are entered from the correct sides as shown in Fig. 10.5 (photo).

48 With the choke shafts (5 and 8) in the fully open position, fit the choke valves (3) into their location slots, then close the valves to allow them to centralise. Make sure that the valves are fitted in their previously noted positions with the flat edge facing downward; the stamped line should be uppermost with the valves closed.

49 Insert the valve retaining screws (4) and tighten them evenly. It is recommended that new screws are always fitted as it is quite easy to cross-thread previously peened screws. Lock the screws (4) by peening with the special Weber tool whilst supporting the shafts with a piece of wood. Alternatively, coat the screw threads with a liquid locking agent (fuel resistant) prior to inserting them.

50 Check that the choke valves and links operate fully and smoothly.

51 Locate the automatic choke fast idle cam and weight on the bush and drive the bush fully into the choke housing (27) using a hammer and a plastic or wooden dowel.

52 Insert the spring (13) into the slot in the lever (14), making sure that the angled end locates fully in the special hole.

53 Hold the housing (27) vertical with the cam weight at the bottom, then fit the lever (14) with the plastic prong at the 2 o'clock position, ie the spring extension must be to the left of the internal lever.

54 Locate the Teflon sleeve (12) over the shaft (15), then insert the shaft into the housing (27) so that the short arm engages the slot in the lever (14) and is located below the fast idle cam serrations, ie adjacent to the weight.

55 Hook the spring onto the dowel in the housing, then fit the choke lever (29), lockwasher (30) and nut (31). Note that the lever (29) must be positioned so that it can contact the stop abutment.

56 Tighten the nut (31) whilst holding the plastic lever on the rear of the housing against the spring tension. If this precaution is not taken it is possible to distort the internal arms.

57 Turn the lever (14) anti-clockwise, then insert the operating rod and diaphragm (26) and press the bush firmly into the housing. The diaphragm must be located over the brass dowel.

58 With the housing (27) on end, position the spring (22) on

the diaphragm (26) then lower the cover (23) and press it onto the diaphragm.

59 Insert and tighten the retaining screws (49).

60 Press the rubber O-ring seal (28) to the rear of the housing (27).

61 Engage the choke lever (29) with the primary choke link (11), then insert and tighten the automatic choke housing retaining screws (21).

62 Insert and tighten the fuel return pipe check valve (92) into the carburettor cover (1).

63 Fit the gasket (93) to the needle valve (89) seating then tighten it into the carburettor cover (1).

64 Invert the cover (1) and fit the gasket (32) making sure that it is correctly located.

65 Lower the needle into the needle valve (89) seating.

66 Fit the float assembly (33) between the two fulcrum pivot posts, at the same time insert the tab under the needle hook.

67 Insert the fulcrum pin (90) through the posts and float arm and, if necessary, lightly pinch the slotted post with a pair of flat pliers to retain the pin (photo).

68 The float level adjustment must now be checked in the following manner: Hold the carburettor cover vertically so that the floats hang from the fulcrum pin with the float arm in light contact with the needle ball (ie the ball is not depressed). Obtain a drill or dowel rod of diameter equal to the closed checking dimension (see Adjustment data) and check that the distance from the cover gasket (32) to the nearest part of the floats is correct.

69 If the dimension checked in paragraph 68 is not correct, carefully bend the tab in contact with the needle as necessary.

70 Tilt the carburettor cover so that the floats move away from the cover and the tab on the float arm contacts the needle valve seating. Now, using the same method described in paragraph 68, check the needle valve fully-open dimension (see Adjustment data).

71 If the dimension checked in paragraph 70 is not correct, carefully bend the angled tab as necessary.

72 The difference between the dimensions obtained in paragraphs 68 and 70 is the needle valve stroke, which must be as given in the Adjustment data.

73 Hold the throttle lever open and lower the cover (1) onto the main body, then release the throttle.

74 Insert the cover retaining screws (94) together with spring washers and tighten them evenly in diagonal sequence.

75 Fit and tighten the fuel filter (91).

76 The carburettor is now completely assembled except for the automatic electric choke housing (19). Before fitting this component, the adjustments as given in Section 8 must first be made.

77 To complete the automatic choke assembly, first fit the insulation disc (20) with the location peg at the bottom.

78 Locate the thermostat assembly (19) over the disc, at the same time engage the bi-metallic spring with the choke lever (14).

79 Fit the retaining ring (18) and insert the screws (17).
80 Align the marks on the thermostat assembly (19) and housing (27) (ie centre mark), then tighten the retaining screws (17).
81 Press the limiter cap (65) onto the idle mixture screw (66) with the extension pointing away from the main body abutment.

8 Carburettor adjustments

With the carburettor completely assembled, the following adjustments must be made prior to fitting it to the engine:
1 Fully open the throttle, hold the choke valves fully open and release the throttle. Turn the throttle idling adjustment screw (62) until it just touches the idle stop lever (56), then continue to screw it in 1 complete turn.
2 Turn the idling mixture screw (66) in until it is in light contact with its seat, then back it off 1 complete turn.
3 Turn the secondary throttle adjustment stop (44) until a gap of 0.05 mm (0.002 in) exists between the outer edge of the secondary throttle valve and the secondary barrel. Check the gap with feeler gauges.

Vacuum pull down
4 Fit an elastic band to the choke lever (14) and over the cover (1) so that it holds the choke valves (3) shut. Open the throttle to allow the choke valves to fully close.
5 Using a small electrician's screwdriver, push the contact ring on the diaphragm spindle until the spindle is in firm contact with the adjustment screw (24). Using a drill or metal dowel, check that the distance between the choke valve straight edges and the intake walls is as given in the Adjustment data under maximum vacuum pull down.
6 To check the minimum vacuum pull down, use long nose pliers to hold the diaphragm spindle in firm contact with the adjustment screw (24), but make sure that the modulator spring is compressed fully. Use a drill to make the check in the identical manner to that given in paragraph 5. Note that on some carburettor types the minimum vacuum pull down can be checked by inserting a screwdriver through a hole in the housing (27); on other models this hole is blanked off.
7 If any of the dimensions checked in paragraphs 5 and 6 are not correct, the adjustment screw (24) must be turned as necessary. This will necessitate removing the seal (25) and the owner must be satisfied that no legislation is being contravened by this action.

Choke phasing
8 Open the throttle then release it and position the fast idle adjusting screw (47) on the middle step of the fast idle cam.
9 Close the choke valves as far as possible by turning the choke lever (14) anti-clockwise. Using a drill, check that the distance between the choke valve straight edges and the intake walls is as given in the Adjustment data. If not, carefully bend the short arm on the shaft (15) as necessary (ie the internal arm).

Dechoke adjustment
10 Open the throttle and fully close the choke valves by turning the choke lever (14) anti-clockwise. While holding the lever (14), fully open the throttle. The distance between the choke valve straight edges and the intake walls should be as given in the Adjustment data when checked with a suitable drill. If not, bend the choke lever (29) as necessary.

Fast idle adjustment
11 Open the throttle and position the fast idle adjusting screw (47) on the highest section of the fast idle cam. Using a feeler gauge, check that the distance between the primary throttle valve and the outer barrel wall is as given in the Adjustment data. If not, loosen the locknut (48) and turn the adjusting screw (47) as necessary; tighten the locknut when the adjustment is completed (photo).

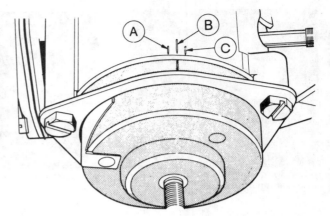

Fig. 10.7 The automatic choke alignment marks (Sec 7)

A Rich position
B Normal position
C Lean position

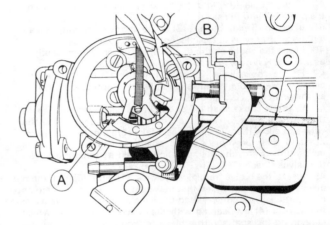

Fig. 10.8 Checking the vacuum pull down adjustment (Sec 8)

A Diaphragm spindle   C Screwdriver (only
B Elastic band   possible on some types)

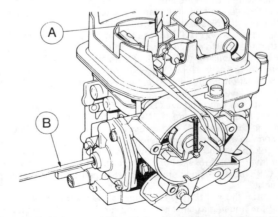

Fig. 10.9 Using a drill to check the vacuum pull down dimension (Sec 8)

A Drill
B Screwdriver

Dashpot adjustment (USA types)

12 Determine the primary throttle opening for adjustment of the dashpot from the Adjustment data.

13 Open the primary throttle, insert the correct size feeler gauge and close the valve onto the gauge.

14 Loosen the dashpot locknut (97) and adjust the dashpot so that its plunger is just touching the throttle lever, then tighten the locknut.

15 Remove the feeler gauge.

9 Tuning

Note: *Refer to Chapter 3 for general notes on tuning.*

1 The idling adjustment screws should be set to their preliminary positions as described in Section 8 paragraphs 1 and 2.

2 Refer to Part 1 of this Manual for information on tamperproofed carburettors.

3 Connect a tachometer to the engine in accordance with the manufacturer's instructions.

4 Connect an exhaust gas analyser to the exhaust pipe in accordance with the manufacturer's instructions.

5 Where an electric fan is fitted, disconnect the sensor wires and connect them together with a further length of wire to ensure that the fan is working continually during the adjustment procedure.

6 Start the engine and run until normal operating temperature has been reached (ie the thermostat has opened).

7 Turn the idling speed adjustment screw so that the engine runs at the recommended idling speed for the particular engine being worked on; this will be approximately 800 rpm.

8 Turn the idle mixture adjustment screw in or out until the engine runs at the highest rpm commensurate with even running. Check that the CO level indicated on the analyser is within the manufacturer's recommended limits and make any fine adjustments to the mixture screw as necessary.

9 If necessary, re-adjust the idle speed screw to bring the engine speed within limits.

10 Switch off the engine and remove the tachometer and

8.11 Showing the throttle lever and the fast idle adjusting screw

analyser, then reconnect the electric fan connections.

11 The automatic choke fast idle setting can be checked if necessary with the engine running. First remove the air cleaner and set the fast idling adjustment screw on the high cam position by fully opening the throttle lever, closing the valves manually and then releasing the throttle. From this stage onward, do not touch the throttle lever otherwise the fast idle cam may move.

12 With the engine at operating temperature and a tachometer connected, check the fast idle engine speed which should be approximately 1800 to 2000 rpm according to the manufacturer's recommendations. If not, loosen the locknut and adjust the fast idle adjusting screw as necessary. When rechecking the speed, always make sure that the adjusting screw is located on the highest section of the fast idle cam.

13 Tighten the locknut, and remove the tachometer.

10 Fault diagnosis

Symptom	Reason
Engine will not start	Faulty automatic choke
	Blocked fuel filter or jets
Uneven idling	Leaking carburettor flange or manifold gasket
	Loose idling jets or auxiliary venturis
	Excessive sediment or water in carburettor
	Worn throttle shaft bushes and seals
	Secondary throttle valve partially sticking open
	Leaking ignition advance tube or EGR tube (USA type)
	Faulty idle cut-off valve
	Faulty vent valve (USA type)
Carburettor floods	Worn needle valve
	Leaking or damaged float assembly
	Incorrect float level adjustment
	Excessive sediment in fuel
Engine lacks performance	Incorrect tuning adjustments
	Incorrect float level adjustments
	Excessive sediment in fuel
	Faulty acceleration pump
	Throttle valves not fully opening
	Faulty vent valves (USA type)
Excessive fuel consumption	Needle valve not seating
	Leaking or damaged float assembly
	Incorrect float level adjustments
	Choked air filter
	Faulty automatic choke

Part 2
Chapter 11 Type 38 to 48 DCOE carburettors

Contents

Adjustment data

Note: *The following information applies to standard Weber fittings only and is not necessarily correct for non-standard fittings.*

Accelerator pump stroke

	in (mm)
40 DCOE Series 2, 4, 24, 27, 28, 32, 33	0·551 (14·0)
45 DCOE Series 15/16	0·551 (14·0)
40 DCOE Series 18, 22/23, 29/30	0·394 (10·0)
42 DCOE Series 8	0·394 (10·0)
45 DCOE Series 9, 14, 14/18, 17	0·394 (10·0)
40 DCOE Series 31, 34/35, 44/45, 76/77	0·630 (16·0)
45 DCOE Series 38/39, 62/63, 68/69	0·630 (16·0)
40 DCOE Series 72/73, 80/81	0·709 (18·0)

Float level setting dimension

	Closed position	Open position	Stroke
40 DCOE Series 2, 4, 18, 22/23, 24, 27, 28, 31, 32, 33, 34/35	0·335 in (8·5 mm)	0·591 in (15·0 mm)	0·256 in (6·5 mm)
45 DCOE Series 14, 14/18, 17	0·335 in (8·5 mm)	0·591 in (15·0 mm)	0·256 in (6·5 mm)
40 DCOE Series 29/30	0·197 in (5·0 mm)	0·453 in (11·5 mm)	0·256 in (6·5 mm)
40 DCOE Series 44/45	0·276 in (7·0 mm)	0·551 in (14·0 mm)	0·276 in (7·0 mm)
40 DCOE Series 72/73, 76/77, 80/81	0·295 in (7·5 mm)	0·551 in (14·0 mm)	0·256 in (6·5 mm)
45 DCOE Series 15/16	0·295 in (7·5 mm)	0·551 in (14·0 mm)	0·256 in (6·5 mm)
42 DCOE Series 8	0·197 in (5·0 mm)	0·532 in (13·5 mm)	0·335 in (8·5 mm)
45 DCOE Series 9: Aston Martin DB4 Vantage GT and Maserati 3500 GT Speciale	0·197 in (5·0 mm)	0·532 in (13·5 mm)	0·335 in (8·5 mm)
Alfa Romeo and Aston Martin DB5	0·276 in (7·0 mm)	0·532 in (13·5 mm)	0·256 in (6·5 mm)
45 DCOE Series 38/39, 62/63, 68/69	0·197 in (5·0 mm)	0·551 in (14·0 mm)	0·354 in (9·0 mm)

1 Introduction

The Weber DCOE carburettor is of the horizontal, side-draught type and has two identical barrels fed by a common centrally located float chamber. The throttle valves are mounted on a common spindle and are of the synchronised, simultaneous operation type.

The carburettor may be fitted on the engine in several different arrangements, the most common being listed as follows:

1 One unit on a four-cylinder in-line engine, ie each barrel feeds two cylinders
2 Two units on a four-cylinder in-line engine, ie each barrel feeds one cylinder via short inlet manifolds
3 Two units on a four-cylinder V-configuration engine, ie each barrel feeds one cylinder
4 Three units on a six-cylinder in-line engine, ie each barrel feeds one cylinder
5 Two units on a six-cylinder in-line engine with one inlet manifold for each carburettor, ie each carburettor feeds three cylinders

The carburettor identification mark is located on the upper cover (photo).

1.3 Identification mark location

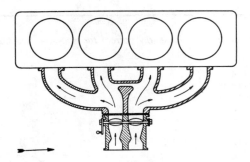

Fig. 11.1 One carburettor fitted to a four-cylinder in-line engine (Sec 1)

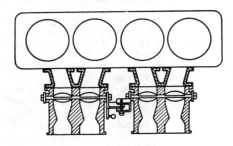

Fig. 11.2 Two carburettors fitted to a four-cylinder in-line engine (Sec 1)

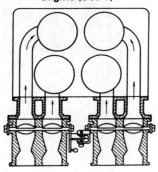

Fig. 11.3 Two carburettors fitted to a four-cylinder V-engine (Sec 1)

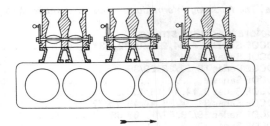

Fig. 11.4 Three carburettors fitted to a six-cylinder in-line engine (Sec 1)

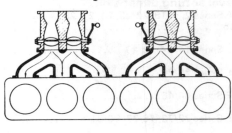

Fig. 11.5 Two carburettors fitted to a six-cylinder in-line engine (Sec 1)

2 Construction

The main body and covers of the Weber DCOE carburettor are of die-cast aluminium construction. The two mounting flanges are machined flat for fitting on the inlet manifold.

Early types are fitted with a brass throttle spindle. Later types have a steel spindle which incorporates two slots to accommodate the two brass throttle valves.

The air horns are of steel construction and are attached to the carburettor body by studs and nuts.

All fuel and air jets and emulsion tubes are of brass construction and are screw fittings into the main body. The internal channels of the main body are mostly drilled and where necessary, sealed with lead plugs.

The throttle spindle is supported by two ball-bearings in most types and spring tensioned seals are incorporated at each end of the spindle to prevent air being drawn through the bearings.

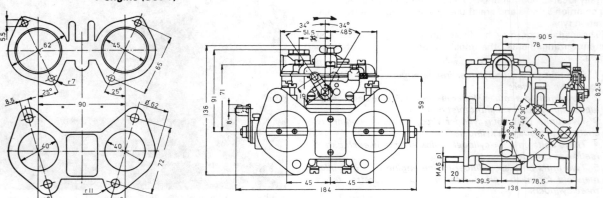

ALL DIMENSIONS IN MILLIMETRES

Fig. 11.6 Overall dimensions of the DCOE carburettor (Sec 2)

The fuel float assembly comprises two semi-floats constructed of thin brass sheet. Each float consists of two halves soldered together.

3 Operation

Cold starting

Not all of the DCOE range of carburettors are fitted with starting devices, the 40 DCOE 20 to 22 and 45 DCOE 12 types being the exception. Where fitted, the starter circuits operate independent of the main circuits and may be considered as separate carburettors within the main carburettor. The system functions as follows:

Operation of the choke (or to be precise cold start) cable moves the starter device lever which, through two intermeshed sector gears, lifts the two starter valves off their seats. Reference to Fig. 11.7 will show that fuel from the float chamber (4) is drawn through the channels (32) to arrive at the starter fuel jets. Air entering the carburettor through hole (29) passes through the top and bottom of the starter jets (30) and emulsifies the fuel which is then drawn through the channels (31), past the starter valves (35), through the channels (33) and into the carburettor throats at the engine side of the throttle valves. It will be observed that additional air is introduced to the emulsified fuel through the starter valve spring retainer guide and through the starter device air filter and channels (34).

Partial operation of the starter device (ie when the engine is warming up) will reduce the amount of fuel admitted to the engine by lowering the starter valves (35) onto their seats and, when completely shut, the supply will cease.

Idling and progression

Refer to Fig. 11.8 and note that when the engine is idling with the throttle valves (17) closed, fuel is drawn from the float chamber (4), through the channels (15) to the bottom of the idling jets (14). On passing through the idling jets, air is introduced through the channels (13) and the holes in the sides of the idling jets and the fuel then becomes emulsified.

The mixture then passes through the channels (20), past the idling adjusting screws (19), through the idling feed holes (18) and into the carburettor throats at the engine side of the throttle valves. The idling adjusting screws (19) have tapered

ends and can therefore be adjusted to admit more or less mixture as necessary.

When the throttle valves are opened slightly to increase the engine speed, the progression holes (16) are brought into action to provide additional fuel. This is necessary in order to prevent a flat spot occuring before the main fuel supply system comes into operation.

Normal running

Under full throttle and high speed cruise conditions, the throttle plates will be sufficiently far from the idling and progression holes to prevent them from admitting fuel and the main supply circuit will be brought into action. Refer to Fig. 11.9 and note that fuel from the float chamber (4) passes through the apertures (6) to the main jets (5) which are located in the bottom of the emulsion tubes (12). Air is drawn through the air corrector jets (11), through the emulsion tube holes and emulsifies the fuel which then passes through the channels (10) to the auxiliary venturis (8). The fuel mixture then passes through the nozzles (7) and mixes with the main air supply as it is drawn through the chokes (9) and into the engine.

It will be observed that under static engine conditions, the fuel levels in the emulsion tubes will be identical to that in the float chambers. As the engine speed increases and the fuel flow is faster, the fuel levels in the emulsion tubes drop. By providing additional holes in the lower part of the emulsion tubes, the necessary air correction is made possible at the higher engine speeds.

Acceleration

To provide the engine with a rich mixture when accelerating, the carburettor is equipped with an accelerator pump. Reference to Fig. 11.10 will show that when the throttle valves are closed, the lever (25) will lift the operating rod (27) against the pressure of the spring (28) and the piston (26) will draw fuel through the intake valve (23), along the channel and into the piston chamber. When the throttle valves are opened, the lever (25) allows the operating rod (27), together with the piston (26), to move down the piston bore under the action of the spring (28). Fuel is therefore forced along the internal channels (22), past the delivery valves (21) and through the pump jets (24) into the carburettor throats. During the pump delivery, the intake valve (23) is closed by the action of the internal ball but a certain amount of fuel is discharged back into the float chamber

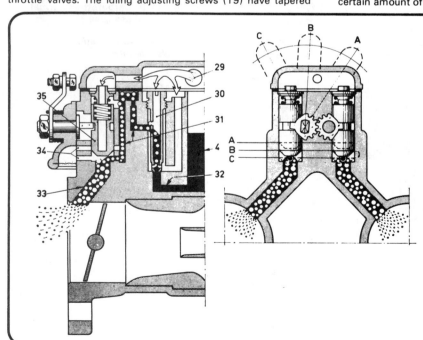

Fig. 11.7 Cold starting device operation (Sec 3)

4   Float chamber
29 Air entry
30 Starting jets
31, 32, 33 and 34 Internal channels
35 Starter valves
A   Cold starting position
B   Warming up position
C   Closed position

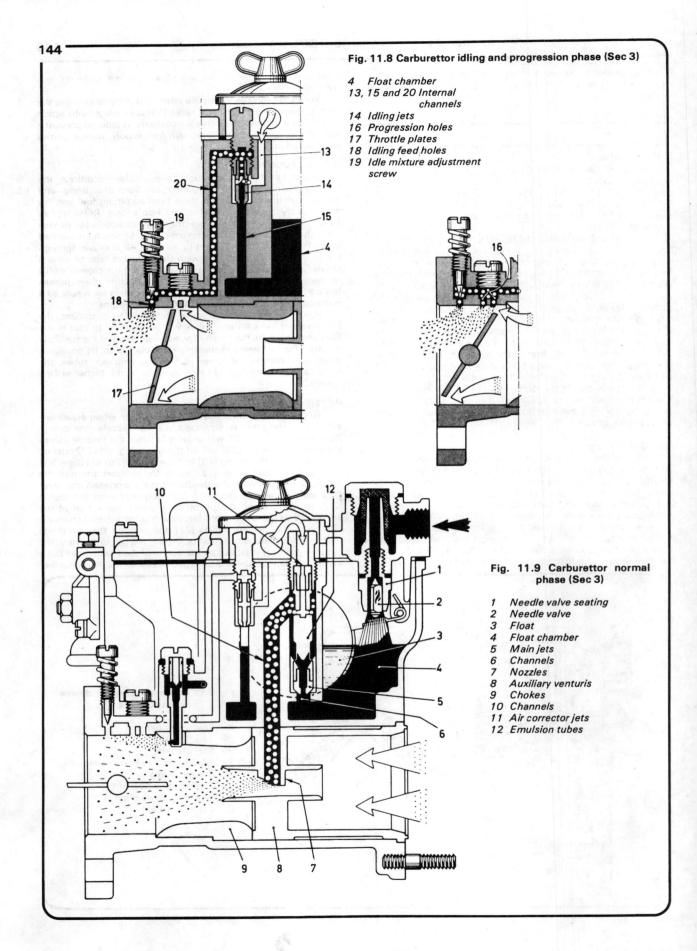

Fig. 11.8 Carburettor idling and progression phase (Sec 3)

4   *Float chamber*
13, 15 and 20 *Internal*
          channels
14   *Idling jets*
16   *Progression holes*
17   *Throttle plates*
18   *Idling feed holes*
19   *Idle mixture adjustment*
      screw

Fig. 11.9 Carburettor normal phase (Sec 3)

1   *Needle valve seating*
2   *Needle valve*
3   *Float*
4   *Float chamber*
5   *Main jets*
6   *Channels*
7   *Nozzles*
8   *Auxiliary venturis*
9   *Chokes*
10   *Channels*
11   *Air corrector jets*
12   *Emulsion tubes*

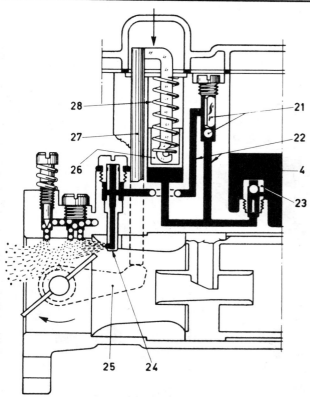

Fig. 11.10 Carburettor acceleration phase (Sec 3)

4	Float chamber	24	Pump jets
21	Delivery valves	25	Pump control lever
22	Channels	26	Piston
23	Intake and discharge	27	Control rod
	valve	28	Pump operating spring

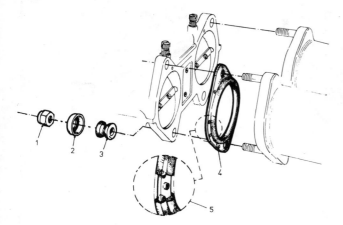

Fig. 11.11 Anti-vibration mounting components (Sec 4)

1	Nylon locknut	4	O-ring gasket
2	Grommet cover	5	Cross-section of O-ring
3	Grommet		gasket

through the discharge hole. By fine calibration of this hole it is possible to determine the exact quantity of fuel injected by the accelerator pump.

4   Removal and refitting

Note: *The following procedure gives a general rather than a specific method of removing and refitting the carburettor, as much will depend on the location of the carburettor within the vehicle. On some applications for instance, the retaining nuts may not be accessible without removing surrounding components.*

1   Unscrew and remove the retaining nuts and withdraw the air cleaner assembly (if fitted).
2   Disconnect the throttle lever operating rod at the lever end by unscrewing the retaining nut.
3   Where necessary, detach the air intake support bracket.
4   Slacken the starter inner cable securing screw and the outer cable securing screw and withdraw the starter cable complete from the carburettor.
5   Unscrew the fuel inlet union bolt and withdraw it together with the two gaskets.
6   Where a common air intake is fitted to more than one carburettor, repeat the procedure given in paragraphs 2 to 5 inclusive on the remaining carburettor(s) and subsequently detach the air intake on the bench.
7   Unscrew and remove the carburettor retaining nuts and spring washers, then carefully withdraw the unit over the mounting studs.
8   Remove the inlet manifold gaskets and clean all traces of gasket from the contact faces of the inlet manifold and carburettor.
9   Protect the inlet manifold from ingress of foreign matter whilst the carburettor is removed by sealing it with masking tape.
10   Refitting is a reversal of removal but the following additional points should be noted:

(a) *Always use new gaskets and spring washers and tighten the retaining nuts in diagonal sequence*
(b) *Where Thackeray double-coil spring washers are fitted, new self-locking nuts must be used. Tighten the self-locking nut to maintain approximately 0.020 in (0.50mm) clearance between adjacent coils of the washer*
(c) *Where an anti-vibration mounting is fitted, first fit both O-ring gaskets, then locate the carburettor over the mounting studs and fit the rubber grommets, covers and locknuts. Tighten the locknuts in diagonal sequence until the covers just contact the grommets which should also be in contact with the carburettor flanges. Now tighten each locknut a further $1\frac{1}{2}$ turns and check that the V-section of each rubber grommet is equal*
(d) *The idling adjustment screws should be set as described in Section 7 and finally turned as described in Section 8*

5   Disassembly

1   Thoroughly clean the carburettor exterior and wipe dry.
2   Referring to Fig. 11.12, unscrew the filter inspection plug (90), remove the gasket (89) and extract the filter and retaining bush (88) (photo).
2   Unscrew the air horn retaining nuts (24A), remove the washers (23A) and retaining plates (25) and withdraw the air intake horns (69) (photo).
4   Unscrew the wing nut and remove the jet inspection cover (1) and gasket (3) (photo) together with the serrated ring (where fitted).
5   Using a large screwdriver, unscrew the carburettor cover retaining screws (2) together with the spring and plain washers (4), then lift off the cover (5) (photo).
6   Remove the plate (13) from the carburettor bowl, then

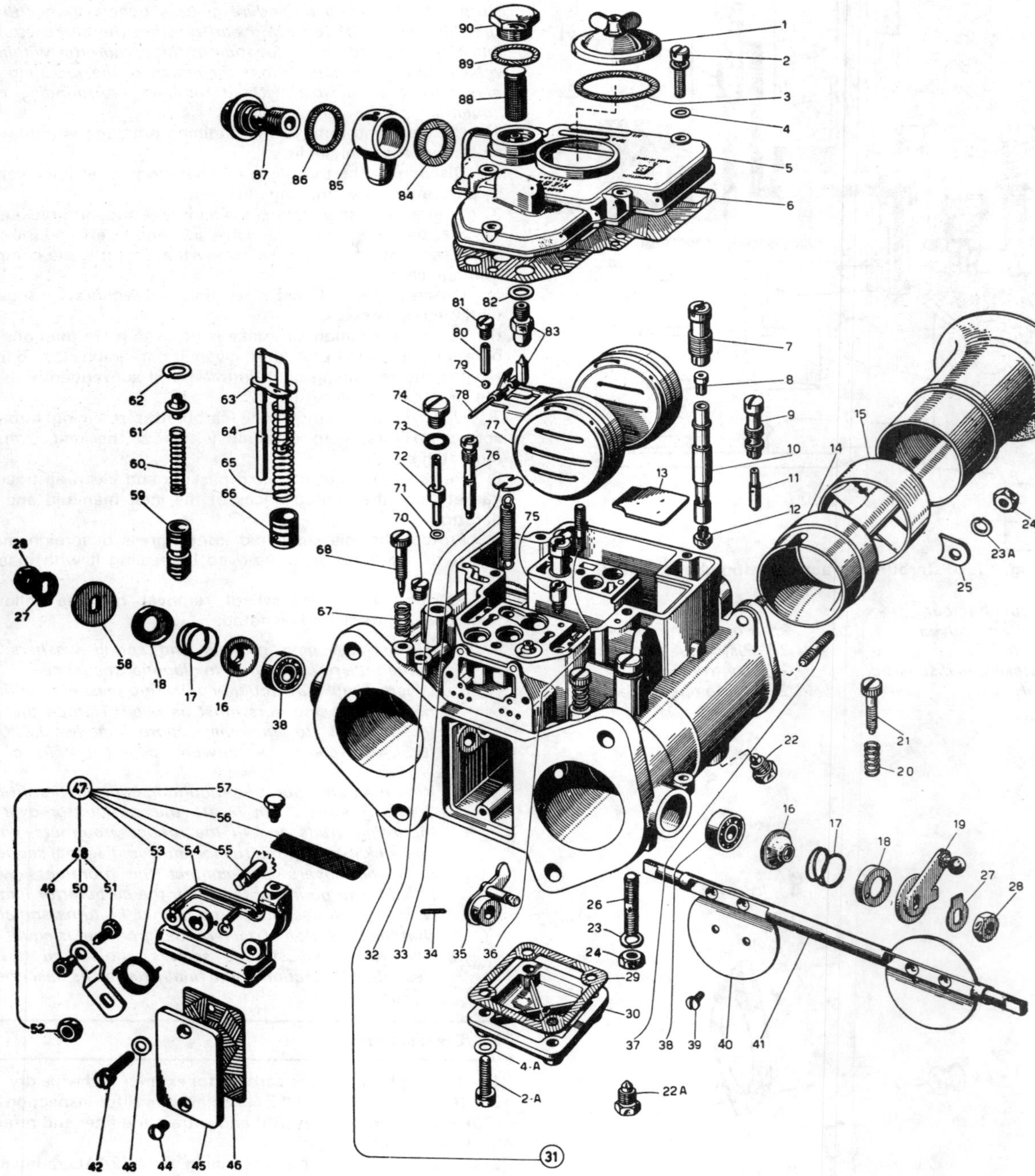
1
2
3
4
5
6
7
8
9
10
11
12
13
14
15
16
17
18
19
20
21
22
22 A
23
23 A
24
24 A
25
26
27
28
29
30
31
32
33
34
35
36
37
38
39
40
41
42
43
44
45
46
47
48
49
50
51
52
53
54
55
56
57
58
59
60
61
62
63
64
65
66
67
68
69
70
71
72
73
74
75
76
77
78
79
80
81
82
83
84
85
86
87
88
89
90
2·A
4·A

5.2 Removing the fuel filter

5.3 Air horn retaining nuts

5.4 Removing the jet inspection cover

5.5 Lifting the carburettor cover

5.6 Location of the carburettor bowl baffle plate

5.7 Removing the well bottom cover

Fig. 11.12 Exploded view of the DCOE carburettor (typical) (Sec 5)

1 Jet inspection cover	30 Well bottom cover	61 Spring retainer and guide
2 and 2A Screw	31 Carburettor body	62 Spring washer
3 Gasket	32 Anchoring plate	63 Retaining plate
4 and 4A Washer	33 Spindle return spring	64 Accelerator pump control rod
5 Carburettor cover	34 Lever fixing pin	65 Spring
6 Gasket	35 Pump control lever	66 Pump piston
7 Emulsion tube holder	36 and 37 Stud	67 Spring
8 Air corrector jet	38 Ball-bearing	68 Idling adjustment screw
9 Idle jet holder	39 Screw	69 Air intake horn
10 Emulsion tube	40 Throttle valve	70 Progression hole inspection screw
11 Idling jet	41 Spindle	71 Gasket
12 Main jet	42 Screw	72 Pump jet
13 Plate	43 Washer	73 Seal
14 Choke	44 Screw	74 Screw plug
15 Auxiliary venturi	45 Cover	75 Intake and discharge valve
16 Dust cover	46 Gasket	76 Starter jet
17 Spring	47 Starter device	77 Float
18 Spring cover	48 Lever	78 Fulcrum pin
19 Throttle lever	49 Nut	79 Valve ball
20 Spring	50 Lever	80 Stuffing ball
21 Throttle adjusting screw	51 Screw	81 Screw plug
22 Auxiliary venturi retaining screw	52 Nut	82 Washer
22A Choke retaining screw	53 Return spring	83 Needle valve
23 and 23A Spring washer	54 Cover	84 and 86 Washer
24 and 24A Nut	55 Sector shaft	85 Union
25 Retaining plate	56 Air filter	87 Union bolt
26 Stud	57 Screw	88 Fuel filter
27 Lockwasher	58 Washer	89 Washer
28 Nut	59 Starter valve	90 Filter inspection plug
29 Gasket	60 Spring	

5.8 Extracting the float fulcrum pin

5.9 Removing the needle and ball from the needle valve seating (40 DCOE 35 type)

5.11a Removing an emulsion tube

5.11b Emulsion tube components

5.12a Removing an idling jet

5.12b Idling jet sections assembled

5.12c Idling jet components

5.14 Removing an idling mixture adjusting screw

5.15 Removing the accelerator pump

5.17a Removing a stuffing ball retaining screw

5.17b Removing a stuffing ball

5.18 Location of the intake and discharge valve

invert the carburettor and unscrew the well bottom cover retaining screws (2A), together with the spring washers and plain washers (4A) (photo).

7 Withdraw the well bottom cover (30) and gasket (29) (photo).

8 Invert the carburettor cover (5) so that the float assembly is uppermost, then extract the float fulcrum pin (78) and withdraw the float assembly (77). If necessary, use a suitable diameter pin punch to tap the pin from the two posts (photo).

9 Remove the needle valve needle and the cover gasket (6) (photo).

10 Using a 10 mm socket, unscrew the needle valve seating (83) and remove the gasket (82).

11 Using a suitable screwdriver, unscrew the emulsion tube assemblies, then separate the tube holders (7), air corrector jets (8), emulsion tubes (10) and main jets (12). Although these parts are a tight fit they must preferably be removed by hand only (photos).

12 Unscrew the idling jet holders (9) and separate the idling jets (11) (photos).

13 Unscrew and remove the throttle idling adjustment screw (21) and spring (20).

14 Unscrew and remove the idling mixture adjusting screws (68) and springs (67) together with the conical washers and O-rings (photo).

15 Carefully prise the accelerator pump retaining plate (63) from the carburettor body and lift out the pump assembly (photo).

16 Disengage the accelerator pump piston (66) from the operating rod (64) and remove the spring (65) and plate (63).

17 Unscrew the stuffing ball retaining screws (81), invert the carburettor body and extract the stuffing balls (80) and the balls for the valves (79) (photos).

18 Unscrew and remove the intake and discharge valve (75) from the bottom of the float chamber (photo).

19 Unscrew the screw plugs (74) and remove the seals (73), pump jets (72) and gaskets (71) (photos).

20 Where a starter device is not fitted, unscrew the retaining screws and remove the blanking plate.

21 Where a starter device is fitted, unscrew and remove the starter jets (76), separate the two sections and follow paragraphs 22 to 25 (photos).

22 Unscrew the starter device retaining screws together with the spring and plain washer and withdraw the starter device assembly (47) from the carburettor (photo).

23 Dismantle the starter device by unscrewing the nut (52) from the shaft (55), then carefully remove the lever (48) and spring (53). Unscrew the cable clamp nut (49) and screw (51), then remove the shaft (55) and filter gauze (56) (photo).

24 Unscrew and remove the progression hole inspection screw plugs (70) (photo).

25 Whilst depressing the starter valve spring retaining guides (61) in turn, prise the spring washers (62) from the carburettor body, then release the guides (61) and extract the return springs (60) and starter valves (59). Note from which bore each valve was taken so that they can be refitted in their original locations (photo).

26 Unscrew and remove the pump opening cover plate retaining screws (44) and withdraw the plate (45) and gasket (46) (photo).

27 Note the location of each throttle plate and mark them if necessary, with a pencil.

28 Unscrew and remove the throttle plate retaining screws (39) with the throttle closed, then open the throttle and withdraw the plates (40) from the spindle (41). If a brass spindle is fitted, be careful not to exert excessive presure with the screwdriver otherwise the spindle will be distorted (photo).

29 Using a pair of pliers, grip the top of the spindle return spring (33), lift it and remove the spring anchoring plate (32).

30 Drive out the lever roll pin (34) with a suitable pin punch; if

5.19a A pump jet retaining screw

5.19b Removing a pump jet

5.21a Removing a starter jet

5.21b The starter jet components

5.22 Removing the starter device, showing the locating lugs

5.23 Removing the starter device air filter gauge, also showing sector alignment marks

5.24 Removing a progression hole inspection screw plug

5.25 Extracting a starter valve, spring and guide

5.26 Removing the accelerator pump opening cover plate and gasket

5.28 Withdrawing a throttle valve from the spindle

5.31 Throttle spindle outer retaining nut and locktab

5.32 Removing a spring cover from the throttle spindle

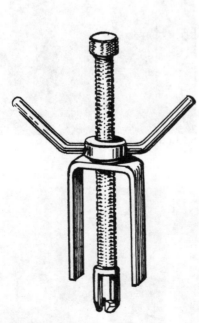
Fig. 11.13 Auxiliary venturi extracting tool (Sec 5)

5.37 Removing an auxiliary venturi, showing the locating spring

5.38 Removing a choke from the carburettor barrel

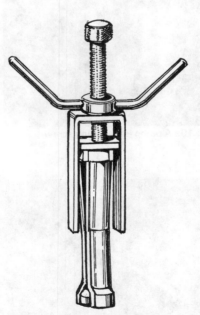
Fig. 11.14 Choke extracting tool (Sec 5)

one is not available obtain the special Weber tool no 98011 400.

31 Bend back the tab washers (27) and unscrew the nuts (28) from each end of the spindle (41). If the nuts are tight use Weber tool no 98023 700 to hold the spindle while the nut is loosened. If this precaution is not taken it is quite possible to distort the spindle, especially if it is a brass one. Should the special tool be unavailable, it is possible to strengthen the spindle by cutting the throttle plates and clamping the middle sections on the spindles while the nuts are loosened. Although the throttle plates will be ruined, they will not cost as much as a new spindle (photo).

32 Remove the nuts (28), tab washers (27), washer (58), lever (19), spring covers (18), springs (17) and dust covers (16) (photo).

33 Using a plastic or hide hammer, tap the spindle (41) out of the carburettor body together with one ball-bearing (38). At the same time withdraw the pump control lever (35) from the carburettor.

34 Place the spindle (41) and bearing (38) loosely in a vice and tap the spindle from the bearing, then reassemble the spindle to the carburettor and tap out the remaining bearing.

35 If the bearings are excessively worn, it is possible for the inner race to separate from the outer race leaving the latter in the carburettor body. If this happens, gently heat the body with a gas blow lamp until the race can be removed. On no account use excessive heat, otherwise the main body may be distorted and this is the only part which is not available as a spare.

36 On series 45 DCOE carburettors, unscrew and remove the auxiliary venturi retaining screws (22).

37 Extract the auxiliary venturis (15) from the carburettor barrels. In most cases these can be pulled out with the fingers, or alternatively Weber tool no 98009 200 can be used (photo).

38 Using Weber tool no 98009 100, extract the chokes (14) from the carburettor barrels. Note from which barrel the auxiliary venturis and chokes are removed in order to ensure

correct refitting, also mark them in relation to the top of the carburettor so that they can be correctly refitted to the locating grooves (photo).

6 Special overhaul procedures

After carrying out the general overhaul procedures given in Chapter 4, the following special procedures should be made:

1 Using a hand chuck and Weber tool no 98006 100, reform the main jet seatings at the bottom of the emulsion tube housing wells by carefully rotating the tool in alternate directions. Finish the seatings by inserting Weber tool no 98010 400 and gently tapping the top of the tool whilst rotating it.

2 Using the same procedure as described in paragraph 1, reform the idling jet seats with Weber tool nos. 98005 800 and 98010 600.

3 Using the same procedure as described in paragraph 1, reform the starter valve seats with Weber tool nos 98004 000 and 98010 400.

4 Using the same procedure as described in paragraph 1, reform the starter jet seats with Weber tool nos 98006 300 and 98010 600.

5 If the internal channels are suspected of being blocked, it will be necessary to drill out the lead plugs as shown in Fig. 11.16, remembering that on 40 DCOE 20 to 22 and 45 DCOE 12 carburettors, the starter device and relative channels are missing. The channels can be checked for obstructions before removing the lead plugs by injecting fuel with a syringe and observing that it emerges freely from the particular channel being tested.

6 The channels are of three diameters, viz 1·0 mm, 1·5 mm and 2·0 mm. The Weber tool nos 98014 300, 98014 400 and 98014 500 should be used to check that the channels are clear for their full lengths.

7 The carburettor body should be thoroughly cleaned after

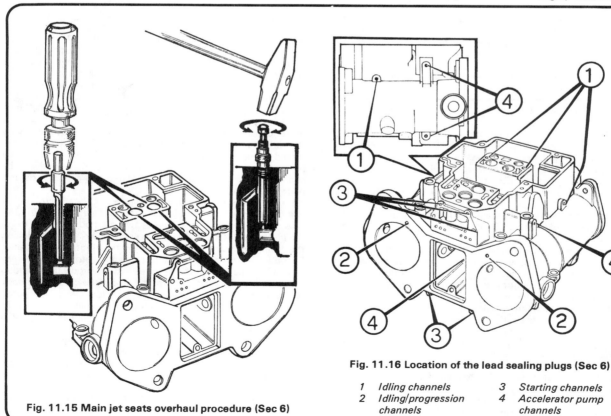

Fig. 11.15 Main jet seats overhaul procedure (Sec 6)

Fig. 11.16 Location of the lead sealing plugs (Sec 6)

1	Idling channels	3	Starting channels
2	Idling/progression channels	4	Accelerator pump channels

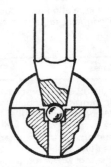

Fig. 11.17 Method of inserting the lead plugs (Sec 6)

7.4a Inserting the throttle spindle return spring and accelerator pump lever

7.4b Fitting the throttle spindle

7.5 Fitting a spindle bearing

7.6 Fitting a throttle spindle dust cover

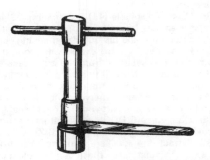

Fig. 11.18 Throttle spindle nut tightening tool (Sec 7)

overhaul to remove any swarf and dirt, preferably using clean fuel and air pressure. The lead plugs should be renewed and retained in position by using the Weber tool no 98010 800 as a punch until the plug is expanded into its bore.

7   Assembly

Note: *All components should be clean and dry before starting the assembly procedure.*

1   If a new spindle (41) or pump control lever (35) is being fitted, first assemble the lever to the spindle to ascertain its fit. If the lever is too tight, use a $\frac{5}{16}$ in expanding reamer to enlarge the lever bore until the spindle is a firm sliding fit.

2   Fit one ball-bearing (38) to the throttle spindle (41) by placing the bearing on an open vice and gently tapping the spindle into it.

3   Fit the remaining ball-bearing (38) into the carburettor body using a plastic hammer and suitable diameter tubing on the outer race.

4   Insert the pump control lever (35) with spring (33) assembled, into the carburettor body, then press the throttle spindle (41) through the locating bore at the same time entering it through the pump control lever (35), making sure that the lever is facing inwards (photos).

5   Tap the spindle bearing (38) into the carburettor body and check that the opposite bearing has not been displaced (photo).

6   Smear a little grease over the spindle bearings (38), then fit the dust covers (16) using a suitable diameter tube to ensure they are correctly seated (photo).

7   Assemble the springs (17), spring covers (18), lever (19), washer (58) and tab washers (27) to their respective ends of the spindle (41), then screw on the nuts (28) finger tight.

8   Screw the throttle adjusting screw (21) and spring (20) into the carburettor body, then tighten the nuts (28) onto the spindle (41). Use the special Weber tool no 98023 700 to do this, but if

not available, tighten the nuts just sufficient to hold the washer (58) and lever (19) firmly on the spindle (41).

9   Lock the nuts (28) by bending the locktabs (27) (photo).

10   With the throttle spindle (41) in the open position, fit the throttle valves (40) into their location slots then close the spindle to allow the valves to centralise within the barrels. Make sure that the valves (40) are fitted the correct way round so that the angled perimeters seat on the bore.

11   With the throttle spindle (41) held closed, insert the valve retaining screws (39) and tighten them evenly but without exerting excessive pressure on the spindle. It is recommended that new screws are always fitted as it is quite easy to cross-thread previously peened screws. Lock the screws (39) by peening with Weber tool no 98010 900 or alternatively, by coating the threads with a liquid locking agent (fuel resistant) prior to inserting them.

12   If a new pump lever (35) or spindle (41) has been fitted, it will be necessary to drill them in order to fit the fixing pin (34). This can be carried out by one of two methods. First by using the gauge no 98015 600 and spacer no 98007 800 and drilling the lever and spindle whilst holding the throttle valves shut. Secondly by fitting the pump rod and piston assembly as described in paragraph 32, then retaining the rod with a bulldog clamp so that the distance from the face of the carburettor body to the underside of the pump rod arch is equal to the pump stroke. By closing the throttle valves and holding the lever (35) against the pump rod (64) the spindle can be drilled using a 2·0 mm or no 46 drill.

13   Drive in the fixing pin (34) using a suitable punch (photo).

14   With a pair of long nose pliers, grip the spindle return spring (33), lift it out of the carburettor body, insert the anchoring plate (32) and locate the plate in its location recess (photo).

15   Check that the spindle operates smoothly, indicating that the bearings are not binding. If there is any tendency to bind, the bearings may not be properly aligned. This may be rectified by gently tapping the carburettor body in their vicinity.

7.9 Throttle lever fitted to the spindle

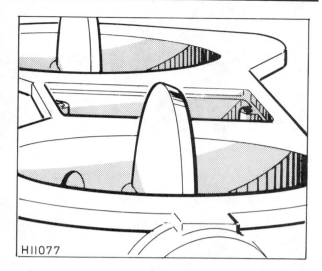

HII077

Fig. 11.19 Angled perimeter of the throttle valves (Sec 7)

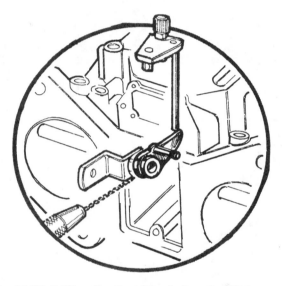

Fig. 11.20 Drilling the throttle spindle using Weber tools (Sec 7)

16 Fit the chokes (14) into the carburettor barrels, making sure that they are located in their original positions and do not obstruct the pump jet (72) apertures (photos).

17 Fit the auxiliary venturis (15) into the carburettor barrels, making sure that the jet cutaway sections are facing the throttle valves.

18 On series 45 DCOE carburettors, fit and tighten the auxiliary venturi retaining screws (22).

19 Fit the pump opening cover plate (45) with a new gasket (46) and tighten the retaining screws (44) evenly.

20 Fit the starter valves (59) into their respective bores, followed by the return springs (60) and retainers (61) (photo).

21 Depress the retainers (61) in turn and locate the spring washers (62) in the carburettor recesses. To do this, first enter the lower leading edge then, whilst keeping this pressed down, close the spring washer and enter the remaining edge.

22 Fit and tighten the progression hole inspection screw plugs (70).

23 Assemble the shaft (55) to the starter device (where fitted) so that the alignment lines on each sector are facing each other, then fit the coil spring (53) locating it in the location hole. Fit the lever (50) over the shaft (55) at the same time hook the end of the spring (53) over the lever, then locate the washer and nut (52) and tighten the nut.

7.13 Fitting the accelerator pump lever fixing pin

7.14 Fitting the throttle spindle return spring anchoring plate

7.16a A carburettor barrel with auxiliary venturi and choke removed showing location groove and accelerator pump jet

7.16b Fitting a choke, showing the location lug

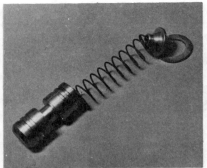
7.20 Starter valve components

7.30 Fitting an accelerator pump delivery valve ball

7.32 Fitted position of the accelerator pump

7.34a Checking the closed-throttle extension of the accelerator pump operating rod with vernier calipers

7.34b Checking the open-throttle extension of the accelerator pump operating rod with vernier calipers

7.38 Needle valve seating location in the carburettor cover

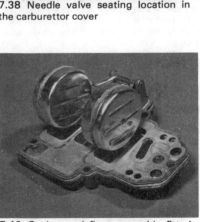
7.40 Gasket and float assembly fitted on the carburettor cover

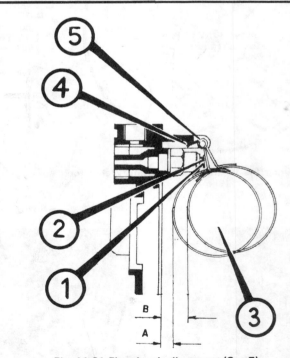
Fig. 11.21 Float level adjustment (Sec 7)

1   Short adjusting tab
2   Spring tensioned ball (not fitted to all types)
3   Semi-floats
4   Long adjusting tab
5   Fulcrum pin
A   Closed dimension
B   Open dimension

7.41 Checking the closed position of the floats using a length of dowel rod

7.43 Checking the open position of the floats using a length of dowel rod

7.49 Fitting an air intake horn

24 Check the operation of the starter device, then fit the cable securing screw (51) and filter gauze (56).
25 Offer the starter device up to the carburettor body and make sure that the sector lugs locate in the starter valve (59) grooves; then insert the retaining screws together with spring and plain washers and tighten them.
26 Check the operation of the starter device and valves then fit and tighten the starter jets (76).
27 Where a starter device is not fitted, fit the blanking plate and tighten the retaining screws.
28 Fit the small gaskets (71) to the pump jets (72), then fit them into the carburettor body and tighten the screw plugs (74) together with new seals (73).
29 Fit and tighten the intake and discharge valve (75) to the bottom of the float chamber.
30 Insert the accelerator pump delivery valve balls (79) and stuffing balls (80), then tighten the retaining screws (81) (photo).
31 Fit the plate (63) and spring (65) to the accelerator pump operating rod (64), compress the spring and engage the piston (66) over the rod.
32 Fit the accelerator pump assembly to the carburettor body and press in the retaining plate (63) using the flat side of a screwdriver blade (photo).
33 Operate the throttle lever and check that the accelerator pump moves freely.
34 The accelerator pump stroke should now be checked using vernier calipers. With the throttle valves shut, measure the distance from the face of the carburettor body to the top of the pump operating rod. Now fully open the throttle and again measure the distance; the difference is the pump stroke which should be as stated in the adjustment data. If the correct stroke is known but the actual reading obtained is incorrect, the length of the operating rod must not be shortened to decrease the stroke by filing, otherwise the hardening will be removed and rapid wear will result; instead a shorter or longer operating rod must be obtained (photos).
35 Fit the conical washers and O-rings together with the springs (67) to the idling mixture adjusting screws (68), then screw them into the carburettor body.
36 Press the idling jets (11) into the holders (9) and tighten them into the carburettor body.
37 Press the air corrector jets (8) into the tops of the emulsion tubes (10) and the main jets (12) into the bottoms of the emulsion tubes, then press the holders (7) to the emulsion tubes and tighten both assemblies into the carburettor body.
38 Tighten the needle valve seating (83) together with a new gasket (82) into the carburettor cover (5) (photo).
39 With the cover (5) inverted, fit the needle then place a new gasket (6) in position.
40 Locate the float assembly (77) and insert the fulcrum pin (78) fully into the two posts. Very carefully pinch the split post to secure the pin using a pair of pliers (photo).

41 The float level adjustment must now be checked in the following manner: Hold the carburettor cover vertical so that the floats are hanging from the fulcrum and the float level arm is in light contact with the needle ball (ie without the ball being depressed). Obtain a drill or dowel rod of diameter equal to the needle valve closed checking dimension and check that the distance from the cover gasket to the nearest part of the floats is correct. The annular seam of the floats should not be taken into consideration for the check and for this reason two small grooves must be filed on the checking rod (photo).
42 If the dimension is not correct, carefully bend the small tab on the float arm accordingly.
43 Tilt the cover so that the floats move away from the cover and the long tab makes contact with the needle valve seating. Now, using the same method as described in paragraph 41, check the needle valve fully open dimension and if necessary bend the long tab to correct (photo).
44 The difference between the dimensions checked in paragraphs 41 and 43 is the needle valve stroke which should be as given in the adjustment data.
45 Fit the well bottom cover (30) with a new gasket (29) to the carburettor body and tighten the retaining screws, (2A) together with the spring washers and plain washers (4A), in diagonal sequence.
46 Press the plate (13) into the top of the carburettor bowl.
47 Lower the cover assembly (5) onto the carburettor body and tighten the retaining screws (2), together with the spring and plain washers (4), in diagonal sequence.
48 Fit the gasket (3) or serrated ring to the cover (5) and tighten the cover (1) with the wing nut.
49 Fit both air intake horns (69), retaining plates (25) and washers (23A), then tighten the retaining nuts (24A) (photo).
50 Insert the fuel filter and retaining bush (88) into the cover (5) and tighten the filter inspection plug (90) fitted with a new gasket (89).
51 With the carburettor completely assembled, the idling adjustment screws should be turned to their preliminary settings. To do this, first screw in the throttle idling adjustment screw until it just touches the throttle lever lug, then continue turning for a further $\frac{1}{2}$ turn. Working on the idling mixture volume screws in turn, fully screw them in until they are in light contact with their seats, then back them off $\frac{3}{4}$ turn. Final adjustments will be necessary when the carburettor is fitted on the engine (refer to Section 8).

8 Tuning

Note: *Refer to Chapter 3 for general notes on tuning.*
1 The idling adjustment screws should be set to their preliminary positions as described in Section 7 paragraph 51.
2 Connect a tachometer to the engine in accordance with the manufacturer's instructions.

Single carburettor unit fittings

3   Start the engine and run until normal operating temperature has been reached (ie the thermostat has opened).

4   Turn the throttle valve adjusting screw so that the engine runs at the recommended idling speed for the particular engine being worked on; this will be between 600 and 800 rpm for touring models and 1000 rpm plus for sports car models.

5   Turn one idle mixture adjustment screw in or out until the engine runs at the highest rpm, then repeat the process on the remaining adjustment screw.

6   Re-adjust the throttle valve adjusting screw if necessary, to bring the engine speed within limits.

7   Repeat the procedure given in paragraphs 5 and 6, switch off the engine and remove the tachometer.

Multiple carburettor fittings (without idle air compensation)

8   The carburettors must be synchronised in order to deliver equal amounts of air/fuel mixture to each individual cylinder. To check the adjustment it will be necessary to obtain a length of tubing (approximately 1 metre long) of about 5 mm to 10 mm (0·25 in to 0·5 in) internal diameter. Alternatively, a synchroniser as shown in Chapter 8 may be used.

9   Remove the air cleaner(s) if fitted, then start the engine and run until normal operating temperature has been reached (ie the thermostat has opened).

10   Switch off the engine and disconnect the accelerator rod connections from the carburettors.

11   Start the engine and place one end of the tube in one air intake of one carburettor, then listen to the amount of hiss present which will indicate the volume of air being passed. Alternatively, press the synchroniser over one of the air intakes and adjust the ring until the air flow indicator is midway up the calibrated tube.

12   Move the tube to the next carburettor and turn the throttle adjustment screw or intermediate synchronising screw until the hiss of the air intakes is identical to that of the original carburettor. If using the synchroniser, turn the screw until the flow indicator is midway up the tube without altering the instrument ring.

13   The procedure given in paragraph 12 must be repeated on all carburettors until all throttle valves are synchronised.

14   Check the engine speed on the tachometer and if necessary, adjust each carburettor adjusting screw by equal amounts to give the correct rpm. Note that where an intermediate synchronizing screw is fitted, it will only be necessary to adjust the carburettor with the fixed adjusting screw; the remaining carburettor will be automatically adjusted.

15   The mixture adjusting screws (2 per carburettor) must all deliver identical amounts of mixture. If necessary, due to uneven engine idling, the screws should be turned half a turn clockwise and the engine rpm noted. This action will weaken the mixture and may cause the engine to stall; if it does, turn each screw anti-clockwise by half a turn. When an adjustment has been reached which gives the highest engine speed, the setting is correct, although it may be necessary to readjust the engine speed on the throttle adjusting screws as previously described.

16   To check that each barrel is delivering equal amounts of idling mixture, temporarily remove each spark plug lead in turn and note the drop in rpm which should be identical on each cylinder.

17   After completing the adjustment procedure, switch off the engine, remove the tachometer and if fitted, fit the air cleaner(s). Finally connect the accelerator rod(s) to the carburettor(s).

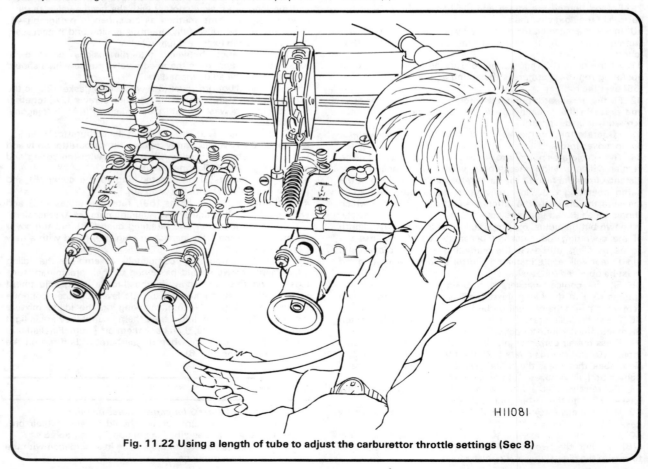

H11081

Fig. 11.22 Using a length of tube to adjust the carburettor throttle settings (Sec 8)

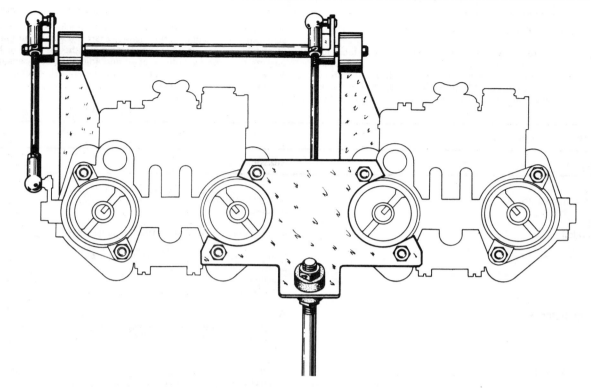

Fig. 11.23 Individual accelerator rod arrangement on a dual carburettor fitting (Sec 8)

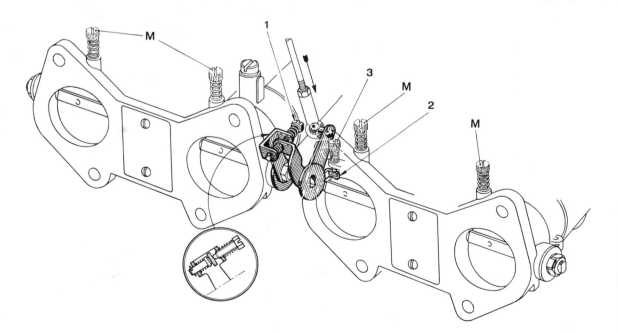

Fig. 11.24 Linked throttle accelerator rod arrangement on a dual carburettor fitting (Sec 8)

1 Synchroniser screw
2 Throttle lever
3 Adjusting screw

M Idle mixture adjusting
   screws

Multiple carburettor fitting (with idle air compensation)
18 Some carburettor types are equipped with adjustable idle air compensation screws which regulate the amount of air bypassing the throttle valves. Where these are fitted, the procedure given in paragraphs 8 to 17 inclusive will apply, but, before starting the two barrels of each carburettor should be syn- chronised together. To do this, first loosen the locknuts and fully screw in each compensation screw. Start the engine and listen to the hiss from each barrel. Determine the barrel which is passing the greatest volume of air and adjust the compensating screw on the remaining barrel to give an identical volume of air. Finally tighten the locknuts.

9 Fault diagnosis

Symptom	Reason/s
Engine will not start	Faulty starter device Blocked fuel filter or jets
Uneven idling	Leaking manifold or carburettor flange gaskets Loose idling jets Excessive sediment or water in carburettor Starter valves not seating Starter device not returning Throttle spindle dust covers broken
Carburettor floods	Worn needle valve Lacking or damaged semi-floats Incorrect float level adjustments Excessive sediment in fuel
Engine lacks performance	Incorrect tuning adjustments Incorrect float level adjustments Excessive sediment in fuel Throttle valves do not fully open Accelerator pump jamming or stroke incorrect
Excessive fuel consumption	Faulty starter device Needle valve not seating Leaking or damaged semi-floats Incorrect float level adjustments Choked air filter

Part 2
Chapter 12 Type 40 IDF,
44 IDF, 48 IDF carburettors

Contents

1 Introduction

The carburettors covered by this chapter are of the vertical downdraught type and each barrel of the carburettor is of identical diameter.

The throttle valves are of the synchronised, simultaneous operation type and are located on a single shaft.

The identification mark is located on the side of the main body just below the fuel inlet filter plug.

2 Construction

The main body and cover of the Weber IDF carburettor are of die-cast aluminium or zinc alloy (Mazak) construction. The mounting flanges are machined flat for fitting on the inlet manifold.

The throttle spindle is of steel and the throttle valve plates of brass.

All fuel and air jets and emulsion tubes are of brass construction and are secured to the main body by screw fittings.

The internal channels of the main body are mainly drilled and where necessary, sealed with lead plugs.

The throttle spindle is supported by two ball-bearings mounted in the main body. Washers are located at each end of the spindle to prevent air being drawn through the bearings.

The fuel float assembly is constructed of plastic and comprises two sections.

The accelerator pump is of the diaphragm type and the operating lever is actuated by a cam attached to the centre section of the throttle spindle.

3 Operation

Cold starting

8 The starting device fitted to type IDF carburettors operates independently of the main circuit and may be considered as a separate carburettor within the main carburettor.

Refer to Fig. 12.1 and note that when the choke cable is pulled the starting device operating lever turns the control shafts, thereby lifting the starting valves off their seats. Fuel from the float chamber (2) is drawn through channels (44) into the starting jets (43) where it is emulsified with air entering through the top of the starting jets (43). The mixture is then drawn through channels (45) where it is further emulsified with air from the hole (50). After passing the starter valves (49) where additional air from the holes (48) weakens the mixture, the final mixture is drawn through channels (47) into the engine below the throttle valves.

The starting device has a progressive action made possible by the tapered end of the valve heads. Lowering the valves will reduce the amount of mixture admitted to the engine until, when shut, the supply will cease.

Idling and progression

Refer to Fig. 12.2 and note that when the engine is idling with the throttle valves (15) closed, fuel is drawn through the main jets and emulsion tube wells (17) to the iding jets (24) where it becomes emulsified with air entering through the calibrated bushes (26). The mixture then travels through the channels (26), past the adjustable mixture screws (27), through the idling feed holes (28) and into the carburettor throats at the engine side of the throttle valves (15). The idling mixture screws (27) have tapered ends and can therefore be adjusted to admit more or less mixture as necessary.

When the throttle valves are opened slightly to increase the engine speed, the progression holes (32) are brought into action to provide additional fuel and to enable the engine to reach the speed when the main system starts to function.

In order to ensure that each carburettor barrel passes identical amounts of air, in particular when the engine is idling, air compensation screws (31) are incorporated in each barrel whereby air can bypass the throttle valves (15). This system ensures identical vacuum below each throttle valve and therefore ensures identical mixtures during idling and progression.

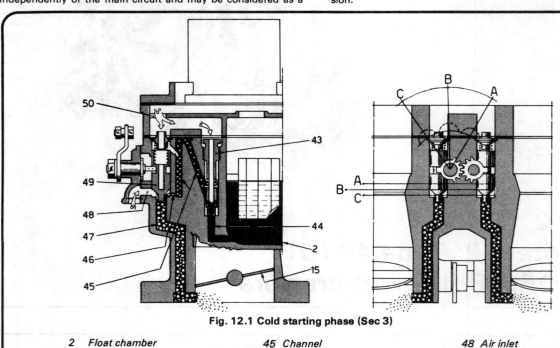

Fig. 12.1 Cold starting phase (Sec 3)

2 Float chamber	45 Channel	48 Air inlet
15 Throttle valves	46 Transfer hole	49 Starter valves
43 Starting jets	47 Channel	50 Air inlet hole
44 Channel		

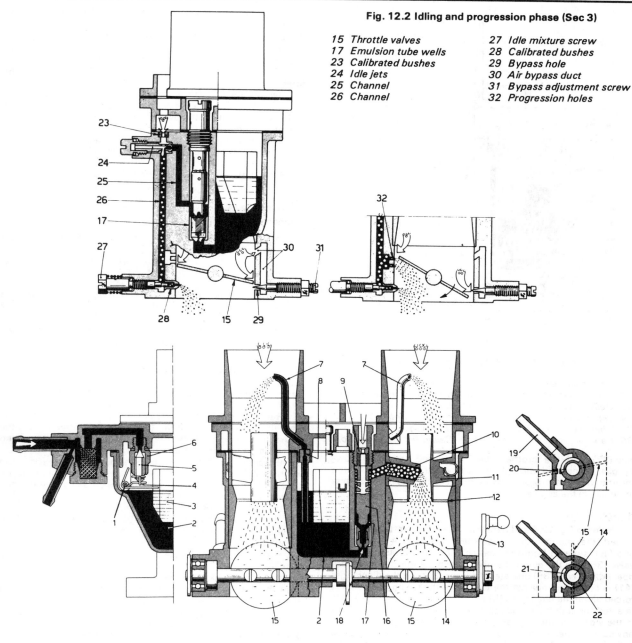

Fig. 12.2 Idling and progression phase (Sec 3)

15	Throttle valves	27	Idle mixture screw
17	Emulsion tube wells	28	Calibrated bushes
23	Calibrated bushes	29	Bypass hole
24	Idle jets	30	Air bypass duct
25	Channel	31	Bypass adjustment screw
26	Channel	32	Progression holes

Fig. 12.3 Normal phase (Sec 3)

1	Fulcrum pin	7	Mixture enrichment tubes	13	Throttle lever	18	Main jets
2	Float chamber	8	Calibrated holes	14	Throttle shaft	19	Crankcase emission tube
3	Float	9	Air corrector jets	15	Throttle valves	20	Calibrated hole
4	Return hook	10	Nozzles	16	Emulsion tubes	21	Crankcase emission valve slot
5	Needle	11	Auxiliary venturis	17	Emulsion tube wells	22	Rotary blanking disc
6	Needle valve seating	12	Chokes				

Normal running

Refer to Fig. 12.3 and note that under full throttle and high speed cruise conditions, fuel is drawn from the float chamber (2) through the main jets (18) to the emulsion tube wells (17) and then past the holes in the emulsion tubes (16). The fuel becomes emulsified with air drawn through the air corrector jets (9) and is then drawn through the nozzle (10), auxiliary venturis (11) and chokes (12) into the engine.

The carburettor also incorporates a high speed mixture enrichment system. Fuel from the float chamber (2) is drawn through the calibrated orifice (8) and spray tubes (7) into the air horns of the carburettor.

The crankcase emission control system is incorporated into one of the carburettor barrels and consists of a rotary blanking

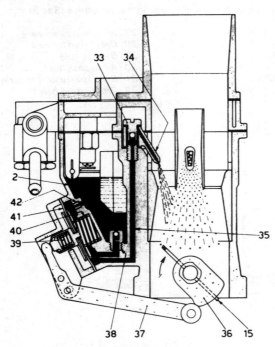

Fig. 12.4 Acceleration phase (Sec 3)

2 *Float chamber*	37 *Lever*
15 *Throttle valves*	38 *Inlet and discharge valve*
33 *Delivery valves*	39 *Reaction spring*
34 *Jet nozzles*	40 *Return spring*
35 *Channel*	41 *Diaphragm*
36 *Cam*	42 *Calibrated discharge hole*

disc (22). With the throttle valves (15) closed, crankcase blow-by gas is metered through the calibrated hole (20). As the throttle valves are progressively opened, the slot (21) admits more gas to the engine.

Acceleration

Refer to Fig. 12.4 and note that when the throttle valves are closed, the spring (40) pushes the diaphragm (41) outwards and fuel is drawn from the float chamber (2), through the inlet valve (38) into the pump chamber. When the throttle valves are opened, the cam (36) operates the lever (37) and the diaphragm (41) is depressed against the tension of the spring (40). Fuel is forced along the channels (35) to the delivery valves (33) and is injected through the pump jets (34) into the carburettor barrels in the vicinity of the auxiliary venturis. The spring (39) dampens any sudden opening of the throttle valves and prolongs the fuel delivery. The calibrated discharge hole (42) determines the maximum pressure of fuel injected into the carburettor and also allows any accumulated air and vapour to escape into the float chamber. The inlet valve (38) may also incorporate a calibrated discharge hole, whereby a further amount of fuel returns to the float chamber. By fine calibration of this hole it is possible to determine the exact quantity of fuel injected by the accelerator pump.

---

4   Removal and refitting

Note: *The following procedure gives a general rather than a specific method of removing and refitting the carburettor, as much will depend on the location of the carburettor within the vehicle. On some applications for instance, the retaining nuts may not be accessible without removing surrounding components.*

1   Where fitted, remove the air cleaner assembly from the carburettor.
2   Disconnect the throttle linkage where necessary.
3   Disconnect the inner and outer choke cable from the starting device.
4   Disconnect the fuel inlet hose; and return hoses where fitted.
5   Remove the crankcase emission hose from the carburettor.
6   Unscrew and remove the carburettor retaining nuts and spring washers and withdraw the carburettor complete over the mounting studs.
7   Remove the gaskets from the inlet manifold and clean all traces of gasket from the contact faces of the manifold and carburettor.
8   Protect the inlet manifold from ingress of foreign matter whilst the carburettor is removed, by sealing it with masking tape.
9   Refitting is a reversal of removal, but the following additional points should be noted:

(a)   Always fit new gaskets and tighten the retaining nuts evenly in diagonal sequence
(b)   The idling adjustment screws should be set as described in Section 7 and finally tuned as described in Section 8
(c)   When refitting the choke (starting device) cable, first secure the outer cable to the support, then insert the inner cable into the operating lever screw and push the instrument panel control knob fully in. Tighten the inner cable retaining nut with the operating lever fully released.

---

5   Disassembly

1   Thoroughly clean the carburettor exterior and wipe dry.
2   Referring to Fig. 12.5, lift the air horns (1) and gasket (2) from the carburettor top cover (photo). Where fitted extract the two split pins and remove the starter device control rod and control lever from the carburettor top cover (82).
3   Unscrew and remove the retaining screws (85) and washers (84) in diagonal sequence and lift the carburettor top cover (82) from the carburettor body (49), making sure that the gasket (81) is not broken (photo).
4   Lift the gasket (81) from the carburettor body (49).
5   Invert the carburettor cover (82) and unscrew the filter cover plug (6) using a 19 mm ring spanner and socket. Remove the washer (5) (photo).
6   Remove the filter gauze (3) and, if necessary, extract the base (4).
7   Using a suitable diameter metal drift, tap the fulcrum pin (7) from the support posts. Do not attempt to prise the split post apart (photo).
8   Note which way round the needle valve return hook is positioned, then lift the float assembly (77) and needle from the cover (photo). Unhook the needle from the float arm.
9   Unscrew and remove the needle valve (78) and washer (79) (photo).
10 Place the carburettor cover (82) to one side, taking care not to damage the high speed enrichment tubes.
11 Unscrew and remove the retaining screws (40A) and washers (71). Remove the starter device (59) from the carburettor (photo).
12 Dismantle the starter device by unscrewing the nut (61) from the shaft (69) together with the washer (62), then carefully remove the lever (65) and spring (67). Unscrew the cable clamp nut (64) and screw (66), then remove the shaft (69) and filter gauze (70).
13 Unscrew and remove the accelerator pump inlet and discharge valve (17) from the bottom of the float chamber (photo).
14 Unscrew the emulsion tube holders (8) from the carburettor body (49) and lift out the emulsion tube assemblies (photos).
15 Separate the emulsion tubes (10) from the holders (8) then

5.2 Removing the air horns

5.3 Removing the carburettor top cover

5.5 Removing the fuel filter and plug

5.7 Removing the float fulcrum pin

5.8 Position of the needle valve on the float assembly

5.9 Needle valve seating location

5.11 Removing the starter device

5.13 Accelerator pump inlet and discharge valve location

5.14a Emulsion tube holders location

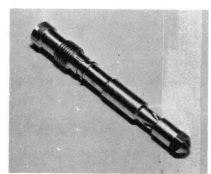

5.14b The emulsion tube assembly

5.15 Component parts of the emulsion tube assembly

5.16a Removing the idling jets

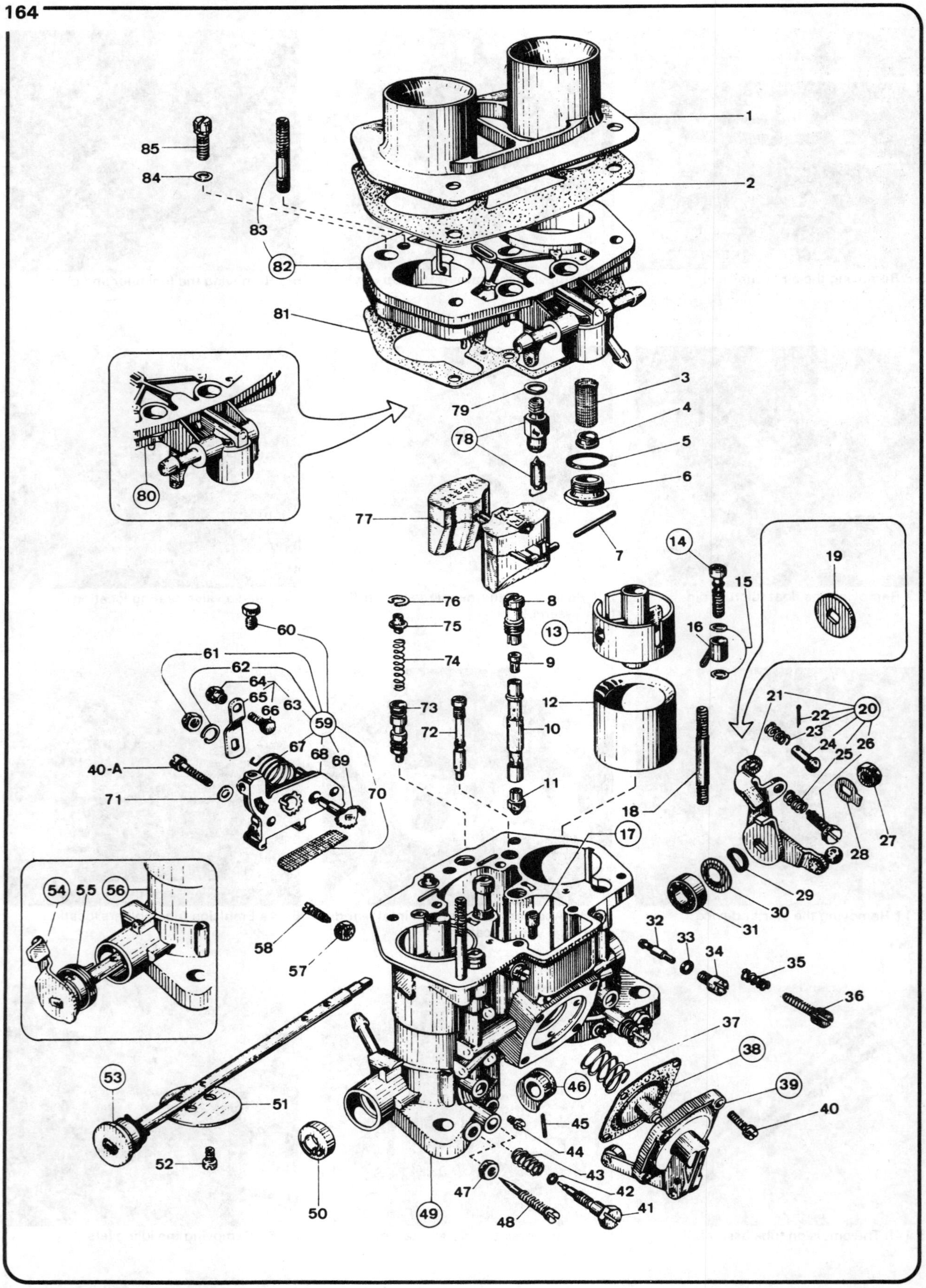
1
2
3
4
5
6
7
8
9
10
11
12
13
14
15
16
17
18
19
20
21
22
23
24
25
26
27
28
29
30
31
32
33
34
35
36
37
38
39
40
40-A
41
42
43
44
45
46
47
48
49
50
51
52
53
54
55
56
57
58
59
60
61
62
63
64
65
66
67
68
69
70
71
72
73
74
75
76
77
78
79
80
81
82
83
84
85

pull the main jets (11) and air corrector jets (9) from the emulsion tubes (10) (photo). Take care not to damage the jets when removing them and, if pliers are used, interpose a piece of paper or card to prevent the brass being scratched.

16 Unscrew the idling jet holders (34) from the side of the carburettor body (49), remove the rubber O-rings (33), then separate the idling jets (32) (photos).

17 Whilst depressing the starter valve spring retaining guides (75) in turn, prise the spring washers (76) from the carburettor body, then release the guides (75) and extract the return springs (74) and starter valves (73) (photos). Note from which bore each valve is taken so that they can be refitted in their original locations. Do not force the valves if they will not come out freely; occassionally a burr may exist at the top of the bore, this must be removed with a fine file.

18 Unscrew and remove the starter jets (72) (photo).

19 Unscrew and remove the accelerator pump delivery valves (14) together with the pump jets (16) and washers (15) (photo), then separate the washers and jets from the valves.

20 Unscrew the retaining screws and washers (40) and carefully prise the pump cover (39) from the carburettor body (photo). Take care not to damage the diaphragm and if necessary, use a blunt knife to release it.

21 Remove the diaphragm (38) and spring (37).

22 Note the location of the auxiliary venturis (13) and mark them if necessary with a pencil to ensure correct refitting, then withdraw them from the carburettor body (49) (photo). If necessary, use a wooden or plastic dowel rod inserted from the throttle valve end of the barrel to tap the auxiliary venturis free. In the unlikely event of their being excessively tight, it will be necessary to obtain the special Weber tool no 9610 150 0035.

23 Loosen the locknuts (57) with a 9 mm ring spanner and unscrew the locking screws (58) (photo).

24 Note the locations of each choke (12) then remove them from the carburettor barrels (photo). Note that the choke ends with the smaller internal diameter are uppermost. If the chokes are excessively tight, it will be necessary to obtain Weber tool no 98009 100.

25 Unscrew and remove the idling mixture adjusting screws (41) together with the springs (43), washers and rubber O-rings (42) (photo).

26 Unscrew and remove the idle speed screw (36) and spring (35), where fitted.

27 Unscrew and remove the blanking screws (44) (photo).

28 Loosen the locknuts (47) with an 8 mm ring spanner, then unscrew and remove the air bypass screws (48) (photo).

5.16b Separating an idling jet from its holder

5.17a Removing a starter valve spring, retaining guide and spring washer

5.17b Removing a starter valve

Fig. 12.5 Exploded view of the 40 IDF carburettor (typical) (Sec 5)

1	Air horns	30	End washer	58	Choke locking screw
2	Gasket	31	Ball-bearing	59	Starter device assembly
3	Filter gauze	32	Idle jet	60	Lock screw
4	Base	33	O-ring	61	Nut
5	Washer	34	Idle jet holder	62	Spring washer
6	Plug	35	Spring	63	Lever assembly
7	Fulcrum pin	36	Idle speed screw	64	Nut
8	Emulsion tube holder	37	Spring	65	Lever
9	Air corrector jet	38	Diaphragm	66	Screw
10	Emulsion tube	39	Accelerator pump cover	67	Spring
11	Main jet	40	Screw	68	Housing
12	Choke	41	Idle mixture screw	69	Sector shaft
13	Auxiliary venturi	42	O-ring	70	Filter gauze
14	Delivery valve	43	Spring	71	Washer
15	Copper washers	44	Blanking screw	72	Starter jet
16	Pump jet	45	Roll pin	73	Starter valve
17	Inlet valve with exhaust orifice	46	Accelerator pump cam	74	Spring
18	Stud	47	Locknut	75	Retaining guide
19	Spacer	48	Air bypass screw	76	Retaining washer
20	Throttle lever assembly	49	Carburettor body	77	Float assembly
21	Throttle lever	50	Emission control valve	78	Needle valve assembly
22	Split pin	51	Throttle valve	79	Gasket
23	Spring	52	Retaining screw	80	Alternative fuel inlet
24	Pressure pin	53	Throttle shaft	81	Gasket
25	Spring	54	Link arm	82	Carburettor cover
26	Adjusting screw	55	Return spring	83	Stud
27	Nut	56	Carburettor body	84	Washer
28	Tab washer	57	Locknut	85	Retaining screw
29	Wave washer				

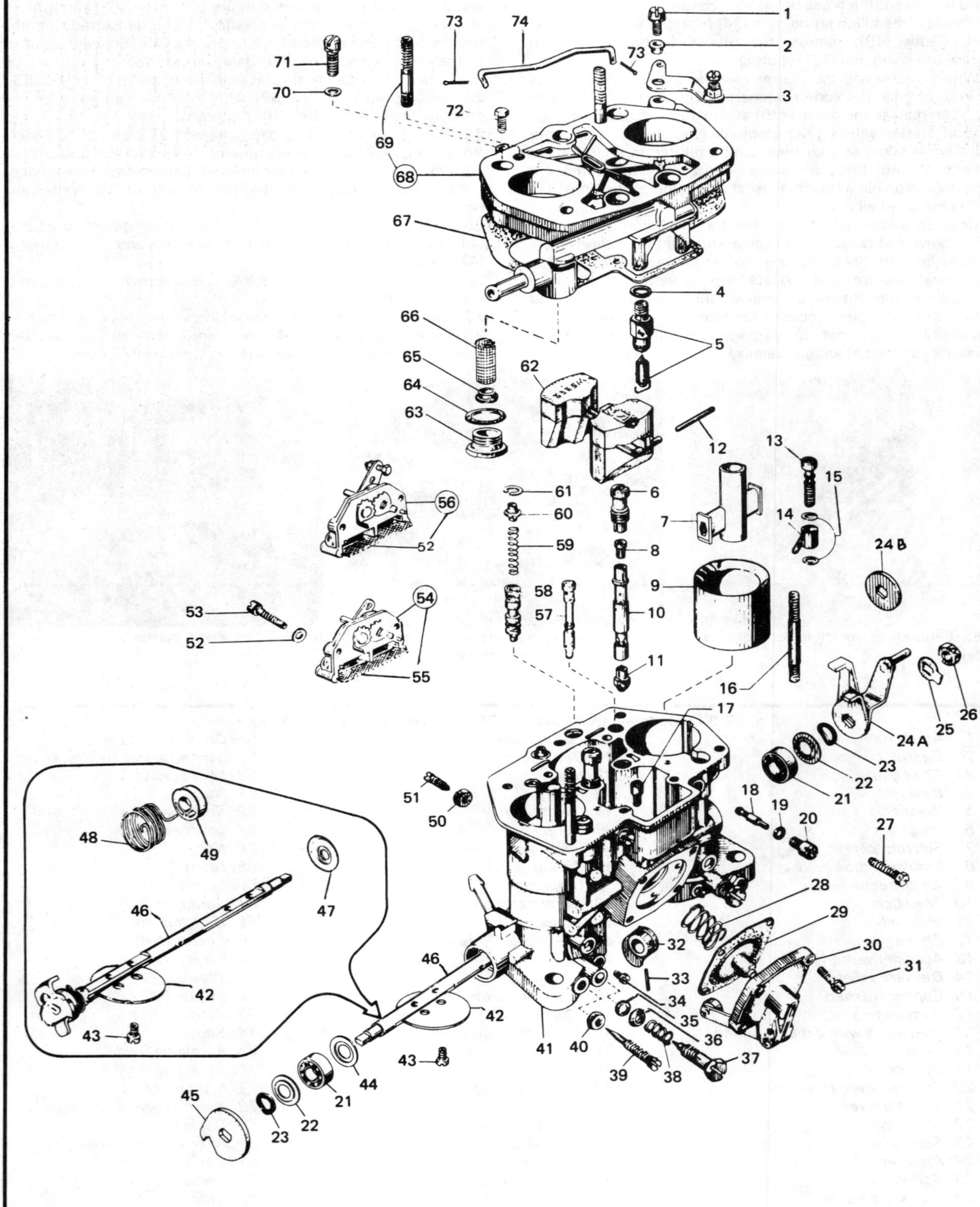
1
2
3
4
5
6
7
8
9
10
11
12
13
14
15
16
17
18
19
20
21
22
23
24 A
24 B
25
26
27
28
29
30
31
32
33
34
35
36
37
38
39
40
41
42
43
44
45
46
47
48
49
50
51
52
53
54
55
56
57
58
59
60
61
62
63
64
65
66
67
68
69
70
71
72
73
74

5.18 Removing a starter jet

5.19 Removing the accelerator pump delivery valve and jet

5.20 Withdrawing the accelerator pump cover from the carburettor

5.22 Removing an auxiliary venturi

5.23 Choke locking screw location

5.24 Removing a choke, showing location indentation

Fig. 12.6 Exploded view of the 40 and 44 IDF carburettor (series 28, 29 and 26, 27) (Sec 5)

1 Screw	26 Nut	52 Washer
2 Bush	27 Idle speed screw	53 Screw
3 Starter control lever	28 Spring	54 Starter device (40 IDF 28 and 44 IDF 26)
4 Gasket	29 Diaphragm	
5 Needle valve assembly	30 Accelerator pump cover	55 Filter gauze
6 Emulsion tube holder	31 Screw	56 Starter device (40 IDF 29 and 44 IDF 27)
7 Auxiliary venturi	32 Cam	
8 Air corrector jet	33 Roll pin	57 Starter jet
9 Choke	34 Blanking screw	58 Starter valve
10 Emulsion tube	35 O-ring	59 Spring
11 Main jet	36 Washer	60 Retaining guide
12 Fulcrum pin	37 Idle mixture screw	61 Retaining washer
13 Delivery valve	38 Spring	62 Float assembly
14 Pump jet	39 Air bypass screw	63 Plug
15 Copper washers	40 Locknut	64 Washer
16 Stud	41 Carburettor body	65 Base
17 Inlet valve with exhaust orifice	42 Throttle plate	66 Filter gauze
18 Idle jet	43 Retaining screw	67 Gasket
19 O-ring	44 Washer	68 Carburettor cover
20 Idle jet holder	45 Anchor plate	69 Stud
21 Ball-bearing	46 Throttle shaft	70 Spring washer
22 End washer	47 Washer	71 Retaining screw
23 Wave washer	48 Return spring	72 Cable locknut
24A Throttle lever	49 Emission control valve	73 Split pin
24B Spacer	50 Locknut	74 Starter control rod
25 Tab washer	51 Choke locking screw	

5.25 Removing an idling mixture adjusting screw

5.27 Removing a blanking screw

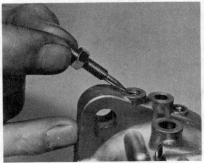

5.28 Removing an air bypass screw

5.29 Throttle spindle end nut location and locktab

5.31 Removing the throttle valve retaining screws

5.33 Removing a throttle valve

5.34 Accelerator pump cam roll pin removal

29 Bend back the locktabs (28) on one or both ends of the throttle spindle (53) depending on the application, then unscrew and remove the nuts (27) (photo). If these are very tight, use Weber tool no 98023 700 to hold the spindle whilst the nut is loosened. If this precaution is not taken, the spindle (53) may become buckled. Do not loosen a tight nut with the throttle valves being forced against the barrel walls.

30 Remove the nut(s) (27), tab washer(s) (28), spacer (19) and throttle lever (21) as applicable to the carburettor.

31 Unscrew and remove the throttle valve retaining screws (52), being careful not to exert excessive pressure on the spindle (53) (photo).

32 Note the position of the throttle spindle and valves in relation to the barrels and if necessary, mark the valves with a pencil.

33 Turn the spindle to the fully open position and withdraw the two throttle valves (51) from their location slots (photo).

34 Using a suitable pin punch, drive the roll pin (45) through

the cam (46) and spindle (53). To ensure correct refitting, mark the cam and spindle in relation to each other (photo).

35 Using a plastic mallet, drive the spindle (53) from the carburettor. Before doing this, check that the spindle is free of any burrs and use a fine file if necessary, to remove them.

36 Recover the wave washer(s) (29) and bearing end washer(s) (30) the accelerator pump cam (46).

37 Drive the remaining bearing (31) from the carburettor body (49). Where the throttle lever (54) is swaged onto the spindle, use a suitable diameter length of metal dowel rod to remove the bearing. Where retaining nuts are located on each end of the throttle spindle, remove the bearing and washer and use the spindle to remove the bearing.

38 When fitted, remove the return spring (55) from the throttle spindle (54).

39 When fitted, remove the crankcase emission rotary disc (50) from the throttle spindle.

40 If necessary, unscrew the idle speed screw (26) and spring

(25) from the throttle lever (21), then remove the split pin (22), pressure pin (24) and spring (23).

6   Special overhaul procedures

After carrying out the general overaul procedures given in Chapter 4, the following special procedures should be completed:

1   Using a hand chuck and the special tool available from Weber r a tool hire agent, reform the main jet seatings at the bottom of the emulsion tube housing wells by carefully rotating the tool in alternate directions. Finish the seatings with the additional special tool by tapping it gently whilst rotating it at the same time.

2   Using the same procedure as described in paragraph 1, reform the idling jet seats.

3   Using the same procedure as described in paragraph 1, reform the starter valve seats.

4   Using the same procedure as described in paragraph 1, reform the starter jet seats.

5   If the emulsion tube wells are discoloured and considerable sediment has accumulated, the bores must be removed using the applicable Weber tool and a hand chuck. Turn the tool carefully until it moves freely, then continue turning it whilst removing it.

6   Check the internal channels of the carburettor body and cover by injecting fuel from a syringe and observing whether it emerges freely. If any channels are blocked, it will be necessary to drill out the lead plugs and use Weber tool nos 98014 300, 98014 400 and 98014 500 to clear them. These tool numbers rfer to the three channel diameters of 1.0 mm, 1.5 mm and 2.0 mm.

7   The carburettor body should be thoroughly cleaned after overhaul, preferably using clean fuel and air pressure. The lead plugs should be renewed and retained in position by using the Weber tool nos 98010 700 or 98010 800 as a punch until the plugs are expanded into their bores.

8   Check the float assembly for damage and leakage. Shake the floats to determine whether fuel has entered. If the floats are damaged or fuel is present, the assembly must be renewed.

9   Check the accelerator pump lever and diaphragm for wear and damage and renew them as necessary.

7   Assembly

Note: *All components should be clean and dry before starting the assembly procedure.*

1   Fit the spring (23) and pressure pin (24) to the throttle lever (21) and secure with the split pin (22).

2   Fit the idle speed screw (26) and spring (25) to the throttle lever (21).

3   When fitted slide the crankcase emission rotary disc (50)

onto the throttle spindle, making sure that the locating pin is fully engaged with the slot (photos).

4   When fitted, locate the return spring (55) over the throttle spindle (54) and engage the hooked end on the throttle lever arm.

5   Using a suitable diameter length of tubing, drive the bearing (31) fully into the carburettor body (49). Make sure that the inner bearing washer is inserted into the body, where fitted.

6   If a new cam (46) or spindle (53) is being fitted, ream the cam as necessary so that it is a firm sliding fit on the spindle.

7   On throttle spindles fitted with two end nuts, place the remaining ball-bearing on an open vice and gently tap the spindle into it. Where necessary, the inner washer must be located on the spindle first.

8   Insert the throttle spindle (53) into the carburettor body (49), at the same time locate the accelerator pump cam (46) between the two barrels with its shoulder as shown in Fig. 12.5 (photo). Also insert the return spring (55) in the location hole where applicable.

9   Using a length of tubing, support the bearing (31) in the main body then tap the spindle (53) fully into position (photo).

10 Fit the bearing end washer(s) (30) and wave washer(s) (29) after lubricating the bearings with a little grease.

11 Turn the throttle spindle (53) to its approximate closed position then, with the accelerator pump cam (46) facing away from the diaphragm face, align the holes in the cam (46) and spindle (53) and drive in the roll pin (45) until it is in a central position.

12 Turn the spindle (53) (against the tension of spring 55 if already fitted) until the throttle valve slots can be seen from the flange end of the carburettor, then insert one throttle valve (51) in the location previously noted and close the valve. Make sure that the throttle valve is fitted the correct way round so that the angled perimeter seats in the barrel.

13 Snap the valve shut several times in order to centralise it, then insert and tighten the valve retaining screws (52) without exerting excessive pressure on the spindle. It is recommended that new screws are always fitted as it is quite easy to crossthread previously peened screws. Lock the screws by peening with Weber tool no 98010 900 whilst supporting the spindle with a length of wood. Alternatively, coat the threads with a liquid locking agent (fuel resistant) prior to inserting them.

14 Repeat the procedure described in paragraphs 12 and 13 for the remaining throttle valve.

15 If a new spindle (53) or cam (46) is being fitted, both must be drilled with a 0.078 in (2.0 mm) drill to accommodate the roll pin (45). To do this, it is essential to obtain the special Weber fixture.

16 Fit the throttle lever (21), spacer (19), tab washer(s) (28) and nut(s) (27) and lock them to the carburettor.

17 Tighten the nut(s) (27) and lock them by bending the locktabs (28). Do not overtighten the nuts otherwise the spindle may be distorted.

18 Insert the air bypass screws (48) and screw them in until

7.3a Crankcase emission rotary disc locating peg ...

7.3b ... and slot

7.8 Fitting the throttle spindle through the accelerator pump cam

7.9 Fitting the throttle spindle bearing

7.31 Fitting a starter valve spring, retainer and spring washer

they are fully seated, then tighten the locknuts (47).

19 Insert and tighten the blanking screws (44).

20 Fit the idle speed screw (36) and spring (35), where fitted.

21 Fit the idling mixture adjusting screws (41) together with the rubber O-rings (42), washers and springs (43).

22 Insert the chokes (12) into the barrels with the smaller internal diameter ends uppermost.

23 Align the indentations in the chokes (12) with the holes in the carburettor body (49), then lightly tighten the locking screws (58) into position and tighten the locknuts (57).

24 Fit the auxiliary venturis (13) in their original locations, making sure that the location springs engage with the grooves in the barrels and that the supply of channels are in alignment with those in the carburettor body. The extended venturis must also be uppermost.

25 Support the carburettor body (49) with the pump diaphragm face uppermost, then locate the spring (37) on the face in a central position.

26 Place the diaphragm (38) against the pump cover (39) and retain with the fingers and thumb, then insert the retaining screws and washers (40) through the diaphragm.

27 Locate the diaphragm and cover on the carburettor and engage two or three threads of the retaining screws. Operate the pump lever several times then hold it so that the diaphragm is not tensioned. Tighten the retaining screws (40) evenly in diagonal sequence. Check the operation of the pump by operating the throttle lever.

28 Assemble the accelerator pump jets (16) to the delivery valves (14) with the copper washers (15), then tighten them into the carburettor body (49).

29 Insert and tighten the starter jets (72) into the carburettor body (49).

30 Fit the starter valves (73) into their respective bores, followed by the return springs (74) and retainers (75).

31 Depress the retainers (75) in turn and locate the spring washers (76) in the carburettor recesses (photo), fully pressing them in with the flat blade of a screwdriver.

32 Press the idling jets (32) into the holders (34), fit the rubber O-rings (33), then tighten the holders into the carburettor body.

33 Press the air corrector jets (9) and main jets (11) into the emulsion tubes (10), then press the holders (8) onto the top of the emulsion tubes (10).

34 Insert and tighten the emulsion tube assemblies into the carburettor body (49).

35 Insert and tighten the accelerator pump inlet and discharge valve (17).

36 Assemble the shaft (69) to the starter device so that the alignment lines on each sector are facing each other, then fit the

coil spring (67) with its end in the location hole. Fit the lever (65) over the shaft (69) and at the same time hook the end of the spring (67) over the lever, then locate the washer (62) and nut (61) and tighten the nut.

37 Check the operation of the starter device, then fit the cable securing nut (64) and screw (66) and filter gauze (70).

38 Offer the starter device up to the carburettor body and make sure that the sector lugs locate in the starter valve grooves, then insert the retaining screws (40A) and washers (71) and tighten the screws. Check that the starter device operates smoothly.

39 Tighten the needle valve seating (78), together with a new gasket (79), into the carburettor cover (82).

40 Hook the needle (78) onto the float arm (77) then lower the needle into the seating. Insert the fulcrum pin (7) through the posts and float assembly (77). If necessary, gently pinch the split post to secure the pin using a pair of pliers.

41 The float level adjustment must now be checked in the following manner: Hold the carburettor cover vertical so that the floats are hanging from the fulcrum pin with the float level arm in light contact with the needle ball (ie without the ball being depressed). Using a vernier caliper, check that the distance from the float to the cover face as shown in Fig. 12.7 is 0.394 in (10.0 mm) without the gasket in place (photo). If not, bend the tab retaining the needle hook as necessary.

42 Tilt the cover so that the floats move away from the cover and the tab makes contact with the needle valve seating. Now, using the same method as described in paragraph 41, check that the needle valve fully open dimension is 1.280 in (32.5 mm) (photo). If not, bend the tab which contacts the needle valve seating as necessary.

43 The difference between the dimensions checked in paragraphs 41 and 42 is the needle valve stroke which should be 0.886 in (22.5 mm).

44 Fit the base (4) to the filter gauze (3). With the carburettor cover (82) inverted, press the filter gauze into the inlet cavity.

45 Fit the washer (5) to the filter cover plug (6), then tighten the plug into the cover (82).

46 Place the gasket (81) onto the top face of the carburettor body (49).

47 Lower the carburettor cover (82) onto the main body (49) over the studs, then insert the retaining screws (85) and washers (84) and tighten them a little at a time in diagonal sequence.

48 Fit the starter device control rod and lever (where fitted) using new split pins.

49 Locate the gasket (2) and air horns (1) over the studs and onto the carburettor cover (82).

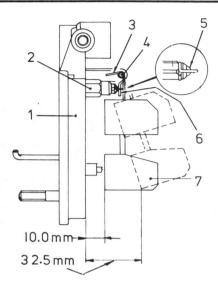

Fig. 12.7 Float level adjustment dimensions (Sec 7)

1 Carburettor cover
2 Needle valve assembly
3 Stroke adjusting tab
4 Fulcrum pin

5 Needle and return hook
6 Height adjusting tab
7 Float assembly

7.41 Checking the float level closed position

7.42 Checking the float level open position

50 With the carburettor completely assembled, the idling adjustment screws should be turned to their preliminary settings. To do this, first screw in the throttle idling adjustment screw (where fitted) until it just touches the throttle lever, then continue turning for a further 2 turns. Working on the idling mixture volume screws in turn, fully screw them in until they are in contact with their seats, then back them off 2 complete turns. Final adjustments will be necessary with the carburettor fitted on the engine (refer to Section 8).

8 Tuning

Note: *Refer to Chapter 3 for general notes on tuning.*
1 Set the idling adjustment screws to their preliminary positions as described in Section 7.
2 Connect a tachometer to the engine in accordance with the manufacturer's instructions.
3 It is now important to understand that each barrel of each carburettor must be synchronized in order to deliver equal amounts of air/fuel mixture to each individual cylinder. To check this, it will be necessary to obtain a length of tubing (approximately 1 metre) of about 5 mm to 10 mm (0.25 in to 0.50 in) internal diameter. Alternatively a synchroniser as illustrated in Chapter 8 may be used.
4 Remove the air cleaner(s) if fitted, then run the engine until normal operating temperature is reached. To ensure that the engine is really hot enough, drive it hard over a 5 mile distance.
5 Switch off the engine and disconnect the accelerator rod connections from each carburettor.
6 Where two carburettor throttle spindles are linked, turn the adjustment screw on the link 2 turns from the fully shut position.
7 Start the engine and adjust each idling speed adjusting screw (except link adjustments) by equal amounts until the engine is idling at the approximate recommended speed. This will vary according to the application and state of tune of the engine but an average will be around 800 rpm.
8 The barrels of each individual carburettor must now be synchronised to pass identical quantities of air during idling. To do this, loosen the locknuts and check that the bypass screws are both in light contact with their seats. Place one end of the synchronising tube in the middle of one air intake and listen at the other end to the amount of hiss present. Alternatively, use the synchroniser to record the air flow through the air intake. Check both air intakes of the carburettor to determine which one is passing the greatest amount of air, then adjust the remaining barrel to give an identical volume. Finally, tighten the adjustment locknuts. Carry out this procedure independently on each carburettor fitted to the engine.
9 Each carburettor must now be synchronised with the remaining carburettors. To do this, allow the engine to idle and check the volume of air flowing through one air intake of each carburettor, using the length of tube or the synchroniser. Determine the carburettor which is passing the medium volume of air and adjust the idle speed adjustment screws of the remaining carburettors until they also pass identical volumes of air. Where the throttle linkage is arranged from a common shaft, the individual throttle levers will have to be adjusted by loosening the locknuts.
10 If necessary, from each idling speed adjustment screw by equal amounts to bring the engine speed within the recommended idling limits.
11 The mixture screw adjustments on each carburettor must now be set and synchronised. Since each screw was turned to

its preliminary setting, it can be assumed that they are reasonably synchronised to start with. With the engine idling, turn all the screws by equal amounts ($\frac{1}{2}$ a turn initially) and observe whether the engine speed falls or increases. Make several adjustments in a similar manner until the engine runs at the highest speed commensurate with even firing.

12 If necessary, again turn each idling speed adjustment screw by equal amounts to bring the engine speed within the recommended idling limits.

13 The final mixture screw synchronisation can be determined by allowing the engine to idle, then to remove each spark plug lead in turn and observe the reduction in engine rpm on the tachometer. The reduction should be identical for each cylinder, thus proving that the mixture strength is also identical for each cylinder. A further check can be made by removing the spark plugs after the engine has been idling for approximately 15 minutes. Any with black sooty deposits indicate that the particular cylinder is running rich. Normally if the mixture screw has not been set correctly, weakening it by half a turn during idling will cut the relevant cylinder.

14 If necessary adjust the idling speed screws on each carburettor by equal amounts to obtain the correct engine idling speed.

15 Note that on some applications it may be advisable to fit 'hotter' spark plugs whilst adjusting the carburettors to prevent misfiring. However the original plugs must always be refitted after completing the adjustment.

16 Switch off the engine and reconnect the throttle linkages, making adjustments as necessary to prevent the carburettor settings from being affected.

17 Remove the tachometer from the engine and refit the air cleaner(s), if fitted.

9 Fault diagnosis

Symptom	Reason
Engine will not start	Blocked fuel filter or jets
	Flooded engine as a result of depressing accelerator pedal
Uneven idling	Leaking manifold or carburettor flange gaskets
	Loose idling jets or auxiliary venturis
	Excessive sediment or water in carburettor
	Worn throttle spindle
	Incorrect tuning adjustments
Carburettor floods	Worn needle valve
	Leaking or damaged float(s)
	Incorrect float level adjustments
	Excessive sediment in fuel
Engine lacks performance	Incorrect tuning adjustments
	Incorrect float level adjustments
	Excessive sediment in fuel
	Throttle valves not fully opening
	Accelerator pump faulty or leaking
Excessive fuel consumption	Needle valve not seating
	Leaking or damaged float(s)
	Incorrect float level adjustments
	Choked air filter (if fitted)

Part 2
Chapter 13 Type 36 DCNF,
40 DCNF, 42 DCNF, 44 DCNF carburettors

Contents

1   Introduction

The carburettors covered by this Chapter are of vertical downdraught type and each barrel of the carburettor is of identical diameter.

The throttle valves are of the synchronised, simultaneous operation type and are located on a single shaft.

The identification mark is located on the main body on the outer face of the float chamber wall.

2   Construction

The main body and cover of the Weber DCNF carburettor are of die-cast aluminium or zinc alloy (Mazak) construction. The mounting flange is machined flat for fitting on the inlet manifold.

The throttle spindle is made of steel and the throttle valve plates of brass.

All fuel and air jets and emulsion tubes are of brass construction and are secured to the main body by screw fittings.

The internal channels of the main body are mainly drilled and where necessary, sealed with lead plugs.

The throttle spindle is supported by two ball-bearings mounted in the main body. Washers are located at each end of the spindle to prevent air being drawn through the bearings.

The fuel float assembly isconstructed of thin brass sheet and comprises two halves soldered together.

The accelerator pump is of the diaphragm type and the operating lever is actuated by a cam plate attached to the end of the throttle shaft.

3   Operation

Cold starting

The starting device fitted to type DCNF carburettors operates independently of the main circuit and may be considered as a separate carburettor within the main carburettor.

Refer to Fig. 13.1 and note that when the choke cable is pulled, the starting device operating lever turns the control shafts which lift the starting valves off their seats. Fuel from the float chamber (8) is drawn through channels (34) into the starting jets (32) where it is emulsified with air entering through the top of the starting jets (32). The mixture is then drawn through channels (33) where it is further emulsified with air from the hole (31). After passing the starter valves (37) where additional air from holes (36) weakens the mixture, the final mixture is drawn through channels (35) into the engine below the throttle valves (14).

The starting device has a progressive action made possible by the tapered end of the valve heads and lowering the valves will reduce the amount of mixture admitted to the engine until, when completely shut, the supply will cease.

Idling and progression

Refer to Fig. 13.2 and note that when the engine is idling with the throttle valves (14) closed, fuel is drawn through the main jets and emulsion tube wells (6), along channels (18) to the idling jets (19) where it becomes emulsified with air entering through the calibrated bushes (20). The mixture then travels through the channels (17), past the adjustable mixture screws (16), through the idling feed holes (15) and into the carburettor throats at the engine side of the throttle valves (14). The idling mixture screws (16) have tapered ends and can therefore be adjusted to admit more or less mixture as necessary.

When the throttle valves are opened slightly to increase the engine speed, the progression holes (13) are brought into action to provide additional fuel and to enable the engine to reach the speed when the main system starts to function.

In order to ensure that each carburettor barrel passes

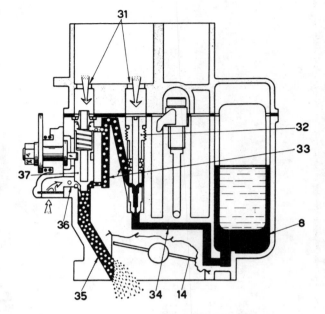

Fig. 13.1 Cold starting phase (Sec 3)

8 Float chamber	34 Channel
14 Throttle valves	35 Channel
31 Air holes	36 Channel
32 Starting jets	37 Starting valves
33 Channel	

identical amounts of air, in particular when the engine is idling, the majority of DCNF carburettors incorporate air compensation screws in each barrel, whereby air can bypass the throttle valves (14) via the starting device ducts (35). This system ensures identical vacuum below each throttle valve and therefore ensures identical mixtures during idling and progression.

Normal running

Refer to Fig. 13.3 and note that under full throttle and high speed cruise conditions, fuel is drawn from the float chamber (8), through the main jets (7) to the emulsion tubes (6). The fuel becomes emulsified with air drawn through the air corrector jets (1) and is then drawn through the nozzles (2), auxiliary venturis (3) and chokes (4) into the engine.

Acceleration

Refer to Fig. 13.4 and note that when the throttle valves are closed, the spring (24) pushes the diaphragm (28) outwards and fuel is drawn from the float chamber (8), through the ball valve (30) into the pump chamber. When the throttle valves are opened, the cam (25) operates the lever (26) and the diaphragm (28) is depressed against the tension of the spring (24). Fuel is forced along the channel (23) to the delivery valve (22) and is injected through the pump jets (21) into the carburettor barrels in the vicinity of the auxiliary venturis. The spring (27) dampens any sudden opening of the throttle valves and prolongs the full delivery. The calibrated discharge hole (29) allows excess fuel and any accumulated air and vapour to escape into the float chamber.

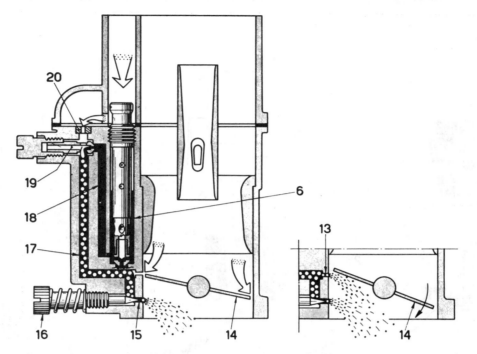

Fig. 13.2 Idling and progression phase (Sec 3)

6 Emulsion tube wells	15 Idle feed holes	18 Channel
13 Progression holes	16 Idle mixture screw	19 Idle jets
14 Throttle valves	17 Channel	20 Calibrated bushes

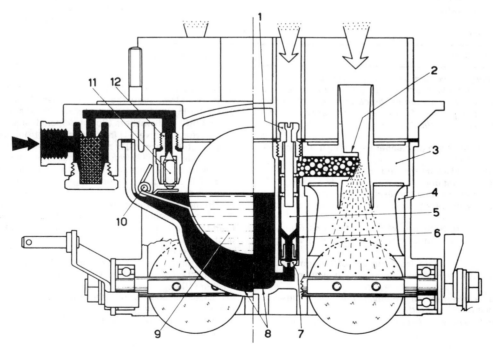

Fig. 13.3 Normal phase (Sec 3)

1 Air corrector jets	5 Emulsion tubes	9 Float
2 Nozzles	6 Emulsion tube wells	10 Fulcrum pin
3 Auxiliary venturis	7 Main jets	11 Needle
4 Chokes	8 Float chamber	12 Needle valve seating

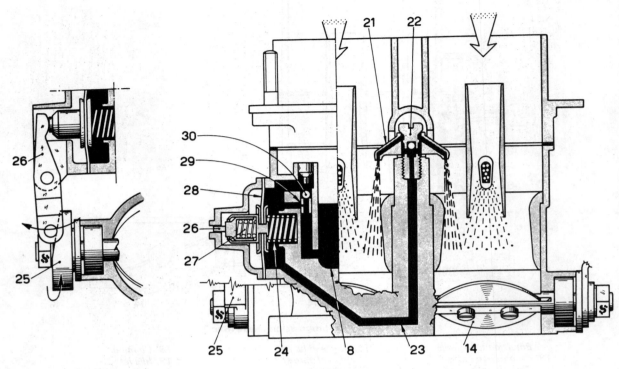

Fig. 13.4 Acceleration phase (Sec 3)

8	Float chamber	23	Channel	27	Reaction spring
14	Throttle valves	24	Return spring	28	Diaphragm
21	Pump jets	25	Cam	29	Calibrated discharge hole
22	Delivery valve	26	Operating lever	30	Ball valve

4 Removal and refitting

Note: *The following procedure gives a general rather than a specific method of removing and refitting the carburettor, as much will depend on the location of the carburettor within the vehicle. On some applications for instance, the retaining nuts may not be accessible without removing surrounding components.*

1   Where fitted, remove the air cleaner assembly from the carburettor.
2   Disconnect the throttle linkage and choke cable.
3   Unscrew the fuel inlet union and recover the two gaskets.
4   Unscrew and remove the carburettor retaining nuts and spring washers and withdraw the carburettor complete over the mounting studs.
5   Remove the gasket from the inlet manifold and clean all traces of gasket from the contact faces of the manifold and carburettor.
6   Protect the inlet manifold from ingress of foreign matter whilst the carburettor is removed by sealing it with masking tape.
7   Refitting is a reversal of removal but the following additional points should be noted:
    (a)   Always fit a new gasket and tighten the retaining nuts evenly in diagonal sequence
    (b)   The idling adjustment screws should be set as described in Section 7 and finally tuned as described in Section 8
    (c)   When refitting the choke (starting device) cable, first secure the outer cable to the support, then insert the inner cable into the operating lever nut and push the instrument panel control knob fully in. Tighten the inner cable retaining screw with the operating lever fully released.

5 Disassembly

1   Thoroughly clean the carburettor exterior and wipe dry.
2   Where air horns are fitted, remove the retaining screws and washers and withdraw the air horn assembly.
3   Referring to Fig. 13.5, unscrew and remove the retaining screws (86) and washers (85) in diagonal sequence and lift the carburettor top cover (1) from the carburettor body (51), making sure that the gasket (3) is not broken (photo).
4   Lift the gasket (3) from the carburettor body (51).
5   Invert the carburettor cover (1) and unscrew the filter cover plug (78), using a 19 mm ring spanner or socket (photo). Remove the washer (79).
6   Remove the filter gauze (81) and extract the base (80).
7   Using a suitable diameter metal drift, tap the fulcrum pin (9) from the support posts (photo). Do not attempt to prise the split post apart.
8   Lift the float assembly (18) from the cover and extract the needle from the needle valve seating (11) (photo).
9   Unscrew and remove the needle valve seating (11) and washer (10).
10 Unscrew and remove the retaining screw (7) and remove the washer and bush (8) (photo).
11 Lift the operating arm (13) and disengage the rod (4 or 6) from the starter device.
12 Extract the split pin (5) and remove the rod from the operating arm (14) (photo). Remove the clamp screw (15) if necessary.
13 Unscrew and remove the retaining screws (69) and washers (70) and remove the starter device (61) from the carburettor (photo).
14 Dismantle the starter device by unscrewing the nut (68) from the shaft (62) together with the washer (67), then carefully

5.3 Removing the carburettor top cover

5.5 Removing the fuel filter and plug

5.7 Removing the float fulcrum pin

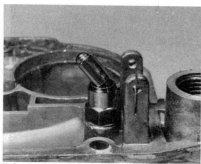
5.8 Removing the needle from the needle valve seating

5.10 Starter device operating rod and lever location

5.12 Starter device operating rod split pin location

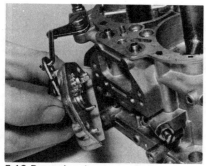
5.13 Removing the starter device

5.15 Removing an emulsion tube

5.16 Separating the main jet and air corrector jet from the emulsion tube

remove the lever (66) and spring (65). Withdraw the shaft (62) and filter gauze (64).

15 Unscrew and remove the air corrector jets (12) from the carburettor body (51) and lift out the emulsion tube assemblies (photo).

16 Separate the emulsion tubes (17) from the air corrector jets (12) and main jets (25) (photo). Take care not to damage the jets when removing them and, if pliers are used, interpose a piece of paper or card to prevent the brass being scratched. Alternatively, insert a small drill through the emulsion tube holes to retain it whilst the jets are turned off each end.

17 Unscrew the idling jet holders (28) from the sides of the carburettor body (51), remove the rubber O-rings (27), then separate the idling jets (26) (photos).

18 Whilst depressing the starter valve spring retaining guides (75) in turn, prise the spring washers (74) from the carburettor body, then release the guides (75) and extract the return springs (76) and starter valves (77) (photos). Note from which bore

each valve is taken so that they can be refitted in their original locations. Do not force the valves if they will not come out freely; if a burr exists at the top of the bore, remove it with a fine file.

19 Unscrew and remove the starter jets (73) (photo).

20 Unscrew and remove the accelerator pump delivery valve (16) together with the pump jet (23) and copper washers (24) (photo), then separate the washers and jet from the valve.

21 Unscrew the retaining screws and washers (31) and withdraw the pump cover (22) from the carburettor body (photo). Take care not to damage the diaphragm and if necessary, use a blunt knife to release it from the body.

22 Remove the diaphragm (30) and spring (29) (photo). Note that the gasket must not be separated from the diaphragm.

23 Mark the accelerator pump lever (21) in relation to the cover (22) to ensure correct refitting, then, using a suitable diameter metal drift, drive the pin (20) up out of the cover (22). On some models it will be necessary to remove a split pin,

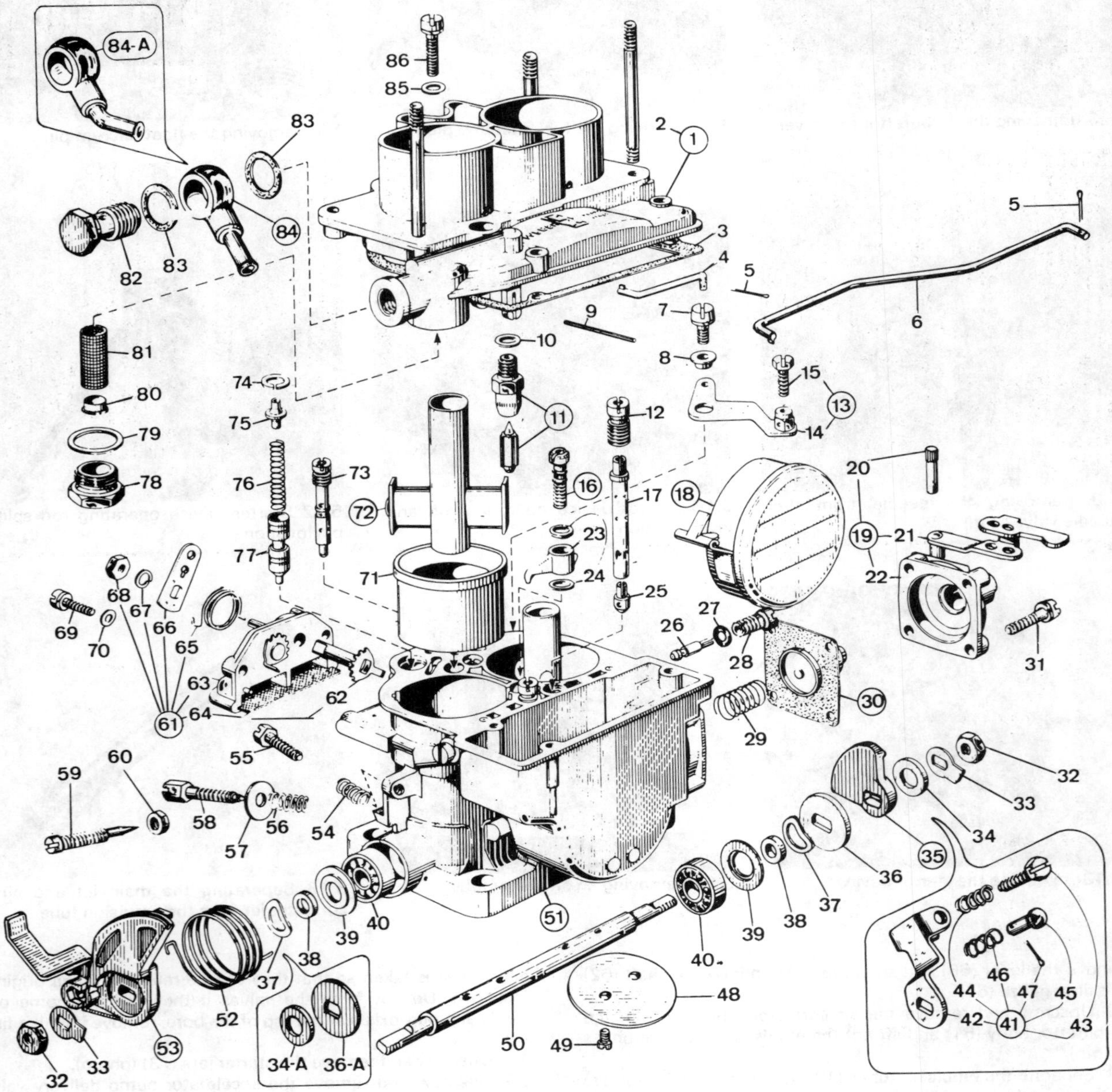
84-A
86
85
83
2
1
5
84
82
83
3
4
5
6
9
7
81
10
8
15
74
80
11
13
75
12
14
79
20
73
78
16
17
18
76
72
19
21
23
77
71
22
68
67
24
25
69
66
26
27
70
65
28
31
63
62
30
61
64
29
55
32
60
59
33
58
56
54
35
34
57
36
37
40
39
51
39
38
37
38
40
37
44
46
47
45
52
48
53
34-A
36-A
42
41
43
32
33
50
49

5.17a Removing the idling jets

5.17b An idling jet and holder

5.18a Removing the starter spring components ...

5.18b ... and starter valves

5.19 Removing a starter jet

5.20 Removing the accelerator pump delivery valve and jet

Fig. 13.5 Exploded view of the 36 DCNF carburettor (typical) (Sec 5)

1 Top cover	30 Diaphragm	59 Air bypass screw
2 Stud	31 Screw	60 Locknut
3 Gasket	32 Nut	61 Starting device assembly
4 Operating rod	33 Tab washer	62 Shaft and sector
5 Split pin	34 Spacers	63 Housing
6 Operating rod link	35 Cam	64 Filter gauze
7 Screw	36 Spacers	65 Return spring
8 Bush	37 Wave washer	66 Lever
9 Fulcrum pin	38 Spacer	67 Washer
10 Gasket	39 End washer	68 Nut
11 Needle valve assembly	40 Ball-bearing	69 Screw
12 Air corrector jet	41 Throttle lever assembly	70 Washer
13 Starting device lever assembly	42 Lever	71 Choke
14 Starting device lever	43 Adjustment screw	72 Auxiliary venturi
15 Clamp screw	44 Spring	73 Starter jet
16 Delivery valve	45 Pressure pin	74 Retaining clip
17 Emulsion tube	46 Spring	75 Retaining guide
18 Float	47 Split pin	76 Spring
19 Accelerator pump cover assembly	48 Throttle valve	77 Starter valve
20 Pivot pin	49 Retaining screw	78 Plug
21 Lever	50 Throttle spindle	79 Gasket
22 Cover	51 Carburettor body	80 Base
23 Pump jets	52 Return spring	81 Filter
24 Washers	53 Throttle lever	82 Fuel inlet bolt
25 Main jet	54 Spring	83 Gasket
26 Idle jet	55 Idle speed screw	84 and 84A Inlet union
27 Rubber O-ring	56 Spring	85 Washer
28 Idle jet holder	57 Washer	86 Screw
29 Return spring	58 Idle mixture screw	

5.21 Withdrawing the accelerator pump cover

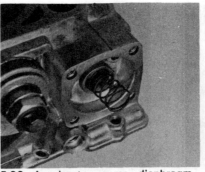
5.22 Accelerator pump diaphragm return spring location

5.25 Removing a choke

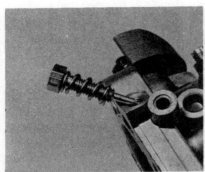
5.26 Removing an idling mixture adjusting screw

5.27 Idle speed screw location

5.28 Removing an air bypass adjusting screw

5.30a Throttle lever and end nut with locktab

5.30b Accelerator pump cam and end nut with locktab

5.32 Throttle return spring location

5.33 Accelerator pump cam and sector

5.36 Removing a throttle valve

5.39 Removing the throttle spindle

washer and clevis pin.

24 Note the location of the auxiliary venturis (72) and mark them if necessary, with a pencil to ensure correct refitting. The auxiliary venturis (72) are lightly staked into the carburettor body and to remove them, it will be necessary to insert a wooden or plastic dowel rod through the throttle valve end of the barrels to tap them free. If they are excessively tight it will be necessary to obtain the special Weber tool no 98009 200.

25 Using a fine file, remove the staking from the two barrels, then note the locations of each choke (71) and slide them out of the barrels. Note that the choke ends with the smaller internal diameters are uppermost (photo).

26 Unscrew and remove the idling mixture adjusting screws (58) together with the springs (56) and washers (57) where fitted (photo).

27 Unscrew and remove the idle speed screw (55), spring (54) and sleeve, where fitted (photo).

28 Loosen the locknuts (60) with an 8 mm ring spanner, then unscrew and remove the air bypass screws (59) (photo).

29 Where fitted, unhook the throttle return spring from the accelerator pump end of the throttle spindle (50).

30 Bend back the locktabs (33) on each end of the throttle spindle (50), then unscrew and remove the nuts (32) (photos). If these are very tight, use Weber tool no 98023 700 to hold the spindle whilst they are loosened; this will prevent the spindle from being buckled. Do not loosen a tight nut with the throttle valves being forced against the barrel walls; instead, use a screwdriver to hold the throttle lever (53) in the open position.

31 Remove the nuts (32), tab washers (33) and spacer (34) from the throttle spindle (50), together with the throttle return spring lever where fitted.

32 Turn the throttle lever (53) against the tension of the coil spring (52) then ease it from the throttle spindle (50) and remove the coil spring (photo). Remove the wave washer (37) together with washers (34A and 36A) where fitted.

33 Using a screwdriver, prise the accelerator pump cam and sector (35) from the throttle spindle (50), together with the spacer (36) when fitted (photo). Remove the wave washer (37).

34 Unscrew and remove the throttle valve retaining screws (49), being careful not to exert excessive pressure on the spindle (50).

35 Note the position of the throttle spindle and valves in relation to the barrels and if necessary, mark the valves with a pencil.

36 Turn the spindle to the fully open position and withdraw the two throttle valves (48) from their location slots (photo).

37 Mark one end of the throttle spindle (50) in relation to the carburettor body (51) to ensure correct refitting.

5.40 Throttle spindle wave washer, spacer and bearing washer

38 Check that the spindle (50) is free of any burrs in the vicinity of the valve retaining screw holes and if necessary, remove them with a fine file.

39 Using a plastic mallet, drive the spindle (50) from the carburettor (photo).

40 Remove the spacers (38) and end washers (39) from the spindle and carburettor body (photo).

41 Tap the spindle (50) through the bearing (40) with the bearing placed on a vice.

42 Re-insert the spindle (50) and drive the remaining bearing (40) from the carburettor body (51). Remove the bearing from the spindle.

43 Where fitted, unscrew the idle speed screw (43) and spring (44) from the throttle lever (42), then remove the split pin (47), pressure pin (45) and spring (46).

6 Special overhaul procedures

After carrying out the general overhaul procedures given in Chapter 4, the following special procedures should be completed:

1 Using a hand chuck and the special tool available from Weber or a tool hire agent, reform the main jet seatings at the bottom of the emulsion tube housing wells by carefully rotating the tool in alternate directions. Finish the seatings with the special drift by tapping it gently whilst rotating it at the same time.

2 Using the same procedure as described in paragraph 1, reform the idling jet seats.

3 Using the same procedure as described in paragraph 1, reform the starter valve seats.

4 Using the same procedure as described in paragraph 1, reform the starter jet seats.

5 If the emulsion tube wells are discoloured and considerable sediment has accumulated, the bores must be reamed using the special Weber tool and a hand chuck. Turn the tool carefully until it moves freely, then continue turning it whilst removing it.

6 Check the internal channels of the carburettor body cover by injecting fuel from a syringe and observing whether it emerges freely. If any channels are blocked, it will be necessary to drill out the lead plugs and use Weber tool nos 98014 300, 98014 400 and 98014 500 to clear them. These tool numbers refer to the three channel diameters of 1.0 mm, 1.5 mm and 2.0 mm.

7 Check that the accelerator pump ball valve is free by shaking the carburettor body and listening to the ball movement.

8 After overhaul, the carburettor body should be thoroughly cleaned, preferably using clean fuel and air pressure. The lead plugs should be renewed and retained in position by using the Weber tool no 98010 700 or 98010 800 as a punch until the plugs are expanded into their bores.

9 Check the float assembly for damage and leakage; shake the float to determine whether fuel has entered. If the float is damaged or fuel is present, it must be renewed.

10 Check and renew if necessary, the accelerator pump lever and diaphragm.

7 Assembly

Note: *All components should be clean and dry before starting the assembly procedure.*

1 Where fitted, fit the spring (46) and pressure pin (45) to the throttle lever (42) and secure with the split pin (47).

2 Fit the idle speed screw (43) and spring (44) to the throttle lever (42), when fitted.

3 Using a suitable diameter length of tubing, drive one bearing (40) fully into the carburettor body (51) at the accelerator pump end.

4 Place the remaining ball-bearing (40) on an open vice and gently tap the spindle (50) into it, entering the end with the

shorter recess first.

5   Insert the throttle spindle (50) into the carburettor body (51), then make sure that the bearings (40) are fully seated on the spindle by supporting one in a suitable diameter length of tubing and using a further length of tubing to tap the opposite bearing.

6   Fit the end washers (39) and spacers (38) over the ends of the spindle (50) after lubricating the bearings with a little grease.

7   Turn the throttle spindle (50) so that the throttle valve retaining screw head recesses are facing the carburettor mounting flange. Place the carburettor body (51) on the accelerator pump end then locate the wave washer (37) over the spindle, together with the washers (34A and 36A) where fitted.

8   Locate the return spring (52) in the hole on the body and hook the remaining end over the flat edge of the throttle lever (53). Tension the spring and press the throttle lever (53) fully onto the spindle (50).

9   Fit the tab washer (33) and nut (32), then tighten the nut and lock it by bending the tab onto a flat; do not overtighten the nut.

10 Turn the throttle lever (53) fully open so that the throttle valve slots can be seen from the flange end of the carburettor, then insert one throttle valve (48) in the location previously noted and close the valve. Make sure that the throttle valve is fitted the correct way round so that the angled perimeter seats in the barrel.

11 Snap the valve shut several times in order to centralise it, then insert and tighten the valve retaining screws (49) without exerting excessive pressure on the spindle. It is recommended that new screws are always fitted as it is quite easy to cross-thread previously peened screws. Lock the screws by peening with Weber tool no 98010 900 whilst supporting the spindle with a length of wood. Alternatively, coat the threads with a liquid locking agent (fuel resistant) prior to inserting them.

12 Repeat the procedure described in paragraphs 10 and 11 for the remaining throttle valve.

13 Locate the wave washer (37) over the spindle (50) and fit the spacer (36) when fitted.

14 Press the sector into the nylon accelerator pump cam (35), then fit the cam over the spindle with the lowest cam contour uppermost.

15 Fit the spacer (34) throttle return spring lever where fitted, tab washer (33) and nut (32). Tighten the nut (32) whilst holding the throttle lever (53) open with a screwdriver, then lock it by bending the locktab; do not overtighten the nut.

16 Where fitted, hook the throttle return spring onto the lever on the end of the spindle (50).

17 Insert the air bypass screws (59) and screw them in until they are fully seated, then tighten the locknuts (60).

18 Fit the idle speed screw (55), spring (54) and sleeve where fitted.

19 Fit the idling mixture adjusting screws (58) together with the springs (56) and washers (57), where fitted.

20 Insert the chokes (71) into the barrels with the smaller internal diameter ends uppermost.

21 Fit the auxiliary venturis (72) in their original locations, making sure that the location springs engage with the grooves in the barrels and that the supply channels are in alignment with those in the carburettor body. The extended venturis must also be uppermost (photos).

22 With the auxiliary venturis (72) fully seated, lightly stake the carburettor upper face to retain them. Use a blade pinch and not a centre punch to do this.

23 Assemble the lever (21) to the accelerator pump cover (22) in its previously noted position, then drive the pin (20) through the cover and lever until fully entered. Where a clevis pin is fitted, insert it through the cover and lever and retain it with the washer and split pin.

24 Support the carburettor body (51) with the pump diaphragm face uppermost, then locate the spring (29) on the face in the central position.

25 Place the diaphragm (30) over the spring (29), then locate the pump cover (22) over the diaphragm (30).

26 Insert the retaining screws and washers (31) and tighten them evenly in diagonal sequence. Operate the throttle lever and make sure that the pump lever runs smoothly and is in contact with the cam.

27 Assemble the accelerator pump (23) to the delivery valve (16) with a copper washer (24) either side, then tighten the assembly into the carburettor body.

28 Insert and tighten the starter jets (73).

29 Fit the starter valves (77) into their respective bores followed by the return springs (76) and retainers (75).

30 Depress the retainers (75) in turn and locate the spring washers (74) in the carburettor recesses, pressing them fully in with the flat blade of a screwdriver (photo).

31 Press the idling jets (26) into the holders (28), fit the rubber O-rings (27), then tighten the holders into the carburettor body.

32 Press the emulsion tubes (17) onto the main jets (25) and into the air corrector jets (12). Insert and tighten the air corrector jets (12) into the carburettor body together with the emulsion tubes.

33 Assemble the shaft (62) to the starter device body so that the alignment lines on each sector are facing each other, then fit the coil spring (65) with its end in the location hole. Fit the lever (66) over the shaft (62) and at the same time hook the end of the spring (65) over the lever, then locate the washer (67) and nut (68), and tighten the nut.

34 Fit the filter gauze (64) and check that the starter device operates smoothly.

35 Offer the starter device (61) up to the carburettor body and make sure that the sector lugs locate in the starter valve grooves, then insert the retaining screws (69) and washers (70) and tighten the screws. Check that the starter device operates smoothly.

36 Fit the clamp screw (15) to the starter device operating arm (14).

7.21a Fitting an auxiliary venturi, showing the location spring

7.21b Showing the auxiliary venturi channel which must face the emulsion tube well

7.30 The starter valves fitted in the main body

37 Insert the operating rod (4 or 6) into the arm (14) and screw with the split pin (5).
38 Insert the rod into the starter device arm (66), then assemble the bush (8) and washer and tighten the retaining screw (7) into the carburettor body.
39 Tighten the needle valve seating (11) together with a new gasket (10) into the carburettor cover (1).
40 Lower the needle into the needle valve seating (11), tapered end first.
41 Lower the float assembly (18) onto the cover (1) and insert the fulcrum pin (9) through the support posts and float arm. If necessary, gently pinch the split post to secure the pin using a pair of pliers.
42 The float level adjustment must now be checked in the following manner: Hold the carburettor screw vertical so that the float is hanging from the fulcrum pin with the float level arm in light contact with the needle ball (ie without the ball being depressed). Using a vernier caliper, check that the distance from the cover face (without gasket) to the top of the float as shown in Fig. 13.6 is 1.890 in (48 mm) for 42 DCNF models and 1.969 in (50 mm) for other DCNF models (photo). If not, bend the needle operating tab as necessary.
43 Tilt the cover so that the float moves away from the cover and the tab makes contact with the needle valve seating. Now, using the same method as described in paragraph 42, check that the needle valve fully open dimension is 2.224 in (56.5 mm) for 42 DCNF models and 2.303 in (58.5 mm) for other DCNF models (photo). If not, bend the tab which contacts the needle valve seating as necessary.
44 The difference between the dimensions checked in paragraphs 42 and 43 is the needle valve stroke which should be 0.335 in (8.5 mm).
45 Fit the base (80) to the filter gauze (81). With the carburettor cover (1) inverted, press the filter gauze into the inlet cavity.
46 Fit the washer (79) to the filter cover plug (78), then tighten the plug into the cover (1).
47 Place the gasket (3) onto the top face of the carburettor body (51).
48 Lower the carburettor cover (1) onto the main body (51), then insert the retaining screws (86) and washers (85) and

tighten them a little at a time in diagonal sequence.
49 Fit the air horn assembly, where fitted. Insert the retaining screws and washers and tighten them evenly in diagonal sequence.
50 With the carburettor completely assembled, the idling adjustment screws should be turned to their preliminary settings. To do this, first screw in the idling speed adjustment screw until it just touches the throttle lever, then continue turning for a further ½ turn. Working on the idling mixture volume screws in turn, fully screw them in until they are in contact with their seats, then back them off 2 complete turns. Final adjustments will be necessary with the carburettor fitted on the engine (refer to Section 8).

8 Tuning

Note: *Refer to Chapter 3 for general notes on tuning.*
1   Set the idling adjustment screws to their preliminary positions as described in Section 7.
2   Connect a tachometer to the engine in accordance with the manufacturer's instructions.
3   It is now important to understand that each barrel of each carburettor must be synchronised in order to deliver equal

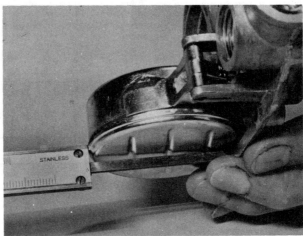

7.42 Checking the float closed position with vernier calipers

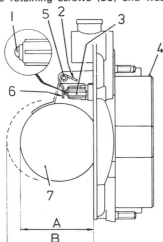

Fig. 13.6 Float level adjustment dimensions (Sec 7)

1   Spring loaded ball
2   Stroke adjusting tab
3   Needle valve assembly
4   Carburettor cover
5   Fulcrum pin
6   Height adjusting tab
7   Float
A   Needle valve fully closed dimension
B   Needle valve fully open dimension

7.43 Checking the float open position with vernier calipers

amounts of air/fuel mixture to each individual cylinder. To check this, it will be necessary to obtain a length of tubing (approximately 1 metre) of about 5 mm to 10 mm (0.25 in to 0.5 in) internal diameter. Alternatively, a synchroniser as illustrated in Chapter 8 may be used.
4   Remove the air cleaner(s) if fitted, then run the engine until normal operating temperature is reached. To ensure that the engine is really hot enough, drive it hard over a 5 mile distance.
5   Switch off the engine and disconnect the accelerator rod connections from each carburettor.
6   Where two carburettor throttle spindles are linked, turn the adjustment screw on the link $\frac{1}{2}$ a turn in from the fully shut position.
7   Start the engine and adjust each idling speed adjusting screw (except link adjustments) by equal amounts until the engine is idling at the approximate recommended speed. This will vary according to the application and state of tune of the engine but on average will be around 800 rpm.
8   The barrels of each individual carburettor must now be synchronised to pass identical quantities of air during idling. To do this, loosen the locknuts and check that the bypass screws are both in light contact with their seats. Place one end of the synchronising tube in one air intake and listen at the other end to the amount of hiss present. Alternatively, use the synchroniser to record the air flow through the air intake. Check both air intakes of the carburettor to determine which one is passing the greatest amount of air, then adjust the remaining barrel to give an identical volume and finally tighten the adjustment locknuts. Carry out the procedure independently on each carburettor fitted to the engine.
9   Each carburettor must now be synchronised with the remaining carburettors. To do this, allow the engine to idle and check the volume of air flowing through one air intake of each carburettor, using the length of tube or the synchroniser. Determine the carburettor which is passing the medium volume of air and adjust the idle speed adjustment screws of the remaining

carburettors until they also pass identical volumes of air.
10   If the engine idling speed is not now within the recommended limits, turn each idling speed adjustment screw by equal amounts as necessary.
11   The mixture screw adjustments on each carburettor must now be set and synchronised. Since each screw was turned to its preliminary setting, it can be assumed that they are reasonably synchronised to start with. With the engine idling, turn all the screws by equal amounts ($\frac{1}{2}$ a turn initially) first in one direction, then in the reverse direction. Observe whether the engine speed falls or increases and make several adjustments until the engine runs at the highest speed commensurate with even firing.
12   If necessary, again turn each idling speed adjustment screw by equal amounts to bring the engine speed within the recommended limits.
13   To check whether the final mixture screw synchronisation is correct, allow the engine to idle, then remove each spark plug lead in turn and observe the reduction in engine rpm on the tachometer. The reduction should be identical for each cylinder, thus proving that the mixture strength is also identical for each cylinder. A further check can be made by removing the spark plugs after the engine has been idling for approximately 15 minutes. Any with black sooty deposits indicate that the particular cylinder is running rich. Normally, if the mixture screw has been set correctly, weakening it by half a turn during idling will cut the relevant cylinder.
14   Note that on some applications it may be advisable to fit 'hotter' spark plugs whilst adjusting the carburettors to prevent misfiring. However, the original plugs must always be refitted after completing the adjustment.
15   Switch off the engine and reconnect the throttle linkages, making any adjustments as necessary to prevent the carburettor idling settings from being affected.
16   Remove the tachometer from the engine and refit the air cleaner(s), if fitted.

9 Fault diagnosis

Symptom	Reason
Engine will not start	Blocked fuel filter or jets Flooded engine as a result of faulty needle valve or depressing accelerator pedal
Uneven idling	Leaking manifold or carburettor flange gaskets Loose idling jets or auxiliary venturis Excessive sediment or water in carburettor Incorrect tuning adjustments
Carburettor floods	Worn needle valve Leaking or damaged float Incorrect float level adjustments Excessive sediment in fuel
Engine lacks performance	Incorrect tuning adjustments Incorrect float level adjustments Excessive sediment in fuel Throttle valves not fully opening Accelerator pump faulty or leaking
Excessive fuel consumption	Needle valve not seating Leaking or damaged float Incorrect float level adjustments Choked air filter (if fitted)

Part 3
Appendix 1   Original equipment jet setting list

This list gives details of calibration and jet sizes on carburettors fitted as original equipment:

A	*Model details*
B	*Number of cylinders*
C	*Capacity in cc*
D	*Carburettor type*
E	*Number of carburettors*
F	*Choke sizes*
G	*Auxiliary venturi*
H	*Main jet*
I	*Idle jet*
J	*Air idle jet or hole*

K	*Emulsion tube*
L	*Air corrector jet*
M	*Starter jet*
N	*Accelerator pump jet*
O	*Accelerator pump back bleed*
P	*Needle valve*

Note:

Where two sets of data are tabulated against the car model, the first line refers to the primary barrel and the second line refers to the secondary barrel

A	B	C	D	E	F	G	H	I	J	K	L	M	N	O	P
ALFA ROMEO															
Giulietta Sprint Veloce	4	1290	40 DCOE 2	2	29	4·50	1·10	0·50 F11	–	F16	2·00	0·60 F5	0·35	0·70	1·50
1300 GT Junior Super	4	1290	40 DCOE 28	2	28	4·50	1·12	0·50 F11	–	F16	2·10	0·65 F5	0·35	0·60	1·50
Giulia 1600 SS	4	1570	40 DCOE 2	2	30	4·50	1·20	0·55 F11	–	F16	1·80	0·65 F5	0·35	0·70	1·50
Giulia 1600 TI Super	4	1570	45 DCOE 14	2	30	4·50	1·20	0·55 F8	–	F16	1·80	0·65 F5	0·35	0·50	1·50
Giulia 1600 Sprint GT	4	1570	40 DCOE 4	2	30	4·50	1·27	0·50 F11	–	F16	2·20	0·65 F5	0·35	0·50	1·50
Giulia 1600 Super	4	1570	40 DCOE 24	2	27	4·50	1·10	0·50 F11	–	F16	1·80	0·65 F5	0·35	0·50	1·50
Giulia 1600 Super	4	1570	40 DCOE 33	2	30	4·50	1·20	0·50 F14	–	F9	2·00	0·65 F5	0·35	0·60	1·50
1600 Junior Z, Giulia															
1600 Super	4	1570	40 DCOE 44/55	2	30	4·50	1·17	0·50 F15	–	F16	1·80	0·65 F5	0·35	0·60	1·50
Giulia 1600 GTV/Spider	4	1570	40 DCOE 27	2	30	4·50	1·17	0·50 F14	–	F16	1·80	0·65 F5	0·35	0·60	1·50
Giulia 1600 GTA	4	1570	45 DCOE 14	2	30	4·50	1·35	0·50 F8	–	F16	2·20	0·65 F5	0·35	0·50	1·50
Giulia 1600 Sprint GTA	4	1570	45 DCOE 18	2	30	4·50	1·20	0·50 F8	–	F9	2·20	0·65 F5	0·35	0·50	1·50
1750 Berlina/Coupé GT															

A	B	C	D	E	F	G	H	I	J	K	L	M	N	O	P
Veloce/Spider Veloce Giulia 1600, Alfetta	4	1779	40 DCOE 32	2	32	4·50	1·30	0·50 F8	—	F9	2·00	0·65 F5	0·35	0·60	1·50
1600	4	1570	40 DCOE 106/107	2	30	6·00	1·32	0·55 F21	—	F41	1·80	0·85 F9	0·30	none	1·50
Alfetta 1·6	4	1570	40 DCOE 82/83	2	30	6·00	1·32	0·55 F21	—	F41	1·80	0·85 F9	0·35	0·35	1·50
Alfetta 1·8	4	1779	40 DCOE 72/73	2	32	4·50	1·35	0·55 F17	—	F34	2·10	0·85 F9	0·35	0·60	1·50
2000 GT Spider Europa	4	1962	40 DCOE 76/77	2	32	4·50	1·35	0·55 F17	—	F34	2·10	0·85 F9	0·35	0·60	1·50
2600 Sprint-Coupé	6	2584	45 DCOE 9	3	36	4·50	1·45	0·55 F8	—	F16	1·55	0·60 F5	0·45	0·40	2·00
ASTON MARTIN															
DB4 GT	6	3670	45 DCOE 9	3	40	3·50	1·55	0·55 F6	—	F2	1·50	0·60 F5	0·55	none	2·00
DB5 GT, DB6 Vantage	6	3995	45 DCOE 9	3	40	4·50	1·50	0·50 F6	—	F2	1·25	0·60 F5	0·45	none	2·00
DB 6MK Coupé	6	3995	45 DCOE 9	3	40	4·50	1·45	0·50 F6	—	F7	1·25	0·60 F6	0·45	none	2·00
DBS V8 Europa	8	5340	42 DCNF 27/100	4	36	4·50	1·35	0·55	1·10	F33	1·80	0·80 F5	0·45	0·40	2·00
DBS V8 Europa	8	5340	42 DCNF 27/150	4	36	4·50	1·35	0·55	1·10	F39	1·80	0·80 F5	0·45	0·40	2·00
DBS V8 USA	8	5340	42 DCNF 27/200	4	36	4·50	1·35	0·55	1·10	F39	2·20	0·80 F5	0·45	0·40	2·00
BMW															
1800 T1/SA	4	1773	45 DCOE 15/16	2	38	5·00	1·25	0·45F8	—	F9	1·70	1·40 F5	0·40	0·70	2·25
1600 Alpina	4	1573	40 DCOE 84/85	2	27	4·50	1·10	0·50 F8	—	F9	2·00	0·60 F5	0·35	0·70	1·50
1800 Alpina	4	1766	40 DCOE 86/87	2	32	4·50	1·20	0·55 F8	—	F9	2·10	0·60 F5	0·35	0·60	1·75
2000 Alpina	4	1990	40 DCOE 88/89	2	34	4·50	1·25	0·55 F8	—	F16	1·70	0·60 F5	0·40	0·60	2·00
CHRYLSER UK															
Avenger Tiger	4	1725	40 DCOE 70/71	2	30	4·50	1·10	0·45 F11	—	F15	2·40	1·00 F5	0·35	1·00	1·50
CHRYSLER FRANCE															
1100 Special H	4	1294	36 DCNF 15	1	28	3·50	1·55	0·50	1·60	F27	1·65	0·80 F1	0·40	none	1·75
1100 TI	4	1294	36 DCNF 17/18	2	29	3·50	1·20	0·45	1·30	F36	1·85	0·70 F100	0·40	0·40	1·75
1100 Special Austria	4	1294	36 DCNF 21	1	28	3·50	1·55	0·50	1·60	F27	1·65	0·80 F1	0·40	none	1·75
1100 Special	4	1294	36 DCNF 24	1	28	3·50	1·55	0·45	1·40	F27	1·65	0·80 F1	0·40	none	1·75
1100 Special	4	1294	36 DCNF 33/34	2	28	4·50	1·50	0·45	1·35	F27	1·75	0·80 F4	0·40	none	1·75
1100 T1/1307 S	4	1294	36 DCNF 49-50/100	2	29	3·50	1·25	0·45	1·35	F36	2·00	0·70 F100	0·40	0·40	1·75
FERRARI															
Dino 246 GT	6	2418	40 DCNF 13-20, 13(2)-20(1)	3	32	4·50	1·25	0·50	1·20	F24	2·20	0·60 F6	0·50	0·40	1·75
Dino 246 GT USA	6	2418	40 DCNF 19	3	32	4·50	1·25	0·55	1·20	F24	2·20	0·60 F6	0·50	0·40	1·75
Dino 208 GT4 '75	8	1991	34 DCNF 53/54/55/56/100	4	29	3·50	1·20	0·45	1·80	F36	2·00	0·80 F5	0·45	0·40	1·75
Dino 308 GT4	8	2926	40 DCNF 35/36/37/38	4	32	4·50	1·30	0·45	1·60	F24	2·20	0·60 F6	0·45	0·40	1·75
Dino 308 GT4 '75	8	2926	40 DCNF 57/58/59/60	4	32	4·50	1·30	0·50	1·50	F36	2·00	1·00 F6	0·45	0·40	1·75
308 GTB/GT4 '77	8	2926	40 DCNF 57/58/59/60/150	4	32	4·50	1·30	0·50	1·50	F36	2·00	1·00 F6	0·45	0·40	1·75
308 GT4 USA	8	2926	40 DCNF 45/46/47/48	4	32	4·50	1·35	0·55	1·70	F36	2·20	0·60 F6	0·45	0·70	1·75
308 GT4 Australia	8	2926	40 DCNF 64/65/66/67	4	32	4·50	1·25	0·55	1·60	F36	1·90	1·00 F6	0·45	0·40	1·75
365 GTC/4	12	4390	38 DCOE 59-60	6	30	4·50	1·25	0·60 F8	—	F29	2·10	0·65 F5	0·35	none	1·50
365 GTC/4 USA	12	4390	38 DCOE 59A/60A	6	30	4·50	1·25	0·55 F9	—	F29	2·10	0·65 F5	0·35	none	1·50
400 GT	12	4823	38 DCOE 110M/11M	6	30	6·00	1·40	0·45 F24	1·55	F41	1·90	0·65 F5	0·35	none	1·50
400 GT (auto)	12	4823	38 DCOE 110/111	6	30	6·00	1·40	0·45 F23	1·25	F41	1·90	0·65 F5	0·35	none	1·50
FIAT															
124 Sport 1600	4	1608	40 IDF 13-15	2	32	4·50	1·25	0·55	1·15	F11	2·10	0·80 F5	0·40	0·50	1·75
124 Sport/Rally	4	1997	44 IDF 20/200/21/200	2	36	4·50	1·45	0·60	1·15	F9	1·90	0·90 F5	0·40	0·80	1·75
Dino Coupé Spider	6	2418	40 DCNF 12	3	32	4·50	1·25	0·50	1·20	F24	2·20	0·75 F5	0·45	0·40	1·75
Dino Coupé Spider	6	2418	40 DCNF 22/23	3	32	4·50	1·25	0·50	1·25	F24	2·20	0·75 F5	0·50	0·40	1·75
FIAT – ABARTH															
124 Sport/Rally	4	1756	44 IDF 20-21/200	2	36	4·50	1·45	0·60	1·15	F9	1·90	0·90 F5	0·40	0·80	1·75
FORD															
Anglia	4	997	28/36 DCD 41	1	23	4·50	1·20	0·40	2·00	F30	2·30	1·00F1	0·55	0·35	1·75
					24	4·50	1·30	0·50	0·70	F30	1·80				
Escort L/GL	4	940	28/30 DGV 14A	1	21	4·50	1·15	0·55	1·50	F50	2·00	—	0·50	0·40	2·00
					22	4·00	1·05	0·50	0·70	F50	2·00				
Escort GT	4	1098	32 DGV 16B	1	21	3·50	1·05	0·45	1·50	F66	1·70	—	0·50	0·30	2·00
					24	4·50	1·15	0·40	1·40	F50	1·70				
Escort GT	4	1098	32 DGV 16C/16D	1	21	3·50	1·05	0·45	1·50	F66	1·70	—	0·50	0·30	2·00
					24	4·50	1·15	0·40	1·40	F50	1·70				
Escort GT Sport	4	1298	32 DGV 15C	1	23	3·50	1·20	0·45	1·65	F66	1·90	—	0·45	0·30	2·00
					24	4·50	1·05	0·45	1·50	F50	1·60				
Escort GT	4	1599	32 DGAV 5C	1	23	3·50	1·20	0·45	1·85	F50	1·60	—	0·45	0·30	2·00
					24	4·50	1·15	0·45	1·50	F50	1·20		0·45		
Escort GT	4	1599	32 DGAV 6C	1	23	3·50	1·15	0·45	1·85	F50	1·60	—	0·50	0·30	2·00
					24	4·50	1·20	0·45	1·50	F50	1·20				
Escort GT	4	1599	32 DGAV 5D	1	23	3·50	1·20	0·45	1·85	F50	1·60	—	0·45	0·30	2·00
					24	4·50	1·15	0·45	1·50	F50	1·20		0·45		
Escort GT	4	1599	32 DGAV 6D	1	23	3·50	1·15	0·45	1·85	F50	1·60	—	0·50	0·30	2·00
					24	4·50	1·20	0·45	1·50	F50	1·20				
Escort GT	4	1599	32 DGAV 5E	1	23	3·50	1·20	0·45	1·65	F50	1·60	—	0·45	0·30	2·00
					24	4·50	1·15	0·45	1·50	F50	1·20		0·45		
Escort GT	4	1599	32 DGAV 6E	1	23	3·50	1·15	0·45	1·65	F50	1·60	—	0·50	0·30	2·00
					24	4·50	1·20	0·45	1·50	F50	1·20				
Escort GT/Capri/1300GT	4	1298	32 DFE 2	1	23	4·50	1·20	0·50	2·00	F6	1·40	—	0·65	0·40	2·00
					24	4·50	1·20	0·45	1·10	F6	1·65				
Escort/Capri 1300/GT	4	1298	32 DGV 7A	1	23	3·50	1·25	0·55	1·50	F50	1·80	—	0·55	0·40	2·00
					24	3·50	1·30	0·50	0·70	F6	1·80				
Cortina Special/ Corsair GT	4	1500	28/36 DCD 23	1	26	4·50	1·40	0·50	2·00	F30	2·30	2·05 F1	0·70	0·50	1·75
					27	4·50	1·55	0·70	0·70	F30	1·80				
Cortina Special GT	4	1500	28/36 DCD 36	1	26	4·50	1·40	0·55	2·00	F30	2·30	2·05 F1	0·70	0·50	1·75
					27	4·50	1·55	0·70	0·70	F30	1·80				

A	B	C	D	E	F	G	H	I	J	K	L	M	N	O	P
Cortina Special GT	4	1500	28/36 DCD 38	1	26	4·50	1·40	0·55	2·00	F30	2·30	2·05 F1	0·70	0·50	1·75
					27	4·50	1·55	0·70	0·70	F30	1·80				
Cortina 1600 GTE	4	1596	32 DFM 4	1	26	4·50	1·42	0·50	1·80	F6	1·65	–	0·65	0·40	2·00
					27	4·50	1·65	0·45	0·70	F6	1·65				
Cortina GT - Export	4	1596	32 DFD	1	26	4·50	1·40	0·55	1·75	F6	1·60	–	0·65	0·40	2·00
					27	4·50	1·62	0·50	0·70	F6	1·40				
Capri 1600 GT	4	1599	28/36 DCD 22	1	26	4·50	1·40	0·50	2·00	F30	2·30	2·05 F1	0·70	0·50	1·75
					27	4·50	1·55	0·70	0·70	F30	1·80				
Capri 1600 GT	4	1599	32 DFM 5	1	26	4·50	1·42	0·50	1·80	F6	1·65	–	0·65	0·40	2·00
					27	4·50	1·65	0·45	0·70	F6	1·65				
Capri 1600 GT	4	1599	32 DFM 3	1	26	4·50	1·45	0·45	1·80	F6	1·50	–	0·55	0·40	2·00
					27	4·50	1·55	0·45	0·70	F6	1·40				
Capri 1600 GT	4	1599	32/36 DGV 5A/05A	1	26	3·50	1·40	0·55	1·60	F50	1·65	–	0·50	0·30	2·00
					27	3·50	1·35	0·50	0·70	F6	1·60				
Capri 1600 GT	4	1599	32/36 DGAV 8A/08A	1	26	3·50	1·40	0·55	1·70	F50	1·70	–	0·50	0·30	2·00
					27	3·50	1·40	0·45	0·70	F50	1·40				
Capri 1600 GT	4	1599	32 DGAV 9A/09A	1	26	3·50	1·35	0·55	1·70	F50	1·70	–	0·50	0·30	2·00
					27	3·50	1·50	0·45	0·70	F50	1·40				
Capri 1600 GT	4	1599	32/36 DGAV 8B/8B1	1	26	3·50	1·30	0·50	1·50	F66	1·60		0·50	0·30	2·00
					27	4·50	1·25	0·45	1·50	F66	1·25				
Capri 1600 GT	4	1599	32/36 DGAV 9B/9B1	1	26	3·50	1·30	0·45	1·50	F66	1·60		0·50	0·30	2·00
					27	4·50	1·25	0·45	1·50	F66	1·25				
Capri 1600 GT	4	1599	32/36 DGAV 8C	1	26	3·50	1·30	0·50	1·50	F66	1·60		0·50	0·30	2·00
					27	4·50	1·25	0·45	1·50	F66	1·25				
Capri 1600 GT	4	1599	32/36 DGAV 9C	1	26	3·50	1·30	0·45	1·50	F66	1·60		0·50	0·30	2·00
					27	4·50	1·25	0·45	1·50	F66	1·25				
Capri 1600 GT	4	1599	32/36 DGAV 8C1	1	26	4·50	1·37	0·45	1·50	F50	1·70	–	0·45	0·30	2·00
					27	3·50	1·25	0·45	1·50	F50	1·20		0·45		
Taunus/Cortina 1600	4	1599	32/36 DGAV 1A/01A, 1B/01B	1	26	3·50	1·40	0·55	1·70	F50	1·70	–	0·50	0·30	2·00
					27	3·50	1·40	0·45	0·70	F6	1·40				
Taunus/Cortina 1600	4	1599	32/36 DGAV 2A/02A, 2B/02B	1	26	3·50	1·35	0·55	1·70	F50	1·70	–	0·50	0·30	2·00
					27	3·50	1·45	0·45	0·70	F6	1·40				
Taunus/Cortina 1600	4	1599	32/36 DGAV 1C/1C1	1	26	3·50	1·30	0·50	1·50	F66	1·60	–	0·50	0·30	2·00
					27	4·50	1·25	0·45	1·50	F66	1·25				
Taunus/Cortina 1600	4	1599	32/36 DGAV 2C/2C1	1	26	3·50	1·30	0·45	1·50	F66	1·60	–	0·50	0·30	2·00
					27	4·50	1·25	0·45	1·50	F66	1·25				
Taunus/Cortina 1600	4	1599	32/36 DGAV 1D	1	26	3·50	1·30	0·50	1·50	F66	1·60	–	0·50	0·30	2·00
					27	4·50	1·25	0·45	1·50	F66	1·25				
Taunus/Cortina 1600	4	1599	32/36 DGAV 2D	1	26	3·50	1·30	0·45	1·50	F66	1·60	–	0·50	0·30	2·00
					27	4·50	1·25	0·45	1·50	F66	1·25				
Taunus/Cortina 1600	4	1599	32/36 DGAV 1D1	1	26	4·50	1·37	0·45	1·50	F50	1·70	–	0·45	0·30	2·00
					27	3·50	1·25	0·45	1·50	F50	1·20		0·45		
Taunus/Cortina Svezia	4	1599	32 DGAV 24A	1	23	3·50	1·15	0·50	1·50	F50	1·85	–	0·50	0·30	2·00
					24	3·50	1·05	0·45	0·70	F50	1·40				
Taunus/Cortina Svezia	4	1599	32 DGAV 25A	1	23	3·50	1·12	0·55	1·50	F50	1·85	–	0·55	0·30	2·00
					24	3·50	1·10	0·45	0·70	F50	1·40				
Corsair 2000 E GT	4	1997	32 DAF 1	1	26	4·50	1·55	0·45	1·50	F6	1·80	–	0·65	0·40	2·00
					27	4·50	1·40	0·45	0·70	F6	1·80				
Corsair 2000 E GT	4	1997	32 DIF 4	1	26	4·50	1·55	0·50	1·50	F6	1·80	–	0·65	0·40	2·00
					27	4·50	1·40	0·45	0·70	F6	1·80				
Cortina 2000 V4	4	1997	32 DIF 5	1	26	4·50	1·55	0·50	1·50	F6	1·80	–	0·65	0·40	2·00
					27	4·50	1·40	0·45	0·70	F6	1·80				
Taunus/Cortina 2000	4	1997	32/36 DGAV 3A/03A, 3B/03B	1	26	3·50	1·40	0·60	1·70	F50	1·70	–	0·50	0·30	2·00
					27	3·50	1·40	0·50	0·70	F50	1·60				
Taunus/Cortina 2000	4	1997	32/36 DGAV 4A/04A, 4B/04B	1	26	3·50	1·40	0·55	1·70	F50	1·70	–	0·50	0·30	2·00
					27	3·50	1·40	0·50	0·70	F50	1·60				
Taunus/Cortina 2000	4	1997	32/36 DGAV 3C/3C1	1	26	3·50	1·37	0·45	1·75	F66	1·70	–	0·50	0·30	2·00
					27	4·50	1·27	0·60	1·40	F66	1·25				
Taunus/Cortina 2000	4	1997	32/36 DGAV 4C/4C1	1	26	3·50	1·35	0·45	1·75	F66	1·70	–	0·50	0·30	2·00
					27	4·50	1·27	0·60	1·40	F66	1·25				
Taunus/Cortina Granada	4	1997	32/36 DGAV 3D	1	26	3·50	1·37	0·45	1·75	F66	1·70	–	0·50	0·30	2·00
					27	4·50	1·27	0·60	1·40	F66	1·25				
Taunus/Cortina Granada	4	1997	32/36 DGAV 4D	1	26	3·50	1·35	0·45	1·75	F66	1·70	–	0·50	0·30	2·00
					27	4·50	1·27	0·60	1·40	F66	1·25				
Taunus/Cortina Granada	4	1997	32/36 DGAV 3D1	1	26	3·50	1·35	0·45	1·60	F66	1·70	–	0·45	0·30	2·00
					27	4·50	1·30	0·45	1·60	F66	1·25		0·45		
Taunus/Cortina Granada	4	1997	32/36 DGAV 4D1	1	26	3·50	1·32	0·45	1·60	F66	1·75	–	0·45	0·30	2·00
					27	4·50	1·40	0·45	1·60	F66	1·25		0·45		
Taunus/Cortina Svezia	4	1997	32/36 DGAV 18A	1	26	3·50	1·32	0·55	1·50	F66	1·75	–	0·45	0·30	2·00
					27	4·50	1·27	0·50	0·70	F66	1·45		0·45		
Taunus/Cortina Svezia	4	1997	32/36 DGAV 19A	1	26	3·50	1·32	0·55	1·50	F66	1·75	–	0·50	0·30	2·00
					27	4·50	1·27	0·50	0·70	F66	1·45				
Capri 2000 GT	4	1997	32/36 DFV	1	26	4·50	1·45	0·45	1·50	F6	1·70	–	0·65	0·40	2·00
					27	4·50	1·45	0·50	0·70	F6	1·80				
Capri 2000 GT	4	1997	32/36 DFAV	1	26	4·50	1·35	0·45	1·50	F6	1·70	–	0·65	0·40	2·00
					27	4·50	1·40	0·50	0·70	F6	1·80				
Capri 2000	4	1997	32/36 DGAV 12A	1	26	3·50	1·40	0·60	1·70	F50	1·70	–	0·50	0·30	2·00
					27	3·50	1·35	0·50	0·70	F50	1·50				
Capri 2000	4	1997	32/36 DGAV 13A	1	26	3·50	1·40	0·55	1·70	F50	1·70	–	0·50	0·30	2·00
					27	3·50	1·35	0·50	0·70	F50	1·50				
Capri 2000	4	1997	32/36 DGAV 12A1	1	26	3·50	1·40	0·60	1·70	F50	1·70	–	0·50	0·30	2·00
					27	3·50	1·35	0·50	0·70	F50	1·50				
Capri 2000	4	1997	32/36 DGAV 13A1	1	26	3·50	1·40	0·55	1·70	F50	1·70	–	0·50	0·30	2·00
					27	3·50	1·35	0·50	0·70	F50	1·50				
Capri 2000	4	1997	32/36 DGAV 12C	1	26	3·50	1·37	0·45	1·75	F66	1·70	–	0·50	0·30	2·00
					27	4·50	1·27	0·60	1·40	F66	1·25				
Capri 2000	4	1997	32/36 DGAV 13C	1	26	3·50	1·35	0·45	1·75	F66	1·70	–	0·50	0·30	2·00
					27	4·50	1·27	0·60	1·40	F66	1·25				
Capri 2000	4	1997	32/36 DGAV 12C1	1	26	3·50	1·35	0·45	1·60	F66	1·70	–	0·45	0·30	2·00
					27	4·50	1·30	0·45	1·60	F66	1·25		0·45		

A	B	C	D	E	F	G	H	I	J	K	L	M	N	O	P
Capri 2000	4	1997	32/36 DGAV 13C1	1	26	3·50	1·32	0·45	1·60	F66	1·75	–	0·45	0·30	2·00
					27	4·50	1·40	0·45	1·60	F66	1·25		0·45		
Capri 2000 Svezia	4	1997	32/36 DGAV 22A1	1	26	3·50	1·32	0·55	1·50	F66	1·75	–	0·45	0·30	2·00
					27	4·50	1·30	0·50	0·70	F66	1·35		0·45		
Capri 2000 Svezia	4	1997	32/36 DGAV 23A	1	26	3·50	1·32	0·55	1·50	F66	1·75	–	0·50	0·30	2·00
					27	4·50	1·27	0·50	0·70	F66	1·45				
Capri 2000 Giappone	4	1997	32/36 DGAV 27A	1	26	3·50	1·32	0·55	1·10	F66	1·75	–	0·50	0·30	2·00
					27	4·50	1·10	0·50	0·70	F66	1·25				
Granada 2000 Svezia	4	1997	32/36 DGAV 20A1	1	26	3·50	1·32	0·55	1·50	F66	1·75	–	0·45	0·30	2·00
					27	3·50	1·30	0·50	0·70	F66	1·35		0·45		
Consul/Granada 2000	4	1997	32/36 DGAV 10A/010A	1	26	3·50	1·40	0·60	1·70	F50	1·70	–	0·50	0·30	2·00
					27	3·50	1·35	0·50	0·70	F50	1·25				
Consul/Granada 2000	4	1997	32/36 DGAV 11A/011A	1	26	3·50	1·40	0·55	1·70	F50	1·70	–	0·50	0·30	2·00
					27	3·50	1·35	0·50	0·70	F50	1·25				
Consul/Granada 2500	6	2551	34 DGAS 8A	1	24	4·00	1·22	0·45	1·95	F50	1·80	–	0·55	0·40	2·50
Consul/Granada 2500	6	2551	38 DGAS 1A	1	27	4·00	1·45	0·50	2·00	F50	1·75	–	0·60	0·30	2·50
Consul/Granada 3000	6	2994	38 DGAS 3A/03A	1	27	4·00	1·45	0·45	1·85	F50	1·85	–	0·60	0·30	2·50
Consul/Granada 3000	6	2994	38 DGAS 4A/04A	1	27	4·00	1·45	0·45	1·95	F50	1·85	–	0·70	0·30	2·50
Granada 3000	6	2994	38 DGAS 4A2	1	27	4·00	1·42	0·45	1·95	F50	1·85	–	0·70	0·30	2·50
Granada 3000	6	2994	38 DGAS 3B	1	27	4·00	1·42	0·45	1·95	F50	1·85	–	0·55	0·45	2·50
Granada 3000	6	2994	38 DGAS 3C	1	27	4·00	1·42	0·45	1·95	F50	1·85	–	0·55	0·45	2·50
Capri 3000 GT	6	2994	38 DGAS 7A/07A	1	27	4·00	1·45	0·45	1·95	F50	1·85	–	0·70	0·30	2·50
Capri 3000	6	2994	38 DGAS 6A1	1	27	4·00	1·42	0·45	1·95	F50	1·85	–	0·70	0·30	2·50
Capri 3000	6	2994	38 DGAS 7A1	1	27	4·00	1·42	0·45	1·95	F50	1·85	–	0·70	0·30	2·50
Capri 3000	6	2994	38 DGAS 6B	1	27	4·00	1·42	0·45	1·95	F50	1·85	–	0·55	0·45	2·50
Capri 3000	6	2994	38 DGAS 6C	1	27	4·00	1·42	0·45	1·95	F50	1·85	–	0·55	0·45	2·50
Fiesta 1600 (49 States)	4	1598	32 DFTA	1	22	4·00	1·00	0·60	1·20	F22	2·50	–	0·45	0·40	1·50
					22	4·00	1·05	0·60	0·70	F22	2·50				
Fiesta 1600 (California)	4	1598	32 DFTA 1	1	22	4·00	1·05	0·60	1·10	F22	2·50	–	0·45	0·40	1·50
					22	4·00	1·00	0·60	0·70	F22	2·50				
Escort GT, twin cam	4	1558	40 DCOE 31	1	30	4·50	1·10	0·45 F8	–		F11	1·55	1·00 F5	0·35	0·40	1·75
Escort 2000 RS	4	1993	44 IDF 40/41	2	34	4·50	1·45	0·55	1·30	F19	1·80	0·90 F55	0·40	0·80	1·75

IKA

A	B	C	D	E	F	G	H	I	J	K	L	M	N	O	P
Torina GS Coupé	6	3770	45 DCOE 17	3	33	4·50	1·30	0·55 F8	–		F11	2·00	0·60 F5	0·45	0·60	2·00

LAMBORGHINI

A	B	C	D	E	F	G	H	I	J	K	L	M	N	O	P
Urraco USA	8	2462	40 IDF 30-31/32/33	4	30	3·00	1·20	0·65	1·00	F7	1·60	–	0·35	1·00	1·75
Urraco SS	8	2462	40 DCNF 42/43	4	34	4·50	1·35	0·60	1·30	F24	2·20	0·60 F5	0·35	0·40	1·75
Urraco P200	8	1973	36 IDF 34/35/36/37	4	27	3·00	1·15	0·55	1·25	F7	1·70	–	0·35	1·00	1·75
Urraco P250	8	2462	40 IDF 22/23/24/25	4	30	3·00	1·20	0·60	1·00	F7	1·60	0·80 F5	0·35	1·00	1·75
Urraco P300 USA	8	2996	40 DCNF 70/71	4	32	4·50	1·30	0·55	1·65	F27	1·80	0·55 F5	0·35	0·45	1·75
Urraco P300 Silhouette	8	2996	40 DCNF 62/63	4	32	4·50	1·35	0·55	1·30	F27	1·90	0·60 F5	0·35	0·45	1·75
Islero GT/Espada GT Jarama	12	3929	40 DCOE 22/23	6	30	4·50	1·15	0·45 F9	–		F3	2·10	0·60 F5	0·35	0·70	1·75
Espada-Jarama USA	12	3929	40 DCOE 22A/23A	6	30	4·50	1·20	0·50 F9	–		F9	2·10	–	0·35	1·00	1·75
Espada-Jarama GTS '77	12	3929	40 DCOE 92-93/150	6	30	4·50	1·15	0·45 F19	–		F3	2·10	–	0·35	1·00	1·75
Countach	12	3929	45 DCOE 96-97/150	6	38	4·50	1·50	0·50 F19	–		F3	2·10	–	0·45	0·70	1·75

LANCIA

A	B	C	D	E	F	G	H	I	J	K	L	M	N	O	P
Stratos	6	2418	40 IDF 28-29, 28(2)-29(1)	3	32	4·50	1·25	0·50	1·20	F3	2·20	0·60 F6	0·40	0·40	1·75

LOTUS

A	B	C	D	E	F	G	H	I	J	K	L	M	N	O	P
Elan S4-SE	4	1558	48 DCOE 18	2	30	4·50	1·15	0·45 F9	–		F11	2·00	1·00 F5	0·40	0·50	1·75
Cortina GT	4	1558	40 DCOE 31	2	30	4·50	1·10	0·45 F8	–		F11	1·55	1·00 F5	0·35	0·40	1·75

MASERATI

A	B	C	D	E	F	G	H	I	J	K	L	M	N	O	P
Merak 2000	6	1999	42 DCNF 78-78/1, 78(2) 78/1	3	32	3·50	1·25	0·50	1·45	F36	1·80	0·80 F7	0·40	0·40	2·00
Merak	6	2995	42 DCNF 31(2), 32(1)	3	36	3·50	1·40	0·60	1·30	F25	1·60	0·80 F7	0·40	0·40	2·00
Merak SS	6	2965	44 DCNF 44	3	36	3·50	1·40	0·65	1·45	F25	1·70	1·10 F7	0·40	0·40	2·00
Merak SS '77	6	2965	44 DCNF 69-69/1, 69(2)-69/1(1)	3	36	3·50	1·40	0·65	1·45	F25	1·70	1·10 F7	0·40	0·40	2·00
3500 GT	6	3485	42 DCOE 8	3	32	3·50	1·35	0·55 F2	–		F15	1·55	0·60 F5	0·45	none	2·00
Khamsin	8	4930	42 DCNF 41	4	34	3·50	1·30	0·60	1·30	F25	1·55	0·80 F7	0·40	0·40	2·00
Khamsin '77	8	4930	42 DCNF 68	4	34	3·50	1·35	0·60	1·35	F25	1·55	0·80 F7	0·40	0·40	2·00
Kyalami 4200	8	4136	42 DCNF 76	4	34	3·50	1·30	0·60	1·35	F25	1·55	0·80 F7	0·40	0·40	2·00
Quattro Porte 11	6	2965	44 DCNF 61	3	34	3·50	1·40	0·65	1·65	F25	1·70	1·10 F7	0·40	0·40	2·00
Bora-Indy 4700	8	4719	42 DCNF 35(3)-36	4	36	3·50	1·40	0·60	1·60	F25	1·55	0·80 F7	0·40	0·40	2·00
Bora 4900	8	4930	42 DCNF 68	4	34	3·50	1·35	0·60	1·35	F25	1·55	0·80 F7	0·40	0·40	2·00

MATRA-SIMCA

A	B	C	D	E	F	G	H	I	J	K	L	M	N	O	P
Baghera	4	1294	36 DCNF 49-50/100	1	29	3·50	1·25	0·45	1·35	F36	2·00	0·70 F10	0·40	0·40	1·75
Baghera S	4	1294	36 DCNF 51-52/100	1	30	3·50	1·30	0·47	1·35	F36	2·10	0·70 F10	0·40	0·40	1·75

PORSCHE

A	B	C	D	E	F	G	H	I	J	K	L	M	N	O	P
904 GTS Carrera	4	1956	46 IDA 2/3	2	40	4·50	1·70	0·60 F10	–		F14	1·30	–	0·50	none	3·00
911L	6	1991	40 IDA 3C/1	2	30	4·50	1·25	0·55	1·10	F26	1·80	–	0·50	none	1·75
911 USA	6	1991	40 IDAP 3C/1	2	30	4·50	1·25	0·52	1·10	F26	1·80	–	0·50	none	1·75
911S	6	1991	40 IDS 3C/1	2	32	4·50	1·30	0·55	1·10	F3	1·80	–	0·50	none	1·75
911T	6	1991	40 IDT 3C/1	2	27	4·50	1·10	0·50	1·10	F2	1·85	–	0·50	none	1·75
911T	6	1991	40 IDTP 3C/1	2	27	4·50	1·10	0·45	1·45	F1	1·85	–	0·50	none	1·75
Carrera 6	6	1991	46 IDA 3C/1	2	42	4·50	1·70	0·70	0·80	F24	1·45	–	0·50	0·40	1·75
914/6	6	1991	40 IDTP 13C/1	2	27	4·50	1·05	0·50	1·45	F1	1·70	–	0·50	none	1·75

SUNBEAM (Rootes)

A	B	C	D	E	F	G	H	I	J	K	L	M	N	O	P
Rapier H 120	4	1725	40 DCOE 90/91	2	30	3·50	1·15	0·50 F18	–		F34	2·00	1·40 F5	0·35	1·00	1·50

Part 3

Appendix 2
Conversion equipment jet setting list

This list gives details of calibration and jet sizes on carburettors fitted as conversion equipment:

A	Model details	K	Accelerator pump inlet valve with exhaust orifice
B	Carburettor type	L	Needle valve
C	Number of carburettors		
D	Choke size		
E	Auxiliary venturi		
F	Main jet		
G	Emulsion tube		
H	Air corrector jet		
I	Idle jet		
J	Accelerator pump jet		

A	B	C	D	E	F	G	H	I	J	K	L
Alfasud	40 IDF 42/43	2	28	4·50	1·10	F11	2·25	0·50	0·40	0·50	1·75
Austin Mini Cooper 'S' 1070 cc and 1275 cc	45 DCOE 13	1	34	3·5	1·30	F2	1·75	0·50 F9	0·50	0·50	2·00
Austin Mini Cooper 'S' 1275 cc	45 DCOE 13	1	38	5·00	1·60	F16	1·70	0·45 F9	0·50	1·00	2·25

A	B	C	D	E	F	G	H	I	J	K	L
Austin America	45 DCOE 9	1	34	3·5	1·30	F2	1·75	0·50 F9	0·50	0·50	2·00
Austin Marina	45 DCOE 9	1	36	4·5	1·65	F16	1·60	0·50 F8	0·60	closed	2·00
Austin Healey Sprite Mk 1	45 DCOE 9	1	32	5·0	1·40	F16	1·80	0·45 F6	0·40	0·50	2·00
Austin Healey Sprite Mk 2 and 3	45 DCOE 9	1	32	5·0	1·40	F16	1·80	0·45 F6	0·40	0·50	2·00
Austin Healey Sprite Mk 4	45 DCOE 9	1	34	3·5	1·30	F2	1·75	0·50 F9	0·50	0·50	2·25
Austin Healey 3000 Mk 2 and 3	45 DCOE 9	3	36	4·5	1·65	F16	1·50	0·55 F8	0·45	closed	2·00
BMW 1600	40 DCOE 18	2	32	4·5	1·30	F9	1·85	0·45 F12	0·35	0·45	1·75
BMW 2002	45 DCOE 15/16	2	34	5·0	1·30	F9	1·80	0·50 F8	0·40	0·45	2·25
Capri 1600	40 DCOE 2	2	32	4·5	1·20	F16	1·80	0·50 F9	0·40	0·50	2·00
Capri 2000	45 DCOE 13	1	34	3·5	1·45	F2	1·85	0·55 F4	0·50	0·50	2·25
Capri 2000	42 DCOE 8	2	32	4·5	1·25	F16	1·80	0·50 F9	0·40	0·50	2·00
Colt 1600	45 DCOE 9	1	32	5·0	1·25	F20	1·60	0·50 F8	0·45	0·50	2·00
Datson B110	40 DCOE 2	1	27	4·5	1·10	F7	1·65	0·50 F9	0·50	0·50	2·00
Datsun B210 F10	40 DCOE 2	1	33	4·5	1·30	F11	1·80	0·50 F8	0·60	closed	2·00
Datsun 510	45 DCOE 13	1	33	4·5	1·30	F16	1·90	0·50 F8	0·50	0·55	2·25
Datsun 510	40 DCOE 12	2	32	4·5	1·35	F15	1·70	0·55 F2	0·40	0·55	2·00
Datsun 610	45 DCOE 13	1	34	3·5	1·30	F16	1·80	0·50 F8	0·50	closed	2·25
Datsun 610	40 DCOE 2	2	33	4·5	1·50	F16	2·00	0·50 F6	0·45	0·55	2·00
Datsun 710	45 DCOE 13	1	34	3·5	1·30	F16	1·80	0·50 F8	0·50	closed	2·25
Datsun 710	40 DCOE 2	2	33	4·5	1·50	F16	2·00	0·50 F6	0·45	0·55	2·00
Datsun 240Z and 260Z	40 DCOE 18	3	30	4·5	1·30	F2	1·75	0·50 F9	0·45	0·55	1·75
Datsun 521 PU (1595 cc)	45 DCOE 13	1	33	4·5	1·30	F16	1·90	0·50 F8	0·50	0·55	2·25
Datsun 521 PU (1595 cc)	40 DCOE 2	2	32	4·5	1·35	F15	1·70	0·55 F2	0·40	0·55	2·00
Datsun 620 PU (1595 cc)	45 DCOE 13	1	33	4·5	1·30	F16	1·90	0·50 F8	0·50	0·55	2·25
Datsun 620 PU (1595 cc)	40 DCOE 2	2	32	4·5	1·35	F15	1·70	0·55 F2	0·40	0·55	2·00
Datsun 620 PU (1770 cc and 1952 cc)	45 DCOE 13	1	34	3·5	1·30	F16	1·80	0·50 F8	0·50	closed	2·25
Datsun 620 PU (1770 cc and 1952 cc)	40 DCOE 2	2	33	4·5	1·50	F16	2·00	0·50 F6	0·45	0·55	2·00
Fiat 126 Gruppo 2	40 DCOE 102	1	28	4·5	1·10	F11	2·50	0·45 F8	0·45	1·00	1·75
Fiat 124 Sport/Rally GR4	48 IDF 1-2/100	2	40	4·5	1·65	F11	1·90	0·65	0·40	1·00	2·00
Ford Cortina 1500	40 DCOE 2	2	33	4·5	1·25	F16	1·70	0·45 F9	0·35	closed	2·00
Ford Cortina 1600 (cross flow) and Pinto 1600	40 DCOE 2	2	32	4·5	1·20	F16	1·80	0·50 F9	0·40	0·50	2·00
Ford Pinto 2000	45 DCOE 13	1	34	3·5	1·45	F2	1·85	0·55 F4	0·50	0·50	2·25
Ford Pinto 2000	42 DCOE 8	2	32	4·5	1·25	F16	1·80	0·50 F9	0·40	0·50	2·00
Honda Civic (except CVCC)	40 DCOE 2	1	33	4·5	1·40	F2	1·85	0·45 F9	0·45	0·55	2·00
Jaguar XKE (3·8 and 4·2)	45 DCOE 9	3	38	3·5	1·65	F2	1·90	0·65 F8	0·40	0·50	2·00
Lancia Stratos	44 IDF 26(2)-27	3	36	4·5	1·50	F11	1·80	0·55	0·40	0·80	1·75
Lotus Europa (Renault engine)	45 DCOE 13	1	34	3·5	1·50	F2	1·80	0·45 F8	0·40	0·50	2·25
Mercedes Benz 190 SL	40 DCOE 18	2	30	4·5	1·35	F2	2·00	0·50 F9	0·45	closed	1·75
MG Midget Mk 1 and 2	45 DCOE 9	1	32	5·0	1·40	F16	1·80	0·45 F6	0·40	0·50	2·00
MG Midget Mk 3	45 DCOE 13	1	34	3·5	1·30	F2	1·75	0·50 F9	0·50	0·50	2·25

A	B	C	D	E	F	G	H	I	J	K	L
MG 1100 Saloon	45 DCOE 9	1	32	5.0	1.40	F16	1.80	0.45 F6	0.40	0.50	2.00
MGA (except twin cam)	45 DCOE 13	1	34	3.5	1.60	F16	1.70	0.50 F8	0.60	closed	2.25
MGB and MGB GT	45 DCOE 9	1	36	4.5	1.65	F16	1.60	0.50 F8	0.60	closed	2.00
Opel Kadette and Rallye (to 1970)	40 DCOE 2	2	33	4.5	1.15	F16	1.50	0.50 F9	0.35	0.55	2.00
Opel Kadette, Rallye and Manta (1971 on)	40 DCOE 2	2	33	4.5	1.15	F16	1.50	0.50 F9	0.35	0.55	2.00
Opel GT 1900	40 DCOE 2	2	33	4.5	1.15	F16	1.50	0.50 F9	0.35	0.55	2.00
Porsche 356A, B, C and 912	48 IDA 4	2	37	4.5	1.35	F7	1.20	0.70 F10	0.50	0.50	2.00
Renault R12 Gordini	45 DCOE 68/69	2	34	4.5	1.35	F9	2.00	0.55 F8	0.45	0.60	1.50
Toyota Corolla 1100 and 1200	40 DCOE 2	1	27	4.5	1.05	F7	1.55	0.50 F11	0.50	0.50	2.00
Toyota Corolla 1600 (2TC)	40 DCOE 18	1	30	4.5	1.10	F11	2.00	0.45 F9	0.50	0.50	1.75
Toyota Corolla 1600 (2TC)	40 DCOE 18	2	30	4.5	1.15	F11	2.00	0.50 F9	0.40	0.50	1.75
Toyota Carina 1600 (2TC)	40 DCOE 18	1	30	4.5	1.10	F11	2.00	0.45 F9	0.50	0.50	1.75
Toyota Carina 1600 (2TC)	40 DCOE 18	2	30	4.5	1.15	F11	2.00	0.50 F9	0.40	0.50	1.75
Toyota Celica (8RC and 18RC)	40 DCOE 2	1	33	4.5	1.60	F2	1.65	0.40 F9	0.60	closed	2.00
Toyota Celica (8RC and 18RC)	40 DCOE 2	2	33	4.5	1.40	F2	1.70	0.45 F6	0.35	closed	2.00
Toyota Corona (8RC and 18RC)	40 DCOE 2	1	33	4.5	1.60	F2	1.65	0.40 F9	0.60	closed	2.00
Toyota Corona (8RC and 18RC)	40 DCOE 2	2	33	4.5	1.40	F2	1.70	0.45 F6	0.35	closed	2.00
Toyota Corona Mk2 (8RC and 18RC)	40 DCOE 2	1	33	4.5	1.60	F2	1.65	0.40 F9	0.60	closed	2.00
Toyota Corona Mk2 (8RC and 18RC)	40 DCOE 2	2	33	4.5	1.40	F2	1.70	0.45 F6	0.35	closed	2.00
Toyota Hi-Lux PU (8RC and 18RC)	40 DCOE 2	1	33	4.5	1.60	F2	1.65	0.40 F9	0.60	closed	2.00
Toyota Hi-Lux PU (8RC and 18RC)	40 DCOE 2	2	33	4.5	1.40	F2	1.70	0.45 F6	0.35	closed	2.00
Toyota PU (18RC)	40 DCOE 2	1	33	4.5	1.60	F2	1.65	0.40 F9	0.60	closed	2.00
Toyota PU (18RC)	40 DCOE 2	2	33	4.5	1.40	F2	1.70	0.45 F6	0.35	closed	2.00
Triumph Dolomite Sprint	48 DCOE	2	42	4.5	1.65	F16	1.75	0.60	0.45	0.40	3.00
Triumph GT6	40 DCOE 2	3	29	4.5	1.20	F16	1.90	0.45 F9	0.40	closed	2.00
Triumph GT6 + Mk 2 and GT6 Mk 3	40 DCOE 2	3	27	4.5	1.30	F2	1.60	0.50 F11	0.45	closed	2.00
Triumph TR2, 3, 3A, 3B, 4 and 4A	42 DCOE 8	2	32	4.5	1.40	F15	1.50	0.50 F2	0.50	0.50	2.00
Triumph TR 250 and TR6	40 DCOE 2	3	27	4.5	1.30	F2	1.60	0.50 F11	0.45	closed	2.00
Volvo 122S, 144 and P1800	42 DCOE 8	2	32	4.5	1.25	F15	1.60	0.50 F8	0.50	0.50	2.00
Volkswagen 1200	36 IDF 16/17	2	27	4.5	1.10	F11	2.15	0.50	0.40	0.50	1.75
Volkswagen 1600	40 IDF 18/19	2	28	4.5	1.15	F11	2.00	0.50	0.50	0.50	1.75
Volkswagen 2000	44 IDF 38/39	2	36	4.5	1.70	F11	2.00	0.50	0.55	0.80	1.75
Volkswagen Saloon 1600 (dual port) stock	40 DCNF 12	1	32	4.5	1.60	F24	2.20	0.55	0.50	none	1.75
Volkswagen Saloon 1600 (dual port) – 1800 cc modification	40 DCNF 12	2	32	4.5	1.55	F24	2.20	0.55	0.45	none	1.75
Volkswagen Saloon 1600 (dual port) – 1800 cc modification	42 DCNF 9	2	34	4.5	1.40	F25	1.80	0.60	0.40	none	2.00
Volkswagen Saloon 1600 (dual port) – 1800 cc modification	40 IDF 19	2	28	4.5	1.15	F11	2.00	0.50	0.50	0.55	1.75
Volkswagen Transporter 1600 (dual port) – stock	40 DCNF 12	1	32	4.5	1.60	F24	2.20	0.55	0.50	none	1.75
Volkswagen Transporter 1600 (dual port) – 1800 cc modification	40 DCNF 12	2	32	4.5	1.55	F24	2.20	0.55	0.45	none	1.75
Volkswagen Transporter 1600 (dual port) – 1800 cc modification	40 DCNF 9	2	34	4.5	1.40	F25	1.80	0.60	0.40	none	2.00
Volkswagen Transporter 1600 (dual port) – 1800 cc modification	40 IDF 19	2	28	4.5	1.15	F11	2.00	0.50	0.50	0.55	1.75
Volkswagen Transporter 1700 (type 4)	40 IDF 19	2	28	4.5	1.15	F11	2.00	0.50	0.50	0.55	1.75
Volkswagen Saloon and Transporter 1600 – highly modified	48 IDA 4	2	37	4.5	1.35	F7	1.20	0.70 F10	0.50	0.50	2.00
Volkswagen Fastback and Squareback 1600 (dual port)	40 DCNF 12	2	32	4.5	1.55	F24	2.20	0.55	0.45	none	1.75
Volkswagen Fastback and Squareback 1600 (dual port)	42 DCNF 9	2	34	4.5	1.40	F25	1.80	0.60	0.40	none	2.00
Volkswagen 411 and 412 1700 and 1800	40 IDF 19	2	28	4.5	1.15	F11	2.00	0.50	0.50	0.55	1.75

Safety first!

Regardless of how enthusiastic you may be about getting on with the job at hand, take the time to ensure that your safety is not jeopardized. A moment's lack of attention can result in an accident, as can failure to observe certain simple safety precautions. The possibility of an accident will always exist, and the following points should not be considered a comprehensive list of all dangers. Rather, they are intended to make you aware of the risks and to encourage a safety conscious approach to all work you carry out on your vehicle.

Essential DOs and DON'Ts

DON'T rely on a jack when working under the vehicle. Always use approved jackstands to support the weight of the vehicle and place them under the recommended lift or support points.

DON'T attempt to loosen extremely tight fasteners (i.e. wheel lug nuts) while the vehicle is on a jack — it may fall.

DON'T start the engine without first making sure that the transmission is in Neutral (or Park where applicable) and the parking brake is set.

DON'T remove the radiator cap from a hot cooling system — let it cool or cover it with a cloth and release the pressure gradually.

DON'T attempt to drain the engine oil until you are sure it has cooled to the point that it will not burn you.

DON'T touch any part of the engine or exhaust system until it has cooled sufficiently to avoid burns.

DON'T siphon toxic liquids such as gasoline, antifreeze and brake fluid by mouth, or allow them to remain on your skin.

DON'T inhale brake lining dust — it is potentially hazardous (see *Asbestos* below)

DON'T allow spilled oil or grease to remain on the floor — wipe it up before someone slips on it.

DON'T use loose fitting wrenches or other tools which may slip and cause injury.

DON'T push on wrenches when loosening or tightening nuts or bolts. Always try to pull the wrench toward you. If the situation calls for pushing the wrench away, push with an open hand to avoid scraped knuckles if the wrench should slip.

DON'T attempt to lift a heavy component alone — get someone to help you.

DON'T rush or take unsafe shortcuts to finish a job.

DON'T allow children or animals in or around the vehicle while you are working on it.

DO wear eye protection when using power tools such as a drill, sander, bench grinder, etc. and when working under a vehicle.

DO keep loose clothing and long hair well out of the way of moving parts.

DO make sure that any hoist used has a safe working load rating adequate for the job.

DO get someone to check on you periodically when working alone on a vehicle.

DO carry out work in a logical sequence and make sure that everything is correctly assembled and tightened.

DO keep chemicals and fluids tightly capped and out of the reach of children and pets.

DO remember that your vehicle's safety affects that of yourself and others. If in doubt on any point, get professional advice.

Asbestos

Certain friction, insulating, sealing, and other products — such as brake linings, brake bands, clutch linings, torque converters, gaskets, etc. — contain asbestos. *Extreme care must be taken to avoid inhalation of dust from such products since it is hazardous to health.* If in doubt, assume that they *do* contain asbestos.

Fire

Remember at all times that gasoline is highly flammable. Never smoke or have any kind of open flame around when working on a vehicle. But the risk does not end there. A spark caused by an electrical short circuit, by two metal surfaces contacting each other, or even by static electricity built up in your body under certain conditions, can ignite gasoline vapors, which in a confined space are highly explosive. Do not, under any circumstances, use gasoline for cleaning parts. Use an approved safety solvent.

Always disconnect the battery ground (−) cable *at the battery* before working on any part of the fuel system or electrical system. Never risk spilling fuel on a hot engine or exhaust component.

It is strongly recommended that a fire extinguisher suitable for use on fuel and electrical fires be kept handy in the garage or workshop at all times. Never try to extinguish a fuel or electrical fire with water.

Torch (flashlight in the US)

Any reference to a "torch" appearing in this manual should always be taken to mean a hand-held, battery-operated electric light or flashlight. It DOES NOT mean a welding or propane torch or blowtorch.

Fumes

Certain fumes are highly toxic and can quickly cause unconsciousness and even death if inhaled to any extent. Gasoline vapor falls into this category, as do the vapors from some cleaning solvents. Any draining or pouring of such volatile fluids should be done in a well ventilated area.

When using cleaning fluids and solvents, read the instructions on the container carefully. Never use materials from unmarked containers.

Never run the engine in an enclosed space, such as a garage. Exhaust fumes contain carbon monoxide, which is extremely poisonous. If you need to run the engine, always do so in the open air, or at least have the rear of the vehicle outside the work area.

If you are fortunate enough to have the use of an inspection pit, never drain or pour gasoline and never run the engine while the vehicle is over the pit. The fumes, being heavier than air, will concentrate in the pit with possibly lethal results.

The battery

Never create a spark or allow a bare light bulb near a battery. They normally give off a certain amount of hydrogen gas, which is highly explosive.

Always disconnect the battery ground (−) cable *at the battery* before working on the fuel or electrical systems.

If possible, loosen the filler caps or cover when charging the battery from an external source (this does not apply to sealed or maintenance-free batteries). Do not charge at an excessive rate or the battery may burst.

Take care when adding water to a non maintenance-free battery and when carrying a battery. The electrolyte, even when diluted, is very corrosive and should not be allowed to contact clothing or skin.

Always wear eye protection when cleaning the battery to prevent the caustic deposits from entering your eyes.

Mains electricity (household current in the US)

When using an electric power tool, inspection light, etc., which operates on household current, always make sure that the tool is correctly connected to its plug and that, where necessary, it is properly grounded. Do not use such items in damp conditions and, again, do not create a spark or apply excessive heat in the vicinity of fuel or fuel vapor.

Secondary ignition system voltage

A severe electric shock can result from touching certain parts of the ignition system (such as the spark plug wires) when the engine is running or being cranked, particularly if components are damp or the insulation is defective. In the case of an electronic ignition system, the secondary system voltage is much higher and could prove fatal.

Printed by
J H Haynes & Co Ltd
Sparkford Nr Yeovil
Somerset BA22 7JJ England